In Pursuit of the White House 2000

In Pursuit of the White House 2000: How We Choose Our Presidential Nominees

William G. Mayer
Northeastern University

CHATHAM HOUSE PUBLISHERS
SEVEN BRIDGES PRESS, LLC
NEW YORK • LONDON

Seven Bridges Press, LLC
135 Fifth Avenue, New York, NY 10010-7101

Publisher: Robert J. Gormley
Managing editor: Katharine Miller
Production supervisor: Melissa A. Martin
Cover design: Inari Information Services, Inc.
Composition: Ashdod Associates
Printing and binding: Versa Press, Inc.

Library of Congress Cataloging-in-Publication Data

In pursuit of the White House 2000 : how we choose our presidential
nominees / edited by William G. Mayer.
    p. cm.
Includes bibliographical references and index.
ISBN 1-889119-17-2
1. Presidents—United States—Nomination. I. Mayer, William G., 1956-
JK521 .I52 1999
324.6'3'0973—dc21
                                                                99-6575
                                                                CIP

Manufactured in the United States of America
10 9 8 7 6 5 4 3 2 1

To Our Children

Natalie Logan Mayer
Anna and Thomas Ericksen Hagen
Katherine Noelle Busch
Rachel Shoshana and Miriam Joanna Bernstein
Alexander Kiliman Best
William Robert Atkeson Cary

Contents

Preface

LIKE THE FIRST volume in the series, this book has two principal objectives: to present a broad overview of the presidential nominating process through a detailed examination of some of its most significant components; and to showcase some of the most interesting work now being done on the politics of presidential selection. In every other respect, this book is new: new topics, mostly new contributors, and nine completely new chapters.

For an author, finishing a book is usually a cause for celebration. In this case, that joy is greatly diminished by the knowledge that Ed Artinian is not here to share it with us. As the founder, owner, publisher, and Prime Mover at Chatham House, Ed leaves behind him both an impressive list of books and a legion of friends and admirers. For years, Ed was a fixture at political science conferences. Especially at regional meetings, participants could always count on finding three things: a printed program, a plastic badge, and Ed Artinian. My personal history with Ed is a particularly treasured one: he published my first academic article, he commissioned both volumes in this series, he was a wonderful source of gossip and cigars; he even sent a teddy bear to my newly born daughter. We will miss him.

That this book is being published approximately on time, even though much of the manuscript was sent in several months after the deadline, is a tribute to the people who have guided Chatham House through a difficult transition. The contributors to this book are especially grateful to Pat Artinian, Bob Gormley, Melissa Martin, and Katharine Miller.

As an attempt to stay abreast of ongoing developments in both the presidential nominating process and the political science literature on that subject, this book owes much to a small group of people with whom I have had regular conversations on both topics. I particularly wish to express my appreciation to Tony Corrado, Nelson Polsby, Gerald Pomper, David Shribman, and Alan Silverleib.

Most of all, I thank my family, which continues to be an extraordinary source of support, encouragement, and inspiration. My love and gratitude, as always, go to my parents, Mary Rose and Joseph Mayer, and to Joe, Rita, Lauren, and Joseph Michael Mayer; Mary Beth, Joe, Allie, and Kate King; Jack; Tom; and Rosemary, Scott, Andy, Steve, Dana, and Renee Kryk. And to my in-laws: Maury and Natalie Logan; Brian, Coralee, and Adam Logan; Nancy; and Maureen, Bill, and Andrew Ferrari.

Unfortunately, much of the burden of writing this book has fallen upon my wife, Amy Logan, and our daughter, Natalie. To them especially I express my gratitude and devotion.

CHAPTER ONE

The Modern Politics of Presidential Selection: How Changing the Rules Really Did Change the Game

by Michael G. Hagen and William G. Mayer

THOUGH NO ONE seems to have thought the day worth celebrating, 27 August 1998 marked the thirtieth anniversary of the beginning of the modern era in presidential nominations. Of course, no important process of historical transformation is ever consummated in a single day. The groundwork and preconditions for change had inevitably been laid during the preceding years and decades; many important events and decisions were yet to take place. But neither is this date as "precisely arbitrary" as is, according to some observers, the current craze over the beginning of the next millennium.[1] For in this case, the date does correspond to something real, concrete, and verifiable. Late on the evening of 27 August 1968, the Democratic National Convention approved a minority report from its rules committee that, along with several other resolutions passed earlier in the week, set in motion a sweeping overhaul of the rules governing national conventions and presidential nominations.

The specific text approved by the convention that night gives only the barest hint of what was to come. As ultimately interpreted, it authorized a special commission created by another resolution to rewrite the delegate selection rules that were to be used for the 1972 convention. Its uncertain mandate notwithstanding, the Commission on Party Structure and Delegate Selection—more commonly known as the McGovern-Fraser Commission, after George McGovern and Donald Fraser, the two men who served as its chairmen—set about its work in a way that showed little evidence of hesitation or second thoughts. In just four years, it managed to put together a comprehensive set of recommendations that entirely recast the ground rules for delegate selection, got these recommendations approved by the Democratic National Committee, and then compelled fifty different state parties to abide by their provisions. As Byron Shafer concludes in his definitive history of these events:

> The minority report of the Rules Committee, as augmented
> by developments in the Credentials Committee and in the
> Democratic National Committee itself, was to become the "mandate"—the hunting license, really—for the greatest systematic
> change in presidential nominating procedures in all of American
> history.[2]

The members of the McGovern-Fraser Commission were not the only people in this period who were interested in rewriting the rules and procedures of American presidential politics. Just two years after the 1972 election, the U.S. Congress, anxious to show some responsiveness to the series of scandals known collectively as Watergate, passed a law (technically, a set of amendments to the Federal Election Campaign Act of 1971) that completely restructured the ways that candidates raised and spent money while running for president. Again, a superlative is not out of place: the 1974 law was, without a close competitor, the most significant change in campaign finance regulations in American history.

Neither academics nor journalists were paying much attention at the beginning of this process—but they were when it ended. Changes of this magnitude eventually penetrate even the thickest ivory tower and the most insulated editorial boardroom. By the late 1970s, a large and growing literature had emerged about the nature of the presidential nominating process and the consequences of trying to change it. And, particularly with respect to the McGovern-Fraser Commission, most of this early work was highly critical of the reformers' efforts.[3] The substance of the criticism varied a bit from author to author, but a number of common themes ran through it. The modern-day reformers, it was argued, had been overly concerned with philosophical abstractions and procedural niceties, and insufficiently attentive to the way the nominating process functioned as a whole and its intimate connections to other important features of the American system. They had focused too narrowly on the immediate issues and controversies of the late 1960s and not enough on long-term needs and objectives. Above all, they had severely weakened political parties, with important repercussions both for the kinds of candidates that were likely to be nominated and their subsequent ability to govern.[4]

In the early 1980s, however, a revisionist view of these issues began to develop. It is a telling commentary on the state of contemporary American politics that almost none of this later work seemed very anxious to defend the way the current nominating process worked as a whole. What the revisionists tended to argue, instead, was that the impact of the new rules on presidential politics had been greatly overstated. The most important features of the current system were attributable to other factors and forces, beyond the control of party reformers. Far and away the best statement of the revisionist position can be found in Howard Reiter's excellent book *Selecting the President: The Nominating Process in Transition*, published in 1985; but many of the same themes have been developed and defended in work by Kenneth Bode and Carol Casey, Donald Fraser, Mathew McCubbins, and David Adamany.[5]

The purpose of this chapter is to add one more layer to the literature on party reform: a reply to the revisionists, so to speak. Our argument, simply put, is that the delegate selection rules and campaign finance regulations enacted in the early 1970s had a very significant impact on the nature of the presidential nominating process: changing the rules really did change the game.

Beyond that rather narrow, academic purpose, this chapter attempts to provide an answer to a question that is often asked but rarely answered in clear or precise terms: What really is distinctive about the current era in presidential nominating politics? As we will see in the next section, almost everyone who works on this topic believes that the contemporary nominating process is significantly different from the one that existed during the 1930s and 1950s, but the nature of those differences has been, in general, neither described very specifically nor documented very carefully. As an introduction to the other studies in this volume, we hope to fill that gap.

The Issues in Dispute

The central point at issue between the critics and defenders of the reform initiatives is *not* whether the basic rules of the nominating process have changed. Quite clearly, they have. When the McGovern-Fraser Commission issued its principal report in April 1970, the full sweep and consequences of its proposals were perhaps not immediately obvious, even to many commission members.[6] But in retrospect, there is little doubt that the commission was recommending a dramatic break with past practices. Before 1972, neither party's national rules said very much at all about how national convention delegates were to be selected. Since the 1830s, state parties (and after 1900, state legislatures) had generally been allowed to handle that task in any way they wanted. Not until 1968, for example, did the Democratic Party require state parties to certify that they had not practiced overt discrimination in selecting their delegations.

In stark contrast to that sort of regime, the centerpiece of the McGovern-Fraser initiatives was a sweeping assertion of the national party's authority to control its state and local affiliates. Specifically, the commission promulgated eighteen "guidelines" that were designed to regulate state delegate selection practices in remarkable detail. Most important, the new rules required all state parties that hoped to have their delegates seated at the 1972 convention to

- have "explicit, written rules,"
- "forbid proxy voting,"
- "forbid the use of the unit rule,"
- ensure that party meetings were held "on uniform dates, at uniform times, and in public places of easy access,"
- "ensure adequate public notice" of all meetings involved in the delegate selection process,
- "prohibit the ex-officio designation of delegates,"
- "conduct the entire process of delegate selection . . . within the calendar year of the Convention."[7]

Still other guidelines took aim at filing fees, petition requirements, quorum provisions, intrastate apportionment, and slate-making procedures.

Of the eighteen guidelines, *every* state was in violation of *at least six*. Before the commission's formation, there were five basic institutional mechanisms used by state parties for selecting national convention delegates. The commission's final report effectively banned two of the five and severely restricted the use of a third.[8] By any reasonable standard, this was no mere "tinkering" with the rules.

Much the same verdict can be rendered about the Federal Election Campaign Act amendments passed by Congress in 1974. That law, too, has both its critics and its defenders, but few deny that the system it sought to create was a significant departure from its predecessor. In particular, the new law

- established contribution limits of $1,000 for individuals and $5,000 for political action committees,
- provided federal matching funds to all candidates who met certain minimum requirements,
- established both overall and state-by-state spending limits for all candidates who accepted government money,
- demanded strict accounting and full disclosure of all monies raised and spent by presidential candidates.

As is well known, a series of Supreme Court decisions have invalidated parts of this law and thereby created some important loopholes in the system. But the effects of those loopholes—exploited heavily for the first time in 1996—are confined largely to the general election. For the presidential primaries, the provisions listed above remain very much in effect. Of all the people who have actively pursued a major party's presidential nomination over the last six election cycles, only one—Steve Forbes in 1996—has not found his campaign decisively shaped by these provisions.[9]

So the rules have changed. Where the critics and the revisionists part company is in their assessment of the larger consequences of these changes. The critics blamed the new rules for a long list of maladies currently besetting the American political system, including the weakening of political parties, the increasing power of special-interest groups, the nomination of candidates who were ideological extremists or who lacked governing experience (or both), increasing tension between the legislative and executive branches, declining voter turnout, and the remarkably central role in nomination politics played by the news media.

The revisionists, especially Howard Reiter, attacked such claims on both methodological and substantive grounds. On the methodological side, Reiter et al. argued that much of the work attacking the new selection process fell well short of the canons of proof usually demanded of scholarly writing in the social sciences. Claims were made about previous periods in American politics without benefit of data or documentation; arguments about causality were asserted without more than token efforts to see if the facts bore them out.[10]

A particularly good example of Reiter's analysis concerns the role of national conventions in the nominating process. According to many critics, one effect of the new rules was to transform conventions from an arena of serious deliberation and bargaining among state party leaders into an empty ritual, put on largely for the benefit of television, that did little more than ratify a decision actually made months earlier by primary

TABLE 1.1   NUMBER OF PRESIDENTIAL ROLL CALL BALLOTS AT
             NATIONAL CONVENTIONS, 1900–96

	Year	Democrats	Republicans
Pre-reform	1900	1	1
	1904	1	1
	1908	1	1
	1912	46	1
	1916	1	3
	1920	44	10
	1924	103	1
	1928	1	1
	1932	4	1
	1936	0[a]	1
	1940	1	6
	1944	1	1
	1948	1	3
	1952	3	1
	1956	1	1
	1960	1	1
	1964	0[a]	1
	1968	1	1
Post-reform	1972	1	1
	1976	1	1
	1980	1	1
	1984	1	1
	1988	1	1
	1992	1	1
	1996	1	1

[a] No roll call vote was taken; candidate was nominated by acclamation.

voters and caucus attendees. There are several possible ways of measuring this trend, but one important indicator—often cited by critics of the contemporary nominating process—is the number of ballots it takes a convention to nominate a presidential candidate. When conventions were in their heyday, the argument goes, parties often had to take a number of roll call votes before finally settling upon a nominee. After the first ballot or two made clear who the principal contenders were and what sort of support they enjoyed, state party leaders had an important opportunity to reassess the candidates and their prospects. Depending on the circumstances, these leaders might then decide to rally around one of the original front-runners, or they might turn to a lesser-known "dark horse" candidate who seemed to have fewer enemies and thus a better prospect of uniting the party. By contrast, if conventions are merely a counting mechanism that registers a decision reached weeks or months earlier, it should presumably require just one ballot to accomplish that task.

Table 1.1 shows the number of roll call ballots each major party has required to nominate its presidential candidate in every convention since 1900. Clearly, there has been a decline in the frequency of multi-ballot conventions. But the change occurred long *before* the creation of the McGovern-Fraser Commission; the last convention that held more than one presidential ballot took place in 1952. At least according to this particular measure, there is no evidence at all that the new rules had an effect on the larger nominating process.

More generally, after collecting and analyzing a vast array of data, Reiter argued that few significant nomination-related behaviors and outcomes were changed by the efforts of recent reformers. The number of ballots it takes to nominate the presidential candidates, the percentage of uncommitted delegates, the rise of independent candidate organizations, the ease with which incumbents are renominated, the relationship between party and president—all *have* changed substantially during the twentieth century. The changes, however, did not begin in 1972 but decades earlier. A few aspects of the selection system were affected by reform, Reiter acknowledged, but not many. The outstanding characteristics of the current process—and the most important and noteworthy changes in it—are simply one manifestation of a larger, long-term decline in American political parties. As Reiter put it:

> . . . the hypothesis underlying this book is that *the nominating process has evolved since the early 1950s gradually into one in which state and local party leaders can no longer control nominations, and this is due to the long-term decay of party organization in the United States.* While no single hypothesis that attempts to explain so complex a set of phenomena can explain all of it, . . . this one comes closer than any other.[11]

"Even if the McGovern-Fraser Commission and its successors had never held a meeting," Reiter concluded, "we would have ended up with roughly the system we now have."[12]

Mathew McCubbins has offered a similar assessment:

> In summary, I find little evidence one way or the other on the effects of the post-1968 party reforms. While convention delegations

seem to have become more demographically representative, they apparently had little or no impact on nominations.[13]

It is with this conclusion that we wish to take issue. For while we agree that there has been a long-term decline in partisan strength in the United States that has wrought a number of significant changes in the presidential nominating process, we also see the McGovern-Fraser Commission and the 1974 Federal Election Campaign Act as having played an important, independent role in changing the nature of presidential selection. In this chapter, we focus on three particular changes that have, in our judgment, two things in common. All three have played a prominent part in popular criticism of the current process; and all three can be linked, as we hope to show, quite directly to the reform initiatives.[14] Those three consequences of reform are as follows:

1. It transformed the nominating process from one in which formal party organizations and party leaders played a major role into one that is, for all practical purposes, a plebiscitary system, in which the nomination is conferred on that candidate who is most successful in winning the support of whatever activists and ordinary voters happen to show up for the primaries and caucuses.
2. It led to the development of the contemporary presidential marathon, in which the quest for nomination begins a year or more before the opening of the party conventions.
3. It produced a system characterized by an extraordinary rush to judgment—that is, a system in which enormous power is entrusted to one or two early caucuses and primaries; in which candidates who do poorly in those early contests are forced to drop out of the race within days after the delegate selection process begins; and in which there is little or no opportunity for second thoughts, voter education, or public deliberation.

The method we employ is taken directly from Reiter.[15] For each of the changes described above, we began by trying to define and measure the hypothesized effects of the new rules as carefully and objectively as possible. (For details, see the appendix to this chapter.) We then collected data on each of these measures from the last five nomination cycles *before* the rules were changed (i.e., the elections of 1952 through 1968) and the first seven elections *after* the reforms (1972 through 1996). If the new rules really did produce the hypothesized effects, then as Reiter notes, we should observe "no change until 1972" and a "sharp change" thereafter. Alternatively, if no change occurs at all, or if the changes begin in the 1950s (as they do in table 1.1), we have strong evidence for the revisionist argument.[16]

One small caveat is in order. While we accept Reiter's argument that any change attributable to the new rules should not appear in the nomination races of the 1950s and 1960s, we do not think the hypothesized changes need to appear in precisely 1972. On the one hand, as we will demonstrate, many important characteristics of the new process were not immediately obvious to the candidates, their supporters, the media, or party leaders; it took an election cycle or two before the new features clearly asserted themselves. In addition, as the preceding discussion should indicate, our conception of "changes in the rules" is broader than just the work of the McGovern-Fraser Commission. The shape of the new presidential nominating process, in our view, also owes much to the campaign finance law of 1974. Assuming this to be the case, we should expect that some important consequences of the new-rules environment will become visible only in 1976 or even later.

Taking Out the Parties

As any introductory text on the subject will tell you, one of the most important functions traditionally performed by political parties in democratic systems is selecting candidates. And, at one time, American political parties actually did perform this task. Today, however, parties *select* presidential candidates only in the most strained sense of the word. A more accurate description would be that parties are simply the arena within which the presidential candidates fight for title to the party's nomination.[17]

Before 1972, parties as institutions—that is, state party organizations and major governmental officeholders elected under the party label— had a major, even decisive, role in determining who would receive the party's nomination for president. But the new rules put in place by the McGovern-Fraser Commission changed all that. And though some effects of those rules can reasonably be described as "unanticipated consequences," this one was largely anticipated and intended. As Austin Ranney, an eminent political scientist who was a member of that commission, has noted:

The commission rejected the notion that past party service should give any special advantage to a person seeking to be a national convention delegate. Most of the guidelines were consciously

designed to maximize participation by persons who are enthusiasts for a particular presidential aspirant or policy *in the year of
the convention*. Whatever the would-be delegate has done for the
party in the past was considered irrelevant to his chances for
selection in the convention year. The commission sought these
goals by banning all devices which in the past had especially
favored party regulars or "insiders": e.g., the reservation of ex
officio delegate slots for the party's governors, senators, congress-
men, state chairmen, and national committeemen and committee-
women. The commission also tried to eliminate any secrecy and
complexity in the selection procedure that might give old hands
an advantage over new enthusiasts.[18]

Or as another commission member put it, in less scholarly terms:

You've got to get these party people out of the process, you've
got to, or at least you've got to have a system which is so open
they get overwhelmed. I think most reformers now agree that
you cannot allow these regular party people to have any control
over anything, and still hope that you will have democracy in the
parties.[19]

As noted earlier, state parties in 1968 used five principal methods to
select national convention delegates; the McGovern-Fraser Commission
banned two of the five entirely and did its best to discourage a third.
What the three proscribed mechanisms had in common was that each
provided the institutional party with a special, privileged role in the delegate selection process. The two approved selection methods, on the
other hand, were both designed to set old party veterans and first-time
participants on an equal footing.

The most celebrated indicator of this transformation is the explosion
in the number of presidential primaries. By their very nature, primaries
give an equal voice—one vote—to every participant, regardless of previous service or experience. Hence, primaries have always been seen, at
least in part, as a way of undermining established party organizations.

Why the McGovern-Fraser reforms fostered an increase in the number of presidential primaries is the subject of some dispute, since there
was nothing in the guidelines that explicitly urged or commended primaries. According to some accounts, the new rules were so complicated
and difficult to implement that many states decided that the easiest way
to comply—and thus to avoid a challenge to their delegations at the next

convention—was to hold a primary.[20] Other scholars contend that with the new rules governing nonprimary selection procedures, party regulars worried about having their local meetings and state conventions overrun by issue activists and ideological zealots. From this perspective, primaries were a way to "separate national convention delegate selection from all other party processes."[21]

Whatever the exact causal mechanism, the statistical evidence is unambiguous.[22] As the data in table 1.2 indicate, from 1952 to 1968, an average of about eighteen states held presidential primaries. Moreover, there is no sign that this number was increasing; if anything, the number of primaries declined slightly in the last few presidential campaigns before the onset of the new rules. And then, in 1972, the number of primaries began a sharp and sustained increase. Looking just at the Democratic figures (the trend for Republicans is similar), the number of primaries jumped from seventeen in 1968, to twenty-three in 1972, to twenty-nine in 1976, and then to thirty-three in 1988. In 1984, in a deliberate effort to "reform the reforms," the Democrats created a new category of delegates, generally

TABLE 1.2　　PRESIDENTIAL PRIMARIES AS A MEANS OF SELECTING NATIONAL CONVENTION DELEGATES, 1952–96

Year	Democrats		Republicans	
	No. of Primaries[a]	% of Delegates Selected by Primary	No. of Primaries[a]	% of Delegates Selected by Primary
1952	18	48	14	45
1956	20	48	19	49
1960	18	43	16	44
1964	18	43	17	46
1968	17	41	16	43
1972	23	65	22	56
1976	29	75	28	67
1980	30	71	33	75
1984	24	54	28	63
1988	33	67	34	72
1992	35	67	38	79
1996	34	62	41	81

Note: All figures include the District of Columbia but exclude territories, such as Puerto Rico and the Virgin Islands, as well as Alaska and Hawaii in 1952 and 1956.
[a] Includes only primaries that were used to select and/or bind delegates (i.e., excludes primaries that were purely advisory).

known as "superdelegates," by granting automatic delegate status to certain types of party leaders and elected officials. In each of the last four Democratic conventions, superdelegates have accounted for about one-sixth of the total votes. Yet even with this innovation in place, more than two-thirds of the delegates to the 1988 and 1992 Democratic conventions were selected through primaries.[23] In the Republican Party, which still bans ex officio delegates, primaries now account for about 80 percent of all convention delegates.

These data notwithstanding, Kenneth Bode and Carol Casey, two former staff members of the McGovern-Fraser Commission, have argued that it is a "myth" that the "reforms spawned primaries." It is true, they acknowledge, that "after the [reform] guidelines were adopted, many states enacted presidential primary laws," but it is "simplistic and inaccurate . . . to say that primaries were adopted *because* of the guidelines." In Bode and Casey's view:

> Historically, the result of public dissatisfaction with acrimonious, divisive nominating contests has been the adoption of new primaries. . . . After the Stevenson-Kefauver contest in 1952, states once again looked toward presidential primaries as a means of giving greater public legitimacy to the selection of delegates. Thus, the adoption of new primaries after 1968 is in keeping with the flux of American political history.[24]

But as the figures in table 1.2 clearly indicate, there is an enormous difference between what took place within the Democratic Party after 1952 and what occurred after 1968. Between 1952 and 1956, the number of Democratic presidential primaries increased by just two—from eighteen to twenty—and there was no further increase after that. By 1960, the number was back down to eighteen. The increase after 1968 was, by comparison, both dramatically larger and far more enduring. Nothing in the data of table 1.2 suggests that the balance between primary and nonprimary selection systems was significantly altered by the events of 1952. The same cannot be said of 1968.

With all of the attention that has been focused on the growth of presidential primaries, most analyses of the new nominating process have missed an equally significant change in the delegate selection procedures used by nonprimary states.[25] Before 1972, states that declined to hold presidential primaries generally chose their delegates through a procedure that began with local party meetings and culminated in a state convention. In other states, the decision was entrusted to a state committee. Whatever the details, the important point is that the process was operated and closely supervised by state party leaders and party organizations. In many states, for example, the local party meetings were open only to party functionaries who had been elected several years earlier. In other cases, these meetings were held in private homes or were poorly publicized or had no written rules of procedure.

Such practices were sharply challenged by the McGovern-Fraser Commission. The commission did not ban nonprimary selection procedures, but it did demand that all such procedures be held during the election year; that they be publicized well in advance; that they abide by written, clearly defined rules of procedure; and most important, that they allow any interested Democrat the right to participate on full and equal terms. Simply put, the effect of such rules was to convert nonprimary selection methods from a party-controlled system to a plebiscitary one, open to anyone who wanted to participate and highly responsive to mass opinion. A fair amount of ink has been expended over the last thirty years discussing (usually in quite theoretical terms) the respective advantages and disadvantages of caucuses and primaries. But most of this writing, in our judgment, misses the far more consequential point that under the new-rules regime, there really is not that much difference between the two. The highly publicized Iowa caucuses, the first major delegate selection event in most recent nomination races, are often described as "the functional equivalent of a primary."[26] In our view, the same may be said of most caucuses.

One way of appreciating the effect of this transformation is shown in table 1.3. For every contested presidential roll call vote since 1952, we have calculated the mean vote percentage that each major candidate received from primary and nonprimary states. Since a state's decision to hold a primary or a convention varied according to its political and demographic circumstances, the final column in table 1.3 presents a set of estimates that show how much better or worse each candidate did in convention states, after controlling for such variables as region, ideology, demographic composition, and the home states of the major candidates.

As these figures show, between 1952 and 1968, it clearly *did* make a difference whether a state used a primary to select its delegates. Even though the presidential primaries of this era often made it difficult for voters to elect delegates who agreed with their presidential preferences, states that held primaries and states that used nonprimary selection procedures quite often differed in the presidential candidates they supported.

The divergence is particularly striking in a number of Democratic nomination races and corresponds closely to the standard historical

TABLE 1.3   MEAN CONVENTION VOTE PERCENTAGE FOR CANDIDATES IN
CONTESTED NOMINATION RACES, BY DELEGATE SELECTION
METHOD, 1952-96

Candidate or Position	Caucus-Convention States	Primary States	Difference (Caucus-Convention minus Primary)	Difference, Controlling for Region and Other Factors
1952 Democratic				
Kefauver[a]	14	53	-39	-46**
Russell[a]	30	13	17	5
Stevenson[a]	25	9	16	31**
Harriman[a]	6	7	-1	4
Favorite son/ other[a]	24	18	6	
1952 Republican				
Yes on seating of La. delegation[b]	60	43	17	3
No on seating of La. delegation[b]	40	57	-17	-3
Eisenhower	47	40	7	17
Taft	50	42	8	1
Favorite son/other	2	18	-16	
1956 Democratic				
Stevenson	65	87	-22	-15
Harriman	10	8	2	4
Favorite son/other	25	5	20	
1960 Democratic				
Kennedy	44	66	-22	-7
Johnson	39	8	31	21*
Stevenson	5	4	1	-2
Symington	6	5	1	-3
Favorite son/other	6	14	-8	
1964 Republican				
Goldwater	75	63	12	-9
Scranton	12	27	-15	-2
Rockefeller	1	9	-8	-9
Favorite son/other	12	1	11	
1968 Democratic				
Humphrey	79	43	36	31**
McCarthy	13	36	-23	-24**
McGovern	4	11	-7	-1
Favorite son/other	3	9	-6	

TABLE 1.3   *(continued)*

Candidate or Position	Caucus-Convention States	Primary States	Difference (Caucus-Convention minus Primary)	Difference, Controlling for Region and Other Factors
1968 Republican				
Nixon	60	68	-8	-25*
Rockefeller	16	12	4	17*
Reagan	11	8	3	7
Favorite son/other	14	12	2	
1972 Democratic				
Yes on Calif. resolution[c]	48	63	-15	-16*
No on Calif. resolution[c]	52	37	15	16*
McGovern	47	60	-13	-12
H. Jackson	27	10	17	16*
Wallace	3	21	-18	-25**
1976 Democratic				
Carter	73	78	-5	-4
Udall	14	9	5	4
Brown	7	8	-1	0
1976 Republican				
Ford	46	56	-10	1
Reagan	54	44	10	-1
1980 Democratic				
Yes on binding delegates[d]	41	41	0	-1
No on binding delegates[d]	59	59	0	1
Carter	68	65	3	2
Kennedy	27	34	-7	-5
1980 Republican				
Reagan as of 26 May 1980[e]	68	72	-4	-7
Bush as of 26 May 1980[e]	14	20	-6	-4
Uncommitted as of 26 May 1980[e]	16	3	13	13*

(continued)

TABLE 1.3   *(continued)*

Candidate or Position	Caucus-Convention States	Primary States	Difference (Caucus-Convention minus Primary)	Difference, Controlling for Region and Other Factors
1984 Democratic				
Mondale	54	53	1	7
Hart	34	33	1	-10*
J. Jackson	9	13	-4	2
1988 Democratic				
Dukakis	65	72	-7	-16**
J. Jackson	31	27	4	14**
1992 Democratic				
Clinton	79	84	-5	0
Brown	12	11	1	-2
Tsongas	5	3	2	0

Note: For details on how the figures in column five were computed, see the appendix to this chapter.

[a] Figures are for the first ballot voting; Stevenson was ultimately nominated on the third ballot.

[b] A "yes" vote supported the pro-Taft position on a credentials dispute; a "no" vote endorsed the pro-Eisenhower position.

[c] A "yes" vote was the position endorsed by McGovern; a "no" vote supported the position of McGovern's principal opponents.

[d] A "yes" vote was the position endorsed by Kennedy; a "no" vote supported the position of Carter.

[e] At the Republican convention, the presidential roll call produced a unanimous vote for Reagan. The results shown here are based on a tally of all delegates selected through 26 May 1980, shortly after Bush withdrew from the race, as reported in *Congressional Quarterly Weekly Report*.

* $p < .05$. ** $p < .01$.

accounts of those elections. In the 1952 Democratic contest, for example, Estes Kefauver demonstrated considerable support among primary voters but had very little rapport with party leaders. The result was that on the first ballot at the national convention, Kefauver won 53 percent of the votes from an average primary-state delegation but averaged only 14 percent in convention states. After controlling for region and a number of demographic variables, we estimate that Kefauver received 46 percent less support in convention states than in states that held primaries. Adlai Stevenson, by contrast, became a reluctant aspirant for the 1952

Democratic nomination only after the national convention was under way. His support, especially after allowances are made for its regional character, came overwhelmingly from convention states. A similar pattern characterized the Democratic nomination race of 1968. Hubert Humphrey, who did not contest a single presidential primary that year, not surprisingly drew disproportionate support from convention states. Eugene McCarthy, on the other hand, garnered about one-third of the delegates selected in primary states but only about one-eighth of the delegates selected through conventions.

Not every nomination race from this period can be characterized as a showdown between primary states and states that held conventions. In the 1952 Republican nomination race, for example, both Robert Taft and Dwight Eisenhower registered a number of impressive victories in the presidential primaries (Taft won six of them, Eisenhower five), and both had considerable support among party leaders (though from different regions of the country). After controlling for region, there is essentially no difference in the way primary and convention states voted on an early credentials dispute at the 1952 national convention, which is probably the best single test of strength between the Taft and Eisenhower forces. Still, the basic pattern is clear: in the "old" nominating process, delegation selection procedures frequently *did* matter. In four of seven races shown in table 1.3, at least one major candidate ran 20 percentage points better in one kind of selection system than in the other.

After 1968, however, that pattern changes. Two important conclusions emerge from the post-reform results shown in table 1.3. First, in most races, it did not matter whether delegates were selected by primary or by caucus, for both were essentially plebiscitary systems. In the Democratic nomination contests of 1976, 1980, and 1992, and the Republican races of 1976 and 1980, no major candidate did very much better in one type of delegate selection procedure than in the other. Second, where differences do occur, they generally run in the opposite direction from that of the 1952–68 races. Whereas the old convention systems tended to aid mainstream, "establishment" candidates and the regular party organization, modern-day caucuses are, if anything, a more favorable arena for candidates supported by issue activists and ideological extremists.

If there is any kind of candidate who ought to receive preferential treatment from the regular organization, it is an incumbent president. Yet, of the two recent incumbents who faced serious opposition in their quests for renomination—Gerald Ford in 1976 and Jimmy Carter in 1980—neither ran significantly better in caucuses than in primaries. Of all the candidates between 1976 and 1996 who might plausibly be dubbed "the candidate of the party regulars," only Walter Mondale in 1984 seems to have derived any perceptible advantage from the caucuses. Yet, even with the AFL-CIO, NOW, and a host of state and national party leaders all solidly in his corner, Mondale's advantage in the caucus states was a remarkably narrow one, especially when compared with the experiences of Adlai Stevenson in 1952 and Hubert Humphrey in 1968. With region, ideology, and a number of other factors held constant, we estimate that Mondale ran about 7 percent better in caucus states than in those that held primaries, while Gary Hart gained an edge of about 10 percent in the primaries (only the latter figure is statistically significant).

The type of delegate selection system a state used also appears to have mattered in the Democratic nomination race of 1988—but the candidate who ran especially well in the caucuses that year was not Michael Dukakis or Al Gore but Jesse Jackson, whose entire campaign was cast as an attack upon the party establishment on behalf of various minorities and issue activists. The relationship is partially obscured by the fact that most of the 1988 caucuses were held in small states that had no significant minority populations and that were therefore not generally sympathetic to Jackson's candidacy. But after controlling for such influences, we estimate that Jackson derived an advantage of about 14 percent from the caucus procedure.

In the 1988 Republican contest, all major candidates except George Bush had withdrawn from the field before the national convention began, with the result that Bush received a unanimous vote from both primary and caucus states on the presidential roll call. But while that race was still being actively contested, the initial voter preference results from primaries and caucuses suggest a pattern quite similar to that of the Democratic race. The two candidates in the Republican contest with the strongest ties to the established party leadership, Vice President Bush and Senate Majority Leader Robert Dole, actually fared better in primaries than in caucuses. The candidate who received a noticeable boost from states using a caucus system was the Reverend Pat Robertson, who had no backing from the regular party organization but was supported by millions of devoted followers of his television ministry.[27]

The only exception to these patterns—the only post-reform race in which an insurgent candidate ran better in the primaries than in the caucuses—was the Democratic nomination race of 1972. This is not to say George McGovern fared poorly in the caucus states; he won, on average, 47 percent of the votes from caucus-state delegations, more than three times the success rate achieved by Kefauver in 1952 and McCarthy in

1968. But McGovern did even better in primary states, where he received an average convention vote of 60 percent.

A closer look at the 1972 race suggests two general explanations for this anomaly. In part, it may simply be that McGovern was lucky. Many of his victories in the primaries came in states whose delegate allocation rules allowed him to take maximum advantage of the votes he received. McGovern won more than 87 percent of the delegates selected in Massachusetts, Nebraska, Oregon, Rhode Island, California, and New York—even though he received no more than 53 percent of the presidential preference vote in any of these states.[28]

Second—and more important to the general argument of this chapter—because its candidate had chaired the Democratic reform commission, the McGovern campaign seems to have had a significantly greater understanding of the new delegate selection rules. Thus, in a number of states, McGovern won substantially more delegates than he might have against better-prepared opponents.[29] In Pennsylvania, for example, McGovern came in third in the preference tally, getting 20 percent of the vote to Hubert Humphrey's 35 percent and George Wallace's 21 percent. But because McGovern fielded an entire slate of delegate candidates, while Wallace had only 4 such candidates pledged to him, McGovern won 37 of the 137 delegates chosen in the Pennsylvania primary, while Wallace received exactly 2 delegates for his showing. Similarly in Tennessee: Wallace was the overwhelming winner in the presidential preference poll, with 68 percent of the vote, but his organization failed to file candidates for *any* of the actual delegate positions. McGovern, by contrast, won a sizable bloc of delegates in the Volunteer State even though he received a bare 7 percent of the votes in the "beauty contest" section of the ballot. As a result, on what is generally regarded as the most important vote of the 1972 Democratic convention—the credentials challenge to the McGovern delegation from California—23 of 49 delegates from Tennessee supported the pro-McGovern position.[30]

Several other indicators are available to show the declining influence of state party leaders and party organizations in the post-reform nominating process.[31] One such measure is the number of "favorite son" candidates in each election. A favorite son is a candidate for the presidency who receives substantial support from his home state but very little support from anywhere else.[32] In a small number of instances, a candidate who started out as a favorite son gradually gained strength in other states and went on to win the nomination.[33] But the chief significance of favorite son candidacies in the pre-reform nominating process was as a mechanism for establishing and maintaining organizational control of a state delegation. By committing its votes to a local favorite, a state could remain neutral among the major contenders, at least for a time, and thus enhance its long-term bargaining position.

While there is broad agreement on the general definition of a favorite son candidate, the methodology we employ in this chapter requires us to convert that idea into more specific and quantitative terms. In the analysis that follows, we define a favorite son as any candidate who receives (1) at least 50 percent of the first-ballot convention votes cast by his or her home state and (2) less than 2 percent of the remaining convention votes. As the figures in table 1.4 indicate, in the pre-reform system, favorite son candidacies were a fairly common occurrence. There were four such candidates in the Republican nomination contest of 1964 and six in 1968. The Democrats had only one favorite son in 1968, but this was probably because Hubert Humphrey had been so clearly designated as the anointed heir of an incumbent president; in 1952–60, the Democrats had averaged five favorite son candidates per convention. In the post-reform nominating process, by contrast, favorite son candidates have gone the way of the dinosaur. There were three such candidates in the 1972 Democratic nomination race; since this last, dying gasp, there have been none in either party. Whereas favorite son candidacies were once an important feature of American presidential

TABLE 1.4   NUMBER OF FAVORITE SON PRESIDENTIAL CANDIDATES, 1952–96

Year	Democrats	Republicans
1952	5	2
1956	6	0
1960	4	0
1964	—[a]	4
1968	1	6
1972	3	0
1976	0	0
1980	0	0
1984	0	0
1988	0	0
1992	0	0
1996	0	0

Note: Favorite sons are candidates who (1) received at least half of the first ballot convention votes cast by their home state, and (2) received less than 2 percent of the remaining convention votes.

[a] No presidential roll call was ever held; Johnson was nominated by acclamation.

politics, most introductory textbooks on the topic no longer even bother to mention them.[34]

In summary, the first important consequence of the new rules governing presidential nominations was to take the parties out of the process. Whatever may be said about a general trend toward party decline during the 1950s and 1960s, the data in tables 1.2-1.4 suggest that when it came to selecting a presidential candidate, party organizations and party leaders were still major players—perhaps *the* central players—all the way up through 1968. Beginning in 1972, two sharp changes are clearly visible: there is a dramatic increase in the number of presidential primaries, and nonprimary selection procedures are so significantly restructured as to be no longer controllable by state party organizations. If the American parties had already begun to weaken by 1972, the new nominating rules were a severe additional blow.

The Advent of the Marathon

Another important effect of the rules changes has been a dramatic lengthening of the presidential nomination race. Once confined to the election year itself, the race now stretches through most of the preceding year and not infrequently involves substantial activity in the year before that. In table 1.5, we have listed the date on which each major presidential candidate of the last fifty years formally announced his candidacy. To allow for an easier comparison across years, we have also calculated the number of days between a candidate's announcement and the start of his party's national nominating convention. These figures are summarized in table 1.6.

As these tables make clear, it was once the case that aspirants for the presidency announced their candidacies at the beginning of the election year itself or at the end of the preceding year. Of all the major candidates who ran for the presidency between 1952 and 1968, Robert Taft had the earliest announcement date—and it came in mid-October of 1951.

The pattern is clearly different in the nomination races since 1968. The first person to understand the incentive structure of the new rules was George McGovern (here again, McGovern seems to have derived an important advantage from chairing his party's reform commission). In a dramatic break with all recent precedents, McGovern announced his candidacy in January of 1971, almost a year and a half before the Democratic National Convention. McGovern's decision was widely ridiculed at the time—but the laughing stopped when, 541 days later, McGovern won the nomination. Not surprisingly, as the candidates

TABLE 1.5   ANNOUNCEMENT DATES FOR MAJOR PRESIDENTIAL CANDIDATES
IN CONTESTED NOMINATION RACES, 1952-96

Democrats

Year	Candidate	Announcement Date	No. of Days before Start of Convention
1952	Estes Kefauver	23 January 1952	180
	Richard Russell	28 February 1952	144
	Robert Kerr	31 March 1952	112
	Averell Harriman	22 April 1952	90
	Alben Barkley	6 July 1952	15
	Adlai Stevenson	None	0
1956	Adlai Stevenson	15 November 1955	272
	Estes Kefauver	16 December 1955	241
	Averell Harriman	9 June 1956	65
1960	Hubert Humphrey	30 December 1959	194
	John Kennedy	2 January 1960	191
	Stuart Symington	24 March 1960	109
	Lyndon Johnson	5 July 1960	6
1964	George Wallace	6 March 1964	173
	Lyndon Johnson	None	0
1968	Eugene McCarthy	30 November 1967	270
	Robert Kennedy	16 March 1968	163
	Hubert Humphrey	27 April 1968	121
	George McGovern	10 August 1968	16
1972	George McGovern	18 January 1971	539
	Henry Jackson	19 November 1971	234
	Eugene McCarthy	17 December 1971	206
	John Lindsay	28 December 1971	195
	Edmund Muskie	4 January 1972	188
	Hubert Humphrey	10 January 1972	182
	George Wallace	13 January 1972	179
	Terry Sanford	8 March 1972	124
1976	Morris Udall	23 November 1974	597
	Jimmy Carter	12 December 1974	578
	Fred Harris	11 January 1975	548
	Henry Jackson	6 February 1975	522
	Sargent Shriver	20 September 1975	296
	Birch Bayh	21 October 1975	265
	George Wallace	12 November 1975	243
	Jerry Brown	12 March 1976	122
	Frank Church	18 March 1976	116

TABLE 1.5   *(continued)*

Democrats

Year	Candidate	Announcement Date	No. of Days before Start of Convention
1980	Edward Kennedy	7 November 1979	278
	Jerry Brown	8 November 1979	277
	Jimmy Carter	4 December 1979	251
1984	Alan Cranston	2 February 1983	530
	Gary Hart	17 February 1983	515
	Walter Mondale	21 February 1983	511
	Reubin Askew	23 February 1983	509
	Ernest Hollings	18 April 1983	455
	John Glenn	21 April 1983	452
	George McGovern	13 September 1983	307
	Jesse Jackson	3 November 1983	256
1988	Richard Gephardt	23 February 1987	511
	Bruce Babbitt	10 March 1987	496
	Gary Hart	13 April 1987	462
	Michael Dukakis	29 April 1987	446
	Paul Simon	18 May 1987	427
	Joseph Biden	9 June 1987	405
	Al Gore	29 June 1987	385
	Jesse Jackson	10 October 1987	282
1992	Paul Tsongas	30 April 1991	440
	Tom Harkin	15 September 1991	302
	Bob Kerrey	30 September 1991	287
	Bill Clinton	3 October 1991	284
	Jerry Brown	21 October 1991	266

Republicans

Year	Candidate	Announcement Date	No. of Days before Start of Convention
1952	Robert Taft	16 October 1951	265
	Earl Warren	14 November 1951	236
	Harold Stassen	27 December 1951	193
	Dwight Eisenhower	4 June 1952	33
1964	Nelson Rockefeller	7 November 1963	249
	Barry Goldwater	3 January 1964	192
	Margaret Chase Smith	27 January 1964	168
	William Scranton	12 June 1964	31

(continued)

TABLE 1.5   *(continued)*

Republicans

Year	Candidate	Announcement Date	No. of Days before Start of Convention
1968	George Romney	18 November 1967	261
	Richard Nixon	1 February 1968	186
	Nelson Rockefeller	30 April 1968	97
	Ronald Reagan	5 August 1968	0
1976	Gerald Ford	8 July 1975	405
	Ronald Reagan	20 November 1975	270
1980	Philip Crane	2 August 1978	712
	John Connally	24 January 1979	537
	George Bush	1 May 1979	440
	Robert Dole	14 May 1979	427
	John Anderson	8 June 1979	402
	Howard Baker	1 November 1979	256
	Ronald Reagan	13 November 1979	244
1988	Pierre du Pont	16 September 1986	699
	Alexander Haig	24 March 1987	510
	Jack Kemp	6 April 1987	497
	Pat Robertson	1 October 1987	319
	George Bush	12 October 1987	308
	Robert Dole	9 November 1987	280
1992	Pat Buchanan	10 December 1991	251
	George Bush	12 February 1992	187
1996	Phil Gramm	24 February 1995	535
	Lamar Alexander	28 February 1995	531
	Pat Buchanan	20 March 1995	511
	Arlen Specter	30 March 1995	501
	Robert Dole	10 April 1995	490
	Richard Lugar	19 April 1995	481
	Pete Wilson	15 June 1995	424
	Steve Forbes	22 September 1995	325

Source: Compiled from contemporary reports in the *New York Times* and *Facts On File*.

TABLE 1.6   TIMING OF CANDIDATE ANNOUNCEMENT DATES: A SUMMARY

Year	Average No. of Days before Start of Convention for All Candidates Listed	
	Democrats	Republicans
1952	90	182
1956	193	—
1960	125	—
1964	86	160
1968	142	136
1972	231	—
1976	365	338
1980	269	431
1984	442	—
1988	427	436
1992	316	219
1996	—	475

Note: Data are reported only for contested nomination races.

began to gear up for the 1976 nomination contests, many followed his example. Indeed, both the eventual Democratic nominee (Jimmy Carter) and the person who would prove to be his toughest opponent (Morris Udall) went McGovern one better, by announcing their candidacies in the waning months of *1974*.

Not all candidates, it must be said, are required to announce quite this early. Incumbent presidents are generally spared the ordeal, even when they expect to face substantial opposition (as Jimmy Carter did in 1980). Also spared are a few candidates with substantial name recognition and an established national following, such as George Wallace, Ronald Reagan, Jesse Jackson, and George Bush when he was the incumbent vice president. In the 1992 election cycle, the Gulf War and its aftermath led most Democratic contenders to delay their entrance into the race until the fall of 1991.

But such exceptions do not mar the basic pattern shown in tables 1.5 and 1.6. At a minimum, we can draw four conclusions from these data:

1. A very large proportion of recent presidential contenders have announced their candidacies at least 400 days before the opening of their parties' national convention—in other words, at least a year and a half before the November election.

2. These early announcers are not just long shots and also-rans. They include the eventual Democratic nominees in 1972, 1976, 1984, and 1988, the Republican nominees in 1976 and 1996, and the second-place finishers in the 1976 and 1984 Democratic races and the 1980 Republican contest. The last of these, of course, parlayed his second-place finish into a vice presidential nomination in 1980 and ultimately into a four-year term in the White House.

3. Of the first two trends described here, neither has any precedent in the nomination races of 1952–68.

4. Many of the candidates who delayed their announcement dates— in particular, Frank Church and Jerry Brown in 1976 and Edward Kennedy and Howard Baker in 1980—would subsequently claim that their late announcement dates had severely hurt their candidacies, denying them a sufficient opportunity to raise money, build an organization, and line up the support of party activists.[35]

By the late 1990s, we have become so accustomed to marathon races for the presidential nomination that we often lose sight of the many disadvantages they present for our system of government. But the difficulties are real and serious. The most obvious problem is the dilemma a long nomination race poses for any current governmental officeholder who is contemplating a run for the presidency: how can he attend to his governing responsibilities while spending three or four days a week raising money, meeting with party activists, and campaigning in Iowa and New Hampshire? There are three ways of dealing with this conflict, all of which pose problems for the ongoing operations of American government.

In the first place, many highly qualified presidential prospects simply decide not to run. It is impossible, of course, to provide a definitive list of such noncandidates, since we will never know for certain if various individuals would have entered the race even if it were a good deal shorter. It surely is worth noting, however, the widespread perception in 1976 and 1992 (and, to a lesser extent, in 1988) that the field of announced Democratic candidates was a distinctly "second-tier" group that did not include many of the best-known and most highly regarded leaders of the Democratic Party.

Alternatively, many of our most talented public officials leave government—are, in effect, driven out of it—because they are thinking about a run for the presidency and have been told that if they are serious about making the race, they should not be tied down with any real governing responsibilities. Consider, as one especially telling example, the contrasting career decisions made by two eminent Democratic politicians from Minnesota. When Hubert Humphrey lost the presidential election of 1968, he clearly entertained some thoughts about seeking the White House again in 1972. Under the rules of the old system, Humphrey saw no conflict between that ambition and serving in the U.S. Senate;[36] so when one of the Minnesota Senate seats came up for election in 1970, he unhesitatingly ran for it and won. By contrast, when Walter Mondale left the vice presidency in 1980 and set his sights on the 1984 Democratic nomination, he recognized quite clearly that his best chance of attaining that goal was to be unencumbered with a government job. Hence, when a Republican-held Senate seat came before the Minnesota voters in 1982, Mondale declined to run for it. Similarly, Howard Baker in 1984 and Gary Hart in 1986 decided not to run for reelection to the U.S. Senate. While a number of factors may have influenced these decisions, contemporary press reports suggest that one of the chief considerations was the likelihood that these men would soon be running for president.[37] If one believes that political talent is a relatively rare and valuable commodity, one has to wonder about a system that encourages so much of that talent to sit on the sidelines, at just the moment when they have finished serving their apprenticeships and seem best able to make significant contributions.[38]

A final alternative, of course, is to attempt both tasks at once: to continue serving in one's current office *and* to run for the presidency. But in most cases, this is likely to be a false choice. As long as days last only twenty-four hours, it is probably impossible to mount a vigorous, national presidential campaign and to fulfill one's duties as governor, senator, or representative. One responsibility or the other will inevitably suffer.

For this third way of handling the conflict between campaigning and governing, we can quantify at least the general dimensions of the problem. For all sitting U.S. senators and representatives who have actively run for the White House since 1952, table 1.7 shows their congressional voting-participation rate—the percentage of all roll call votes in which they took part—for the election year and the three years prior to that. Table 1.8 provides a rough summary of these figures by showing the average participation rates for candidates in the five pre-reform election cycles (1949-68) and the seven post-reform elections (1969-96).[39] As these data indicate, it has always been difficult to be a senator and a presidential candidate at the same time. Robert Taft in 1952, Estes Kefauver in both 1952 and 1956, John Kennedy and Hubert Humphrey in 1960, Barry Goldwater in 1964, Eugene McCarthy and Robert Kennedy in 1968—all attended fewer than half the roll call votes held while they campaigned for the presidency. Even candidates who waged less active

TABLE 1.7   CONGRESSIONAL VOTING-PARTICIPATION RATES FOR PRESIDENTIAL
CANDIDATES, 1949-96 (IN PERCENTAGES)

1952	*Senate Average*	*Taft*	*Kefauver*	*Russell*	*Kerr*
1949	n.a.[a]	70	72	85	87
1950	n.a.	74	73	89	78
1951	n.a.	76	65	78	93
1952	n.a.	47	22	43	49

1956	*Senate Average*	*Kefauver*
1953	84	76
1954	85	50
1955	86	79
1956	89	49

1960	*Senate Average*	*Kennedy*	*Humphrey*	*Symington*	*Johnson*
1957	85	79	87	87	87
1958	86	85	89	94	89
1959	89	77	81	89	95
1960	82	35	49	58	95

1964	*Senate Average*	*Goldwater*	*Smith*
1961	87	69	100
1962	80	63	100
1963	83	71	100
1964	85	28	100

1968	*Senate Average*	*McCarthy*	*Kennedy*	*McGovern*
1965	85	59	84	87
1966	79	83	74	86
1967	82	66	83	88
1968	76	5	28[b]	62

1972	*Senate Average*	*McGovern*	*Jackson*	*Muskie*	*Humphrey*
1969	85	89	87	89	—
1970	77	84	85	74	—
1971	83	52	65	59	75[c]
1972	80	22	74	48	53

TABLE 1.7   *(continued)*

1976	*Senate Average*	*Jackson*	*Bayh*	*Church*	*Udall*
1973	87	99	86	85	91
1974	86	99	69	71	85
1975	89	95	56	81	47
1976	83	84	65	62	47

1980	*Senate Average*	*Kennedy*	*Dole*	*Baker*	*Crane*	*Anderson*
1977	88	89	97	91	88	84
1978	87	89	95	79	72	71
1979	90	74	93	62	54	28
1980	87	18	96	79	68	14

1984	*Senate Average*	*Cranston*	*Hart*	*Hollings*	*Glenn*
1981	93	88	92	94	94
1982	94	89	94	92	82
1983	92	56	63	50	64
1984	91	78	37	79	80

1988	*Senate Average*	*Simon*	*Gore*	*Biden*	*Dole*	*Gephardt*	*Kemp*
1985	95	93	99	92	99	91	88
1986	95	99	99	94	99	70	81
1987	94	42	43	62[d]	95	18	31
1988	92	72	61	—	86	80	39

1992	*Senate Average*	*Harkin*	*Kerrey*
1989	98	98	100
1990	97	100	99
1991	97	75	77
1992	95	74	84

1996	*Senate Average*	*Gramm*	*Specter*	*Dole*	*Lugar*
1993	98	93	86	98	99
1994	97	90	97	99	100
1995	97	89	98[e]	99	96
1996	98	93	—	92	99

Source: All data are taken from *Congressional Quarterly Almanac* (Washington, D.C.: Congressional Quarterly), various issues.

[a] Average Senate voting-participation figures are not available for 1949–1952.

[b] Includes only roll calls taken before Kennedy's assassination on 5 June 1968.

[c] Humphrey was not a member of the U.S. Senate in 1969 and 1970.

[d] Biden withdrew from the 1988 race on 23 September 1987.

[e] Specter withdrew from the 1996 race on 22 November 1995.

TABLE 1.8   CONGRESSIONAL VOTING-PARTICIPATION RATES FOR PRESIDENTIAL
CANDIDATES (IN PERCENTAGES): A SUMMARY

Year of the Election Cycle	Average for Pre-Reform Candidates (1949-68)	Average for Post-Reform Candidates (1969-96)
Year 1	81	92
Year 2	80	88
Year 3	82	65
Year 4	48	66

races, such as Richard Russell in 1952 and Stuart Symington in 1960, registered sharp declines in their attendance at Senate roll call votes.

But—and this is the key point—up through 1968, congressional voting-participation rates were affected *only during the election year itself*. In particular, there is no indication for any of the pre-reform candidates listed in table 1.7 that their congressional attendance declined significantly in the year before the election. John Kennedy, for example, participated in 79 percent of the roll call votes held in 1957, 85 percent in 1958, and 77 percent in 1959. Not until 1960 did his participation rate plunge to 35 percent.

Once again, however, there is a sharp change in the post-reform nomination races. In the 1972 election cycle, as we have seen, far and away the earliest entrant in the field was George McGovern, who announced his candidacy in January 1971. Table 1.7 shows one consequence of that decision: McGovern took part in only 52 percent of the Senate roll call votes held in 1971, as compared with 89 percent in 1969 and 84 percent in 1970. (In 1972, his participation rate fell even further, to 22 percent.) Indeed, even those candidates who entered the 1972 contest at a much later point in the cycle, such as Henry Jackson and Edmund Muskie, showed up for substantially fewer Senate votes in 1971 than they had in 1970.

And so it has been in almost every subsequent nomination race. Candidates with early announcement dates—Udall in 1976; Crane and Anderson in 1980; Cranston, Hart, Hollings, and Glenn in 1984; Simon, Gore, Biden, Gephardt, and Kemp in 1988—usually did not make it to even 60 percent of the congressional roll call votes held in the year before the election. Those few candidates who had better attendance records—such as Jackson and Church in 1976 and Dole and Kennedy in 1980—generally found their campaigns hamstrung as a result.

As we will see in the next section, another important characteristic of the post-reform nominating process is that many candidates get forced out of the race within just a few days or weeks after the first primary. While that development poses a number of important problems for the presidential selection process, from the perspective of table 1.7, it does have one compensating advantage. Candidates who withdraw early— such as Baker and Crane in 1980, and Cranston, Hollings, and Glenn in 1984—are generally able to attend a significantly higher percentage of the roll call votes held during the election year. But even for these candidates, the election-year participation rates still lag well behind the rates in the first two years of the election cycle. As for candidates who stay in the race to the bitter end—Udall in 1976, Anderson in 1980, Hart in 1984—their congressional duties continue to suffer.

One final point is worth making about the data in table 1.7. While an active presidential campaign clearly curtailed a candidate's attendance at congressional roll calls between 1952 and 1992, the effect seems, at first glance, to be considerably smaller in the 1996 election cycle. Of the four sitting senators who sought the Republican nomination that year, none had conspicuously poor attendance records in either 1995 or 1996. Does this mean that running for president no longer requires a huge commitment of a candidate's time and resources?

The news coverage of the 1996 race certainly provides no reason for thinking this to be the case. All the now-familiar routines of contemporary nomination races—the fund raisers and cattle shows, the regular trips to Iowa and New Hampshire—were every bit as much in evidence in 1996 as in previous contests. What seems to have occurred instead was a significant change in Senate and House procedures. During the late 1970s and early 1980s, a number of congressional challengers adopted the tactic—reputedly with great success—of attacking incumbents for missing a substantial proportion of roll call votes. To forestall such charges, "House and Senate leaders have in recent years made it easier for members to compile [a record of diligence] by avoiding votes on Mondays and Fridays, 'stacking' votes back-to-back in midweek, and promising no votes several evenings each week."[40] A good measure of the total change that occurred is provided by the average Senate participation rates, shown in the second column of table 1.7. Whereas the average senator cast a vote in 86 percent of the roll calls held between 1973 and 1976, the *average* participation rate during the 1996 election cycle was almost 98 percent.

This does not mean, we think, that being a U.S. senator has become a less demanding job and that there is no longer any conflict between serving in Congress and running for president. What it shows, rather, is that roll call participation rates are no longer an especially good indicator of a senator's or representative's attention to his congressional duties.[41] The price of a presidential campaign is paid elsewhere: in missed committee meetings, diminished effort in drafting bills and amendments, nonattendance at debates, and so forth. Unfortunately for our purposes, these other forms of dereliction are less easy to document—which is precisely why they, rather than the more visible roll call votes, are the sorts of things likely to be neglected.

The Rush to Judgment

The transformation of the presidential nomination race into a two-year-long marathon has been commented upon and lamented many times. But the fact that many candidates begin their quest for the White House a year before the first delegates are selected is only half the story, for once the actual delegate selection activities begin, the presidential race has grown progressively *shorter*. To track this development, table 1.9 lists the withdrawal dates of all presidential candidates since 1952 who actively contested at least one primary outside their home state.

As these data make clear, the pattern in pre-1972 presidential races was that once the candidates had announced, they were able to remain in the race for a reasonably extended period of time, at least to the end of the primary season and usually up to the actual convention balloting. In the end, of course, only one candidate could get the nomination, but the losers could at least feel that their case had received a reasonably full hearing, that they had been able to run in a number of primaries in a variety of locations. And this, in turn, gave the candidates' audience—voters, party leaders, and the press—an important opportunity for second thoughts and extended deliberation. A partial exception to this pattern was the long-shot, underfunded candidacy of Hubert Humphrey in 1960. Yet even Humphrey was able to stay in the race for more than two months after the New Hampshire kickoff and to run in two primaries (he skipped a number of others) held in states thought to be especially sympathetic to his candidacy.[42]

In 1976, one sees the emergence of a quite different pattern. Candidates who did poorly in one or two early contests—in particular, the New Hampshire primary and (after 1980) the Iowa caucuses—were withdrawing from the field just days after the race had formally begun. In 1984, for example, five of the eight announced Democratic candidates had withdrawn within just twenty-five days of the Iowa caucuses. In

TABLE 1.9   WITHDRAWAL DATES OF CANDIDATES WHO CONTESTED THE
PRIMARIES, 1952-96

Democrats

Year	Candidate[a]	Withdrawal Date	No. of Days after Start of Delegate Selection Season[b]
1952	Estes Kefauver	None	137
	Robert Kerr	None	137[c]
	Richard Russell	None	137
1956	Estes Kefauver	31 July 1956	140
1960	Hubert Humphrey	10 May 1960	63
1964	George Wallace	19 July 1964	131
1968	Lyndon Johnson	31 March 1968	19
	Eugene McCarthy	None	169
1972	John Lindsay	4 April 1972	28
	Edmund Muskie	27 April 1972	51[d]
	Henry Jackson	2 May 1972	56
	Hubert Humphrey	11 July 1972	126
	Eugene McCarthy	12 July 1972	127
	George Wallace	None	127
	Terry Sanford	None	127[c]
	Shirley Chisholm	None	127
1976	Birch Bayh	4 March 1976	9
	Milton Shapp	12 March 1976	17
	Sargent Shriver	16 March 1976	21
	Fred Harris	8 April 1976	44
	Henry Jackson	1 May 1976	67
	George Wallace	9 June 1976	106
	Morris Udall	14 June 1976	111
	Frank Church	14 June 1976	111[c]
	Jerry Brown	None	141[c]
1980	Jerry Brown	1 April 1980	35
	Edward Kennedy	11 August 1980	167
1984	Alan Cranston	29 February 1984	9
	Reubin Askew	1 March 1984	10
	Ernest Hollings	1 March 1984	10

(continued)

TABLE 1.9   *(continued)*

Democrats

Year	Candidate[a]	Withdrawal Date	No. of Days after Start of Delegate Selection Season[b]
1984	George McGovern	14 March 1984	23
	John Glenn	16 March 1984	25
	Gary Hart	None	149
	Jesse Jackson	None	149
1988	Bruce Babbitt	18 February 1988	10
	Gary Hart	11 March 1988	32
	Richard Gephardt	28 March 1988	49
	Paul Simon	7 April 1988	59
	Al Gore	21 April 1988	73
	Jesse Jackson	None	163
1992	Bob Kerrey	5 March 1992	24
	Tom Harkin	9 March 1992	28
	Paul Tsongas	19 March 1992	38
	Jerry Brown	None	156

Republicans

Year	Candidate[a]	Withdrawal Date	No. of Days after Start of Delegate Selection Season[b]
1952	Robert Taft	None	122
	Earl Warren	None	122
	Harold Stassen	None	122
1964	Nelson Rockefeller	15 June 1964	97
	Margaret Chase Smith	None	127
1968	Ronald Reagan	None	149[c]
1976	Ronald Reagan	None	177
1980	Howard Baker	5 March 1980	8
	John Connally	9 March 1980	12
	Robert Dole	15 March 1980	18
	Philip Crane	17 April 1980	51
	John Anderson	24 April 1980[c]	58
	George Bush	26 May 1980	90

TABLE 1.9   *(continued)*

Republicans

Year	Candidate[a]	Withdrawal Date	No. of Days after Start of Delegate Selection Season[b]
1988	Alexander Haig	12 February 1988	4
	Pierre du Pont	18 February 1988	10
	Jack Kemp	10 March 1988	31
	Robert Dole	29 March 1988	50
	Pat Robertson	6 April 1988	58
1992	Pat Buchanan	17 August 1992	189
1996	Phil Gramm	14 February 1996	2
	Lamar Alexander	6 March 1996	23
	Richard Lugar	6 March 1996	23
	Steve Forbes	14 March 1996	31
	Pat Buchanan	None	184

Source: Compiled from contemporary reports in the *New York Times* and *Facts On File*.
[a] Includes all candidates who actively contested at least one primary outside their home state.
[b] The start of the delegate selection season is the day of the New Hampshire primary in the nomination races of 1952–80; in the 1984–96 contests, it is the day of the Iowa caucuses. For candidates who did not withdraw, figure given is the number of days between the start of the delegate selection season and that party's final presidential roll call vote.
[c] Indicates the candidate announced his candidacy after the first primary had taken place.
[d] On 14 June, Muskie made an attempt to resume active campaigning. He withdrew for the second (and final) time on 11 July.
[e] Date given is the day on which Anderson announced he was running for president as an independent candidate.

1992, three of five Democratic aspirants were out by the third week of March. The name that has been given to this process is *winnowing*, and as the data in table 1.9 make clear, it is entirely a post-1968 phenomenon.

To make matters worse, once this general pattern had become clear, many states responded in a way that, while perhaps rational from their own perspective, only exacerbated the problem. If most of the candidates dropped out of the race so early, if the contest was effectively settled five or six weeks after it had begun, why schedule a primary in May or June, when it would have little or no effect on the final outcome? It was far more sensible to move a primary to a much earlier date, a few weeks after Iowa and New Hampshire, and thus get at least a small share of the candidate and media attention.

That states understood the crazy logic of the new system and reacted accordingly is demonstrated in table 1.10, which shows the cumulative percentage of primary-state delegates that had been selected by the end of each week of the primary season. Again, one notes a distinct break between the 1952–68 nomination races and those held under the new rules. In the earlier period, especially in the contests of 1960, 1964, and 1968, the nomination race started up rather slowly. By the end of the seventh week after New Hampshire, about halfway through the primary season, only about 20 percent of the primary-state delegates had been selected. Most primaries—especially those in larger states—were scheduled in late April, May, or June.

Beginning in 1976, however, and accelerating rapidly in each subsequent nomination race, there is a clear trend of states' moving their primaries to earlier and earlier dates in the delegate selection season. By 1988, half of the primary delegates to both party conventions had been selected by the fifth week of the primary season. In the 1996 Republican race, 65 percent had been chosen by week five. This process also has a name. It is called *front-loading*, and as the data in table 1.10 make clear, it, too, is entirely a post-1968 phenomenon.

Why is this a problem? After all, every candidate but one has to drop out eventually. Who cares if these withdrawals come early or late in the primary season? To provide an answer to these questions, three other points need to be made about the pattern of withdrawals in contemporary nomination contests.

First, while some of these early withdrawal decisions were made by long-shot candidates who never had much chance of winning the nomination, that fate was also suffered by candidates who were widely thought—by both the media and party insiders—to be among the top contenders for their party's nomination. Many had also demonstrated considerable popularity among ordinary voters. Through the last months of 1979 and much of January 1980, Howard Baker, then the Senate minority leader, consistently ran second or third in national polls of rank-and-file Republicans as their choice for the party's nomination. A well-designed selection process need not have guaranteed Baker the nomination on that basis, of course. Indeed, as many commentators have pointed out over the years, congressional leaders have never fared well in presidential nomination contests.[43] But it is not unreasonable to suggest that the process should have given Baker's candidacy a better and more thorough appraisal than it received; in the end, he withdrew just eight days after the

TABLE 1.10   THE RISE OF FRONT-LOADING, 1952–96. Figures are the cumulative percentage of delegates chosen via primary that had been selected by the end of each week in the primary season.

Democrats

	1952	1956	1960	1964	1968	1972	1976	1980	1984	1988	1992	1996
Week 1	1%	1%	2%	1%	2%	1%	1%	1%	1%	1%	1%	1%
Week 2	6	6	2	1	2	5	5	6	1	1	1	1
Week 3	6	6	2	1	2	13	9	14	18	1	8	15
Week 4	13	10	2	1	8	13	17	22	27	42	31	44
Week 5	22	18	6	6	8	17	19	36	29	49	41	59
Week 6	27	24	14	11	8	17	19	41	41	49	43	73
Week 7	53	39	20	18	15	17	35	43	49	51	43	73
Week 8	63	47	35	33	22	29	35	43	49	54	56	73
Week 9	80	64	56	53	43	43	35	51	49	54	56	73
Week 10	86	68	62	59	49	51	43	51	53	63	56	80
Week 11	86	68	66	66	49	61	54	61	74	70	62	80
Week 12	86	72	73	71	58	64	57	64	77	79	68	86
Week 13	99	100	73	100	84	64	65	66	77	81	70	88
Week 14	99		100		89	85	73	70	77	83	72	90
Week 15	100				100	85	76	100	100	83	75	92
Week 16						100	100			83	100	100
Week 17										100		

(continued)

TABLE 1.10   (continued)

Republicans

	1952	1956	1960	1964	1968	1972	1976	1980	1984	1988	1992	1996
Week 1	3%	2%	2%	2%	1%	2%	1%	1%	2%	1%	1%	1%
Week 2	8	7	2	2	1	7	4	4	2	3	2	7
Week 3	8	7	2	2	1	14	9	14	18	3	10	22
Week 4	17	11	2	2	7	14	15	20	24	49	36	51
Week 5	26	19	8	7	7	17	19	30	26	54	44	65
Week 6	33	25	16	15	7	17	19	35	37	54	46	77
Week 7	61	40	23	22	16	17	30	37	43	56	46	77
Week 8	68	41	40	36	22	28	30	37	43	59	56	77
Week 9	78	61	56	53	38	42	30	42	43	59	56	77
Week 10	81	64	63	58	44	55	35	42	47	65	56	81
Week 11	84	67	63	64	44	64	52	57	72	70	60	81
Week 12	84	71	71	70	53	68	55	61	75	78	66	88
Week 13	100	100	71	100	77	68	64	68	77	80	67	89
Week 14			100		86	90	75	72	77	82	71	91
Week 15					100	90	78	100	99	83	75	93
Week 16						100	100		100	83	99	100
Week 17										99	100	
Week 18										100		

New Hampshire primary. A similar assessment can be made about the candidacies of Birch Bayh in 1976, John Connally in 1980, and John Glenn in 1984.

Second, early withdrawal was not just the fate of candidates who lost the early contests. It also befell many candidates who showed considerable strength in the early going. Consider the campaign of Richard Gephardt in 1988. Gephardt came in first in the hotly contested Iowa caucuses, placed second in the New Hampshire primary (given its location, first place had long been conceded to Michael Dukakis), and won the South Dakota primary a week after that. That record notwithstanding, the Gephardt campaign limped into "Super Tuesday" and was forced to shut down entirely in late March, about a month and a half after the race formally commenced, with three and a half months still to go before the start of the Democratic convention.

Even more remarkable was the experience of Paul Tsongas in 1992. Tsongas won the New Hampshire primary on 18 February, the Maryland primary and the Utah and Washington caucuses on 3 March, the Arizona caucuses on 7 March, the Massachusetts and Rhode Island primaries and the Delaware caucuses on 10 March, and finished second in a large number of other primaries and caucuses. Yet, just nine days after his last set of victories—and a bare thirty-eight days after Iowa—he withdrew from the race entirely.

Third, in a significant number of cases, candidates have been forced to withdraw before having a chance to run in the kinds of primaries and caucuses in which their strength might have been most evident. The 1984 Democratic nomination race, for example, included two well-regarded southern politicians: Ernest Hollings, senator from South Carolina, and Reubin Askew, former governor of Florida. What was remarkable about the candidacies of these two men was not just that they withdrew ten days after the Iowa caucuses, but that they withdrew before a single southern caucus or primary had taken place. Both men had based their candidacies, in part, on the premise that to win the presidency, the Democratic Party had to nominate someone who would run well in the South. Again, nothing in a well-designed nomination process would guarantee that the Democratic Party had to accept this argument, but the process should at least have given it a proper hearing by allowing these candidates to demonstrate their popularity (or lack thereof) with southern voters and caucus participants. As it turned out, by the time the first three southern states voted on 13 March (one of them was Askew's home state of Florida), both southerners had dropped out of the race twelve days earlier. As a result, Mondale won the Alabama and Georgia primaries, and

Gary Hart carried Florida, even though neither man stood much of a chance of carrying these states in November.

In short, while early withdrawals are often treated by pundits as an indication that a candidate simply did not catch on with the voters, there are far too many cases that do not fit this pattern to accept it as a general explanation. In fact, it is almost always a lack of *money*, rather than votes, that forces these candidates to drop from the race.[44] Because any individual is now prohibited from contributing more than $1,000 to a campaign, a candidate's financial health depends on raising money from a very large number of contributors. Most contributors—like most voters and party activists—are reluctant to support a candidate whose viability is in question. Candidates who do poorly in the early primaries and caucuses thus suffer a double blow. Not only are they written off by the press, which deprives them of extensive "free media" coverage; they are also unable to raise enough money to conduct the kind of campaign that might reverse their downward momentum.

Whatever the causal mechanism, the combination of early withdrawals and increased front-loading greatly accelerates the voters' decision process and thus makes the whole system less deliberative, less rational, less flexible, and more chaotic. To be sure, as we have seen in the last section, most presidential candidates have been campaigning for nine months or a year before the first caucus or primary is held. The problem is that during most of this time, voters are paying little attention to the campaign. Remarkable though it may seem to hard-core political junkies, a substantial part of the primary electorate approaches the beginning of the delegate selection season with very little solid information about most of the candidates who are seeking their party's presidential nomination. In mid-January of 1992, for example, seven out of ten registered voters said they had not heard enough about Bill Clinton to form an opinion of him. As late as March of 1988, one-third of registered voters still did not know enough about Michael Dukakis to offer an evaluation.[45]

Eventually, the voters do learn more about the candidates; the problem is that, given the dynamics of the current nominating process, it is increasingly likely that they will learn it too late.[46] Within about five weeks of the New Hampshire primary, most delegates have already been selected and most candidates have already withdrawn. A good presidential selection process, in short, ought to allow for second thoughts, for reconsideration, for the possibility that initial impressions may be wrong or incomplete. The net effect of the recent rules changes, however, has been to propel the system in precisely the opposite direction.

As this account should also indicate, another problematic feature of the contemporary presidential selection process is the enormous weight it places on two early delegate selection events: the Iowa caucuses and the New Hampshire primary. Neither of these states, as is well known, is very representative of the national electorate. Each also has other idiosyncrasies that further complicate its ability to render such important judgments. But a debate about whether the winnowing function should be performed by Iowa and New Hampshire or by two other states misses the real point: no two states should have the ability to make or break the fortunes of so many presidential contenders.

And before 1972, no pair of states did possess such extraordinary power. The Iowa caucuses did not even exist in anything like their present form or place in the election calendar. As for New Hampshire, which has been the first presidential primary since 1920, it was regarded from 1952 to 1968 as a useful, but not essential, step on the road to the White House. Six of the ten major-party nominees during this period won the New Hampshire contest, but in only two of the ten races (Eisenhower in 1952, McCarthy and Johnson in 1968) could one say that the New Hampshire results played a major role in shaping the final outcome. More striking is how many serious candidates decided to bypass the New Hampshire primary (Stevenson in 1956, Humphrey in 1960), announced their candidacies after it had already taken place (Kennedy in 1968), or did not enter any primaries at all (Stevenson in 1952, Johnson in 1960, Humphrey in 1968).[47] It was not until the reforms went into effect that Iowa and New Hampshire became such an extraordinary media event and make-or-break colossus.

Conclusion

What really is distinctive about the contemporary era in presidential nominating politics? How does the current system differ from the one that existed in the 1950s and 1960s? Our answer to these questions is summarized in table 1.11, which lists six major ways in which the nominating process has changed.

As we have indicated at several points in this chapter, we certainly recognize that the 1950s and 1960s were difficult times generally for America's two major parties and that some measures of party strength— such as the number of partisans in the electorate and the loyalty of those partisans in the voting booth—had started to decline before 1972.[48] More than that, we believe that there are many distinct features of contemporary presidential politics to which Reiter's thesis does apply, and

TABLE 1.11   MAJOR DIFFERENCES BETWEEN THE PRESIDENTIAL NOMINATING
PROCESS OF 1952–68 AND THAT OF 1972–96

	Pre-Reform	*Post-Reform*
1. Use of primaries	Limited	Predominant mode of delegate selection
2. Nonprimary selection procedures	Party-controlled	Public: open to anyone who who wants to participate
3. Favorite son candidates	Common	Nonexistent
4. When most candidates announce	In the election year itself or the final months of the preceding year	More than a year before the convention starts
5. When most candidates withdraw	After the end of the primary season	Shortly after the primaries begin
6. Primary calendar	Back-loaded	Front-loaded

that party reforms have sometimes been blamed for problems for which they are not responsible. Having said that, however, we are struck by the fact that, according to all the data presented here, *none* of the changes we are concerned with shows any signs of appearing in the last few nomination races of the pre-reform era. At least in the presidential nominating process, the parties seemed to be holding up pretty well—until the onset of reform.

Indeed, greater attention to the historical context of the late 1960s and early 1970s, in our judgment, only raises further questions about the basic philosophy animating many of the reform initiatives. Given that parties were declining generally, it is surely not unreasonable to think that those who were rewriting the rules during this period might have viewed their work, at least in part, as an opportunity to revive and strengthen party institutions. Instead, the effect of their labors was to accelerate the downward trend.[49]

None of this, of course, implies that there is now a large and vocal constituency actively seeking to undo all these rules changes. Moreover, even if both parties were somehow willing to readopt the rules they had used in 1968, that alone would not restore the pre-reform nominating process. Too many other important features of that system have been allowed to wither and die in the meantime. But our analysis is sufficient, we believe, to show that reform does have an impact: changing the rules does change the game, and people, not just social forces, effect political change.

Appendix: A Note on Measurement Issues and Data Sources

In many subfields of political science, there is an extensive literature on how best to measure and quantify such concepts as party identification, the incumbency advantage in congressional elections, and a president's success in getting his legislative program through Congress. In studies of the presidential nominating process, by contrast, there has been, in general, surprisingly little appreciation of the complexities involved in defining certain variables and of the limitations of many data sources.[50] In the hope of promoting further discussion of such issues, and for those interested in replicating our results, this appendix provides details about the construction of the tables in this chapter.

Number of Primaries (Table 1.2, p. 11)

It is surprisingly difficult to get accurate data on the number of states holding meaningful presidential primaries and the number of delegates selected through those primaries. Most scholars and journalists rely on two sources: *America Votes*[51] and various publications by Congressional Quarterly, particularly its *Guide to U.S. Elections.*[52] Both sources list all presidential primaries in which there was a presidential preference vote, but this criterion is problematic in two respects. On the one hand, it excludes primaries that were used to select national convention delegates but that did not have a specific presidential preference line on the state ballot. For example, in every presidential election between 1952 and 1976, New York Democrats and Republicans selected most of their delegates by primary. But since these primaries never included a presidential preference vote, there is no mention of them in either source.

On the other hand, both *America Votes* and Congressional Quarterly do include primaries held for purely advisory purposes, even though the delegates were actually selected through a caucus-convention procedure. From 1976 to 1988, for example, the Vermont presidential primary—in both parties—played no role in the selection of national convention delegates.

The only way to deal with this problem is to make a detailed study of each party's delegate selection procedures for every nomination race with which one is concerned. That is what we have done for all elections between 1952 and 1996.

Our criterion for inclusion in table 1.2 was whether a primary was used to select and/or bind national convention delegates. Thus, we included all states that elected delegates directly by primary, regardless of whether that primary produced a presidential preference vote. Also included are states that selected their delegates at state or district conventions but formally pledged them to vote in accord with the results of a presidential primary. In Indiana, for example, the system in operation between 1956 and 1968 used state conventions to select the delegates but bound those delegates to vote for the candidate who had won a plurality of their district's vote in the presidential primary.

To add yet one more level of complexity to the analysis, a number of states—in both the pre- and post-reform periods—selected some of their delegates by primary and some by convention, without in any way requiring the convention-selected delegates to vote for the winner(s) of the primary. In every such case, we managed to determine the exact number of delegates selected or bound by the primary results; and it is these figures (rather than simply the total number of delegates from states holding primaries) that were used to calculate the percentage figures in table 1.2. For that reason, our figures may differ slightly from other tabulations of these data.

Mean Vote Percentage by Delegate Selection Method (Table 1.3, p. 14)

The second and third columns in table 1.3 represent the mean vote percentage each candidate received at the national convention in, respectively, states that selected their delegates by a caucus-convention or committee system and states that used a presidential primary. The fourth column is simply the difference between these two figures.

As indicated in the text, however, the states that decide to hold primaries or caucuses are not, in most years, randomly distributed across the country. During the 1950s and 1960s, the vast majority of presidential primaries were held in the Northeast and Midwest. In the years since 1972, caucuses have more often been held in the West and in states with smaller, less urban populations. Hence, to get a proper estimate of how each candidate was helped or hurt by a particular delegate selection procedure, it is necessary to control for other factors that might be correlated with both the candidate's vote and the selection system employed.

The general procedure used to produce the estimates in table 1.3 was to calculate a regression equation in which the dependent variable was the percentage of each state's convention vote received by a particular candidate or position. The independent variables were somewhat different from equation to equation, but they generally broke down into six categories: selection system used, region, ideology, the candidate's home state, the home states of other leading candidates, and other demographic variables.

Selection system was defined through two dummy variables, one for convention states (1 if yes, 0 if no) and one for the states that used mixed selection systems (i.e., states that selected a substantial number of delegates by both primary and convention). The coefficient for the convention-state variable thus represents the average difference between a candidate's vote in the convention states and that candidate's vote in the "pure" primary states, with all other influences held constant. It is the value of this coefficient that is reported in the fifth column of table 1.3, along with an indication of its statistical significance.

For further details on all other variables in these equations, see the appendix to William G. Mayer, "Caucuses: How They Work, What Difference They Make," in *In Pursuit of the White House: How We Choose Our Presidential Nominees*, ed. William G. Mayer (Chatham, N.J.: Chatham House, 1996), 149–51.

Favorite Sons (Table 1.4, p. 20)

As noted in the text, there is broad agreement on the general definition of a favorite son candidacy. Literally every source we consulted emphasized two characteristics: (1) favorite sons receive substantial support from their home state; (2) they receive little support elsewhere. To count the number of favorite son candidates in any particular nomination race, then, it is necessary only to provide a more mathematically precise definition of these two attributes.

The criterion that a favorite son must receive at least 50 percent of the votes from his home state seems to us straightforward enough. On the one hand, nothing in the definition requires a favorite son to receive *every* vote from his home state. But if the vote he receives falls below 50 percent, it is difficult to maintain that he is still that state's *favorite* son. The second criterion, that the candidate receive less than 2 percent of the remaining convention votes, is perhaps somewhat more arbitrary, but it does distinguish, we believe, between candidates whom contemporary press reports regarded as favorite sons and those who were considered to be legitimate national contenders.

In any event, slight changes in these thresholds do not change the general picture presented in table 1.4. In particular, under no reasonable definition of favorite son can one claim that there have been many such candidates in recent nomination races.

Our principal source for convention roll call data is *National Party Conventions 1831–1996* (Washington, D.C.: Congressional Quarterly, 1997). For conventions held before 1960, however, this source generally does not provide state-by-state breakdowns of the vote received by minor candidates. To determine whether candidates in 1952 and 1956 met the criteria stated above, we have therefore consulted the *Official Proceedings*, published by the national committees.

Announcement Dates (Tables 1.5, p. 22, and 1.6, p. 25)

With a few exceptions to be noted below, it is generally pretty easy to identify an announcement date for all presidential candidates—that is, *the day on which they publicly declare themselves to be candidates actively seeking their party's presidential nomination.* As indicated in the note to table 1.5, we have taken these data from contemporary reports in the *New York Times* and *Facts On File*, and these sources concur in essentially every case.

The more difficult question concerns the meaningfulness of this date. In a number of cases, one might argue, a candidate had clearly been pursuing the presidency long before his formal announcement. In the 1988 election cycle, for example, George Bush did not announce his candidacy until 12 October 1987, but there is little doubt that he had been laying the groundwork for his campaign for many years before that. For the years after 1974, a more revealing measure of when a presidential campaign begins might be the day on which a candidate files papers with the Federal Election Commission establishing a campaign finance committee, because until that step is taken, the law imposes at least some restrictions on what candidates can do and how much money they can spend. Unfortunately, such data are not available for elections before 1974. Since our purpose in identifying announcement dates is precisely to provide a basis for comparing the pre- and post-reform nomination races, such a measure is clearly not appropriate for our analysis.

For all their shortcomings, however, candidate announcement dates are still a very meaningful piece of information. The purpose of these data, it should be emphasized, is not to establish when potential candidates first thought about running for the presidency, nor when they actually arrived at their personal decisions to enter the race. What we seek to measure, instead, is the time when a candidacy becomes an active, public concern: when the candidate openly begins to solicit votes, money, and endorsements; to put together an organization; and so forth. And for most candidates, both before and after the reforms, the formal announcement date seems to provide a quite good indication of when this phase of the nomination race begins. Particularly worth noting in this connection is the close correlation between the announcement data in table 1.5 and the congressional voting-participation data in table 1.7. Whatever kinds of private, behind-the-scenes maneuvering may be going on, a candidate's attention to congressional duties generally does not begin to decline until after he has formally entered the race.

A few notes on some ambiguous cases: Three dates might reasonably be claimed as *the* day on which Dwight Eisenhower launched his first presidential campaign. On 7 January 1952, while still serving as General of the Army in France, Eisenhower said he would accept the Republican nomination if he were drafted at the convention, but he also indicated that he would not actively seek the nomination or participate in any pre-convention political activities. On 12 April, the White House announced that, at his own request, Eisenhower would be relieved of his command of the NATO forces in Europe on 1 June, so that he could return to the United States. But Eisenhower specifically noted at that time that he had not yet made any plans for an active political campaign. Finally, on 4 June, Eisenhower delivered his first campaign speech in his home town of Abilene, Kansas. Though that speech did not contain a formal declaration of candidacy (by this time, Eisenhower's interest in the Republican nomination seems to have been openly acknowledged), it is this third date that seems closest to our definition of an announcement date.[53]

Strange as it may seem by contemporary standards, Lyndon Johnson never made a formal announcement of his presidential candidacy in 1964. One is tempted to say that this further demonstrates the irrelevance of formal announcement dates—except that Johnson's behavior during the first half of 1964 provides little evidence that an active campaign was then in progress. For example, according to Theodore White, Johnson made only two "political" speeches during the first five months of 1964—"both at fund-raising dinners to which John F. Kennedy had previously committed the President."[54] Similarly, Johnson did not enter a single presidential primary in 1964, nor did he authorize anyone else to organize a primary campaign on his behalf. The only primary in which Johnson's name actually appeared on the ballot was in Oregon, where it was put on at the initiative of Oregon's secretary of state. (There was also a slate of delegates in Florida that, again without his authorization, was "pledged" to vote for Johnson.) Indeed, there is evidence that, up to the eve of the actual convention voting, Johnson was seriously entertaining the idea of not running at all.[55]

In 1988, two candidates announced their candidacies in two stages. Paul Simon and Jesse Jackson both delivered speeches in which they announced that they would definitely be running for the 1988 Democratic presidential nomination but that they would not formally launch their campaigns until a month later.[56] In table 1.5, we use the date of the formal campaign opening for both candidates. Using the earlier date would, of course, only strengthen the argument we are attempting to make.

Congressional Voting-Participation Rates (Tables 1.7, p. 28, and 1.8, p. 30)

As indicated in the text, what we are seeking to measure with the data in table 1.7 is the extent to which a U.S. senator or representative attends to his congressional duties while running for president. There is no one, perfect measure of this concept, but for most of the period we are concerned with, far and away the best indicator is a candidate's participation rate in congressional roll call votes.

More specifically, *voting participation* is defined as the number of times each senator or representative voted "yea" or "nay" on a roll call vote, divided by the total number of such votes held in a given year.[57] All data in table 1.7 are taken from the *Congressional Quarterly Almanac*, published annually since 1945.

Withdrawal Dates (Table 1.9, p. 33)

By *withdrawal date*, we mean the day on which candidates declare they are no longer actively seeking their party's presidential nomination. Candidates describe this pivotal decision in a variety of ways, however. Some candidates specifically say they are "withdrawing" from the race; others say they are "suspending" all further campaign activities.[58] Whatever the exact wording, there seems in practice to be little ambiguity as to the candidate's own intentions or the message communicated to supporters, opponents, and the media.

Though some candidates who have "suspended" their campaigns have intimated that they might get back into the race at a later date, the only candidate during this period who actually did so was Edmund Muskie in 1972. After doing poorly in a string of early primaries, Muskie announced on 27 April that he was "withdraw[ing] from active participation in the remaining presidential primaries." But on 14 June, with the primaries all but over, Muskie launched what the *New York Times* called "a new campaign," directed principally at uncommitted delegates. Though Muskie himself described the effort as a "long shot," he apparently hoped to establish himself as a "viable alternative" if a deadlock developed at the Democratic convention. To judge from contemporary press coverage, Muskie waged a moderately active campaign over the next month; his efforts, however, brought him few new delegates. On 11 July, one day after George McGovern's victory in the California credentials fight, Muskie withdrew for the second and final time.[59]

Front-Loading (Table 1.10, p. 37)

As indicated in table 1.10, the figures we report deal only with delegates who were selected and/or bound by presidential primaries. Delegates selected through caucus-convention systems are excluded, for several reasons.

First, unlike the situation in primaries, it is misleading to imply that states employing a caucus-convention system select their national convention delegates on a single day. A caucus-convention system is a multistage affair.[60] An initial set of meetings, usually held at the town or precinct level, selects delegates to district and state conventions, and only at these latter meetings are the national convention delegates chosen. In general, the actions of the district and state conventions are neither rigidly determined nor completely unbound by what takes place at the precinct caucuses. On the one hand, the caucuses determine who can participate in later conventions and thus the kinds of candidates and policies they are likely to support. At the same time, delegates to the district and state conventions are not required to vote for the candidate they supported when first elected. Especially if one or more candidates withdrew from the race at some time between the caucuses and the state convention, the composition of a state's national convention delegation may bear only a faint resemblance to the original caucus results. In such circumstances, to single out one date as *the day* when a caucus-convention system selects its delegates is a bit like claiming to know the specific day on which Rome was built.

In addition, because caucus-convention systems were almost completely unregulated by national party rules before 1972, it is difficult—in fact, usually impossible—to get reliable information on when the various stages of the process were held in most states. In particular, the initial round of meetings that selected delegates to the state convention were generally left to the discretion of local party organizations, with no requirement that such meetings be publicized or that they be held on the same day throughout the state.

The only way to get meaningful, comparative data on trends in front-loading, then, is to limit the calculations to delegates selected by primary. For each week in the primary season—week one is, of course, the week of the New Hampshire primary—we have determined the total number of delegates selected or bound by presidential primaries. In 1976, for example, 2,232 delegates to the Democratic National Convention were selected via primary. In week one, New Hampshire chose 17 of them, about 1 percent of the total. By the end of the second week, 121 primary delegates had been selected (the 17 from New Hampshire plus 104 in the Massachusetts primary)—5 percent of the total. Week three added 81 more delegates (from the Florida primary), for a cumulative total of 202 delegates, or 9 percent of the total. And so on through week sixteen, when the final set of Democratic primaries was held that year.

Acknowledgments

We would like to thank Gerald M. Pomper, Nelson W. Polsby, and Amy Logan for helpful comments on various early drafts of this chapter. A special word of thanks is owed to Howard Reiter, who chaired the conference panel at which this paper was originally presented. His assistance—that day and ever since—has been a model of grace and academic collegiality.

Notes

1. See, in particular, Stephen Jay Gould, *Questioning the Millennium: A Rationalist's Guide to a Precisely Arbitrary Countdown* (New York: Harmony Books, 1997).
2. Byron E. Shafer, *Quiet Revolution: The Struggle for the Democratic Party and the Shaping of Post-Reform Politics* (New York: Russell Sage Foundation, 1983), 28.
3. As the following discussion suggests, remarkably few academic analysts have taken a clearly positive view of the McGovern-Fraser Commission and its handiwork. Perhaps the most prominent exception is William J. Crotty; see especially *Decision for the Democrats: Reforming the Party Structure* (Baltimore: Johns Hopkins University Press, 1978).
4. See especially William Cavala, "Changing the Rules Changes the Game: Party Reform and the 1972 California Delegation to the Democratic National Convention," *American Political Science Review* 68 (March 1974): 27–42; James I. Lengle and Byron Shafer, "Primary Rules, Political Power, and Social Change," *American*

Political Science Review 70 (March 1976): 25-40; Everett Carll Ladd, Jr., "'Reform' Is Wrecking the U.S. Party System," *Fortune*, November 1977, 177-88; Jeane Jordan Kirkpatrick, *Dismantling the Parties: Reflections on Party Reform and Party Decomposition* (Washington, D.C.: American Enterprise Institute, 1978); Austin Ranney, "The Political Parties: Reform and Decline," in *The New American Political System*, ed. Anthony King (Washington, D.C.: American Enterprise Institute, 1978), 213-47; James W. Ceaser, *Presidential Selection: Theory and Development* (Princeton, N.J.: Princeton University Press, 1979); Edward C. Banfield, "Party 'Reform' in Retrospect," and James W. Ceaser, "Political Change and Party Reform," both in *Political Parties in the Eighties*, ed. Robert A. Goldwin (Washington, D.C.: American Enterprise Institute, 1980); James I. Lengle, *Representation and Presidential Primaries: The Democratic Party in the Post-Reform Era* (Westport, Conn.: Greenwood, 1981); Nelson W. Polsby, *Consequences of Party Reform* (New York: Oxford University Press, 1983); and Shafer, *Quiet Revolution*.

5. The works referred to are Howard L. Reiter, *Selecting the President: The Nominating Process in Transition* (Philadelphia: University of Pennsylvania Press, 1985); Kenneth A. Bode and Carol F. Casey, "Party Reform: Revisionism Revised," and Donald M. Fraser, "Democratizing the Democratic Party," both in *Political Parties in the Eighties*, ed. Robert A. Goldwin (Washington, D.C.: American Enterprise Institute, 1980); Mathew D. McCubbins, "Party Decline and Presidential Campaigns in the Television Age," in *Under the Watchful Eye: Managing Presidential Campaigns in the Television Era*, ed. Mathew D. McCubbins (Washington, D.C.: CQ Press, 1992), 9-57; and comments by David W. Adamany in *Parties, Interest Groups, and Campaign Finance Laws*, ed. Michael J. Malbin (Washington, D.C.: American Enterprise Institute, 1980), 314-21. Another scholar who seems generally in agreement with the revisionist argument is John H. Aldrich. See Aldrich, *Why Parties? The Origin and Transformation of Political Parties in America* (Chicago: University of Chicago Press, 1995), 269-74; and idem, "Presidential Campaigns and Party- and Candidate-Centered Eras," in *Under the Watchful Eye: Managing Presidential Campaigns in the Television Era*, ed. Mathew D. McCubbins (Washington, D.C.: CQ Press, 1992), 59-82.

6. This is a major theme in Byron Shafer's history of the commission; see *Quiet Revolution*, especially chap. 7.

7. All guidelines are quoted from the commission's principal report: Commission on Party Structure and Delegate Selection, *Mandate for Reform* (Washington, D.C.: Democratic National Committee, 1970), 33-5.

8. Shafer, *Quiet Revolution*, 197-9, 223.

9. Forbes took advantage of a loophole carved out by the Supreme Court's *Buckley* v. *Valeo* decision in 1976, which allows candidates to spend unlimited amounts of their own money on their campaigns. (The original law had limited personal expenditures to $50,000.) John Connally in 1980 evaded the state spending limits, but this was because he declined to accept federal matching funds, an option that was specifically provided for in the 1974 law.

10. For details, see Reiter, *Selecting the President*, 15-20.

11. Ibid., 14 (emphasis in original).

12. Ibid., 142.

13. McCubbins, "Party Decline," 48.

14. We are not necessarily claiming that these are the *only* important consequences the new rules produced. As noted in the text, we decided to focus on these three changes, at least in part, because they can be documented. But many of the effects

attributed to party reform are, in the nature of things, not capable of being measured very precisely or quantified over an extended period of time. There is an unfortunate tendency in contemporary political science that seems to argue that if we can't quantify something, it can't be very real or important. Reiter is quite careful not to fall into this trap, but parts of McCubbins's essay are, in our view, more problematic.

15. For Reiter's own description of his method, see *Selecting the President*, 20-3. McCubbins seems to commend a similar procedure; see "Party Decline," 38.

16. Reiter, *Selecting the President*, 20. Reiter actually distinguishes four different causal theories about how and when the current nominating process came into existence. In this chapter, however, we are concerned only with showing that party reform did have an impact, and we accordingly treat all evidence to the contrary as support for the null hypothesis.

17. Similar terminology has been employed by other writers on this topic; see, for example, Ranney, "Political Parties," 236-41. Another way of interpreting this development is to say that American political parties have often been characterized as having three major components: the party organization, the party in government, and the party in the electorate. Under the pre-reform rules, all three elements played a role in presidential nominations, with the first two generally regarded as most important. In the new system, effective power came to reside in the party in the electorate and in such nonparty entities as the news media. The party organization and the party in government were almost entirely stripped of any significant voice in the decision. What our phrasing attempts to emphasize is that the so-called party in the electorate is not an organization or institution; it is just a loosely defined collection of individuals.

18. Austin Ranney, *Curing the Mischiefs of Faction: Party Reform in America* (Berkeley: University of California Press, 1975), 153-4 (emphasis in original).

19. McGovern-Fraser Commission transcripts, 19-20 November 1969, as quoted in Kirkpatrick, *Dismantling the Parties*, 2-3.

20. See Polsby, *Consequences of Party Reform*, 55-6.

21. Austin Ranney, "The Democratic Party's Delegate Selection Reforms, 1968-76," in *America in the Seventies: Problems, Policies, and Politics*, ed. Allan P. Sindler (Boston: Little, Brown, 1977), 184.

22. Reiter clearly acknowledges this point; see *Selecting the President*, 2-3.

23. The number of Democratic presidential primaries declined slightly in 1996, but this seems to have occurred only because Clinton was running unopposed and a few states therefore decided not to bother with the effort and expense of a primary.

24. Bode and Casey, "Party Reform," 16.

25. The following analysis draws on William G. Mayer, "Caucuses: How They Work, What Difference They Make," in *In Pursuit of the White House: How We Choose Our Presidential Nominees*, ed. William G. Mayer (Chatham, N.J.: Chatham House, 1996), 136-45.

26. The phrase apparently originated with Howard Baker; see Jack W. Germond and Jules Witcover, *Blue Smoke and Mirrors: How Reagan Won and Why Carter Lost the Election of 1980* (New York: Viking, 1981), 96.

27. These conclusions are based on an analysis of primary votes and first-round caucus preferences and hence are not included in table 1.3, which uses only convention roll call votes. For details, see Mayer, "Caucuses," 144.

28. The New York primary did not have a presidential preference vote in 1972. McGovern's average in the other five states was 46 percent.

29. In a sense, this is perhaps the most striking finding in Lengle and Shafer's well-known article "Primary Rules, Political Power, and Social Change." Though the authors emphasize that McGovern would have done best under districted rules, Wallace under proportional representation, and Humphrey under winner-take-all, the actual delegate totals for the fifteen primaries they analyze show that McGovern did significantly better (and Humphrey and Wallace significantly worse) than he would have under any of the pure systems. See their comments on pp. 29–30, n. 8. A similar point is made in Ripon Society and Clifford W. Brown, Jr., *The Jaws of Victory* (Boston: Little, Brown, 1973), 121–31.

30. The peculiar character of the Tennessee Democratic delegation in 1972 is discussed in Ranney, "Democratic Party's Delegate Selection Reforms," 180–1.

31. One such indicator, which we do not attempt to duplicate here, is the percentage of governors with expressed presidential preferences who were able to deliver a majority of the votes from their home-state delegations. Reiter has collected such data, however, for all contested nomination races between 1952 and 1984, and his results show a clear decline in gubernatorial success rates after 1968; see *Selecting the President*, 42–5.

32. Every political dictionary we have consulted provides a similar definition. See, for example, William Safire, *Safire's New Political Dictionary* (New York: Random House, 1993), 239; Jay M. Shafritz, *The Dorsey Dictionary of American Government and Politics* (Chicago: Dorsey, 1988), 210; Edward C. Smith and Arnold J. Zurcher, *Dictionary of American Politics*, 2nd ed. (New York: Barnes & Noble, 1968), 144; and Jack C. Plano and Milton Greenberg, *The American Political Dictionary*, 7th ed. (New York: Holt, Rinehart & Winston, 1985), 150.

33. The only two examples in the twentieth century are Warren G. Harding in 1920 and John W. Davis in 1924.

34. See, for example, John S. Jackson III and William Crotty, *The Politics of Presidential Selection* (New York: HarperCollins, 1996); Nelson W. Polsby and Aaron Wildavsky, *Presidential Elections: Strategies and Structures of American Politics*, 9th ed. (Chatham, N.J.: Chatham House, 1996); and Stephen J. Wayne, *The Road to the White House 1992: The Politics of Presidential Elections* (New York: St. Martin's Press, 1992).

35. Accounts of the 1976 and 1980 elections routinely note that the candidacies of Brown (in 1976), Church, Baker, and Kennedy were hurt because they launched their campaigns too late in the election cycle. See, for example, Jules Witcover, *Marathon: The Pursuit of the Presidency, 1972-1976* (New York: Viking, 1977), 264, 331–2; Elizabeth Drew, *American Journal: The Events of 1976* (New York: Random House, 1977), 231–2; Germond and Witcover, *Blue Smoke and Mirrors*, 103–6, 121–2, 145–8, 165; and Jonathan Moore, ed., *The Campaign for President: 1980 in Retrospect* (Cambridge, Mass.: Ballinger, 1981), 7–9, 24–7, 43–4.

36. As it turned out, of course, the old rules were in the process of being changed, but Humphrey, like many others in the Democratic Party, was unable to appreciate the significance of those changes at the time.

37. On Baker's decision not to seek reelection, see *New York Times*, 22 January 1983, 7; *Congressional Quarterly Weekly Report*, 22 January 1983, 166; *Newsweek*, 12 September 1983, 37–8; and *Time*, 24 January 1983, 26. On Hart's decision, see *New York Times*, 5 January 1986, 1, and 6 January 1986, A18; *Congressional Quarterly Weekly Report*, 11 January 1986, 61–2; *New Republic*, 27 January 1986, 4; *Time*, 13 January 1986, 21; and *Newsweek*, 13 January 1986, 33.

38. Robert Dole could arguably be added to this list. Dole, however, did not resign from the U.S. Senate until 11 June 1996, several months after he had already clinched the Republican nomination. It was, in short, more the anticipated strains of the general election than the rigors of the nomination race that drove Dole into retirement.

39. Several recent papers by Dickinson and Tenpas provide evidence of a similar pattern in the executive branch. Since the onset of party reform in 1968, they argue, there has been a significant increase in the turnover rate of top presidential staff, as a result of the heightened conflict between the needs of campaigning and the imperatives of governing. See Kathryn Dunn Tenpas and Matthew J. Dickinson, "Governing, Campaigning, and Organizing the Presidency: An Electoral Connection?" *Political Science Quarterly* 112 (spring 1997): 51–66; and Matthew J. Dickinson and Kathryn Dunn Tenpas, "The Revolving Door at the White House: Explaining Increasing Turnover Rates among Presidential Advisors, 1933–1997" (paper presented at the annual meeting of the American Political Science Association, Washington, D.C., September 1997).

40. Roger H. Davidson and Walter J. Oleszek, *Congress and Its Members*, 4th ed. (Washington, D.C.: Congressional Quarterly, 1994), 360.

41. Although a senator or representative's absolute participation rate is no longer very meaningful, his relative ranking may be. In 1995, for example, Phil Gramm's participation rate of 89 percent was actually the lowest in the U.S. Senate.

42. For a vivid account of Humphrey's difficulties in 1960, see Theodore H. White, *The Making of the President 1960* (New York: Atheneum, 1961), 29–36, 86–93, 109–12.

43. This is a long-standing complaint about the American presidential selection process that unquestionably predates the reform era. See, in particular, James Bryce's essay "Why Great Men Are Not Chosen Presidents," in *The American Commonwealth*, 3rd ed. (New York: Macmillan, 1900), 1:78–85. Similarly, in *Politics in America* (New York: Harper & Brothers, 1954), D.W. Brogan noted, "No congressional leader of the very first rank, save James Madison, has ever been elected President" (p. 198).

44. For extensive documentation of this point, see William G. Mayer, *The Divided Democrats: Ideological Unity, Party Reform, and Presidential Elections* (Boulder, Colo.: Westview, 1996), 35–41.

45. Both results are reported in Kathleen A. Frankovic, "Public Opinion in the 1992 Campaign," in *The Election of 1992: Reports and Interpretations*, ed. Gerald M. Pomper (Chatham, N.J.: Chatham House, 1993), 114–6.

46. For a particularly careful analysis of what national voters learn and when they learn it, see Henry E. Brady and Richard Johnston, "What's the Primary Message: Horse Race or Issue Journalism?" in *Media and Momentum: The New Hampshire Primary and Nomination Politics*, ed. Gary R. Orren and Nelson W. Polsby (Chatham, N.J.: Chatham House, 1987), 127–86.

47. For an elaboration of this point, see William G. Mayer, "The New Hampshire Primary: A Historical Overview," in *Media and Momentum: The New Hampshire Primary and Nomination Politics*, ed. Gary R. Orren and Nelson W. Polsby (Chatham, N.J.: Chatham House, 1987).

48. For details, see William G. Mayer, "Mass Partisanship, 1946–1996," in *Partisan Approaches to Postwar American Politics*, ed. Byron E. Shafer (New York: Chatham House, 1998), 186–219.

49. A similar observation was made by Everett Ladd in the late 1970s; see "'Reform' Is Wrecking the U.S. Party System," 179.

50. An important exception is the literature on measuring voter-participation rates in presidential primaries. See especially Barbara Norrander, "Measuring Primary

Turnout in Aggregate Analysis," *Political Behavior* 8 (1986): 356-73; Michael G. Hagen, "Voter Turnout in Primary Elections," in *The Iowa Caucuses and the Presidential Nominating Process*, ed. Peverill Squire (Boulder, Colo.: Westview Press, 1989), 51-87; and Lawrence S. Rothenberg and Richard A. Brody, "Participation in Presidential Primaries," *Western Political Quarterly* 41 (June 1988): 253-71.

51. This series of books has been published every two years since 1956, originally by Macmillan, now by Congressional Quarterly. The principal editor since the beginning has been Richard M. Scammon.

52. The latest edition of this book is *Congressional Quarterly's Guide to U.S. Elections*, 3rd ed. (Washington, D.C.: Congressional Quarterly, 1994). Data on presidential primaries also appear in *Presidential Elections 1789-1996* (Washington, D.C.: Congressional Quarterly, 1997).

53. For details on each of these three milestones, see *New York Times*, 8 January 1952, 1; 12 April 1952, 1; and 5 June 1952, 1.

54. Theodore H. White, *The Making of the President 1964* (New York: Atheneum, 1965), 252.

55. The most detailed account of Johnson's own thinking about the 1964 campaign is in his memoirs; see Lyndon Baines Johnson, *The Vantage Point: Perspectives on the Presidency, 1963-1969* (New York: Holt, Rinehart & Winston, 1971), 88-98. Most Johnson biographers are also convinced that his reluctance was sincere, if a bit bizarre. See, for example, Robert Dallek, *Flawed Giant: Lyndon Johnson and His Times, 1961-1973* (New York: Oxford University Press, 1998), 122-7.

56. For details on the Simon campaign, see *New York Times*, 10 April 1987, A16, and 19 May 1987, A20. On Jackson's announcements, see *New York Times*, 8 September 1987, A16, and 11 October 1987, 36.

57. During the first few years of the period we are concerned with, Congressional Quarterly used a slightly different definition of participation. For all such years, we have recomputed the figures to ensure comparability.

58. Candidates say they are "suspending" their campaign, rather than "withdrawing" from the race, primarily for legal reasons. In particular, under Democratic Party rules, a presidential candidate who has withdrawn from the race is prohibited from winning any more at-large convention delegates, even though that candidate may be entitled to them on the basis of votes already received in previous primaries. (See Rule 9C of the Democratic Party's delegate selection rules.) Suspending a campaign thus allows a candidate's supporters to continue filling convention delegate positions even though the candidate is no longer actively campaigning.

59. For further details, see *New York Times*, 28 April 1972, 1; 10 June 1972, 1; 15 June 1972, 36; and 12 July 1972, 1.

60. For a more detailed explanation of how the caucus system works, see Mayer, "Caucuses," 105-18.

CHAPTER TWO

New Features of the 2000 Presidential Nominating Process: Republican Reforms, Front-Loading's Second Wind, and Early Voting

by Andrew E. Busch

EVERY FOUR YEARS for the past three decades, political parties in the United States have made their presidential nominations amid both great fanfare and great disillusionment. No nominating season has been complete without a chorus of complaints about the nature of the nominating process and a host of proposals to reform that process. Since 1968, more often than not, at least some of those proposals have been enacted by at least one of the parties, though the rules have remained fundamentally the same since the mid-1970s. At the same time, other changes have taken place in the way nominees are chosen—not through centralized manipulation of the party rules, but through the aggregate effects of decentralized decisions at the state level.

The 1996 presidential nominating process was the first since 1968 that was not preceded and shaped by some sort of attempt at central rules reform. Republicans had never been eager for reform, and Democrats—having actually won the presidency in 1992—lost the sense of urgency they had felt in the aftermath of recent election fiascoes. Instead, the greatest change in the nominating process of 1996 was a significant acceleration of the phenomenon of "front-loading," the trend since the mid-1970s of states' moving their primaries closer to the front of the primary calendar. Among the several states that moved their primaries forward in 1996 were California, New York, and Ohio. As a result of this accelerated trend, 77 percent of Republican delegates and 73 percent of Democratic delegates had been selected by the end of March 1996, compared with only 46 percent and 43 percent at a comparable point in 1992.[1] March of 1996 alone saw twenty-five primaries or caucuses in twenty-four days.

If front-loading was the great innovation of 1996, the great question of 2000 was whether front-loading would be at least partially reversed or whether it would continue, perhaps even increase. The extreme compression of the primary schedule in 1996 produced growing unease and another call for change in the system, prompting a new round of central party reforms—this time originating in the Republican Party. Some smaller states, concluding that in 1996 the front-loaded system had buried their influence in a virtual avalanche of simultaneous primaries, moved toward establishing new regional primaries. The number of states utilizing "early voting" also reached an all-time high—and seemed destined to continue growing—with the potential of mitigating the effects of "momentum" in the first few weeks of the primary season. Yet the dynamics that produced front-loading have not fundamentally changed, and serious pressures continue to be exerted to move state primaries and new regional ones as close to the front of the calendar as possible. This chapter examines some of these new features of the 2000 nominating system and their potential effect on presidential campaigns in 2000 and beyond.

Front-Loading and Republican Reforms in 1996

Reform of the presidential nominating process has been a central concern of political parties and of students of political parties for much of the last thirty years. Most scholarly attention has focused on Democratic Party reform, largely because Democrats have initiated the most important changes in rules and rule making. The Republicans, meanwhile, have been largely pulled along into the reform system. Democratic control of most state legislatures led to election-law changes and the establishment of primaries with little say by the Republicans. In some respects, the Republicans have avoided the reforms; most importantly, they still permit plurality elections, and they allow the regular party a greater degree of influence in their caucuses than the Democrats do in theirs.[2] Until 1996, to the extent that Republicans did try to change their nominating system through central direction, their efforts largely mimicked those of the Democrats and were, in many respects, not particularly effective. For the most part, neither the Republican National Committee (RNC) nor the Republican National Conventions chose to disturb state autonomy.[3]

That historical pattern was broken in 1996. With the Republican National Committee Task Force on Primaries and Caucuses as the spearhead, Republicans considered and adopted a set of rules changes for the 2000 presidential nominating cycle. The 1996 RNC task force represented a new variant of nominating reform in two respects: it was the Republicans' first serious attempt to modify their nominating process by means of enforceable central direction, and the plan that Republicans adopted was the first set of reforms in either party to rely primarily on incentives rather than mandates.

Concern about the possible effects of front-loading led Republican National Committee chairman Haley Barbour to appoint the eight-member Task Force on Primaries and Caucuses in January 1996 to assess the impact of front-loading and, if necessary, to offer recommendations for change. In Barbour's words, "There is some concern that our nominating process may have become so compressed that it does not serve the party or the voters very well. . . . [V]oters don't have much time to reflect as some candidates drop out and others emerge."[4] The RNC chairman also charged the task force with maintaining the "Republican Party's longstanding tradition of respect for the independence of the state parties."[5] Barbour later explained that he deliberately appointed the task force before the onset of the primary season so that "nobody could make [a] credible argument" that it was directed for (or against) a particular candidate or outcome, adding that the task force's "obligation was not to a candidate . . . [but] to the Republican voters of the United States."[6]

The task force was headed by Jim Nicholson, national committeeman from Colorado and now RNC chairman, and included seven other RNC members who represented a balance of regional interests.[7] The task force mechanism was a new approach and an unusual departure for the Republicans, since it assumed the RNC to be in a position of leadership vis-à-vis the state parties, rather than a relatively passive instrument of the states and a clearinghouse for information.

Although the task force was appointed in January 1996, it did not begin deliberations until April. Because only the Republican National Convention is authorized to change nominating rules, the task force had to complete its deliberations and make recommendations before August if it wished to affect the nominating process in 2000. And before recommendations could be presented to the convention, they had to navigate a complex procedural route, going through the RNC's rules committee, the full RNC, and the national convention's rules committee.

After an organizational teleconference in April, only three formal meetings were held before recommendations were made in July. The task force also held only two days of formal hearings, one of which was timed to coincide with the annual Washington meeting of Republican state chairmen on 30 May. The sparsity of formal hearings disguised an extensive search for input and information. Voting turnout data were compiled and examined, several academics were consulted, and all Republican governors, secretaries of state, and members of the U.S. House or Senate were invited to comment in person or in writing. The task force also sought and received input from fellow RNC members (state chairmen and national committeepeople), from notable Republican strategists like Lyn Nofziger and Charlie Black, and from all serious 1996 Republican presidential candidates or their representatives. Even before the meetings began, Nicholson declared, "I have not talked to one presidential candidate who doesn't think this process has problems. They all think something has to be done."[8]

Ultimately, the concerns about front-loading that had led to the formation of the task force in January were only amplified by the actual operation of the front-loaded system. A consensus was reached in the organizational teleconference that the current system was defective and that possible solutions should be explored.[9] The concerns shared by Barbour, Nicholson, and other task force members fell into two basic categories: front-loading's impact on voters and its impact on candidates and campaigns.

The interests of voters were hurt in a variety of ways, but the common theme was that voters were deprived of meaningful participation. Nicholson defined the central question as "whether or not enough people are represented in the process. . . . Are enough people really involved?"[10] The 1996 nomination was decided by mid-March, leaving the bulk of states—including many that had moved up their primary dates to gain influence—without any effective say in the nomination. Consequently, while voter turnout rose to record heights in five of the first six contests, turnout in later states fell to record lows.[11] Low primary turnout was not only bad in itself, Nicholson argued, but also hurt the party: "Primaries are a good way to get people involved with the party, and where fewer people vote, the party loses strength."[12] Additionally, the rapid-fire sequence of primaries meant that the quality of participation even for those Republicans who did vote was reduced significantly:

> As the primary results from one state shifted the strength of candidates within the field, voters in the states next on the schedule

often did not have time to thoroughly assess the field of candidates. They didn't have the opportunity to make a well-informed decision. They didn't see those candidates very much, if at all.[13]

Believing there could be little meaningful dialogue in a "tarmac" campaign and little prospect of careful deliberation by voters, Nicholson described the front-loaded system as an "insect dance" in which "candidates just flit about . . . [and are] never in any one state long enough to have meaningful discussion about the issues of that state or region."[14] Perhaps surprisingly, the prominent role of Iowa and New Hampshire in the nominating process was not a major concern of most task force members and remained essentially unaddressed.

Members of the task force argued that front-loading also harmed candidates and potential candidates in a variety of ways. The bunching of primaries at the beginning of the process made both a well-known name and a $20 million war chest a virtual prerequisite for any serious candidacy, a financial hurdle that discouraged numerous "first-tier" Republicans from entering the 1996 race (including Dan Quayle, Jack Kemp, and Richard Cheney). The task force was also concerned that the race to the front had a negative effect on candidate strategy. As Nicholson said, "The candidates themselves found that once the gun went off there was no way to catch their breath, change any strategy, relate to local voters." Furthermore, candidates and campaigns expressed frustration that developing a coherent strategy was increasingly difficult in an atmosphere dominated by uncertainty over the very order of primaries and caucuses. One by-product of the race to the front was an unprecedented degree of jockeying for position among states at the very beginning of the process, jockeying that continued nearly until the start of the primary season. Alaska and Louisiana caucuses edged ahead of Iowa, while Delaware, North Dakota, and South Dakota primaries crowded right behind New Hampshire. Nicholson argued, "For candidates to make sure voters have an ample opportunity to learn their views and assess their candidacies, they must be able to make strategic and tactical decisions based on a definite primary schedule, one that doesn't change up until the last minute."[15]

It also became clear that the intense spending requirements of the new system had emptied Bob Dole's war chest, leaving him victorious but highly exposed for an unprecedented five-month "interregnum" between the time the nomination was practically secured and the national convention. Finally, as Bill Clinton widened his lead over Dole, some observers speculated—though Republicans denied it—that

Republicans were experiencing a case of "buyer's regret," which magnified their existing concerns about the speed of the process.[16] By late spring of 1996, a wide variety of outside political analysts had concurred that the front-loaded system was "madness," "insane," "warped and virtually mindless," "absurdly accelerated," "self-defeating," "debilitating," a "high speed demolition derby," and a "parody of participatory democracy" in which "candidates have rushed through the country like airline passengers late for a connection."[17]

No limits were placed on initial discussions in the task force, and a variety of options were put forward. A national primary was considered undesirable; indeed, many task force members disliked the front-loaded system precisely because they believed it was moving in the direction of a de facto national primary. Serious consideration was given to a system of rotating regional primaries, similar to that proposed by Senator Slade Gorton (R-Wash.) and Senator Joseph Lieberman (D-Conn.) in S. 1589 in the 104th Congress. However, such a plan could be imposed only with the cooperation of the Democrats and at the expense of the traditional independence of state parties. Some party leaders, such as Texas GOP chairman Tom Pauken, suggested that some of the larger states (including Texas) should simply move back their primary dates voluntarily, but others in those states balked at the prospect of "unilateral disarmament." While the purely voluntary approach appealed to the decentralized tradition of Republican intraparty governance, it also seemed inadequate to the scope of the problem.

Finally, the task force agreed upon a proposal that struck a balance between activism and decentralization: a system of bonus delegates to provide an incentive to states to move back their primaries and caucuses. States holding their primaries and caucuses between 15 March and 14 April would receive additional delegates equal to 10 percent of their original delegations; states holding their contests between 15 April and 14 May would get a 15 percent bonus; and states selecting delegates between 15 May and the third Tuesday in June would receive a 20 percent bonus. Contrasting this "carrot" approach with the "stick" of Democratic rules mandates, Barbour, Nicholson, and other task force members cited Republican philosophy as a motivating factor behind the proposal of the incentive system. While the practical difficulties of imposing a uniform rule on the states was clearly a factor, the philosophical or ideological dimension of the discussion seemed paramount.[18] In the words of one task force member, "Democrats tell the states how they will run their nominating processes; Republicans fundamentally have an aversion to that [approach]."[19]

As a means of further discouraging a race to the front of the calendar and providing greater stability and certainty for the benefit of voters and candidates alike, the task force made two additional recommendations: (1) states must certify with the RNC the date and manner of their delegate selection process by 1 July of the year preceding the nomination contest (1 July 1999 for the 2000 race); and (2) all contests must be held in a window between the first Monday in February and the third Tuesday in June. Failure by states to abide by these limitations could lead to a challenge that would disqualify their delegates at the convention. In the words of Nicholson, states would disregard the rules "at their peril."[20]

New Hampshire and Iowa Republican officials pleaded for special treatment—specifically a guarantee that their states' positions as first in the nation would be ensured—but no such guarantee was included in the task force's recommendations. If Iowa and New Hampshire are at the beginning of the window, no one can precede them; but there is no assurance that others will not hold their contests at the same time or shortly thereafter. As some analysts noted, however, these two states may continue to be protected by Democratic Party rules, specifically the primary/caucus window that prohibits delegate selection before 1 March except in Iowa and New Hampshire.

After the task force released its recommendations on 2 July, the recommendations had to be approved by the RNC's rules committee, the full RNC, the rules committee of the national convention, and the full national convention, in that order. Only in the rules committee of the national convention did opponents nearly succeed in derailing the recommendations. The recommendations were finally approved by a vote of fifty-four to thirty-two, but only after substantial negotiations and compromise over the system of bonus delegates.

Led by national committeeman Morton Blackwell of Virginia, small states and some conservatives on the national convention's rules committee objected to the bonus delegate system. Several complaints were heard. For example, opponents argued that the bonus system reflected a dangerous deviation from the Republicans' traditional allocation of delegates on the basis of Electoral College votes, with bonuses for electoral performance. Arguments were also heard that the incentive system would prove unfair to states where the legislature—and hence the power to determine primary dates—was controlled by Democrats. As Clarke Reed, national committeeman from Mississippi, argued, "It's easy to change the rules; it's hard as hell to change the legislatures."[21] Opponents claimed (in retrospect, rather incredibly) that the bonus system could lead to a new move toward "back-loading," in which a de facto national primary might become a reality at the end of the process rather than the beginning.

Most crucial, though, was Blackwell's argument that the proposed system contained a bias in favor of large states. While the percentage incentives applied equally to all the states within each time bracket, states that already had large delegations would have much more to gain than those with small delegations. Although unable to defeat the plan, Blackwell succeeded in persuading the convention's rules committee to cut what he called the bonus "monster" in half.[22] It was this reduced incentive system, offering bonuses of 5 percent, 7.5 percent, and 10 percent, that was ultimately approved by the Republican National Convention and that governs the Republican nominating process in 2000. The bonus delegates will be added to each state's at-large delegate total. The 1 July 1999 deadline for primary scheduling and the February–June window were approved without modification.[23]

Many on and off the task force were confident that front-loading would indeed be reversed either because of the delegate incentives or because of the disillusionment of states with the consequences of their move up in 1996. Several other party officials and outside observers also voiced the opinion that there would likely be some movement away from front-loading even without the incentives.[24] At a news conference held on 2 July 1996 to unveil the task force's proposal, Nicholson and Barbour acknowledged that small states would have little to gain directly from the bonuses, but held that if several large states moved back, small states would not feel so pressured to remain in the front. Barbour argued that

> what a lot of states will see is that these primaries are much more spread out and that the best way to get attention, and participation by the campaigns in the state, is not to front-load, but to find a place in the chronology where candidates have time to come to your state. . . . I believe the actual effect of this will be that a lot of smaller states will find [themselves] spacing over the February to June period, because they will know the contest is not going to be over in March, because they'll know a lot of big states will go later.[25]

Nevertheless, as numerous students of the nominating system have observed, reforms sometimes fail and almost always bring with them unanticipated consequences. Many argued that the bonus delegate system, especially in its final form, would not be sufficient to reduce front-loading. Political scientist Nelson Polsby was even more pessimistic, calling the rules changes a "gimmick" that had little chance of success.[26] In the end, the skeptics proved prescient.

1996 RNC Task Force on Primaries and Caucuses in Context

A comparison of the 1996 RNC Task Force on Primaries and Caucuses with the McGovern-Fraser Commission can be instructive for two reasons. First, since reform at the national level has taken place predominantly in the Democratic Party, students of reform have been tempted to conflate the patterns of reform evident in the Democratic Party with all possible modes of reform. Second, party reform can help illuminate important points about the parties themselves. The two reform efforts can be compared along three dimensions: process, motivation, and product. Great differences, as well as some similarities, between the two efforts are evident on each dimension.

In terms of process, the national chairmen—Fred Harris for the Democrats in 1969, Haley Barbour for the Republicans in 1996—were instrumental in both cases.[27] Otherwise, the two processes diverged dramatically. The Democratic commission was big (twenty-eight members) and complex (with an executive committee of ten to direct its actions); the Republican task force was small (eight members) and structurally simple. The Democrats conducted their business for over a year; the Republican task force spent less than three months in active deliberation. The Democrats held seventeen regional hearings on the defects of the pre-reform nominating system; the Republicans had two formal hearings buttressed by considerable informal information gathering. And, in contrast with the GOP task force, which operated with only minimal staff support, Byron Shafer documents how the McGovern-Fraser Commission staff—a permanent body with strong reformist leanings—took the lead in driving the commission in a particular substantive direction.[28]

To some extent, these variations were the result of differences in the time frames and scope of action of the two bodies. Yet they can also be explained by reference to two other factors: the philosophical orientations of the parties and the differences in motivation between the two bodies.

In the broadest sense, the motivation behind the two reform efforts was similar. Both parties perceived problems or potential problems with their nominating processes that were serious enough to require remedy. And, to a surprising extent, one of the perceived problems that was most responsible for driving change in both parties was the level of participation by party voters in the process. The McGovern-Fraser Commission construed the 1968 convention's call for full and timely participation liberally, successfully imposing participation as virtually the sole standard of legitimacy in the modern nominating system.[29] The Republicans were similarly concerned about the ability of the forty states that came last in the primary schedule to influence the outcome and about the reluctance of individual voters to participate in a system that made the winner known so early. Barbour even repeated the McGovern-Fraser language of "effective, meaningful participation" as a central party goal.[30] To this extent, of course, it could be said not that both parties repaired in equal measure to a neutral standard, but rather that the Republicans (while maintaining their unique respect for state sovereignty) had adopted the Democratic standard as their own. No greater testimony can be offered to the fundamental transformation in nominating politics that was ignited by the McGovern-Fraser reforms, which did so much to define not only the structure of the process, but also its underlying ethos.

Yet, a deeper examination of the parties' motives also reveals substantial differences. Most notably, the McGovern-Fraser Commission served not only as a battleground in the factional dispute raging within the Democratic Party in the late 1960s and early 1970s, but also as a weapon wielded by the pro-reform forces against their foes. The factional nature of the commission was largely responsible for its large-scale use of public hearings (which were in no small part an organizing and publicity mechanism for the incipient McGovern campaign), as well as for its complexity and the prominence of its staff (both of which were required to drive the full commission in the desired reform direction). In contrast, the Republican task force in 1996 was driven more by a general dissatisfaction with the system on the part of all candidates and a wide array of party officials that cut across regional and ideological lines.

Consequently, the greatest divergence is evident along the third dimension: the products of the two reform efforts. Again, both circumstance and party philosophy played a role. Democrats, adhering to a more centralized vision of governance, took a much more prescriptive approach. Republicans, too, moved further toward central direction than they ever had before, but fell far short of the extent of centralization practiced by Democrats after 1968. Their approach was far more bottom-up or, as several participants put it, "market-based." Furthermore, Republican reforms were clearly (and deliberately) more incremental in nature. The broader philosophy of each party on such questions as states' rights and incremental versus radical change clearly came into play in their differing approaches to reform. The contrast between the two reform bodies thus serves as an important reminder that ideas matter; as Philip Klinkner argues, party innovation is powerfully influenced by party culture.[31]

Circumstances matter, too, and in most respects the prospect of major change in the nominating system in 1996 was not as strong as after 1968. Historically, major transformations of the nominating system have required a confluence of several factors. These have included the emergence of a change-oriented political movement, such as the Progressives or New Politics movement; a major electoral crisis of legitimacy, such as the five-way split of 1824, the Taft "steamroller" of 1912, or the Chicago disaster of 1968; and the interests of a particular candidate, as in the cases of Andrew Jackson, Theodore Roosevelt, Eugene McCarthy, George McGovern, and others.[32] All three elements were present after 1968. In 1996, the most that can be said is that problems falling well short of a full-scale crisis of legitimacy led one party to determine that its interests were not well served by the current system. Thus, even had Republicans possessed a philosophical inclination to impose massive top-down changes, the circumstances were not aligned for fundamental reform of that nature.

Finally, as Klinkner points out, party innovation is almost always undertaken by the party out of the White House, a pattern repeated in 1996.[33] It is also worth pondering whether the 1996 Republican nominating changes and the McGovern-Fraser reforms (as well as other Democratic reforms) indicate that reform of the nominating system is most likely to be driven by the majority party, as defined by its predominance at the state level and perhaps by its ideological control of the national agenda. Is it possible that the majority party inherently holds the initiative in such matters, either for practical reasons (because control of governorships and state legislatures makes reform a more viable option) or because of more intangible factors, such as greater confidence and a sense of moral authority? Such a supposition may be impossible to prove, but in its favor it can be said that no major nominating reform of the last 170 years has been initiated by a party that was clearly in the minority. Perhaps Samuel Lubbell's famous "sun and moon" analogy of majority and minority parties—that the minority party's moon often passively reflects the energy of the majority sun—applies as well to the capacity or inclination for reforming the presidential nominating system.[34]

Front-Loading in 2000

Until mid-1998, it appeared that the pressure for front-loading had indeed begun to abate. Minnesota and South Dakota had moved their primaries back in the schedule, while in Wisconsin and California, whose early primary dates in 1996 were a one-time experiment, primaries had returned automatically to their pre-1996 place. Bills were introduced in Ohio and Texas to move primaries back into May, and while neither was enacted, both had substantial legislative support and seemed likely to be reintroduced. Missouri added a presidential preference primary to its caucus-convention system for delegate selection, but scheduled the primary for April. All this prompted Massachusetts's secretary of state William J. Galvin to declare that "the rush to the front has been arrested."[35]

Regional primaries also gained support. The southern "Super Tuesday" primary, initiated in the 1980s, was the first of the species and had survived through 1996, though in slimmed-down form compared with its heyday in 1988 when virtually every southern state held its primary or caucus on the same day. The "Yankee primary," a new regional primary consisting of five New England states, made its debut early in the 1996 schedule (5 March). And the 19 March 1996 primaries featured a Great Lakes theme, with Michigan, Illinois, Ohio, and Wisconsin participating. This movement toward regional primaries picked up strength after 1996.

Mike Leavitt, Republican governor of Utah, spearheaded a move to forge a regional primary in the mountain states of the West (the "Big Sky primary"). Leavitt argued, "Currently, we are on the outside looking in on the presidential nominating process. But collectively we could change the landscape. Group the eight mountain states [Arizona, Colorado, Idaho, Montana, Nevada, New Mexico, Utah, and Wyoming] together and you have a powerhouse."[36] The Big Sky idea quickly gained bipartisan support, with its proponents expressing hope that a unified primary date would encourage presidential candidates to focus more seriously on issues like water law, grazing rights, mining, and environmental regulation.[37] More generally, a Rocky Mountain primary "could serve as a platform for a Western politician—or one who would run well in the West."[38] The eight states account for 10 percent of the delegates to the Republican National Convention and 6 percent of Democratic delegates, a total 50 percent larger than the California GOP delegation (242 to 163).[39] Leavitt initially left open the possibility of holding the Big Sky primary late in the primary season, in recognition of the problems inherent in extreme primary compression.

Officials in other parts of the country also floated the idea of regional primaries. For example, talk was heard of a "Prairie primary," a Mid-Atlantic primary, and a Pacific Coast primary. Through mid-1998, it was still an open question whether these regional primaries would actually come to pass and, if they did, whether they would exacerbate front-loading or mitigate it by being spread more evenly through the primary calendar. Massachusetts's William Galvin and New Hampshire's secretary of state Bill Gardner, for example, held the regional trend to be a viable alternative to front-loading, and Galvin even expressed willingness to move the Yankee primary to a later date.[40]

Then everything changed. California election officials announced that they would seek to move California's primary up to the first Tuesday of March (7 March in 2000) and that they would try to convince the states of Oregon and Washington to join them. California state senator Jim Costa, who sponsored the bill changing the primary date, argued, "We've been reduced in presidential politics to being the ATM machine, in the sense that presidential aspirants can raise money here and then take that money to New Hampshire and Iowa and the East and South and Midwest, where the race develops early."[41] California's announcement sent the primary schedule into a chaotic free-for-all, with the almost certain outcome, at least in 2000, a system even more front-loaded than the one in 1996. Even without further changes in the primary calendar, California's addition to the 7 March lineup meant that about 40 percent of the Republican delegates and 50 percent of the Democratic delegates required to win the nomination would be at stake on that one day.[42]

States participating in the Yankee primary, already scheduled for 7 March, expressed grave concern that their regional primary would be eclipsed by the primaries in California and New York. Governor Leavitt of Utah, proponent of the Big Sky primary, declared, "If California moves up, we'll have to position ourselves relative to California."[43] The eight Big Sky governors settled on 10 March, midway through the week between California and the southern Super Tuesday, though several of the state legislatures involved ultimately refused to ratify the new date.[44] Kansas called for the Prairie primary to be held early in the process; four of the targeted seven states (Kansas, Missouri, Minnesota, and Wisconsin) almost immediately set a date of 4 April, while two others (Nebraska and South Dakota) considered joining them.[45] Even 4 April seemed too late for some Kansas lawmakers, one of whom lamented, "It's almost a dead issue by then."[46] Virginia had already indicated that it was considering a primary one week after New Hampshire's. Legislation was introduced in Michigan to hold that state's primary on the same day as the Iowa caucuses, a proposal that met with the hearty approval of Democratic Senator Carl Levin, even though such a proposal would clearly violate national Democratic rules.[47] The states of the original regional primary, the southern Super Tuesday, were hardly going to allow themselves to be rendered impotent in the nominating process. And New Hampshire officials, fearing the loss of their traditional "first primary" status, threatened to move their primary date into early January.[48]

The renewed race for the front set off by California's decision was limited only by the 1 July 1999 deadline established by the 1996 Republican reforms for states to set their primary dates. There will be more regional primaries in 2000 than ever before, but rather than serving as an alternative to front-loading they will almost certainly add to the compression of the schedule. Galvin, so full of hope just a few months earlier, concluded that "this is a bigger mess than ever, a political and civic crisis. . . . It's going to entirely capsize the presidential primary process."[49] Altogether, within six months of California's decision to move its primary forward, some analysts were predicting that thirty-five states might hold their primaries or caucuses by 21 March 2000.[50]

After a modest but promising start to the effort to reverse front-loading, what happened? First and foremost, front-loading is largely a self-perpetuating phenomenon. Like generals who prepare for the last war, state lawmakers base their presumptions about the future on their experience in the recent past. In 1996, no state holding a primary after 12 March had had an influence on the outcome of the presidential nominating race. California, which had moved its primary from June to 26 March, was still left as a bystander. More broadly, front-loading did not cause (though it might have exacerbated) the phenomenon of early winners; it was the tendency of the pre-1996 nominating process to pick a clear winner before many states had yet voted that led states to move their contests up in the calendar. As long as that dynamic remains—and there is little reason to believe it would change even with a shift back to the pre-1996 calendar—the incentive for front-loading will remain.

Second, the attempt to rebalance the primary calendar was always fragile, in that success required several states, including some large states, to move back and *no* large states to move forward. In other words, virtually everyone had to go along. Once California, the proverbial eight-hundred-pound gorilla of American politics, moved forward, all efforts at restraint were doomed. Finally, several states were driven to move up in the calendar by parochial considerations, specifically the desire to vote early enough to help promote the potential candidacies of favorite sons (in California's case, Governor Pete Wilson). Altogether, the bonus delegate incentive offered in the 1996 Republican reforms proved inadequate when measured against the continuing political incentives for holding an early primary. After all, 10 percent more delegates (or even 20 percent more) do not help a state if it votes after the nomination has already been decided.

The short-term consequences of the revivified front-loading frenzy are not easy to predict, aside from the mad scramble for position. Unlike 1996, when states were still revising their primary dates a few months before the New Hampshire primary, the 1 July 1999 filing deadline at least means that the primary schedule will be locked into place and candidates will have time to adjust their strategies to the new calendar. The two greatest areas of speculation have been the effects of an even more front-loaded calendar on internal party struggles and on the relevance of Iowa and New Hampshire. On the Democratic side, several analysts have expressed the opinion that further primary compression would work to the benefit of Vice President Al Gore, since it would put a premium on having campaign resources up front.[51] Indeed, Democratic Senator Paul Wellstone, who had briefly considered a presidential candidacy, complained that "[front-loading] is transparent. It's nothing less than an effort to wire the whole thing."[52] While there is little evidence to support the idea that front-loading in 2000 is the result of a pro-Gore conspiracy, Wellstone would almost certainly have been hurt by it had he chosen to run. On the Republican side, California officials argued that an early California primary combined with the Yankee primary could tilt the balance in favor of a "moderate" Republican, though the chain reaction set in motion by California's move up could easily negate any such effect.[53]

As for the influence of Iowa and New Hampshire, which will remain at the front of the calendar (though perhaps not alone), analysts are divided in their opinions. Some hold that the earliest contests will be even more important, helping to establish momentum that will carry the winner of New Hampshire through California only days later.[54] Others maintain that California will come so quickly on the heels of New Hampshire that candidates will have to campaign in both places simultaneously, in which event "it would end the retail politics of New Hampshire, and you'd get into mass-media politics, which is the politics of California."[55] As one California political analyst put it, "We are such a dominant media state that poor New Hampshire might get drowned out completely."[56] This debate is reminiscent of the debate over front-loading before the 1996 primaries, which featured a "deadlock" school and a "knockout" school. The deadlock school held that no candidate could do well everywhere at once and that because such a highly compressed schedule would not allow time to weed out candidates, it would produce a deadlock. The knockout school held that the primaries were so compressed that whoever won the earliest contests would be carried by the resultant momentum through the decisive segment of the primary calendar. In the actual event, of course, neither scenario played out as envisioned. The Republican nomination was determined early, but the very earliest contests were not the decisive ones; the winner in New Hampshire never won another primary. If nothing else, the failure of the two models in 1996 shows how difficult it is to predict the consequences of shifts in the primary calendar.[57]

Paradoxically, the long-term consequences of increased front-loading are perhaps easier to predict than the short-term consequences, at least in general outline. It is likely that voices will be heard on the Republican National Committee urging that the question of primary reform be reopened. While members of the 1996 task force were reluctant to predict future RNC action, none were willing to rule out additional steps in the future if the incentive plan failed and the front-loading of 1996 was repeated in 2000; half foresaw pressure to revisit the nominating reforms.

The primary system's imminent collapse into chaos also increases pressure on the states to find a solution. Throughout 1998, state election officials spoke increasingly favorably about attempting to adopt a more formal system of regional primaries. Such a system might feature five or six regions, each of which would hold primaries spaced two to four weeks apart. The chronological order of these regional primaries would rotate systematically, although (at least according to some proposals) Iowa and New Hampshire would retain their first position. Indeed, California's secretary of state Bill Jones acknowledged that he hoped California's move up would become "the catalyst" for a system of rotating regional primaries.[58]

Several formidable problems must be overcome for such a system to begin operating, however, and no one expects it to be in place before 2004. Above all, absent federal legislation, this system would require an unprecedented degree of cooperation among every state in the union; in 2000, not even the eight states at the center of the Big Sky proposal succeeded in producing a unified primary date. Many states would be forced to choose between holding a costly separate primary just for presidential selection or allowing primaries for lower office to be shifted along with the presidential primary every four years. Moreover, it is not clear how a system of rotating regional primaries would solve one of the chief problems of the current system, which is that states holding the latest primaries have no say in the nomination. In this case, whole regions could be disenfranchised. If California considers it unjust that the most populous state in America votes after the nomination is decided, it is hard to imagine that it would someday passively agree to vote with the last region on the calendar. Nonetheless, the regional primaries idea has strong and growing support in the abstract, and the extreme front-loading that is shaping up in 2000 will likely provide an additional boost for the idea (as well as an informal and imperfect test of it, minus the rotation).

Early Voting and Presidential Primaries

Scholars debate the precise meaning, the psychological mechanism, and even the full significance of momentum, which is only one of numerous factors contributing to nomination outcomes. Momentum notwithstanding, national poll standings and fund raising in the year prior to the primaries are remarkably good predictors of ultimate success.[59] Nevertheless, few doubt that it can be an important factor in the nominating process under certain conditions.

Generally speaking, momentum in the context of the presidential nominating process refers to the electoral benefits accruing in later primaries to candidates who do well in earlier primaries, as a consequence of those earlier successes. The notion of momentum has become so central to the current presidential selection process that Elaine Kamarck has argued that after the McGovern-Fraser reforms, "the cultivation of momentum became the only real strategy available" to candidates.[60]

The exact nature of the signals sent by early victories remains a matter of academic contention, but momentum seems to be a real prospect only when voters' informational levels are relatively low.[61] This means that the nature of the candidate field has an immense influence on the question of whether substantial swings of momentum are likely to develop in any given race. In races between two major candidates, especially when one is an incumbent president, the effects of momentum are generally less significant than in races in which information about the candidates is scarcer. Momentum has mattered most when there was no major candidate in the race (as in the Democratic race of 1976) and next most when there were one major candidate and a host of lesser candidates.[62] Consequently, the significance of momentum is not uniform across elections. Overall, as the public learns more about the candidates, the effects of momentum are muted. Thus, according to Larry Bartels, "The 'shelf life' of momentum in its most intense and uncritical form may be no more than 2 or 3 weeks."[63]

Momentum that dominates the political scene for two or three weeks is, of course, a more troubling prospect when primaries are so compressed that victory can conceivably be secured three weeks after the New Hampshire vote. While the Republican reforms of 1996 aimed unsuccessfully to reverse primary front-loading, a seemingly unrelated electoral reform undertaken by a large number of states may hold the potential for undermining the "bandwagon effect" in the presidential nominating process—not in spite of front-loading, but because of it.

In search of greater voter convenience and improved voter turnout, more than two dozen states have adopted one or more versions of what may loosely be termed *early voting*. The first variation of early voting was unrestricted absentee voting, pioneered by California and Oregon in 1978, which allowed voters to request and cast a mailed absentee ballot without notarization and without a specified reason, such as illness or travel. In 1990, Texas introduced a second version: a window of time prior to election day during which voters could vote in person at a county clerk's office or satellite voting facility. The third, and in many ways most radical, method of early voting is the mail-ballot election, in which all eligible voters are automatically mailed a ballot, which they can either return by mail or return in person to the county elections office.

While proponents of early voting have touted its potential for higher voter turnout, actual results have been mixed. In some states using unrestricted absentee and walk-in early voting, turnout has edged up modestly; in others, there has been no change at all. Of the three methods, mail-ballot voting seems to increase turnout most reliably. While turnout effects have been inconsistent, early voting has been consistently popular. In many states that allow early voting, early voters regularly make up as much as one-fifth of the electorate (in Texas, the figure has reached one-third).

At the same time, some analysts (as well as some political participants) have expressed a variety of concerns about early voting, ranging from ballot security to the qualitative effects on citizenship. One of the most prominent concerns has been that early voters will cast their ballots before all relevant information about the candidates is available. In this view, early voting "deprives large numbers of voters of the ability to make fully informed decisions by encouraging them to vote before all the information about the candidates and issues has been presented."[64] This sort of "premature voting" may leave a large number of voters regretting their decisions, and could be decisive in a closely fought election. Substantial evidence exists that such effects may have already occurred in selected races. In the closely fought 1990 Texas gubernatorial race, "significant changes in voter sentiment occurred during the final week of the campaign,"[65] while in 1992, Republican officials in California complained that hundreds of thousands of people had already voted before economic statistics were released in late October showing strong national economic growth.[66] In Colorado in 1994, late-breaking revelations led the two Denver daily newspapers to reverse their endorsements of the Democratic candidate for secretary of state. A subsequent analysis of the vote showed that the candidate's Republican opponent did significantly better in election day precinct voting than in early voting; clearly, thousands of early voters had cast their ballots before all the facts were known.[67]

The potential connection between early voting and momentum in presidential nominations should be obvious, especially in the context of a highly compressed schedule. In theory, thousands of voters in states with late primaries could vote before the results of earlier primaries are known. In no sense could the 1996 Republican nomination race be said to have been heavily affected by early voting, but voting results do give some information on which to base an analysis of the potential effects of this reform.

It is possible to divide the Republican primaries held in February and March 1996 into four phases:

1. post–New Hampshire (24 February–2 March, which included the primaries from Delaware through South Carolina),
2. "Junior Tuesday" (5 March),
3. "Super Tuesday" (12 March),
4. "mop-up" (the remainder of March, including the Rust Belt and California primaries).

Of the twenty-seven Republican preference primaries held during this period (excluding Puerto Rico's), eleven (or 41 percent) used at least one version of early voting. Two out of the five states whose primaries occurred in phase 1 had early voting; two out of eight in phase 2 did; four of seven in phase 3; and three of seven in phase 4 (see table 2.1).

It is more difficult to ascertain how many voters actually cast their ballots early in these eleven states, since many early-voting states did not compile data on that question. In North Dakota, which used a mail-ballot system, 90 percent of votes were returned before election day (84 percent by mail and 6 percent in person). Although the other two mail-ballot states (Oregon and Nevada) did not compile official data, other evidence indicates that the vast majority of voters in these states also returned their ballots before election day.[68] Of the eight other early-

TABLE 2.1   STATES WITH EARLY VOTING IN REPUBLICAN PRESIDENTIAL
PRIMARIES, FEBRUARY AND MARCH 1996

State	Primary Date	Method of Early Voting
Arizona	27 February	Unrestricted absentee/walk-in
North Dakota	27 February	Mail ballot
Colorado	5 March	Unrestricted absentee/walk-in
Vermont	5 March	Unrestricted absentee
Oklahoma	12 March	Unrestricted absentee/walk-in
Oregon	12 March	Mail ballot
Tennessee	12 March	Unrestricted absentee/walk-in
Texas	12 March	Unrestricted absentee/walk-in
California	26 March	Unrestricted absentee
Nevada	26 March	Mail ballot
Washington	26 March	Unrestricted absentee

voting states (which used walk-in early voting and/or unrestricted absentee voting), the four that do keep figures on the proportion of voters who voted early ranged from a low of 7 percent (Vermont) to a high of 22.3 percent (Texas) and averaged 12.9 percent (see table 2.2).[69]

A comparison of 1996 primary results from states that used early-voting methods and states that did not yields some interesting conclusions. The results, shown in table 2.3, suggest that early voting does have the potential to mitigate the effects of momentum. Whether a state allowed early voting or not made little difference for Dole except in the 5 March primaries (phase 2), held only three days after his breakthrough win in South Carolina. In the 5 March primaries, Dole did significantly better in

TABLE 2.2   PERCENTAGE OF EARLY VOTERS IN REPUBLICAN PRESIDENTIAL
PRIMARIES, FEBRUARY AND MARCH 1996

State	Primary Date	% of Early Voters
Arizona	27 February	8.3
North Dakota	27 February	90.0
Colorado	5 March	n.a.
Vermont	5 March	7.0
Oklahoma	12 March	n.a.
Oregon	12 March	n.a.[a]
Tennessee	12 March	13.8
Texas	12 March	22.3
California	26 March	n.a.
Nevada	26 March	n.a.[a]
Washington	26 March	n.a.

[a] Mail-ballot states typically have 80 percent or more of the ballots returned before election day.

TABLE 2.3   1996 REPUBLICAN PRESIDENTIAL PRIMARY RESULTS FOR STATES WITH EARLY VOTING AND STATES WITHOUT EARLY VOTING (MEAN RESULTS)

	Phase 1[a]		Phase 2[b]		Phase 3[c]		Phase 4[d]	
	Early Voting (2 States)	No Early Voting (3 States)	Early Voting (2 States)	No Early Voting (6 States)	Early Voting (4 States)	No Early Voting (3 States)	Early Voting (3 States)	No Early Voting (4 States)
Dole	35.9	39.0	42.0	51.1	54.2	55.0	60.4	58.6
Buchanan	23.0	25.5	19.1	23.0	22.4	25.7	18.2	28.0
Forbes	26.5	19.4	18.2	14.5	11.2	13.8	11.8	5.4
Alexander	6.7	10.8	10.2	9.6	5.4	1.8	1.8	1.7
Keyes	2.0	3.6	3.7	2.9	3.1	2.3	3.3	3.2
Other[e]	6.1	1.7	8.7	4.8	2.9	1.3	4.6	3.1

[a] 24 February–2 March (Delaware through South Carolina primaries, Puerto Rico excluded).
[b] 5 March ("Junior Tuesday").
[c] 12 March ("Super Tuesday").
[d] Remainder of March.
[e] Includes all candidates not otherwise listed, plus the uncommitted vote.

states that did not have early voting than in states that did; it is likely that many early voters cast their ballots before the South Carolina results were known. Forbes did significantly better in states with early voting in phase 1 (when early voters may have voted before his late slide in Iowa and New Hampshire), phase 2 (when early voters may have voted before the South Carolina primary), and phase 4 (when early voters may have voted before he dropped out of the race). Indeed, Forbes's campaign manager, Billy Dal Col, attributed Forbes's 27 February victory in Arizona largely to the campaign's effort to collect 14,000 absentee ballots.[70] Alexander did better in states without early voting in phase 1 (early voters may have voted before his surprisingly good showing in Iowa and his near-victory in New Hampshire), but better in states with early voting in phase 2 (held just after South Carolina) and phase 3 (just after he dropped out of the race). Other candidates like Phil Gramm and Richard Lugar, as well as votes for "uncommitted," did better in early-voting states than they did in non–early–voting states in every phase. Interestingly, Buchanan did better in states without early voting in every phase, regardless of his level of previous electoral success.

These figures support the notion that early voting can distort the effects of momentum, either by inflating or deflating the votes of active candidates or by siphoning votes away from active candidates to inactive candidates or the "uncommitted" option. The effects were most severe in the three states using mail-ballot elections (North Dakota, Oregon, and Nevada). In North Dakota, Senator Phil Gramm received nearly 10 percent of the vote even though he had dropped out of the race two weeks earlier; indeed, more than half the ballots in North Dakota were returned before the New Hampshire primary.[71] Though the North Dakota primary was not close enough to be tilted by that distortion, it is not difficult to imagine a situation in which it could be decisive. (In the critical Arizona primary, held the same day as North Dakota's, less than 6 percentage points separated the first-place finisher, Forbes, from the third-place finisher, Buchanan.) Similarly, in Nevada on 26 March, nearly a third of the electorate voted for inactive options (19 percent for Forbes, who had withdrawn on 14 March, and 10 percent for other/uncommitted, including "none of the above").

Oregon's Super Tuesday primary displayed a similar, if less dramatic, pattern. Alexander received 7 percent of the vote despite having dropped out of the race, a share four times greater than his mean vote share in all other Super Tuesday states except his own state of Tennessee (another state with early voting, in which Alexander received 12 percent of the vote). The other/uncommitted vote in Oregon was also greater than in

TABLE 2.4   "OTHER" AND "UNCOMMITTED" VOTES IN MAIL-BALLOT AND ALL
OTHER STATES, BY NOMINATION PHASE

Phase	Mail-Ballot States	All Other States (Mean)
1	10.6% (N.D.)	1.5%
3	4.1 (Ore.)	1.6
4	10.0 (Nev.)	2.7

Note: Votes for "other" candidates include all Republican primary candidates except
Alexander, Buchanan, Dole, Forbes, and Keyes. In Nevada, "other" also includes votes
cast for "none of the above."

any other state but Texas (an early-voting state where favorite son Phil
Gramm garnered some support). Altogether, the votes for minor candidates and uncommitted votes tabulated in mail-ballot states were much
greater than the mean for other states in the same nomination phase (see
table 2.4).

While these data suggest that early voting could profoundly affect
nomination races under certain conditions, the actual impact on the
1996 race was marginal at best. Furthermore, because we are dealing
with aggregate data, we can only infer that differences between states
that have early voting and states that do not are due to a difference
between early votes and votes cast on election day. In the mail-ballot
states, this is indeed highly probable, since almost all voters return their
ballots before election day. In the walk-in and unrestricted absentee
states, such an inference may be logical but cannot be proven. None of
the eleven states using early voting through March 1996 gathered
statewide data separating the results of early votes from the results of
election day votes. More detailed data *are* often available at the county
level, however, making it possible to approach the question with a sampling of results from county election offices.

Early Voting and the 1996 Colorado Republican Primary

Because collection of data at the county level was practical only on a limited scale, I targeted ten key counties in Colorado.[72] Colorado uses both
walk-in early voting and unrestricted absentee voting. Its 1996 primary
was held on 5 March ("Junior Tuesday"), the only phase of the campaign
when Alexander, Forbes, and Dole all seemed to be experiencing significant momentum-driven shifts in support. One would expect that Dole's
support on election day would have been bolstered by the news of his
South Carolina victory. One would expect the converse for Alexander,

TABLE 2.5   1996 COLORADO REPUBLICAN PRIMARY: PERCENTAGES OF EARLY
VOTES AND ELECTION DAY VOTES IN TEN SAMPLE COUNTIES

	Dole	Buchanan	Forbes	Alexander	Keyes	Other
Actual statewide vote	43.6%	21.5%	20.8%	9.8%	3.7%	0.6%
Total vote in sample counties	43.0	21.2	21.4	9.9	3.8	0.7
Early vote in sample counties	40.9	23.1	17.8	14.1	2.9	1.2
Election day vote in sample counties	43.2	21.0	21.7	9.5	3.9	0.7

Note: Sample counties were Adams, Arapahoe, Boulder, Denver, Douglas, El Paso, Jefferson, Larimer, Pueblo, and Weld. Total votes cast in sample counties: 197,538. Early votes cast in sample counties: 15,703 (7.9% of total).

whose disappointing showing in South Carolina was widely held to write the epitaph for his campaign. Forbes could conceivably have gone up or down on election day. Early voters might have been affected by his win in Arizona, though it came too late for many (only one week before election day), and some election day voters—taking Alexander's apparent demise into account—might have shifted strategically to Forbes as the most serious non-Buchanan opponent for Bob Dole. It is also important to note that Forbes targeted Colorado with a large television advertising campaign just before the primary.

The results from the ten Colorado counties confirm these general expectations (see table 2.5). Bob Dole's election day vote was modestly better than his early vote, both in the aggregate and in seven of the ten counties individually. Lamar Alexander's vote fell by one-third from the early vote to the election day vote, and fell in every county. Steve Forbes increased his vote share by about the same percentage that Alexander's declined, providing at least a little evidence that some later voters were affected by strategic calculations. Forbes's surge could also provide evidence that a self-financed candidate running a massive ad campaign can be buffered from the impact of negative momentum, at least for a time. Buchanan lost a bit overall, and Keyes gained a bit overall, in election day voting versus early voting. Finally, the proportion of votes for "other" candidates (mostly Richard Lugar) was cut in half from early voting to election day. In no case was the shift from the early vote to the election day vote dramatic, but in some cases it could have been important had the primary results been closer.

Mitigating the potential consequences was the relatively small proportion of voters who voted early in Colorado in 1996. In the ten sample counties, roughly 8 percent voted before election day, a much smaller proportion than in recent general elections in Colorado (which frequently see one in five voters vote early). This pattern also existed in other states, as the 1996 presidential primaries experienced lower-than-normal early-voting rates. Although there is no firm evidence for it, it is possible that presidential primary voters are sufficiently aware of the shifting tides of the typical nomination campaign that, at least in 1996, they deliberately chose to forgo the early-voting option so they could take into account the latest possible developments.

Overall, early voting can either reduce the scale of a candidate's momentum-driven surge or break a candidate's momentum-driven fall, though in the context of the 1996 nomination race it was insufficient to make a decisive impact. Looking to the year 2000, it is not yet clear whether the movement toward early voting among states and within the electorate has slowed or will continue through the end of the 1990s. In recognition of the obvious mathematics of the calendar, the Democratic National Committee warned Oregon in January 1999 that its 14 March mail-ballot primary could violate the DNC "window," which starts 1 March, because ballots are distributed three weeks prior to election day.[73] Despite DNC concern, a number of states in early 1999 were considering the adoption of mail-ballot primaries, and it seemed quite possible that the move toward early balloting, like the move toward front-loading, had passed the point of easy central control by the parties.

The more states that adopt some form of early voting and the more voters who avail themselves of it, the more likely it is that early voting will significantly affect the 2000 nomination races. If early-voting rates in presidential primaries merely begin to match the rates found in general elections, the impact of early voting would grow considerably. It can already be said that the additional compression of the primary calendar will heighten the potential impact of early voting in such states as North Dakota, California, Colorado, Texas, and Oregon.

Finally, the nature of the candidate fields will almost certainly work to increase the importance of early voting. Both the Republican and Democratic nomination races will be theoretically more subject to momentum in 2000 than their counterparts were in 1996. While in late 1998 Governor George W. Bush of Texas emerged as the pundits' front-runner on the Republican side, there is neither an incumbent president nor an heir-apparent running for the Republican nomination. Indeed, many analysts saw Bush's hold on front-runner status as tenuous, buffeted by the candidacies of Steve Forbes and Elizabeth Dole, among others.[74] The Democratic race is certain to feature an identifiable front-runner (Al Gore), but unlike 1996, it will be a race. This means that both parties' races will be more subject to the potential effects of early voting in early contests.

Conclusion

The presidential nominating system in the year 2000 will feature a variety of innovations. New Republican rules will be tested and will have an effect, even if the chief goal of reversing front-loading is not achieved. Republicans have ventured into the realm of party reform and have placed their distinctive stamp on it. If nothing else, the 1 July 1999 deadline that was part of the reform package will structure states' choices and should end the calendar jockeying seven months before the New Hampshire primary. Front-loading will nevertheless reach new heights, and regional primaries will exert more influence than ever before, perhaps pointing the way to more comprehensive change after 2000. And early voting, which reached a high point in 1996, could be an important factor—the more so as the primary calendar becomes more and more compressed. These developments remind us of both the limits of deliberate reform and the far-reaching potential of decentralized, even accidental, change and evolution in the presidential nominating system.

Acknowledgments

I would like to thank the members of the Republican National Committee Task Force on Primaries and Caucuses and the RNC staff who agreed to be interviewed for this project, including Mark Acton, Alice Algood, Robert Bennett, Jim McGinley, Cindy Moyle, David Norcross, Alec Poitevint, Christopher Quish, and Diemer True.

Notes

1. William G. Mayer, "The Presidential Nominations," in *The Election of 1996*, ed. Gerald M. Pomper (Chatham, N.J.: Chatham House, 1997), 23–4.
2. Nelson Polsby argues that in many respects the Republican nominating system "remains unreformed"; see *Consequences of Party Reform* (New York: Oxford University Press, 1983), 54. Other scholars emphasize the crucial similarities between the nominating systems in each party. See Thomas R. Marshall, *Presidential Nominations in a Reform Age* (New York: Praeger, 1981), 42; and Leon Epstein, *Political Parties in the American Mold* (Madison: University of Wisconsin Press, 1986), 103–4.
3. For a good discussion of Republican reform efforts, see David E. Price, *Bringing Back the Parties* (Washington, D.C.: CQ Press, 1984), 156–9.

4. Republican National Committee, "Nicholson Tapped to Chair National GOP Task Force on Presidential Primary Schedule," news release, 27 February 1996.

5. Republican National Committee, "Republican National Committee to Hold Hearing on Presidential Primary Process," news release, 10 April 1996.

6. "Press Conference with Haley Barbour: Report by Special Task Force on Primaries and Caucuses," Federal News Service, 2 July 1996.

7. The task force members included Alice Algood (national committeewoman, Tennessee), Robert Bennett (state chairman, Ohio), Cindy Moyle (national committeewoman, Idaho), David Norcross (national committeeman, New Jersey), Alec Poitevint (national committeeman, Georgia), Doris Russell (national committeewoman, Maine), and Diemer True (state chairman, Wyoming). RNC Deputy Counsel Jack Connors served as task force counsel.

8. C. David Kotok, "GOP Takes 2nd Look at Primary Schedule," *Omaha World Herald*, 6 March 1996, 10.

9. David S. Broder, "After Quick Decision, GOP Reviewing Primary Schedule," *Washington Post*, 19 April 1996, A8.

10. Peter A. Brown, "GOP Weighs Policy on Primaries," *Rocky Mountain News*, 8 April 1996, 19A.

11. Broder, "After Quick Decision."

12. Ibid.

13. "Press Conference with Haley Barbour."

14. Carolyn Barta, "'Texas' Super Tuesday Participation Rethought," *Dallas Morning News*, 16 March 1996, 25A.

15. "Press Conference with Haley Barbour."

16. Indeed, Haley Barbour specifically denied this motivation, arguing that "you could have tried five different processes, and Bob Dole would still have won the nomination"; see "Press Conference with Haley Barbour."

17. Ronald Brownstein, "GOP Leaders Fear that Frantic Pace of Primaries Leaves Voters Out in Cold," *Los Angeles Times*, 11 March 1996, A5; Gerald F. Seib, "Primary Issue: If It's Broke, Why Not Fix It?" *Wall Street Journal*, 20 March 1996, A16; William Safire, "Primary Reform Now," *New York Times*, 28 March 1996, A25; and David S. Broder, "Primary Madness," *Washington Post*, 3 March 1996, C7.

18. Of the six task force members interviewed, five (Bennett, Moyle, Norcross, Poitevint, and True) explicitly mentioned that the philosophy of the party was "states' rights" and an avoidance of top-down central mandates. The sixth (Algood) did not use such terminology, but mentioned a somewhat more general (though compatible) desire not to be "dictatorial."

19. Diemer True, telephone interview by author, 26 February 1997.

20. "Press Conference with Haley Barbour."

21. Jack Germond and Jules Witcover, "Republicans Rethink Their Front-Loaded Primary Process," *Denver Post*, 22 August 1996, B11.

22. For the objections of opponents to the plan, see Germond and Witcover, "Republicans Rethink"; Cragg Hines, "Republicans Move to Reverse 'Front-Loading' of Primaries," *Houston Chronicle*, 9 August 1996, A21; and Finlay Lewis, "GOP Panel OKs Rewarding States That Hold Later Primaries," *San Diego Union-Tribune*, 10 August 1996, A10.

23. See Rules 31(6), 32(10), and 32(11) in *The Rules of the Republican Party as Adopted by the 1996 Republican National Convention* (San Diego, 1996), 15–24.

24. See David Yepsen, "GOP Goal: A Face Lift for Presidential Race in 2000," *Des Moines Register*, 3 July 1996, 4; and Germond and Witcover, "Republicans Rethink."

25. "Press Conference with Haley Barbour."

26. Mike Dorning, "GOP May Offer States an Incentive to Move Back Their Primaries," *Chicago Tribune*, 3 July 1996, 24.

27. Byron E. Shafer, *Quiet Revolution: The Struggle for the Democratic Party and the Shaping of Post-Reform Politics* (New York: Russell Sage Foundation, 1983), 42. Shafer notes the degree to which the ultimate form and direction of the McGovern-Fraser Commission was shaped by Harris, who deliberately "planned to install the growing 'reform wing' of the party" in the commission—and succeeded.

28. Mark Acton, Staff Director, RNC Counsel's Office, interview by author, 27 February 1997; and Shafer, *Quiet Revolution*, 85, 95.

29. Shafer, *Quiet Revolution*, 117.

30. "Press Conference with Haley Barbour." It should be noted, however, that the participation issue was not as prominent in interviews with task force members as it was in public pronouncements by Barbour and Nicholson.

31. Philip A. Klinkner, *The Losing Parties: Out-Party National Committees 1956–1993* (New Haven, Conn.: Yale University Press, 1994).

32. Andrew E. Busch and James W. Ceaser, "Does Party Reform Have a Future?" in *In Pursuit of the White House*, ed. William G. Mayer (Chatham, N.J.: Chatham House, 1996), 330–55.

33. Klinkner, *The Losing Parties*.

34. Samuel Lubbell, *The Future of American Politics* (New York: Harper & Row, 1967), 16.

35. Chris Black, "Survey Shows End to Trend in 'Frontloading' Primaries," *Boston Globe*, 13 February 1998, A11.

36. Jeff Barker, "Western States' Party Leaders Weigh 'Big Sky' Primary Idea," *Arizona Republic*, 20 May 1998, A3.

37. Peggy Lowe, "Regional Primary Idea Advances," *Denver Post*, 1 April 1998, 2D; and Barker, "Western States' Party Leaders."

38. Barker, "Western States' Party Leaders."

39. Philip Burgess, "'Big Sky' Primary Would Shift Power," *Rocky Mountain News*, 2 June 1998.

40. Black, "Survey Shows End."

41. Siobhan Gorman, "California's Quest for Attention," *National Journal*, 27 June 1998, 1524.

42. Ibid. For California's primary to be meaningful, state officials had to maneuver around the state's new election law introducing a "blanket primary" in which voters could vote for a candidate of one party for one office and a candidate of a different party for another office. Both Republican and Democratic national rules forbid blanket primaries for presidential delegate selection. A referendum on the November 1998 California ballot would have exempted the presidential primary from the blanket primary, but it failed. Few observers doubted, however, that some mechanism would be devised to allow the 2000 presidential primary to be conducted in a fashion consistent with national party rules.

43. Ibid.

44. Peter Blake, "'Rocky Mountain Regional Primary' Gets Badly Shrunk," *Rocky Mountain News*, 6 June 1999, 3B.

45. B. Drummond Ayres, "For Campaign 2000, a Month of Tuesdays," *New York Times*, 8 August 1998, A9. See also Lew Ferguson, "April Presidential Primary in Works for Midwest States," Associated Press Wire, 28 January 1999. Only North Dakota, which already schedules its primary earlier in the process, refused to join the Prairie primary.

46. Ferguson, "April Presidential Primary."
47. B.G. Gregg, "Earlier Presidential Primary Urged: Michigan Lawmakers Seek February Date to Lure Candidates, Money," *Detroit News*, 13 January 1999, D10.
48. "Emerging Calendar: 70% in the First Eight Weeks! Egads!" *Hotline*, 11 December 1998.
49. Ayres, "For Campaign 2000, a Month of Tuesdays"; and "A Challenge for the Yankee Primary," *Boston Globe*, 31 May 1998, B4.
50. "Emerging Calendar."
51. Gorman, "California's Quest."
52. "Primary Reform," *Boston Globe*, 8 December 1998, A2.
53. Michael Kranish, "Calif. Moves to Match Mass. on Primary Date; N.E. States Fret about Losing Voice," *Boston Globe*, 17 July 1998, A1.
54. See Kranish, "Calif. Moves to Match Mass. on Primary Date"; "California Secretary of State Seeks to Hold 2000 Presidential Primary One Week after New Hampshire," *White House Bulletin*, 26 March 1998; and "California Seeks to Dominate 2000 Presidential Primary," *White House Bulletin*, 14 April 1998.
55. Gorman, "California's Quest."
56. Ibid.
57. For an updated version of this debate, see Alan Bernstein, "Primary Candidates Face Squeeze in 2000," *Houston Chronicle*, 15 December 1998, A1.
58. Gorman, "California's Quest."
59. William G. Mayer, "Forecasting Presidential Nominations," in *In Pursuit of the White House*, ed. William G. Mayer (Chatham, N.J.: Chatham House, 1996).
60. Elaine Ciulla Kamarck, "Structure as Strategy: Presidential Nominating Politics since Reform" (Ph.D. diss., University of California at Berkeley, 1986), 23, cited in Larry M. Bartels, *Presidential Primaries and the Dynamics of Public Choice* (Princeton, N.J.: Princeton University Press, 1988). While momentum has been widely discussed as a phenomenon of the modern (post–McGovern-Fraser) nominating system, it should be pointed out that the modern system has reformulated momentum rather than inventing it. Prior to the advent of primaries, state party leaders and delegates were heavily influenced by the bandwagons created by other leaders and delegates at the national convention. After 1912, when the nominating process featured a mixture of primaries and caucuses, primaries often served to provide momentum by transmitting evidence of electability from voters to state party leaders and national convention delegates. Today, momentum takes the form of signals transmitted from primary voters directly to other primary voters.
61. See Bartels, *Presidential Primaries*; William G. Mayer, "The New Hampshire Primary: A Historical Overview," and William C. Adams, "As New Hampshire Goes . . . ," both in *Media and Momentum: The New Hampshire Primary and Nomination Politics*, ed. Gary R. Orren and Nelson W. Polsby (Chatham, N.J.: Chatham House, 1987); Emmett H. Buell, Jr., and James W. Davis, "Win Early and Often: Candidates and the Strategic Environment of 1988," in *Nominating the President*, ed. Emmett H. Buell, Jr., and Lee Sigelman (Knoxville: University of Tennessee Press, 1991); Paul R. Abramson, John H. Aldrich, Phil Paolino, and David W. Rohde, "'Sophisticated' Voting in the 1988 Presidential Primaries," (paper presented at the annual meeting of the American Political Science Association, San Francisco, 1990); and John G. Geer, *Nominating Presidents: An Evaluation of Voters and Primaries* (Westport, Conn.: Greenwood Press, 1989).
62. See Bartels, *Presidential Primaries*, 171; Geer, *Nominating Presidents*, 81; Mayer, "The New Hampshire Primary," 16; and Adams, "As New Hampshire Goes . . . ," 56.

63. Bartels, *Presidential Primaries*, 290.
64. Margaret Rosenfield, *Innovations in Election Administration: Early Voting* (Washington, D.C.: Federal Election Commission, April 1994), 3.
65. Jeanie Stanley, "Bush, Richards Both Gear Campaigns to Women's Vote," *Dallas Morning News*, 6 November 1994, 6J.
66. Daryl Kelly, "Number of Votes by Mail Expected to Break Record," *Los Angeles Times*, 28 October 1992, B1.
67. Andrew E. Busch, "Early Voting: Convenient, But . . . ?" *State Legislatures* 22, no. 8 (September 1996): 27.
68. In Oregon's special senatorial election in January 1996, 87 percent of voters returned their ballots by mail more than two days in advance of election day; 50 percent voted within one week of receiving their ballots. County-level analyses of mail-ballot elections in Washington and Colorado have shown that between 85 and 95 percent of voters returned their ballots before election day. See Phil Keisling, "Final Election Results Released for January Special US Senate Election," Office of Secretary of State, Oregon, 27 February 1996, 2; Margaret Rosenfield, *All-Mail-Ballot Elections* (Washington, D.C.: Federal Election Commission, September 1995), 14–15; "November 2, 1993 Coordinated Election Results," Office of Secretary of State, Colorado; and Brian Weber, "Mail Voting a Hit with Weary Officials," *Rocky Mountain News*, 4 November 1993, 28A.
69. Some of the states that do not compile such figures for presidential primaries do compile them for other races. In California, Colorado, and Washington, early votes typically represent 15 to 20 percent of the total votes cast. See "States Innovate to Battle Low Turnout," *New York Times*, 24 October 1994; "Absentee Ballot Voting Statistics," Office of Secretary of State, Washington, 1995; and "Colorado Voting in 1992 General Election by County," Office of Secretary of State, Colorado, April 1993.
70. Glenn Frankel, "Forbes Optimism Is Selling," *Washington Post*, 28 February 1996, A6.
71. Richard L. Berke, "Forbes Claims Victory in Arizona Race," *New York Times*, 28 February 1996, A1.
72. The counties were Adams, Arapahoe, Boulder, Denver, Douglas, El Paso, Jefferson, Larimer, Pueblo, and Weld. These represent ten of the eleven most populous counties in Colorado and are divided among Republican-leaning (Arapahoe, Douglas, El Paso, Jefferson, Larimer, and Weld) and Democratic-leaning (Adams, Boulder, Denver, and Pueblo) counties.
73. Brad Cain, "Oregon May Lose Voice in Choosing Democratic Nominee," Associated Press State & Local Wire, 15 January 1999.
74. See Ron Fournier, "Bush, Forbes Standing Tall in GOP's Presidential Field," Associated Press Wire, 2 January 1999; and Richard Lowry, "Invincible Ignorance," *National Review*, 8 February 1999, 30–2.

CHAPTER THREE

The Changing Face of the New Hampshire Primary

by Emmett H. Buell, Jr.

AS SO OFTEN happens in New Hampshire, the nation's first Republican primary of 1996 ended on a note of high drama. A contest that once appeared Bob Dole's to lose now looked like one that he would indeed lose. The final week of campaigning (13–20 February) saw remarkable volatility in daily tracking polls of likely New Hampshire voters. Millionaire publisher Steve Forbes abruptly lost half his support after spending millions on attack ads and briefly overtaking Dole in late January. Lamar Alexander soared from a mere 11 percent just before the Iowa caucuses to 23 percent at midweek. Pat Buchanan topped out at 25 percent for most of the week. At first, Dole appeared to profit by his narrow victory in Iowa, going from 25 percent just before the caucuses to 32 percent immediately afterward. Then the trend turned against him. The same tracking polls that showed Buchanan holding steady and Alexander climbing rapidly registered a steady decline in Dole's support.[1] Dole now faced the prospect of losing to Alexander as well as to Buchanan. Since 1952, when the New Hampshire primary first became a major event in the nominating process, no candidate of either party had finished third here and fought on to win the nomination. "You know if I finish third I will drop out," Dole told one aide. "If we're third," he said to another, "we're finished."[2]

Moreover, as Dole fully appreciated, New Hampshire Republicans had never greeted his presidential bids with enthusiasm. His first try for the nomination collapsed after garnering less than 1 percent of the 1980 New

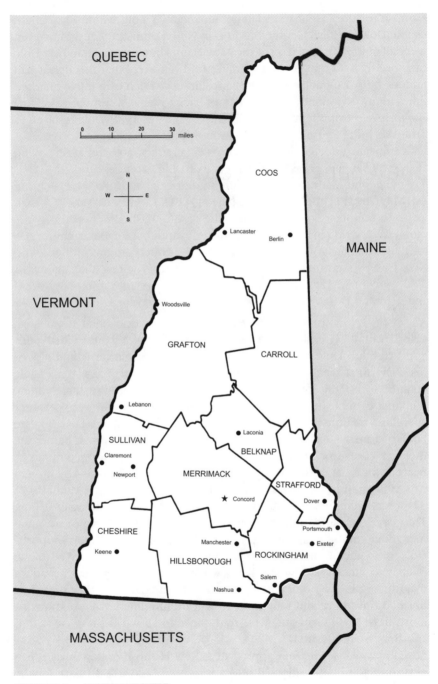

FIGURE 3.1   NEW HAMPSHIRE

Hampshire vote.[3] Eight years later, it looked as if a big win in Iowa might enable Dole to finish George Bush off in New Hampshire. Bush, however, went all out in the final days of the New Hampshire campaign to beat Dole by more than 14,000 votes. Dole later told reporters that this defeat had undone him: "I think it's all New Hampshire. I've been over it five hundred times in my own mind, and it all comes back to what went wrong in New Hampshire."[4] Doubtless haunted by the memory of 1988, Dole resolved to beat Alexander in 1996 even if it meant losing to Buchanan. Accordingly, his campaign directed nearly all of its final attack ads and push-polling against Alexander.[5] Figure 3.2 suggests that Dole's strategy worked.

In keeping with New Hampshire tradition, a handful of voters in tiny Dixville Notch at the northern fringe of Coos County cast the first ballots one minute into 20 February. The results flashed across the wires moments later: 11 votes for Dole, 5 for Alexander, 2 for Buchanan, and 1 for Richard Lugar. As often happens, Dixville Notch did not prefigure the New Hampshire outcome.[6] Out of a total 210,211 votes, Buchanan won 27.2 percent to Dole's 26.2 percent, a difference of 2,136 votes. Alexander trailed Dole by 7,590 votes with 22.4 percent. Forbes finished a distant fourth, and Lugar came in fifth.

The margin between victory and defeat in many places proved exceedingly slim. Buchanan led Dole by fewer than 10 votes in 20 of the

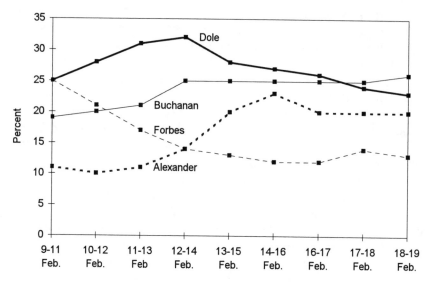

FIGURE 3.2   *USA TODAY*/CNN TRACKING POLL OF CANDIDATE SUPPORT IN FINAL DAYS OF 1996 NEW HAMPSHIRE REPUBLICAN PRIMARY

116 towns he carried. Indeed, he prevailed over Dole by only a single vote in Salem (1,078 to 1,077), Gilmanton (156 to 155), and tiny Wentworth's Location (2 for Buchanan, 1 each for Dole and Alexander). Likewise, Dole bested Buchanan by fewer than 10 votes in 18 of the 94 towns he carried, and he beat Buchanan by only 1 vote in Ellsworth (9 to 8), Orange (14 to 13), and Wentworth (51 to 50), not to be confused with Wentworth's Location.[7]

Table 3.1 provides a more general accounting of the vote for Buchanan, Dole, and Alexander by county and by towns of 10,000 or more inhabitants. Although Buchanan carried only four of the ten counties, they included the two most populous, Hillsborough and Rockingham. Dole won every other county except Merrimack, which he lost to Alexander by less than half a percentage point. Buchanan looked especially strong in the comparatively large towns of Berlin, Manchester, Goffstown, Derry, Londonderry, Pelham, and Claremont, while Dole won handily in Portsmouth, Lebanon, Hampton, Exeter, and Keene. Alexander ran a close second in some of these places, but he prevailed in none.

Responding to network interviews the next morning, a seemingly buoyant Alexander claimed to be the de facto winner. Yet, for all of his bravado, Alexander surely realized that his candidacy had been mortally wounded. As Mike Murphy, one of Alexander's top advisors, later acknowledged, "Our campaign died the day we didn't become the Buchanan alternative to Dole or the Dole alternative to Buchanan."[8]

Murphy went on to characterize New Hampshire as "the closest thing we have to a national primary." Still, if New Hampshire is so significant, one wonders how Buchanan could lose every other 1996 primary, how Forbes was able to win the Delaware and Arizona primaries after finishing fourth in both Iowa and New Hampshire, and how Dole could wrap up the nomination by mid-March.

More generally, what are we to make of New Hampshire's role in presidential nominating politics? Is the state too small, atypical, and unrepresentative for its voters to have so much say in who wins the White House? Is it truly the grim reaper of presidential aspirations, the best springboard for momentum, the ultimate media event of each primary season, one of the few contests where personal contact with voters still matters, and the supreme test of campaigning skills? Will it continue to exercise as much clout in presidential nominating politics well into the next century, or will it lose significance in an increasingly front-loaded calendar?

TABLE 3.1   1996 REPUBLICAN PRIMARY VOTE FOR BUCHANAN, DOLE, AND
ALEXANDER, BY COUNTY AND TOWN

County (Votes Cast)	Buchanan	Dole	Alexander
Belknap (11,094)	24.8%	25.8%	23.5%
Carroll (9,626)	23.6	28.0	24.5
Cheshire (11,338)	22.5	26.6	23.8
Coos (5,011)	41.1	21.1	15.8
Grafton (14,350)	24.0	28.3	21.8
Hillsborough (62,074)	30.5	24.9	22.1
Merrimack (26,958)	22.7	24.1	24.5
Rockingham (48,425)	27.4	27.0	22.0
Strafford (14,480)	24.9	28.5	23.4
Sullivan (6,855)	27.6	27.5	17.6
Total (210,211)	27.2	26.2	22.4

Town (Votes Cast)[a]			
Manchester (14,691)	39.0%	20.3%	20.7%
Nashua (11,247)	26.0	28.3	21.8
Concord (7,260)	18.6	26.4	23.6
Derry (4,480)	32.5	24.1	21.8
Rochester (3,831)	30.8	25.5	19.2
Salem (3,759)	28.7	28.6	16.2
Dover (3,575)	19.9	31.8	22.6
Merrimack (4,531)	30.2	26.7	25.8
Portsmouth (2,985)	17.4	49.3	22.7
Keene (3,381)	23.2	28.9	24.2
Londonderry (4,215)	32.3	25.6	23.0
Hudson (3,239)	28.4	24.4	10.6
Laconia (2,898)	24.2	28.2	21.3
Goffstown (3,195)	36.8	19.6	21.2
Bedford (4,513)	26.5	26.9	26.1
Claremont (1,722)	31.3	25.2	14.2
Exeter (2,923)	26.7	31.3	22.9
Hampton (2,750)	20.2	33.2	23.6
Lebanon (1,752)	16.8	33.4	21.7
Milford (2,549)	28.0	26.3	26.9
Berlin (1,127)	47.4	19.6	12.1
Somersworth (1,189)	26.2	27.5	22.2
Durham (1,353)	13.1	30.3	29.9
Pelham (1,479)	33.2	29.5	17.6

Source: *State of New Hampshire Manual for the General Court*, vol. 55 (Concord,
N.H.: Department of State, 1997).
[a] Towns with more than 10,000 inhabitants, ordered from most to least populous.

Historical Overview

New Hampshire held its first presidential primary ever on the second Tuesday in March (Town Meeting Day) of 1916, as prescribed by state law. Minnesota Republicans and Democrats voted on the same day; Indiana voters had gone to the polls one week earlier. By 1920, Indiana had moved its primary date to May and Minnesota had abandoned primaries altogether; hence, New Hampshire kicked off that nominating season by default.[9] Since then, it has always held the first state primary in the presidential nominating process, and for much of this time, New Hampshire held the only March primary.

Holding the first primary also meant that New Hampshire selected the first delegates to the national conventions in each cycle of presidential nominations. That changed in 1972 when the Iowa Democrats caucused six weeks before the New Hampshire primary.[10] Eventually, political leaders in both states agreed that Iowa would begin its caucus-convention process eight days before the New Hampshire primary. This arrangement laid the foundation for close cooperation in 1984, when New Hampshire and Iowa Democrats won a dispute with the Democratic National Committee over early scheduling of their events.[11]

The concept of holding a presidential primary on the traditional Town Meeting Day worked reasonably well for New Hampshire until the early 1970s. In 1971, when Florida rescheduled its primary to occur on the second Tuesday in March, New Hampshire officials moved their primary date (and Town Meeting Day) up to the first Tuesday of the month. New Hampshire's 1972 primary was the last the state held in the month of March. Three years later, reacting to demands for participation in a New England regional primary, the New Hampshire legislature voted to hold its primary on the first Tuesday in March or, if that date did not give New Hampshire priority in the process, on the Tuesday before any other New England state held a "similar election." New Hampshire officials intended this amendment to give the state at least one week of national acclaim before the next presidential primary. The Tuesday stipulation made sense because at that time all presidential primaries took place on a Tuesday. Eventually, a few states scheduled their primaries to occur on other days of the week and thereby raised the possibility of another state's holding its primary only three or four days after New Hampshire, as finally happened in 1996. One year earlier, the legislature had revised its law yet again to stipulate that New Hampshire vote at least seven days before the next primary state.[12]

Since 1984, both the New Hampshire primary and the Iowa caucuses have taken place in February. In 1984, moreover, the two states had February all to themselves. That arrangement changed in 1988 when South Dakota held its primary one week after New Hampshire. The month grew more crowded in 1996, when Louisiana Republicans caucused less than a week before their counterparts in Iowa, when Arizona and North Dakota moved to the same day as South Dakota, and when Delaware Republicans held their primary on the Saturday following New Hampshire's Tuesday election. As this is written, Delaware party officials appear no more inclined to allow New Hampshire a week unto itself in 2000 than they were in 1996.

Until 1952, the New Hampshire primary ballot allowed no direct expression of voter preference for presidential candidates. Rather, the only official purpose of the primary was to elect delegates to the national nominating conventions. Although the delegates chosen in these primaries went to their respective conventions officially uncommitted to any candidate, many, if not most, made their preferences known to the voters. In 1928, for example, both parties elected officially unpledged slates, even though all the Republican delegates backed Herbert Hoover and all the Democrats supported Al Smith. Franklin D. Roosevelt got a nice boost in 1932 when his delegate-candidates filled up the Democratic slate.[13]

Perhaps the most exciting primary of the delegate-election-only period was the last. In 1948, Senator Charles W. Tobey of New Hampshire stirred up considerable interest by calling on fellow Republicans to elect delegates unofficially committed to General Dwight D. Eisenhower. Having already expressed disinterest in either party's nomination, Ike rightly took Tobey's ploy to be a draft and flatly rejected it. Eisenhower's exit only encouraged supporters of Thomas E. Dewey and Harold Stassen to wage a well-publicized primary battle for delegate-candidates.[14]

The events of 1948 are probably what induced the New Hampshire legislature in 1949 to consider including a nonbinding preference vote, or "beauty contest," on the primary ballot. Passed in time for the 1952 primary, this provision gave presidential hopefuls an opportunity to demonstrate early strength. Now embarked on his third try for the Republican nomination, Senator Robert Taft campaigned for several days in New Hampshire hoping to inflict an early defeat on Eisenhower. New Hampshire governor Sherman Adams and other surrogates won the primary for Eisenhower even though the general remained at his NATO post in Paris. Republican turnout more than tripled from 28,854 in 1948 to 92,530 in 1952. Yet another sign of things to come was the number of *New York Times* stories about the Republican primary, which increased from twenty-one in 1948 to fifty-three in 1952. The *Times* even ran an editorial asking New Hampshire Republicans to support Eisenhower.[15]

The new primary law also affected the 1952 Democratic race. Enticed by the prospect of upsetting President Truman in the preference vote, if not in the selection of delegates, Senator Estes Kefauver virtually took up residence in the state. Aided by Truman's ambivalence and preceded by his own celebrity as a leading foe of political corruption, Kefauver waged the kind of campaign that has since become a New Hampshire tradition:

> Informal gatherings became the trademark of the Kefauver campaign. Tea parties, church breakfasts or fairs, visits to homes of sympathetic Democrats, tours through factories, and canvassing on the street were typical of the methods used to expose Kefauver to New Hampshire voters. Democrats who had never had any formal contact with the party . . . suddenly found themselves considered very important people by the hard-working Kefauver, who considered a group of five to be a "good crowd." He amazed his supporters by his tremendous energy and drive, and would campaign from early morning until late at night, never losing his personal charm.[16]

Kefauver scored an impressive win over Truman in both the delegate elections and the beauty contest. Turnout for the Democratic primary soared from 4,409 in 1948 to 35,995 in 1952, then a record high. Two weeks later Truman announced that he would not seek renomination.[17]

According to William G. Mayer, 1952 marks the beginning of an era in which presidential candidates saw the primary as important, but not essential, to nomination. After 1968, however, major reforms in the Democratic rules of delegate selection enhanced the importance of presidential primaries in general and of the New Hampshire primary in particular. By 1976, the nominating process of both parties had been transformed by passage of the 1974 campaign finance law; increased resort to primaries as the best means of selecting delegates; new rules apportioning delegates on the basis of the preference vote; Iowa's preemption of New Hampshire as the first act in the drama of delegate selection; and a growing recognition among candidates, campaign consultants, and pundits alike that an upset in Iowa or New Hampshire had important consequences for contests in other states.[18]

No presidential aspirant grasped the import of these changes better than Jimmy Carter. Trailing in the national polls and in the money chase,

Carter realized that scoring early wins in Iowa and New Hampshire could give him valuable momentum elsewhere. He campaigned tirelessly in both states, typically staying overnight in supporters' homes and methodically seeking support wherever he went. Carter also benefited from the miscalculations of major rivals. As in 1972, Senator Henry Jackson decided not to run in the New Hampshire beauty contest, figuring that the benefits of victory there would not be worth the effort. He reckoned that a win in Massachusetts would offset the New Hampshire outcome. Former Alabama governor George Wallace also skipped New Hampshire to concentrate on Massachusetts.[19]

With Jackson out of the picture in New Hampshire, Carter positioned himself as the only moderate in an otherwise liberal field. Chief rival Morris Udall competed with Birch Bayh, Fred Harris, and Sargent Shriver for the liberal vote. Helped by a victory of sorts in Iowa, where he ran second to "uncommitted" but ahead of any other Democratic candidate, Carter won New Hampshire, thereby gaining enough momentum to overcome finishing fourth in the Massachusetts primary one week later. A week after his loss in Massachusetts, he all but eliminated Wallace in the Florida primary and was well on his way to the White House.

Since John Connally in 1980, no serious candidate has bypassed New Hampshire, although Democrat Al Gore made only a half-hearted effort there in 1988. Carter's success has inspired many a long-shot candidate, although most of what he did in New Hampshire came straight out of the Kefauver playbook. Carter inspired more admiration, however, for having mastered a process greatly changed since Kefauver's day. Kefauver won virtually every primary in 1952, only to lose at a convention controlled by his foes. Carter lost the Massachusetts, California, and other important primaries and still won a nomination no longer in the convention's power to refuse.[20]

By 1980, according to Mayer, a significant relationship had developed between the Iowa precinct caucuses and the New Hampshire primary in which each contest performed a distinct function for the rest of the nominating process. Writing after the 1984 races and mindful of the perils of generalizing from only the last two nominating cycles, Mayer nonetheless argued that Iowa thinned out the weakest candidates, while New Hampshire posed the first major test for the strongest. True, New Hampshire had lost the distinction of voting before any other state, but it had also taken on an "extraordinarily powerful role" likely to become even more important in each new election.[21]

Subsequent turns of the presidential wheel since the publication of Mayer's essay oblige us to reexamine the Iowa–New Hampshire relationship. Although Iowa remains important, it has never been a sure path to victory either in New Hampshire or at the nominating convention. Of all the candidates competing in contested caucuses since 1972, only Carter (in both 1976 and 1980), Walter Mondale, and Dole (in 1996) have won in Iowa and gone on to capture the nomination, and of this lot, only Carter won the New Hampshire primary.

Moreover, finishing third in Iowa has not proven much of a barrier to success either in New Hampshire or in the race generally. Recall that Bush won the 1988 New Hampshire Republican primary only eight days after losing to both Dole and Pat Robertson in Iowa; that Michael Dukakis scored a similar triumph after running behind Richard Gephardt and Paul Simon in the 1988 Democratic caucuses; and that Bill Clinton won the 1992 Democratic nomination after trailing Tom Harkin, Paul Tsongas, and "uncommitted" in Iowa.[22]

Iowa also has a history of being upstaged by other states. The Michigan GOP decided to start its 1988 caucus-convention process in August of 1986, and Hawaii Republicans caucused a week before their Iowa counterparts in 1988. Iowa Republicans reclaimed their priority in 1992, only to be displaced by Louisiana Republicans in 1996. At this writing, Louisiana means to preempt Iowa again in 2000.[23]

The issue of "winnowing" candidates out of the race also deserves closer scrutiny. What precisely does this term mean? Obviously the causality of elimination gets more complicated when departure does not immediately follow the Iowa or New Hampshire vote. Consider Birch Bayh in 1976 and John Glenn in 1984, both of whom got trounced in Iowa, finished third in New Hampshire, and then suffered another beating before giving up their respective bids for the Democratic nomination. If the definition of winnowing includes wounding as well as eliminating, the roll of the winnowed is long indeed.

A stricter definition of winnowing is that the candidate drops out right after the Iowa and New Hampshire contests and before the next primary is held. The list of candidates meeting this condition includes only four Democrats and one Republican: Reubin Askew, Alan Cranston, Ernest Hollings, Bruce Babbitt, and Pierre du Pont. Askew, Cranston, and Hollings dropped out immediately after the 1984 New Hampshire primary; Babbitt and du Pont withdrew after the 1988 primary. Two other cases also deserve mention in this connection. General Al Haig withdrew from the 1988 Republican race just *before* the New Hampshire primary after finishing dead last in the Iowa caucuses. Twin losses in the Louisiana and Iowa caucuses forced Senator Phil Gramm out of the 1996 Republican race only days before the New Hampshire primary.

Today's extraordinary front-loading, prodigious fund raising, and inordinately expensive invisible primary have made the ascription of winnowing power to any one state problematic. Consider the long run-up to the Republican caucuses and primaries of 1996 (which began more than a year before the *1992* New Hampshire primary).[24] Nine presidential aspirants tested the waters and dropped out before a single caucus or primary ballot had been cast.[25] Some of the surviving candidates, including Dole, had spent most of their campaign money by the end of 1995.[26]

New Hampshire party leaders used to boast that nobody could win the White House without winning their primary. Dating from 1952, that claim expired forty years later when Clinton won his first term. A more telling statistic about New Hampshire's nominating role is how often winners of its primary go on to claim the nomination. Table 3.2 compares New Hampshire's record in this regard with the records of other "perennial" primary states—that is, all other states that have consistently held a presidential primary since 1952.

In examining table 3.2, readers should remember not only that the New Hampshire primary occurred before any other, but also that it frequently preceded the next primary by three weeks or more. Going first naturally increased the probability of error in forecasting the eventual winner, and this was especially so when states back-loaded the calendar, when some candidates skipped New Hampshire, and when win-

TABLE 3.2   NEW HAMPSHIRE'S RECORD OF BACKING EVENTUAL PRESIDENTIAL NOMINEES COMPARED WITH THAT OF OTHER PERENNIAL PRIMARY STATES, 1952-96

	No. of Times out of 12 Primary Voters Backed Eventual Republican Nominee	No. of Times out of 12 Primary Voters Backed Eventual Democratic Nominee
New Hampshire	10	6
California	9	5
Illinois	11	8
Massachusetts	9	5
Nebraska	10	7
New Jersey	9	5
Ohio	8	5
Oregon	11	8
Pennsylvania	10	8
Wisconsin	10	7
West Virginia	7	6

Source: *Presidential Elections 1789-1996* (Washington, D.C.: Congressional Quarterly Press, 1997), 170-227.

ning New Hampshire generated little momentum. Of course, some late-voting states diminished their own standings as bellwethers by backing uncommitted delegates and favorite sons. It is also important to note that the Republicans experienced fewer contested nominations than the Democrats did during the 1952–96 period. Republican incumbents Eisenhower, Nixon, and Reagan encountered little opposition in 1956, 1972, and 1984. Similarly, Nixon piled up 90 percent of the primary vote when, as vice president, he ran virtually unopposed for the 1960 Republican nomination. The only Democratic equivalent is Clinton's uncontested renomination in 1996.[27]

New Hampshire voted for the eventual Republican nominee ten out of twelve times, thereby surpassing the forecasting prowess of California, Massachusetts, New Jersey, Ohio, and West Virginia, but scoring less impressively than Illinois and Oregon and doing no better than Nebraska, Pennsylvania, and Wisconsin. Looking only at contested Republican races, New Hampshire smiled on the future standard-bearer six out of eight times: in 1952, 1968, 1976, 1980, 1988, and 1992. Nebraska, Pennsylvania, Wisconsin, and West Virginia also picked the "right" Republican in six of the eight races, while Illinois, Oregon, and New Jersey backed the eventual winner seven times.

New Hampshire's record of forecasting Democratic nominations looks unimpressive unless one makes allowances for voting first in so many open races. Eventual nominees won only six of the twelve New Hampshire primaries at issue. New Hampshire nonetheless compiled a better record in this respect than California, Massachusetts, New Jersey, and Ohio. The list of Democrats who overcame a loss in New Hampshire includes Adlai Stevenson in 1952, Stevenson again in 1956,[28] George McGovern in 1972, Mondale in 1984, and Clinton in 1992.

Since 1952, the New Hampshire primary has been characterized as the best hope of "outsiders" running against party "establishments."[29] Although not every long-shot candidate has been an outsider, every outsider with the possible exception of Ronald Reagan in 1976 has been a long shot.[30] The list of outsiders who have won the primary since 1952 is lengthy but almost entirely Democratic: Kefauver in 1952 and 1956, Carter in 1976, Hart in 1984, Tsongas in 1992, and Buchanan, the only Republican, in 1996. Eugene McCarthy, McGovern, and Buchanan managed to score moral, if not statistical, victories, in 1968, 1972, and 1992 by running better than expected. Carter is the only outsider so far to win both the New Hampshire primary and his party's nomination.

Whether Buchanan's successes portend a better future for Republican outsiders in the New Hampshire primary can only be guessed at. In any event, by the time Buchanan took on President Bush in 1992, the GOP had developed a corrective for anomalous New Hampshire outcomes. This arrangement surfaced in 1988 when Bush ran poorly in the Iowa caucuses, Dole looked like a winner in New Hampshire, and Robertson boasted that the support of Christian conservatives in the South would make him the nominee. Contrary to Robertson's expectations, however, the party regulars and religious conservatives in Dixie preferred Bush. Indeed, they backed Bush so strongly that the vice president viewed South Carolina and the southern primaries on Super Tuesday as a "fire wall" against unwelcome outcomes in Iowa and New Hampshire. The proposition was not fully tested in 1988, owing to Bush's win in New Hampshire, but both the Dole and Robertson candidacies lay in ruins after the South Carolina and Super Tuesday primaries.[31]

South Carolina has stood as a barrier against the Robertsons and Buchanans of the Republican Party ever since. It corked Buchanan's bottle in 1992 after his strong showing in New Hampshire. Four years later, it put the faltering Dole back on the road to nomination. In each instance, the eventual nominee owed much of his victory in South Carolina to the votes of religious and social conservatives, who were persuaded by party leaders to choose electability over ideological affinity. In 1996, for instance, the Voter News Service (VNS) exit poll showed that New Hampshire voters identifying with the Christian right voted 54 percent for Buchanan, 11 percent for Dole. In the South Carolina primary, such voters split almost evenly, 44 percent for Buchanan to 40 percent for Dole.[32]

In sum, the New Hampshire primary has figured in presidential nominating politics for more than eighty years. Since 1952, it has become a staple, if not a perfect barometer, of presidential nominating politics. New Hampshire's role in the nominating process has been increased rather than diminished with the proliferation of presidential primaries and despite being upstaged by Iowa. Principally because of the Democrats, the New Hampshire primary is regarded as the best hope of "outsider" candidates. Since 1992, however, the South Carolina primary has stood as a barrier against Republican outsiders who do well in New Hampshire. Whether record front-loading of the 2000 Republican primaries will allow South Carolina to continue in this role remains to be seen.

The Ultimate Media Event?

Writing about the 1976 nominating races, political scientist Donald R. Matthews observed that presidential primaries were "made to order" for television news.[33] Typically billed as a showdown that only some survive, New Hampshire satisfies all the requirements of a good news story: a beginning with the onset of the invisible primary; a climax, as notoriously diffident voters reach decisions on which candidacies live or die; and an ending with measurable results and seemingly crucial consequences for what happens next. "Were it not for the media," David Paletz and Robert Entman avowed in 1981, "the Iowa caucuses and New Hampshire primary would be about as relevant to the presidential nomination as opening-day baseball scores are to a pennant race."[34] Yet, because it has been first and so often "right," candidates and pundits alike see New Hampshire as the first reliable indicator of who will win the nomination. As Elizabeth Drew has noted, the press takes New Hampshire seriously because the candidates do, and the candidates take it seriously because the press does.[35]

The New Hampshire primary has thus become a venerable media tradition, "as much a staple in the national political diet as national conventions, election day in November, or a president's inauguration."[36] James Perry of the *Wall Street Journal* described it as "part reunion, part convention, part warm-up for what's to come."[37] Syndicated columnists Jack Germond and Jules Witcover fondly recalled the comforts of the Sheraton Wayfarer, the hostelry most favored by reporters in the 1970s and 1980s, and the ease of covering presidential politics in a small state:

> It is a familiar campaign for them [elite journalists]. They live at the Sheraton Wayfarer in Bedford, just outside Manchester, and most of the voters and campaign events are less than an hour away. It is necessary to run up to Hanover or over to Durham and Portsmouth once or twice, but they are only ninety minutes away. And the obligatory trip all the way up to Berlin, a largely Democratic papermaking center in the isolated north, has to be made only once. It is possible most days to make it back to the Wayfarer and then run over to Daffodil's for a lobster with some of the local politicians, many of whom reporters have known through three or four campaigns.[38]

Part of the New Hampshire media tradition is to lavish coverage on the winner, especially in the case of an upset.[39] Alternatively, if the front-runner prevails by less than the expected margin, the runner-up typically gets as much favorable coverage as the actual winner or more, as did McCarthy in 1968, McGovern in 1972, Clinton in 1992, and Buchanan in 1992.

Commentators have long noted and often decried New Hampshire's hold on the news media. Most measure the extent of this "overkill" by comparing New Hampshire's extraordinary publicity with that of larger primary states where many more delegates are at stake. Proportionate to the number of delegates selected, Doris Graber wrote in the early 1980s, New Hampshire generally gets ten or more times the coverage of any subsequent primary.[40] According to Donald Matthews, New Hampshire got at least twice as much notice on the nightly news in 1976 as any other primary during the next six weeks. By his reckoning, New Hampshire's coverage came out to 2.63 network stories per delegate, compared with .37 stories per delegate for the Wisconsin primary and .07 for New York.[41]

William C. Adams similarly documented New Hampshire's lopsided advantage in an analysis of 1984 Democratic primary coverage: more network news seconds and *New York Times* print lines about New Hampshire than the combined total for twenty-four primaries in the South, the border states, and the Rocky Mountain West; 125 times as much coverage as for the Ohio primary; and less news of the Ohio, Pennsylvania, Illinois, North Carolina, and California primaries combined, where a total of 8,403,000 voted, than of the New Hampshire primary, where 101,000 voted. Indeed, according to Adams, New Hampshire got nearly one-fifth of the total campaign coverage provided by the three traditional networks and the *Times*. When Adams tried to estimate a simple regression equation that predicted how much coverage each state received on the basis of such characteristics as the number of its convention delegates and the number of other primaries held on the same day, his model generated a modest R^2 of .41. With New Hampshire and Iowa omitted from the equation, R^2 soared to .78, with the number of state delegates alone accounting for 71 percent of the variance.[42]

My own analysis of network news notice of the 1984 primaries revealed that from October 1983 through June 1984, ABC, CBS, and NBC together devoted 12,330 news seconds to stories entirely about the New Hampshire primary. Moreover, owing to that year's comparatively modest front-loading, New Hampshire also figured importantly in stories about the earlier Iowa caucuses and about several other primaries held shortly afterward. The grand total of all this coverage on the three networks came to an astounding 19,390 news seconds, or more than five hours of viewing. One way or another, New Hampshire figured in nearly one-fourth of all the primary coverage offered on nightly television newscasts over the period observed.[43]

Based on data for the 1996 Republican race, table 3.3 confirms that the first primary still captures the attention of the national news media

TABLE 3.3   NETWORK EVENING NEWS COVERAGE OF 1996 REPUBLICAN
NOMINATING RACE

Nominating Event (Date)	Delegates	Network Stories Mentioning Event					Stories per Delegate
		ABC	CBS	CNN	NBC	Total	
Louisiana straw poll (1/7/95)	0	0	1	0	1	2	—
Iowa straw poll (8/19)	0	2	2	0	1	5	—
Maine straw poll (11/4)	0	0	1	0	0	1	—
Florida straw poll (11/18)	0	0	3	2	1	6	—
Alaska straw poll (1/27/96)	0	2	1	0	0	3	—
Louisiana caucuses (2/6)	30	5	3	3	1	12	0.40
California straw poll (2/11)	0	0	1	0	0	1	—
Iowa caucuses (2/12)	25	23	21	8	22	74	2.96
New Hampshire primary (2/20)	16	35	32	12	22	101	6.31
Delaware primary (2/24)	12	2	1	3	2	8	0.67
Arizona primary (2/27)	39	8	4	6	5	23	0.59
North and South Dakota primaries (2/27)	36	3	2	3	1	9	0.25
South Carolina primary (3/2)	37	5	7	5	5	22	0.59
Wyoming caucuses (3/2)	20	1	0	0	0	1	0.05
Puerto Rico primary (3/3)	14	1	0	1	1	3	0.21
Yankee-Junior Tuesday (3/5)	259	5	4	2	3	14	0.05
New York primary (3/7)	102	5	4	2	3	14	0.14
Super Tuesday (3/12)	353	9	9	7	10	35	0.10
Midwest regional (3/19)	229	1	0	2	0	3	0.01
California Tuesday (3/26)	197	4	2	3	3	12	0.06
Later primaries (4/23–6/4/96)	621	0	0	1	0	1	0.00
Total	1,990	111	98	60	81	350	0.18

Source: Vanderbilt Television News Abstracts.
Note: Observation period extends from 1 January 1995 through 4 June 1996.

out of all proportion to the number of delegates selected. From 1 January 1995 through 4 June 1996, the number of stories aired about New Hampshire on ABC, CBS, CNN, and NBC amounted to a staggering 101 out of a total 350, averaging out at 6.31 stories per delegate. No other state except Iowa received comparable exposure.[44]

The relationship of voting early to news coverage shows up in this table for other primary states as well. Contrast the coverage accorded Delaware's largely uncontested primary with that of the Midwest regional primary three weeks later. Likewise, the networks mentioned the Arizona primary in nearly twice as many stories as they aired about the later Yankee primary or California Tuesday. Still another sign of front-loading's impact on the news media was the virtual cessation of coverage after Dole clinched the nomination on 26 March. Pennsylvania, Indiana, New Jersey, and nine other late-voting primary states fell into a black hole of media indifference.

Table 3.4 gives a more precise view of the New Hampshire media extravaganza by comparing network news seconds devoted entirely to a

TABLE 3.4   NUMBER OF TELEVISION NEWS SECONDS IN STORIES ABOUT JUST ONE EVENT IN 1996 REPUBLICAN NOMINATING RACE

Event (Date)	ABC	CBS	CNN	NBC	Total
Louisiana straw poll (1/7/95)	0	20	0	20	40
Iowa straw poll (8/19)	290	270	0	30	590
Maine straw poll (11/4)	0	150	0	0	150
Florida straw poll (11/18)	0	390	500	140	1,030
Alaska straw poll (1/27/96)	140	0	0	0	140
Louisiana caucuses (2/6)	0	40	230	0	270
California straw poll (2/11)	0	60	0	0	60
Iowa caucuses (2/12)	2,570	3,130	1,140	2,510	9,350
(Iowa % of total news seconds)	(35.0)	(35.6)	(25.0)	(38.8)	(34.4)
New Hampshire primary (2/20)	3,030	4,209	1,060	3,230	11,529
(N.H. % of total news seconds)	(41.2)	(47.9)	(23.2)	(50.0)	(42.5)
Delaware primary (2/24)	120	0	0	229	349
Arizona primary (2/27)	760	0	220	0	980
South Carolina (3/2)	150	480	940	390	1,960
Tennessee primary (3/12)	0	0	50	0	50
Texas primary (3/12)	0	0	0	140	140
Ohio primary (3/19)	180	0	0	0	180
California primary (3/26)	110	30	190	0	330
Total news seconds	7,350	8,779	4,559	6,460	27,148

Source: Vanderbilt Television News Abstracts.
Note: Observation period extends from 1 January 1995 to 4 June 1996; no single event coverage after 26 March.

single state's role in the 1996 Republican race. The time frame is the same as for the previous table, and, to underscore the media effects of front-loading, I have also noted the news seconds allotted to precaucus and preprimary straw polls conducted in 1995 and early 1996. Consistent with previous research, New Hampshire dominated on every network except CNN, which devoted eighty news seconds more to Iowa. NBC gave New Hampshire fully half of its single-event coverage. On all four networks New Hampshire got 42.5 percent of the total time, amounting to 11,529 news seconds, or more than three hours of viewing.

By now it should be clear that much of the extraordinary media coverage of New Hampshire occurs during the invisible primary, a good part of which is waged in the state. Few other primary or caucus states get more than passing mention on the nightly news a year or more before delegate selection starts. According to Michael J. Robinson and Margaret A. Sheehan, New Hampshire dominated the television and wire-service coverage of what remained of the run-up to the 1980 caucuses and primaries after 1 January 1980.[45] The same pattern surfaced in my longer view of 1996 invisible primary coverage: twenty-eight of the fifty-five stories aired on all four networks pertained to New Hampshire. So long as candidates take the New Hampshire primary seriously, so, too, will the news media.

Momentum

If lopsided publicity generates momentum, New Hampshire should be a veritable catapult for presidential aspirations. Not only do news organizations lavish coverage on this primary; they also hype the surprise winners and runners-up who exceed expectations. As Robinson once put it, front-runners bank on this tradition and challengers borrow on it.[46]

No case better illustrates how much of a difference New Hampshire can make than the 1984 Democratic primary. As reported in table 3.5, the last national poll that Gallup took before New Hampshire (and Iowa) pegged Hart at 3 percent and Mondale at 49. The next poll, taken less than a week after New Hampshire, put Hart at 30 percent, only 3 points behind Mondale.[47]

Newspaper accounts of the 1984 race immediately after New Hampshire corroborated the polls. "People are telephoning at all hours of the day and night," said Hart's cochairman in New York.[48] Reporter Curtis Wilkie wrote that traveling with Hart in the South immediately after New Hampshire was like riding in the eye of a hurricane: "There is serene con-

TABLE 3.5   THE NEW HAMPSHIRE BOUNCE IN NATIONAL POLL STANDINGS

Primary	Polling Dates of Nationwide Gallup Surveys of Candidate Preference	Candidate Standings Just before and Just after New Hampshire Primary
1964 Republican	30 January–5 February 1964 (10 March, N.H. primary)	Lodge 12%, Goldwater 20%
	13–17 March	Lodge 42%, Goldwater 14%
1976 Republican	30 January–2 February 1976 (24 February, N.H. primary)	Ford 55%, Reagan 35%
	27 February–1 March	Ford 51%, Reagan 41%
1976 Democratic	23–26 January 1976 (24 February, N.H. primary)	Carter 4%, Wallace 20%
	27 February–1 March	Carter 16%, Wallace 19%
1980 Republican	1–4 February 1980 (26 February, N.H. primary)	Reagan 47%, Bush 25%
	February–March	Reagan 55%, Bush 25%
1980 Democratic	1–4 February 1980 (26 February, N.H. primary)	Carter 61%, Kennedy 32%
	February–March	Carter 66%, Kennedy 27%
1984 Democratic	10–13 February 1984 (20 and 28 February, Ia. caucuses and N.H. primary)	Hart 3%, Mondale 49%
	2–6 March	Hart 30%, Mondale 33%
1992 Republican	31 January–2 February 1992 (18 February, N.H. primary)	Bush 84%, Buchanan 11%
	19–20 February	Bush 78%, Buchanan 20%
1992 Democratic	31 January–2 February 1992 (18 February, N.H. primary)	Tsongas 5%, Clinton 45%
	19–20 February	Tsongas 31%, Clinton 36%
1996 Republican	26–29 January 1996 (20 February, N.H. primary)	Buchanan 7%, Dole 47%
	23–25 February	Buchanan 27%, Dole 41%

Sources: Annual editions of *The Gallup Poll* (Wilmington, Del.: Scholarly Resources); and William G. Mayer, "The New Hampshire Primary: A Historical Overview," in *Media and Momentum: The New Hampshire Primary and Nomination Politics*, ed. Gary R. Orren and Nelson W. Polsby (Chatham, N.J.: Chatham House, 1987), 15.
Note: Data are shown only for races when Gallup polled before the next primary.

fidence immediately around the candidate, but something is swirling wildly nearby."[49] That same week, Hart roared to victory in the Maine caucuses and the Vermont primary. "It appears that whatever happened in New Hampshire and Maine just went through Vermont," one Mondale aide ruefully admitted.[50] Until the New Hampshire victory, the Hart campaign in Michigan consisted of a makeshift office and a handful of student volunteers. Within two weeks of Hart's win in New Hampshire, hundreds of volunteers had come forth, four offices had opened, television advertising had begun, and Hart had moved within 8 percentage points of Mondale in a *Detroit News* poll. Until New Hampshire, the Minnesota campaign had been run by a single graduate student whose St. Paul apartment doubled as Hart headquarters. Unexpected victory unleashed a flood of money and volunteers, and soon a greatly expanded staff took up new quarters in the same building where the Mondale camp had rented space. Similar accounts flowed in from Alaska, Virginia, Nevada, and other states.[51]

The 1984 Democratic primary in New Hampshire stands out not only for dramatically inflating the support of an upset winner, but also for wreaking havoc on the front-runner. Mondale dropped by 16 percentage points in the Gallup poll, while Hart soared by 27 points. Although other upset winners have gotten a comparable lift out of New Hampshire, their eventually successful rivals held up better in the polls than Mondale did. Table 3.5 shows that Tsongas in 1992 and Buchanan in 1996 nearly matched Hart's surge and that Henry Cabot Lodge got an even bigger bounce in 1964, but that none of the front-runners they defeated in New Hampshire dropped by more than 9 points in the next Gallup poll.

Gallup polls also reveal that front-runners typically gain little or no bounce after winning New Hampshire.[52] Ford dropped a few points after eking out a victory in 1976, as did Bush in 1992. Carter's standing rose by a mere 5 percent after winning the 1980 primary.

It appears, then, that New Hampshire's reputation for momentum is better deserved than its reputation for winnowing. Or, stated another way, New Hampshire generally has a more immediate effect on momentum than on winnowing. Unexpected winners often get an extraordinary bounce from this primary. Whether it propels them to final victory is another matter.

Should New Hampshire Hold the First Primary?

Since 1952, scholars and journalists have challenged the fitness of New Hampshire to hold the first primary of each presidential nominating cycle. Of all the primary's critics, none has matched the ferocity of Neal R. Peirce, a widely recognized authority on state politics. Writing in 1976, Peirce pointed to population size, popular aversion to general income or sales taxes, and other failings of the political culture as reasons to deny New Hampshire's primary its first-in-the-nation status. He excoriated the reliance on liquor, tobacco, lottery, and other "sin" taxes for state revenue and decried the "almost confiscatory" property taxes levied by local communities to fund education and other essential services. A key reason why this folly persisted, Peirce argued, was because the only statewide newspaper—Manchester's "bile-ridden" *Union Leader*—viciously opposed any change in the status quo. Such backwardness led to the provision of "mediocre" public services, perpetuation of an "antediluvian" political culture, and justifiable condemnation of New Hampshire as the most "unresponsive and irresponsible" of the fifty states. And this is the place, Peirce thundered, where every four years presidential aspirants pander to a "minuscule" and "quite unrepresentative" primary electorate.[53]

Atypical Demographics and Benighted Public Policy?

Is New Hampshire as backward and unrepresentative as Peirce maintained? There is no denying that its population is small and unrepresentative of the nation in important respects. In size, New Hampshire ranked forty-first among the fifty states in 1990, with 1,108,882 inhabitants (roughly 100,000 more than Dallas, Texas). Only 24 of the state's 234 towns had estimated populations of 10,000 or more in 1995, and, of these, only Manchester and Nashua boasted populations of 80,000 or more. Whites consistently make up 98 percent of the state population, while African-Americans generally account for 1 percent. Catholics in 1990 constituted a majority of all churchgoers in eight of the state's ten counties. French-Canadians have long been the largest ethnic group, amounting to perhaps a third of the statewide population.[54]

The dependency on local property taxes that aroused Peirce's ire in 1976 remains at the forefront of New Hampshire politics at this writing. The issue gained particular notoriety in 1997, when the state supreme court ruled that reliance on local property taxes imposed an inequitable and therefore unconstitutional burden on poorer towns. Since roughly 90 percent of New Hampshire's public school funding comes from local property taxes, less affluent communities must impose much higher rates than are charged by wealthier towns. Still, most politicians in both parties evidently prefer this method of school funding to any state sales, income, or property tax. In 1998, Governor Jeanne Shaheen, a Democrat and former cochairwoman of Gary Hart's 1984 New Hampshire campaign, joined Republicans in endorsing a constitutional amendment to protect the local property tax against future lawsuits.[55] Tax issues also color presidential primary politics, especially on the Republican side, where local activists routinely demand that candidates commit themselves to vetoing any tax hike passed by Congress.

New Hampshire does not lack defenders on these and other charges. The policies that Peirce derided as primitive seem positively Jeffersonian to many, if not most, residents. As for population, political scientist Niall Palmer rightly notes that race is not the only gauge of diversity. A constellation of white ethnic groups, including French-Canadians, Greeks, Italians, Poles, and Irish, has made New Hampshire one of the most diverse states in New England. Moreover, the state's population increased by 50 percent from 1970 to 1990, giving New Hampshire the most rapid rate of growth of any state east of the Mississippi except Florida. And, for all the talk of small towns, this extraordinary population increase has created a corridor of commerce and industry stretching from Manchester to the Massachusetts border. Moreover, New Hampshire has roughly the same ratio of white- to blue-collar jobs as the rest of the country. Regarding complaints about education and other services, Palmer calls attention to the comparatively low poverty rate, high Scholastic Aptitude Test scores, and high proportion of college-educated citizens in New Hampshire.[56] In February 1999, Vice President Al Gore sounded a similar note while attending a New Hampshire jobs forum. "In terms of the percentage of work force involved in high technology jobs," Gore proclaimed, "New Hampshire is number one out of all fifty states."[57]

Unrepresentative Primary Electorates?

More often than not, critics like Peirce mean "conservative" or "Republican" when denouncing the New Hampshire primary electorate as "unrepresentative." "The state is so conservative and Republican," journalist Elizabeth Drew wrote in 1984, "that the Democratic nominee, who probably spends more time here than anywhere else during the fight for the nomination, doesn't bother to come back for the general election."[58]

Despite Democratic successes in recent presidential and state races, there is no denying that the GOP has dominated New Hampshire elections since the 1850s. Of the thirty-six presidential elections since John C. Fremont headed the first Republican ticket in 1856, the Granite State has voted Republican in twenty-seven, or 75 percent, of them. Sixty years passed between the victory of native son Franklin Pierce in 1852 and that of Woodrow Wilson, the next Democrat to carry New Hampshire. Wilson doubtless owed his 1912 victory to the split between William Howard Taft and Theodore Roosevelt. Facing only one Republican in 1916, Wilson beat Charles Evans Hughes in New Hampshire by a mere 56 votes out of 89,127 cast. Two decades passed before another Democrat, Franklin D. Roosevelt, carried the state. Nationwide, Roosevelt led Governor Alf Landon by 24 percentage points in the popular vote, but in New Hampshire he won by less than 2 percent. Roosevelt carried the state again in 1940 and 1944. Only two Democrats have since captured New Hampshire's electoral votes: Johnson in 1964 and Clinton in 1992 and again in 1996.[59]

All thirteen U.S. senators elected by the state legislature from 1855 until ratification of the Seventeenth Amendment in 1913 were Republicans, as were nine of the thirteen subsequently elected by popular vote through 1998. During all this time, New Hampshire governors appointed nine Republicans as stand-ins for senators who resigned or died while in office. In sum, since the rise of the Republican party in New Hampshire, only four Democrats have represented the state in the U.S. Senate: Henry Hollis in 1913–19, Fred Brown in 1933–39, Thomas McIntyre in 1962–79, and John Durkin in 1975–80.[60]

When Republican candidates first ran for the U.S. House in 1857, New Hampshire had three congressional districts and elected its representatives in odd-numbered years. The state lost a district after the 1880 census and began holding congressional elections in even-numbered years in 1882. All told, Republicans won 84 percent of 153 House races from 1857 through 1998, capturing the entire delegation in 51 elections, achieving dominance (two seats to one) in 3 elections, and winning one of two seats in 11 elections.[61]

From 1857, when the Republicans put up their first candidate for governor, through 1877, the last time a New Hampshire governor was elected to a one-year term, the Republicans prevailed in eighteen of twenty-one gubernatorial races. Since the switch to biennial elections in 1878, Republicans have won fifty-three of sixty-four races, albeit sometimes by slim margins. Of the nine Democratic victories during this period, seven occurred after 1960: John King in 1962, 1964, and 1966; Hugh Gallen in 1978 and 1980; and Jeanne Shaheen in 1996 and 1998.[62]

The Republicans also enjoy a substantial advantage in the number of voters registered to participate in the presidential primary. Since the advent of a new presidential nominating system in 1972, however, the GOP has not claimed an outright majority of registrants. This is partly because New Hampshire law allows voters to register their party affiliation as "undeclared" rather than Republican or Democratic. Undeclared registrants may participate in either party's primary, and the presence of an unusually large group of undeclared voters is always of concern to presidential candidates. It is important not to confuse undeclared voters, many of whom are strong party identifiers, with voters who style themselves "independents" when responding to pollsters.[63] Figure 3.3 charts the Republican plurality in primary voter registration from 1972 through 1996.

Not so long ago pundits saw the Democrats in New Hampshire as scarcely less conservative than the Republicans. This was especially true of Manchester Democrats. For example, one veteran reporter wrote that about 60 percent of the voters in the 1972 Democratic primary had been "conditioned daily" by the ultraconservative *Union Leader*.[64] At least some Democratic candidates took a similar view. In 1984, for instance, Reubin Askew campaigned in New Hampshire as the "different Democrat" in hopes of establishing himself as the only conservative in the race. His campaign manager described New Hampshire as a "moderate-to-conservative state." Aides to Mondale, the 1984 Democratic front-runner, called New Hampshire a "very conservative state." Mondale had already

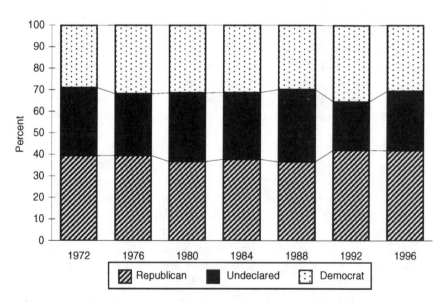

FIGURE 3.3   PARTY REGISTRATION OF NEW HAMPSHIRE PRIMARY VOTERS, 1972–96

Source: *State of New Hampshire Manual for the General Court*, vol. 55 (Concord, N.H.: Department of State, 1997).

revealed his doubts about New Hampshire in a 1975 book, and he later attributed his 1984 defeat there to the baneful influence of the *Union Leader* and to a crossover vote by closet Republicans.[65]

Are Republican and Democratic primary voters in New Hampshire mere peas in the same conservative pod? Table 3.6, which compares the liberalism-conservatism of party identifiers and independents who voted in the 1992 and 1996 primaries, points up some important differences.

Put simply, scarcely any ardent liberals turned up in the 1992 exit poll of Republican primary voters, while few strong conservatives showed up among Democratic primary voters. Ideological commitment correlated with partisan dedication. Twenty-three percent of all strong Republicans described themselves as "very conservative," while one-fifth of the strong Democrats described themselves as "very liberal." (Put another way, 72 percent of the very conservative voters polled just after casting Republican ballots said that they were strong Republicans. Likewise, 61 percent of the very liberal voters in the Democratic primary claimed to be strong Democrats.)

Weak partisans and independents obviously played an important role in tempering each party's ideological inclination by positioning themselves at or near the center of the left-right continuum in 1992. Unfortunately, Voter News Service made no distinction between strong and weak party identifiers when polling 1996 primary voters. But that year's results, though less precise, show a similar pattern: most Republicans described their views as conservative, most Democrats professed liberal views, and about half of all independents voting in either party's primary put themselves in the moderate category.

My next task is to establish how closely New Hampshire primary voters resemble their counterparts in other states, beginning with party identification. Figure 3.4 compares 1992 Republican primary voters in New Hampshire with an aggregate of Republican primary voters in eleven other states. (The aggregate consists of 11,946 voters polled after taking part in the primaries of South Carolina, Florida, Texas, Massachusetts, Illinois, Wisconsin, Pennsylvania, Oregon, New Jersey, Ohio, and California.) Although strong Republicans outnumbered weak Republicans and independents in both New Hampshire and in the aggregate, independents clearly cast a much larger portion of the vote in New Hampshire than in most other primaries.

The 1996 VNS data are quite consistent with the 1992 findings. Republican identifiers cast 64 percent of the New Hampshire primary vote in 1992 and 62 percent in 1996. Independents accounted for 33 percent in 1992 and 34 percent in 1996. Similarly, in a twenty-eight-state

TABLE 3.6   LIBERALISM-CONSERVATISM OF NEW HAMPSHIRE VOTERS BY PRIMARY AND PARTY IDENTIFICATION, 1992 AND 1996

	1992 Strong Party Identifiers	1992 Weak Party Identifiers	1992 Independents	All 1992 Primary Voters	All 1996 Party Identifiers	1996 Independents	All 1996 Primary Voters
Republican Primary							
Very liberal	2%	2%	3%	2%	1%	2%	2%
Somewhat liberal	4	12	12	8	4	11	7
Moderate	25	39	45	35	26	50	35
Somewhat conservative	45	42	31	40	46	29	39
Very conservative	23	5	9	15	22	7	16
Weighted N's	(782)	(352)	(586)	(1,782)	(1,400)	(773)	(2,280)
Democratic Primary							
Very liberal	20%	4%	8%	11%	15%	5%	12%
Somewhat liberal	41	35	28	32	35	30	33
Moderate	32	46	50	42	41	52	44
Somewhat conservative	4	14	13	12	7	12	9
Very conservative	3	1	2	2	1	1	2
Weighted N's	(594)	(244)	(860)	(1,836)	(630)	(322)	(1,004)

Sources: Voter Research and Surveys (VRS) and VNS exit polls obtained from ICPSR.
Note: Some columns do not total 100 percent due to rounding. The 1996 party identification question regrettably did not distinguish between strong and weak party loyalty. The table excludes a small number of voters not responding to one or both questions and a few others voting in the Republican primary who called themselves Democrats, as well as self-identified Republicans voting in the Democratic primary.

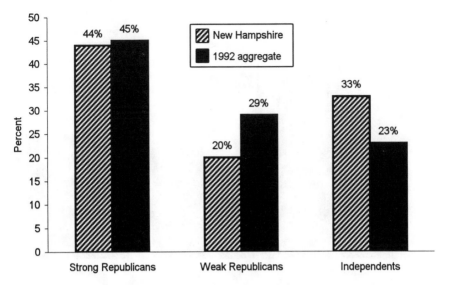

FIGURE 3.4   PARTY IDENTIFICATION OF 1992 REPUBLICAN PRIMARY
VOTERS IN NEW HAMPSHIRE AND AGGREGATE OF ELEVEN
OTHER STATES

Source:VRS exit polls.

aggregate of 1996 Republican primary voters reported by the *New York Times,* Republican identifiers cast 75 percent of the vote, independents 21 percent.[66] In 1992, the aggregate breakdown was 73 and 23 percent.

Figure 3.5 points up dramatic differences between New Hampshire Democratic primary voters in 1992 and 16,080 of their counterparts polled after balloting in the same eleven states used to construct the 1992 Republican aggregate. Even when combined into a single category, strong and weak Democrats cast only 45 percent of the New Hampshire vote, compared with 65 percent in the Democratic primary aggregate. Forty-seven percent of the New Hampshire turnout consisted of independents, a much higher proportion than in the aggregate sample. A *New York Times* recapitulation of the 1992 vote in twenty-nine Democratic primaries corresponds almost exactly to the figures in my aggregation: Democratic identifiers cast 67 percent of the vote, while independents cast 29 percent.[67]

How does the ideological profile of New Hampshire's primary voters compare with other primary electorates from the same party? Allowing for the limitations of how pollsters ask about ideology,[68] the Republican fit in 1992 and 1996 was impressive. Figure 3.6 clearly negates the popular

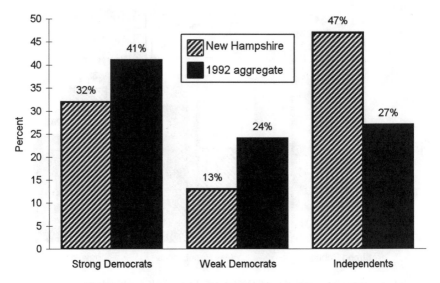

FIGURE 3.5   PARTY IDENTIFICATION OF 1992 DEMOCRATIC PRIMARY
VOTERS IN NEW HAMPSHIRE AND AGGREGATE OF ELEVEN
OTHER STATES

Source: VRS exit polls.

image of New Hampshire as a backwater primary dominated by the
extreme right. Compared with Republican primary voters nationwide,
those in New Hampshire showed up as slightly less likely to describe
their politics as very conservative, slightly more likely to embrace the
somewhat conservative label, slightly less likely to choose the moderate
category, and equally likely to call themselves liberals. No comparison in
this graph produced a difference larger than the sampling error of 5 percent. The final set of bars in this figure shows that Republican voters in
New Hampshire expressed considerably less enthusiasm than their counterparts in other states for putting a constitutional ban on abortions in the
GOP platform.

Another indication of moderation on the part of Republican primary
voters in New Hampshire (not included in the *New York Times* summary
and therefore not shown in figure 3.6) was the relative paucity of
Christian conservatives. Only 18 percent of the New Hampshire primary
voters associated themselves with the religious right, compared with 37
percent of South Carolina voters, 18 percent in the Yankee Tuesday primaries, 39 percent in the Super Tuesday South, and 28 percent in the
Midwestern regional primary.[69]

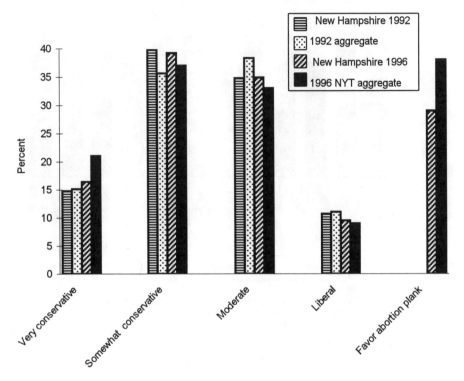

FIGURE 3.6   LIBERALISM-CONSERVATISM OF REPUBLICAN PRIMARY VOTERS
IN NEW HAMPSHIRE AND THE AGGREGATE, 1992 AND 1996

Sources: VRS and VNS exit polls; and *New York Times*, 31 March 1996.

What about the ideological inclinations of Democratic primary voters?
Exit polls have long contradicted the myth of a conservative electorate in
New Hampshire's Democratic primaries. Take 1984, for instance, when
Mondale overcame defeat in New Hampshire to win the nomination.
Figure 3.7 offers a comparison of the voters in a dozen 1984 Democratic
primaries, including New Hampshire's. Contrary to conventional wisdom
at the time, proportionally more liberals voted in New Hampshire than in
all but four of the other primaries. (Ironically, in view of his misgivings
about New Hampshire, Mondale won both of the primaries in which conservatives outvoted liberals.) According to the CBS/*New York Times* exit
polls, only 17 percent of the New Hampshire voters billed themselves as
conservatives, a smaller proportion than was found anywhere else except
Connecticut and New York. Moderates accounted for an outright majority
of the vote in New Hampshire and in eight other primaries.[70]

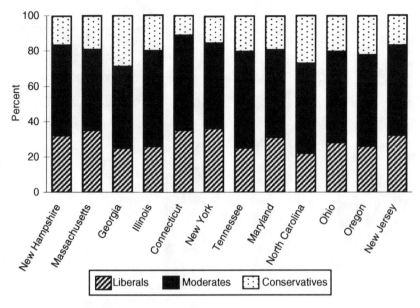

FIGURE 3.7   HOW 1984 DEMOCRATIC PRIMARY VOTERS IN NEW
HAMPSHIRE AND ELEVEN OTHER STATES LABELED THEIR
POLITICAL OUTLOOK

Source: CBS/*New York Times* exit polls.
Note: Party identifiers and independents are combined.

Basically the same ideological pattern emerged in 1992, the last round of contested Democratic primaries of the twentieth century. According to exit polling, liberals constituted 43 percent of the New Hampshire vote, compared with 35 percent in the combined total of voters in twenty-nine Democratic primaries. Moderates made up 42 percent of the vote in New Hampshire and 45 percent in the aggregate, while conservatives cast 14 percent of the ballots in New Hampshire compared with 20 percent in the aggregate.[71]

We have already noted Peirce's argument that New Hampshire hardly reflects national diversity, but the real demographic issue is how much Republican and Democratic voters in New Hampshire look like Republican and Democratic voters in other primaries. The resemblance is closer on the Republican side, although voters in New Hampshire's 1996 primary did stand out as younger, more educated, more affluent, and less Protestant than the Republican norm (see table 3.7). The gender gap characteristic of virtually all Republican primaries surfaced in New Hampshire as well: male voters substantially outnumbered female voters.

TABLE 3.7 DEMOGRAPHIC COMPARISONS OF 1996 REPUBLICAN PRIMARY VOTERS IN NEW HAMPSHIRE AND OTHER STATES

Primary Voters	New Hampshire (N = 2,556)	South Carolina (N = 1,894)	Yankee Tuesday (N = 4,374)	Dixie Super Tuesday (N = 9,911)	Midwest Tuesday (N = 7,477)	Twenty-Eight States Voting before 1 April
% Men	57	53	55	52	53	n.a.
% Women	43	47	45	48	47	n.a.
% Aged 18–29	14	8	9	10	11	10
% 30–44	37	31	31	28	32	30
% 45–59	27	28	27	28	28	28
% 60 or older	22	32	32	34	28	32
Median age	44	50	50	51	48	50
% Did not finish high school	3	5	3	4	3	3
% Graduated high school	19	20	16	19	26	20
% Some college coursework	25	25	25	31	27	30
% Graduated college	31	28	32	27	26	27
% Postgraduate work	22	21	24	18	17	19
% < $15,000 in 1995 family income	7	6	5	7	7	n.a.
% $15,000–$29,999	17	15	16	18	18	n.a.
% $30,000–$49,999	26	30	25	28	30	n.a.
% $50,000–$74,999	25	26	25	25	26	n.a.
% $75,000–$99,999	12	12	13	11	10	n.a.
% $100,000 or more	11	11	15	11	9	n.a.
Median family income	$49,990	$49,380	$53,400	$48,220	$46,980	n.a.
% Protestant	42	69	42	59	46	n.a.
% Catholic	36	11	38	19	32	n.a.
% Other Christian	10	14	8	16	13	n.a.
% Jewish	2	2	3	1	1	n.a.
% Other/none	10	5	8	6	7	n.a.

Sources: VNS exit polls; aggregate of twenty-eight primaries from New York Times, 31 March 1996, A24. Medians computed from grouped data with the kind assistance of Professor Don Bonar, Denison University.

Note: Yankee Tuesday primaries held in Connecticut, Maine, Massachusetts, Rhode Island, and Vermont on 5 March; Dixie Super Tuesday states include Florida, Louisiana, Mississippi, Oklahoma, Tennessee, and Texas, voting on 12 March; Midwest Tuesday states include Illinois, Michigan, Ohio, and Wisconsin. Percentage bases exclude missing cases; n.a. indicates data not reported by the New York Times. All N's are weighted; total N for voters polled in the aggregate of twenty-eight primaries not reported by the Times.

Much has been made of New Hampshire's paucity of nonwhites, but at least for Republicans, the same is true everywhere: 95 percent or more of the votes in GOP primaries are almost always cast by whites. In 1992, for instance, whites cast 97 percent of the vote in the Republican primaries of New Hampshire, South Carolina, Wisconsin, Pennsylvania, and Ohio. (VNS did not even ask Republican primary voters in 1996 to identify themselves by race.) The discrepancy is more serious for Democrats, however. Although African-Americans cast about 14 percent of the aggregate vote in the 1992 Democratic primaries, they accounted for only 1 percent in New Hampshire.[72]

The same gender gap characteristic of other 1992 Democratic primaries showed up in New Hampshire: women outvoted men by a sizable margin. Otherwise, New Hampshire Democratic primary voters stood apart from those in other primaries as overwhelmingly white, younger, better educated, better off financially, and more likely to be Catholic (see table 3.8).

To summarize, the question of representation is not whether the state of New Hampshire reflects the national population's heterogeneity, but whether the voters in each party's presidential primary reasonably resemble their counterparts in other states or in the main. New Hampshire voters in both primaries showed up as somewhat younger, better educated, less likely to be Protestant, and less likely to express loyalty to a political party than voters in other primaries of the same party (see table 3.9). Independents made up a much larger portion of the primary vote in New Hampshire, especially on the Democratic side, than in other states. Republican primary voters in New Hampshire appeared quite representative of other Republican primary voters with respect to race, gender, income, and choice of ideological labels. Yet this last similarity did not preclude significant differences over a constitutional ban on abortion or affiliation with the religious right. Catholics accounted for an unusually large share of the Republican turnout in New Hampshire and an even bigger portion of Democratic voters. Contrary to conventional wisdom, moderates and liberals dominated Democratic primary turnout in New Hampshire.

The Notorious Union Leader

Of all Neal Peirce's criticisms recounted earlier, surely his denunciation of the "bile-ridden" *Manchester Union Leader* is the least contested. Nearly two decades after the death of owner and publisher William Loeb, this newspaper still engenders fear and loathing among liberals and moderates.

TABLE 3.8   DEMOGRAPHIC COMPARISONS OF 1992 DEMOCRATIC PRIMARY
VOTERS IN NEW HAMPSHIRE AND TWENTY-NINE OTHER STATES

Primary Voters	New Hampshire	29-State Aggregate
% Men	46	47
% Women	54	53
% Whites	97	80
% Blacks	1	14
% Other	1	6
% Aged 18–29	17	12
% 30–44	43	33
% 45–59	24	25
% 60 and older	16	30
Median age	41	48
% Did not finish high school	5	8
% Graduated high school	21	27
% Some college coursework	24	27
% Graduated college	26	20
% Postgraduate work	24	18
% < $15,000 in 1991 family income	11	15
% $15,000–$29,999	22	25
% $30,000–$49,999	34	30
% 50,000–$74,999	22	18
% $75,000 or more	12	11
Median family income	$42,580	$36,660
% Protestant	27	50
% Catholic	44	30
% Other Christian	7	n.a.
% Jewish	3	6
% Other/none	18	n.a.

Sources: VRS exit polls; and "Recap of the Primaries: How Democrats in 29 States Voted,"
New York Times, 12 July 1992, A18.
Note: Medians computed from grouped data. Weighted N for voters in the 1992 New
Hampshire Democratic primary same as reported in table 3.6; weighted N for twenty-
nine primary state aggregate not reported.

David W. Moore offered a comparatively benign assessment of the *Union Leader* in 1987, noting that its style of unabashed partisanship had gone out of fashion in the United States but was still common in European democracies. Partisan journalism, he added, should not be equated with old-fashioned "yellow journalism" or distorting news to the point of fabrication.[73] A legion of critics over the years has disputed this interpretation by finding plenty of yellow in Loeb's journalism. The late Theodore H. White, for

TABLE 3.9   SUMMARY OF HOW NEW HAMPSHIRE PRIMARY VOTERS IN THE 1990s
RESEMBLED SAME-PARTY VOTERS IN OTHER STATE PRIMARIES

	Republican Primary Voters	*Democratic Primary Voters*
Race	Close resemblance	Almost no nonwhites
Gender	Close resemblance	Close resemblance
Age	Younger	Younger
Education	Above the norm	Above the norm
Income	Slightly above norm	Considerably above the norm
Religion	More Catholics and fewer Protestants than the norm	More Catholics and fewer Protestants than the norm
Independents	Larger share of primary vote	Much larger share of primary vote
Strong party identifiers	Close resemblance	Much smaller share of primary vote
Weak party identifiers	Smaller share of primary vote	Much smaller share of primary vote
Liberalism/conservatism	Close resemblance in choice of labels, less supportive of abortion plank, and less affinity for religious right	More liberal, less conservative in choice of labels

instance, excoriated the *Union Leader* as "paranoid," "execrable," and a throwback to the "knife-and-kill" reporting of the nineteenth century.[74]

Shortly after Loeb purchased the *Union Leader* and the *New Hampshire Sunday News* in 1946, his basic operating style became clear: wholesale defamation of any presidential candidates and other prominent figures who annoyed him. His targets included "Dopey Dwight" Eisenhower; John F. Kennedy, the "spoiled brat"; Nelson Rockefeller, the "wife swapper"; Eugene McCarthy, the "skunk's skunk's skunk"; Jimmy "the Wimp" Carter; "Jerry the Jerk" Ford; and Henry "Kissinger the Kike."[75]

Senator Edmund Muskie ("Moscow Muskie" in the *Union Leader*) came in for especially rough treatment in 1972, when Loeb repeatedly charged that he was not emotionally stable enough to be president, that he had no real convictions, and that he had denigrated Franco-Americans. Loeb based this last claim on a bogus "Canuck" letter of which he made much ado. He also goaded Muskie to fury by reprinting a *Newsweek* story critical of Muskie's wife. Standing outside the *Union Leader* building with reporters looking on, the enraged Muskie assailed Loeb's tactics until choking up. This outburst amplified doubts about Muskie's fitness for the Oval Office.[76]

Candidates for local, state, and congressional office also felt or feared the sting of Loeb's attacks. The mere threat of such coverage discouraged an untold number from running, as in 1966 when former congressman Louis C. Wyman abandoned plans to seek a U.S. Senate seat. Former governor Walter Peterson acknowledged that many New Hampshire politicians dared not speak out "for fear of being pilloried in the pages of the *Union Leader.*" Still, other politicians like Governor Hugh Gregg and congressional candidate James Cleveland took Loeb on. Cleveland, a veteran of World War II battles, avowed that he would not crawl before "a junior Goebbels" whose only combat experience consisted of "lawsuits and character assassinations."[77] Cleveland won his primary and captured the House seat.

Summing up the *Union Leader*'s importance, Eric Veblen concluded in 1975 that the paper had influenced the campaign strategies of every gubernatorial and congressional candidate of the previous two decades. Although politicians may not have altered their stands to satisfy Loeb, the emphasis they placed on particular issues suggested a common concern not to arouse his enmity. Loeb regarded taxes as the premier issue of every gubernatorial campaign and endorsed only candidates who pledged to veto any bill enacting a state income or general sales tax.[78]

Veblen also adduced plausible evidence of a significant relationship between the *Union Leader*'s readership and the vote for candidates favored by the paper in gubernatorial and senatorial primaries of the 1960s and early 1970s. Endorsed candidates ran strongest in Manchester and surrounding Hillsborough County where most readers of the newspaper lived. Elaborating upon Veblen's data, Christopher Achen confirmed that the slant of *Union Leader* coverage had more effect on the vote in primaries than in general elections, where party loyalties came into play. Achen also concluded that Veblen had successfully disproved competing notions that the newspaper had simply supported candidates who would have carried Manchester anyway, that it backed candidates who campaigned mostly in Manchester, or that subscribing to the *Union Leader* was a surrogate measure of conservatism.[79]

At first glance, the *Union Leader*'s impact on New Hampshire *presidential* primaries appears fairly marginal. The paper's conservative agenda has always appealed more to Republicans than to Democrats, and it is hardly surprising that all but one of the paper's endorsements has gone to a Republican.[80] In three of these races, the paper backed a sure winner who would have easily triumphed in any event: Nixon in 1960 and 1968 and Reagan in 1984. In five others, the endorsed candidate lost: Barry Goldwater in 1964, Congressman John Ashbrook in 1972,

Reagan in 1976, former Delaware governor Pierre du Pont in 1988, and Buchanan in 1992. Ashbrook picked up only 10 percent of the vote; du Pont a mere 9 percent. In 1972, Loeb also backed a Democratic primary candidate, Los Angeles mayor Sam Yorty, who garnered just 6 percent of the vote. Only in 1980 (Reagan) and 1996 (Buchanan) did the *Union Leader*'s choice prevail in a contested presidential primary.[81]

A newspaper's influence, of course, can be gauged in ways other than endorsing eventual winners. The *Union Leader* has sometimes followed a win-by-losing strategy in which backing one candidate mattered less than bashing others. It clearly took this tack when supporting Ashbrook, Yorty, du Pont, and Buchanan in 1992, none of whom had any realistic chance of victory. The main objective in every instance was to inflict as much harm as possible on the front-runner. Supposedly, for example, Loeb played a critical role in "destroying" Muskie's candidacy.[82]

There is ample basis to argue that the *Union Leader* also made a difference in the 1980 Republican primary. According to David Moore, Loeb helped Reagan in at least two ways: first, by diminishing Congressman Phil Crane's challenge to Reagan, and, second, by lavishing favorable coverage on Reagan while panning Bush at every opportunity.[83] Until the *Union Leader* went to work on his personal life, Crane seemed to be catching on as a youthful alternative to Reagan. Bush came under relentless attack once he posed a real threat to Reagan. Reagan received favorable treatment in 46 percent of the *Union Leader* stories that Moore sampled (compared with 5 percent for Bush) and negative publicity in only 2 percent (compared with Bush's 48 percent).

Traditionally, the *Union Leader* has used its front page to promote a favorite while savaging his rivals. True to form in 1980, the paper ran thirty-five favorable stories about Reagan on page one, offered neutral coverage in thirty-two, and criticized him in only one. Conversely, Moore found, forty of fifty-seven front-page stories about Bush were negative; none were positive.

Another *Union Leader* tradition has been to blend editorial opinion with ostensibly more objective news reporting, first, by incessant editorializing, and, second, by running some of these editorials on the front page. In 1980, according to Moore, twenty-three of twenty-nine editorials published over the space of fifty-five days lauded Reagan; not one was critical. The paper even featured Reagan as a guest columnist. Bush came under attack in nineteen of the twenty editorials written about him.[84]

Several polls taken before and immediately after the 1980 primary allowed Moore to assess *Union Leader* influence on Republican vote choice. His analysis divided Republican primary voters into two electorates: *Union Leader* readers and nonreaders. Readers gave Reagan substantially more support in every poll and helped sustain him after being upset by Bush in Iowa. Readers were also much more likely than nonreaders to classify their political outlook as conservative, though not all readers were conservative. Moore identified readership as the most important predictor of vote choice, with more than twice the impact of ideology.[85]

Figure 3.8 shows how voters polled after the 1992 primaries fell out when classified by ideology and whether or not they read the *Union Leader*. Consistent with the findings of Veblen and Moore, readership did not show up as a surrogate measure of conservatism. True, Republican primary voters who read the *Union Leader* were twice as likely to classify themselves as "very conservative" as were nonreaders. Yet it is also clear that the vast majority of Republican primary voters labeled themselves as somewhat conservative or moderate, whether they read the paper or not. No meaningful difference surfaced among readers and nonreaders voting in the Democratic primary.[86]

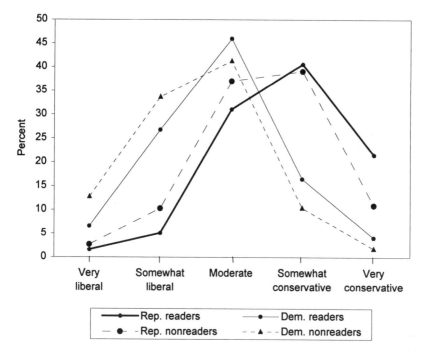

FIGURE 3.8   IDEOLOGICAL PROFILE OF *UNION LEADER* READERS AND NONREADERS VOTING IN THE 1992 REPUBLICAN AND DEMOCRATIC PRIMARIES

Source: VRS exit polls.

Table 3.10 offers a rough test of the two-electorates notion as applied to the 1992 Republican primary. When ideological differences are not taken into account, readers of the *Union Leader* show up in the exit poll as significantly more likely than nonreaders to vote for Buchanan: Buchanan won 50 percent of the reader vote, compared with less than 37 percent of the nonreader vote. Holding ideology constant modified this relationship, however, as can be seen in the varying magnitude of Cramer's V. The reader vote for Buchanan rose from 41 percent of the liberals and moderates to 71 percent of the ultraconservatives. Although nonreader voting varied erratically by ideological category, nonreaders gave Buchanan less support than did readers in every comparison. Though not an exact replication of Moore's regression model, my analysis also finds that readership and ideology exercised a joint influence on voting choice. In 1992, however, ideology appeared to affect the vote as much as reading the *Union Leader* did.[87]

TABLE 3.10   *UNION LEADER* READERSHIP AND CANDIDATE SUPPORT IN 1992 NEW HAMPSHIRE REPUBLICAN PRIMARY

Reported 1992 vote	*Readers (N = 652)*	*Nonreaders (N = 1,141)*
Buchanan	50%	36%
Bush	50%	63%
$X^2 = 31.95$, p < .001,		
Cramer's V = .133		
Self-identified as "somewhat liberal" or "moderate"		
Buchanan	41%	39%
Bush	59%	61%
$X^2 = .198$, n.s.,		
Cramer's V = .016		
"Somewhat conservative"		
Buchanan	47%	31%
Bush	53%	69%
$X^2 = 19.67$, p <.001,		
Cramer's V = .168		
"Very conservative"		
Buchanan	71%	51%
Bush	29%	49%
$X^2 = 11.03$, p <.01,		
Cramer's V = .205		

Source: VRS exit poll.

TABLE 3.11   CORRELATION OF VOTE IN 1992 AND 1996 NEW HAMPSHIRE REPUB-LICAN PRIMARIES WITH *UNION LEADER* SUBSCRIPTION RATES

Candidate and Primary	Pearson's r	Significance
Buchanan 1992	+.401	<.001
Bush 1992	-.382	<.001
Buchanan 1996	+.480	<.001
Dole 1996	-.495	<.001
Alexander 1996	-.021	n.s.

Sources: *New Hampshire Manual for the General Court,* vols. 53, 55; and paid New Hampshire circulation data compiled by *Union Leader* for 1991–92 and 1995–96. Note: Correlation coefficients based only on towns of 1,000 or more.

Additional evidence of the *Union Leader*'s influence on recent Republican primaries emerged from correlating the vote for Buchanan and his rivals with the paper's subscription rate in towns of 1,000 or more. Following Veblen, I hypothesized that the subscription rate would vary positively and significantly with Buchanan's vote in both primaries. I likewise expected readership to vary negatively with the vote for Bush, Dole, and Alexander. Subscription rates were measured as the total number of subscribers in each town divided by the total number of registered primary voters.[88] The findings, reported in table 3.11, upheld every hypothesis, except for Alexander.

The media environment in New Hampshire has changed enormously since William Loeb's day. Nackey Loeb took over the paper after William died in 1981 and, with the help of editor Joseph McQuaid, continued her husband's tradition of dyspeptic editorials, shrill headlines, and the full-court press for favored candidates. McQuaid assumed the responsibilities of publisher and company president when Mrs. Loeb retired in May 1999.[89] The *Union Leader* remains New Hampshire's only statewide newspaper, offering unmatched coverage not only of local politics, but also of weddings, deaths, high school graduations, and other prosaic happenings. Now, however, it must compete with two local television stations, WMUR and WNDS, as well as cable television and a regional edition of the *Boston Globe*.[90]

Up Close and Personal?

Where else except Iowa, defenders of the New Hampshire primary ask, do little-known and poorly funded candidates have any hope of overcoming a front-runner's inordinate advantage? Where else must every candidate, with the possible exception of sitting presidents, actually discuss ideas with ordinary folk and ask for their votes?

David Moore has disputed the actual importance of retail politics in the New Hampshire primary, particularly with respect to frequent and often dramatic swings in preprimary polls. These surges and declines, he maintained in 1985, are not the result of door-to-door campaigning but of campaign events, many external to New Hampshire, such as who runs well in Iowa. Likely voters learn of these developments from the mass media, not from campaign contacts. The notion that candidates must talk to the voters and organize volunteers, he concluded, is a "myth."[91]

Moore is surely right about dramatic poll changes. Moreover, for every Kefauver, Carter, or Hart who seemingly owes his New Hampshire success to retail politics, one also recalls an Askew, Babbitt, or du Pont who pursued voters just as doggedly but to no avail. Indeed, the candidates who rely most on retail politics probably do so to compensate for lack of money and other essential resources.

Still, by lumping all forms of retail politics together, Moore throws the important out with the trivial. What Gary Jacobson wrote about congressional candidates also holds for presidential contenders:"Most politicians have faith in the personal touch; if they can just talk to people and get them to listen, they can win support. Some evidence supports this notion."[92] Time spent talking issues with neighborhood opinion leaders might just pay off at the polls, especially if the candidate effectively projects the presidential equivalent of "homestyle."[93]

In any case, no serious presidential candidate neglects the protracted retail politics of recruiting activist supporters and proficient organizers in New Hampshire. Good organizations build the vote in the towns and get voters to the polls, as Hart staffers and volunteers did in the midst of a blizzard in 1984. One doubts that Hart could have capitalized on finishing second in Iowa without a good organization already in place.

For their part, New Hampshire activists and state officeholders typically talk with most, if not all, of their party's candidates before choosing one. In the small world of New Hampshire politics, where presidential primary outcomes sometimes turn on two thousand or fewer votes, who supports which candidate is taken seriously.[94] Vice President Gore certainly understood this when gearing up for the 2000 primary:

> Minutes after the polls closed last November 3 [1998], the phones started ringing in New Hampshire. It was the vice president on the line and he wanted to talk to New Hampshire Democrats. All

of them. He called state Senator Sylvia Larson, who at first thought it was a practical joke. "He knew my husband's name and the names of both of my children," she marvels. . . . Gore spoke to about 200 people that night and the next day, and he left answering-machine messages for hundreds more. Then, he asked his weary staff for more phone numbers. . . . Gore, of course, isn't dialing for fun; he figures the phone calls and the party invitations will win him the crucial support of Democratic activists like [Greg] Martin in New Hampshire's first-in-the-nation primary a year from now. And he's probably right. "They've made me more of a Gore person," says Martin, who backed Richard Gephardt in '88 but now pledges his support to the vice president.[95]

Other aspects of retail politics plied by the candidates, such as greeting employees at the factory gates or shoppers at the malls, probably have little effect. But effective or not, retail politics is no myth in New Hampshire. Front-loading dictates that candidates come early and often. Gearing up for the 1996 primary, for instance, Alexander made twenty different visits to New Hampshire. Dole logged fifteen visits, and Buchanan made eleven.[96] Clearly, as the 1996 Republican case demonstrates, the most frequent visitor does not always win, but this hardly makes visiting unimportant.

Candidates spend most of their time campaigning in the southern counties, especially Hillsborough and Rockingham, where slightly more than half of all registered Republicans and Democrats reside. Table 3.12 shows how closely Hart, Mondale, and Glenn patterned their visits on the voter registration rolls. (Hart also visited more often than Mondale and Glenn combined.) More recent breakdowns of counties visited would doubtless uphold the 1984 pattern.

Remarkably high percentages of New Hampshire primary voters tell exit pollsters that they met one or more candidates during the campaign. In a 1980 CBS/*New York Times* exit poll, for instance, 15 percent of the Democratic primary voters mentioned candidates as their chief source of information about the campaign, compared with 35 percent who relied mostly on television and 22 percent who relied on newspapers. Table 3.13 reports the percentage of voters in the 1992 Republican and Democratic primaries who said that they actually had met the candidate they voted for. Bush appears to have met more voters than Buchanan, even though Buchanan spent much more time campaigning in New Hampshire. (It is possible that when responding to this question, voters may have recalled meeting Bush in 1988 or even 1980.) Tsongas,

TABLE 3.12   COUNTIES VISITED BY HART, MONDALE, AND GLENN DURING 1984
DEMOCRATIC PRIMARY CAMPAIGN

County	% of Total Democratic Registration	% of Total Undeclared Registration	Hart Visits	Mondale Visits	Glenn Visits
Belknap	3.3	4.9	8	3	1
Carroll	2.0	3.8	1	0	0
Cheshire	6.2	7.1	8	1	4
Coos	4.7	4.0	8	1	2
Grafton	6.0	7.3	9	4	6
Hillsborough	34.7	26.1	52	19	20
Merrimack	9.0	12.0	19	5	7
Rockingham	19.8	22.0	34	10	10
Strafford	10.1	9.5	23	5	10
Sullivan	4.2	3.2	6	0	2
Total	100	99.9	168	48	62

Source: Author's compilation from campaign schedules obtained in 1984.
Note: The first Hart, Mondale, and Glenn visits listed above occurred in 1983.

the Democratic winner, met proportionately fewer of the people who voted for him than was true of most of his rivals. As the Tsongas example illustrates, victory does not always go to the candidate who shakes the most hands. Still, building rapport with hundreds of voters can pay off when the candidate is buffeted by scandal or other setbacks. Arguably, one reason for Clinton's survival in the 1992 primary is that he met one in every five of the people who voted for him.

Voter contact, of course, extends well beyond the candidates to include the efforts of campaign workers who collect names at candidate appearances, make literature drops and phone calls, canvass door to door, raise funds and organize social gatherings, and get out the vote. Unfortunately, exit pollsters do not consistently ask about most of the specific manifestations of retail politics in New Hampshire, nor do they provide a basis for comparison by asking voters whether they have met candidates or been contacted by campaign workers in other primary states. New Hampshire polls indicate that most primary voters come into contact with at least one campaign before casting their ballots. In 1980, according to the CBS/*New York Times* exit poll, 53 percent of all Democratic primary voters had been contacted by the Carter campaign one or more times, 64 percent had heard from Edward Kennedy's organization, and 45 percent had heard from supporters of Jerry Brown.

TABLE 3.13   PERCENTAGE OF 1992 NEW HAMPSHIRE PRIMARY VOTERS WHO MET THE CANDIDATE THEY VOTED FOR

Met Own Candidate?	Voted for Bush	Voted for Buchanan	All GOP Primary Voters	Voted for Brown	Voted for Clinton	Voted for Harkin	Voted for Kerrey	Voted for Tsongas	All Dem. Primary Voters
Yes	13	9	11	19	20	18	12	10	15
No	87	91	88	80	79	81	88	90	85
(N)	(1,049)	(744)	(1,793)	(162)	(495)	(199)	(220)	(659)	(1,735)

Source: VRS exit poll.

Conclusion

Should New Hampshire continue holding the first presidential primary? Until recently, the answer to this question hinged on the type of nominating process desired. Most of the debate occurred in the Democratic Party. Democrats who wanted to minimize the risk to their party's presidential front-runner argued that atypical New Hampshire should not hold the first primary. Big-state Democrats blamed Iowa and New Hampshire for winnowing the field before their voters had any say in the nomination. These issues came to a head in 1984, when the Democratic National Committee tried but failed to strip Iowa and New Hampshire of their first-in-the-nation status.[97]

Recent increases in front-loading have clearly overtaken some of the arguments against letting New Hampshire hold the first primary. Front-loading, the protracted invisible primary it fosters, and the prodigious fund raising it necessitates work in tandem to aid already advantaged front-runners. (According to one estimate, any candidate expecting to win either party's 2000 nomination had to raise $2,893 an hour, or $69,432 every day, for the rest of the year beginning 5 January 1999.) Front-loading and its manifestations now eliminate more candidates than the Iowa caucuses and the New Hampshire primary combined.[98] Moreover, front-loading now renders every late primary almost meaningless because the voters in early primaries have already decided the outcome. In 1996, Republican voters in Pennsylvania, Indiana, New Jersey, and nine other late-voting primary states found themselves in precisely this predicament. In 2000, every primary held after the second Tuesday in March will likely fall into the same "ex post facto" category.

Front-loading may also have overtaken the argument that New Hampshire gives lesser candidates a chance at upsetting front-runners. At this writing, New Hampshire is tentatively set to hold the first presidential primary of the 2000 process on 29 February. Just one week later, a remarkable set of primaries is taking shape, including those in the rest of New England and in California, Washington, Oregon, New York, and possibly a few other states.[99] Based on 1996 apportionment figures, this cluster of primaries will select 43 percent or more of the delegates needed to win the Republican nomination and no less than 52 percent of those needed to decide the Democratic nomination. California alone will account for about 17 percent of the Republican delegates and roughly 20 percent of the Democratic delegates necessary for nomination.[100]

In the opinion of William Galvin, secretary of state of Massachusetts, this massing of big-state power spells "disaster for the traditional presidential primary process as we've known it."[101] Actually, the system has been moving in this direction for some time. But Galvin is certainly correct when he avows that candidates will be stretched to their physical and financial limits by having to campaign in major states on both coasts at the same time. Nor can the candidates rest once California and the other behemoths of 7 March have registered their preferences. South Carolina and perhaps as many as eight western states are scheduled to hold their primaries on 11 March, and those southern states that are part of Super Tuesday will vote on 14 March. The question is not whether New Hampshire will vote first, but whether voting first will matter in a process moving at warp speed. The conventional wisdom at this writing supports numerous possibilities.

One scenario, as articulated by former Iowa governor Terry E. Branstad, holds that the caucuses in his state and the first primary in New Hampshire will actually gain in importance by prefiguring—or at least affecting—the outcome in California and the rest of the bicoastal primary states. "It is critically important for candidates to do well in Iowa and New Hampshire," Branstad maintains, "because they will have very little time to recover before the California primary."[102] Actually, as discussed earlier, history indicates that it is not necessary to do well in Iowa in order to place first or second in New Hampshire or to win the nomination. Indeed, a big win or strong second in New Hampshire following a setback in Iowa might generate the very momentum to impress a bicoastal electorate.

Another scenario is that the "bicoastal blowout" on 7 March will all but extinguish New Hampshire's importance. This could become obvious even before the vote in California if leading candidates decide that the New Hampshire primary is too risky or not worth the trouble of contesting. And, for those electing to take their chances in the first primary, winning or finishing second in New Hampshire would not matter if 7 March proves disastrous. At the very least, nervous candidates will make a major effort in California as well as in New Hampshire and Iowa. Much also depends on whether California's new blanket primary method of selecting delegates can be revised to suit the national parties. At this writing, a solution appears to have been found.[103]

The New Hampshire primary would also lose importance if a favorite son scares off the other candidates. In every New Hampshire primary since 1952 in which one of the candidates hailed from New England and in which no incumbent president sought renomination, the regional son has prevailed: Kennedy of Massachusetts in 1960, Lodge of Massachusetts in 1964, Muskie of Maine in 1972, Dukakis of Massachusetts in 1988, and Tsongas of Massachusetts in 1992. (Bush is omitted from this list because although Connecticut-born and a property owner in Maine, he had claimed Texas as his place of residence long before seeking the nomination.) The prospect of a regional favorite in the 2000 Democratic race expired when Senator John Kerry of Massachusetts decided not to challenge Gore. A local son has entered the Republican race, however, and although few pundits take Senator Robert Smith of New Hampshire seriously at this writing, some Republican leaders worry that he might give more prominent rivals an excuse to discount the first primary.[104]

The most likely scenario for 2000 is that every serious candidate in both parties will campaign hard in New Hampshire. Calendar compression should make this comparatively inexpensive and much-publicized primary irresistible even to risk-averse front-runners. In any event, few candidates will have the means to continue campaigning after mid-March. Doubtless the front-runner in each party will try to claim the nomination as swiftly as possible, and a convincing win in New Hampshire will certainly be instrumental, if not crucial, to that objective.

If anything is clear at this early stage in the 2000 nominating cycle, it is that the Democrats will hold a very different primary in New Hampshire than the Republicans. At this writing, the field of potential Democratic candidates has shrunk to Vice President Gore, the prohibitive favorite, and former senator Bill Bradley. Like Kerry of Massachusetts, Senator Bob Kerrey of Nebraska, Senator Paul Wellstone of Minnesota, and House minority leader Richard Gephardt removed themselves from contention after exhibiting considerable interest in running. In marked contrast, only Senator John Ashcroft of Missouri and former California governor Pete Wilson have dropped out of a burgeoning Republican field. The Republican list now includes most of the candidates who opposed Dole in 1996—Pat Buchanan, Lamar Alexander, Steve Forbes, and Alan Keyes—as well as Dole's wife, Elizabeth; former vice president Dan Quayle; Senator John McCain of Arizona; Representative John Kasich of Ohio; and family-values advocate Gary Bauer. The Republican favorite at this writing is George W. Bush, Texas governor and presidential son, whose support in the polls greatly exceeds popular knowledge of his policy stands or accomplishments.

It follows that finishing second in the New Hampshire Democratic primary will mean nothing unless Gore falls far short of expectations or loses outright. On the Republican side, coming in second in this multi-candidate fray might prove almost as valuable as winning, especially if Buchanan or native son Senator Smith wins. A national favorite who finishes second in New Hampshire might still carry California and some of the other megastates, whereas an upset winner in New Hampshire likely will not have the resources to contest the big-state primaries.

In 2004, the nominating system may change yet again if more states agree to vote together in a series of regional or cluster primaries. Though hardly novel, the idea is being seriously considered by the National Association of Secretaries of State. Unlike earlier plans of this sort, the scheme now under consideration exempts Iowa and New Hampshire from participating in any cluster of primaries and allows them to kick off the process as before.[105]

In any case, even the principal architects of the early California primary now concede that Iowa and New Hampshire perform a function for the nominating system worth preserving. According to Bill Jones, California's secretary of state, both states provide "a viable forum" for lesser candidates and "require" all of the candidates to "practice retail, rather than media-driven politics."[106] Iowa's title to priority in this process appears less certain than New Hampshire's, however, and New Hampshire likely will find it increasingly difficult to enjoy an entire week unto itself once actual voting starts. Still, so long as New Hampshire holds the first of the primaries, it will attract inordinate media coverage as a critical event in an extraordinarily compressed process. Out of necessity, the candidates will visit even earlier and perhaps more often than before. No doubt, old misgivings about giving so much say to so small a state will linger into the new century, but so will the mystique.

Acknowledgments

I greatly appreciate the invaluable assistance provided by New Hampshire secretary of state William M. Gardner, New Hampshire state librarian Michael York, Lee Sigelman of The George Washington University, former New Hampshire governor Hugh Gregg, librarian Terry Dean of the Institute of Governmental Studies at the University of California at Berkeley, James Freeman of the Denison computer center, Denison librarian Mary Prophet, John and Carol Resch of Manchester, David McCuan of the University of California at Riverside, Dartmouth political scientist Linda Fowler, Alan Rines of the New Hampshire Motor Vehicles Department, Martin J. Capodice of the New Hampshire Employment Security Department, and Benjamin Wu of the Inter-University Consortium for Political and Social Research (ICPSR). Data obtained from ICPSR and the Vanderbilt Television News Archives proved invaluable to my analysis. None of the above bears any responsibility for my findings and interpretations.

Notes

1. Data from WMUR-Dartmouth College poll of 29 January–2 February 1996 were kindly provided by Linda Fowler. Other data are from *"USA Today* Tracks the Candidates," www.usatoday.com/elect.
2. Quoted in Bob Woodward, *The Choice* (New York: Simon & Schuster, 1996), 385–6. See also Larry Sabato, *Toward the Millennium: The Elections of 1996* (Boston: Allyn & Bacon, 1997), 45.
3. Dole got only 597 votes out of a total of 146,534 cast, trailing every other Republican candidate and even the write-in total for Jimmy Carter. See Charles Brereton, *First in the Nation: New Hampshire and the Premier Presidential Primary* (Portsmouth, N.H.: Peter E. Randall, 1987), 250.
4. Quoted in Jack W. Germond and Jules Witcover, *Whose Broad Stripes and Bright Stars? The Trivial Pursuit of the Presidency 1988* (New York: Warner Books, 1989), 146.
5. Remarks by Michael Murphy at Symposium on the 1996 Presidential Campaign, George Washington University, 20 April 1996. See also Sabato's account in *Toward the Millennium*, 43.
6. In 1992, for example, Clinton, rather than Tsongas, won the Dixville Democratic vote, and Ernest Hollings led the Democratic vote there in 1984. In 1980, Bush tied with Reagan at five votes each, while Howard Baker got four votes. Henry Cabot Lodge and Richard Nixon tied at three votes each in 1964. Hugh Gregg, former governor of New Hampshire, has succinctly described the tradition: "[T]he New Hampshire primary election begins at midnight in Dixville Notch. . . For Dixville to retain this distinction, state law requires that the ballots of all registered voters be recorded before a count is taken. This famous quadrennial event is held at The Balsams, a world-renowned resort in the North Country. Most of these voters are involved, directly or indirectly, with the hotel and its subsidiary operations." See Hugh Gregg, *The Candidates: See How They Run* (Portsmouth, N.H.: Peter E. Randall, 1990), 33.
7. *State of New Hampshire Manual for the General Court*, vol. 55 (Concord, N.H.: Department of State, 1997).
8. Murphy, remarks; and Sabato, *Toward the Millennium*, 44–5.
9. Niall A. Palmer, *The New Hampshire Primary and the American Electoral Process* (Westport, Conn.: Praeger, 1997), 1–3. Palmer writes that New Hampshire moved into first position in 1920 when Indiana and Minnesota "either moved or abandoned their primaries as the Progressive reform impulse weakened across the nation." According to *Presidential Elections 1789–1996* (Washington, D.C.: Congressional Quarterly Press, 1997), Indiana moved its presidential primary to the first Tuesday in May in 1920 and held to that date until 1932, when it abandoned the primary; it resurrected it in 1956. After 1916, Minnesota did not hold another presidential primary until 1952. Palmer is also a good source for brief accounts of state laws that protect New Hampshire's first-in-the-nation status.
10. For a full account of how this happened, see Hugh Winebrenner, *The Iowa Precinct Caucuses: The Making of a Media Event*, 2nd ed. (Ames: Iowa State University Press, 1998), 35–56.
11. See Emmett H. Buell, Jr., "First-in-the-Nation: Disputes over the Timing of Early Democratic Presidential Primaries and Caucuses in 1984 and 1988," *Journal of Law & Politics* 4 (1987): 311–42; and Palmer, *New Hampshire Primary*, 135–73.

12. Palmer, *New Hampshire Primary,* 2; and William Gardner, New Hampshire secretary of state, telephone interview by author, 28 January 1999.

13. See *Presidential Elections 1789-1996,* 158-9; and Neal R. Peirce, *The New England States: People, Politics, and Power in the Six New England States* (New York: Norton, 1976), 316.

14. This paragraph relies on a close reading of the *New York Times* index of stories about the presidential primaries of 1948. Dewey and Stassen split New Hampshire's eight delegates six to two. See Richard Norton Smith, *Thomas E. Dewey and His Times* (New York: Simon & Schuster, 1982), 486.

15. See *Presidential Elections 1789-1996,* 168-71, for 1952 turnout statistics. The 1948 coverage period runs from 1 January to 9 March and the 1952 period from 1 January to 11 March, as determined from close study of the *New York Times* index listings for presidential primaries. My count includes every story mentioning the primaries as revealed in terse index summaries. For good accounts of the 1952 primary campaigns, see Brereton, *First in the Nation,* 1-34, and Palmer, *New Hampshire Primary,* 3-9.

16. Joseph Bruce Gorman, *Kefauver: A Political Biography* (New York: Oxford University Press, 1971), 124.

17. Truman compounded his problems in New Hampshire by withdrawing from the primary, dismissing primaries as "eyewash," and boasting that the nomination was his if he wanted it. A few days later, he reversed himself and allowed supporters to keep his name on the ballot. In an editorial titled "The Boss Is Insolent," the *Concord Monitor* concluded: "What the President was saying is that the sovereign state of New Hampshire can go to hell"; quoted in Gorman, *Kefauver,* 119. By the time of the New Hampshire primary, Truman had most likely decided not to seek another term and was prepared to announce this as soon as he found a worthy replacement. At a loss for successors after failing to convince Chief Justice Fred Vinson, Governor Adlai Stevenson, and even Eisenhower to run for the Democratic nomination, Truman may have let his name go forward in New Hampshire simply to keep Kefauver at bay until someone better could be found. Truman also resented Kefauver's attacks on his administration. See David McCullough's account in *Truman* (New York: Simon & Schuster, 1992), 887-94. For turnout figures in the 1952 New Hampshire primary, see *Presidential Elections 1789-1996,* 151-70.

18. William G. Mayer, "The New Hampshire Primary: A Historical Overview," in *Media and Momentum: The New Hampshire Primary and Nomination Politics,* ed. Gary R. Orren and Nelson W. Polsby (Chatham, N.J.: Chatham House, 1987), 9-41. The literature on party reform is vast. Leading works include James W. Ceaser, *Reforming the Reforms: A Critical Analysis of the Presidential Selection Process* (Cambridge, Mass.: Ballinger, 1982); Nelson W. Polsby, *Consequences of Party Reform* (New York: Oxford University Press, 1983); Byron E. Shafer, *Quiet Revolution: The Struggle for the Democratic Party and the Shaping of Post-Reform Politics* (New York: Russell Sage Foundation, 1983), and Howard L. Reiter, *Selecting the President: The Nominating Process in Transition* (Philadelphia: University of Pennsylvania Press, 1985). Anthony Corrado has written extensively on the impact of campaign finance reform. See his chapter, "The Changing Environment of Campaign Finance," in *In Pursuit of the White House: How We Choose Our Presidential Nominees,* ed. William G. Mayer (Chatham, N.J.: Chatham House, 1996), 220-53.

19. For a first-hand account of Carter's techniques in New Hampshire, see Brereton, *First in the Nation,* 179-82. Henry Jackson later acknowledged to reporter Jules

Witcover that he had miscalculated. Some staff members had tried to convince him that "New Hampshire as a psychological media state was overwhelming, that it was New Hampshire or bust." Eventually, however, he concluded that "the choice was Massachusetts; it was the kind of state that would provide the kind of acceleration in the campaign effort that would more than offset not going in New Hampshire. Also, New Hampshire involved a long, tedious, one-on-one type of campaign, whereas Massachusetts did not"; see Jules Witcover, *Marathon: The Pursuit of the Presidency, 1972-1976* (New York: Viking Press, 1977), 191. Jackson did contest the selection of New Hampshire delegates, offering his delegate-candidates $1,000 each to promote themselves. "It was as doomed an approach as could ever be devised," Brereton observed; see *First in the Nation*, 183. For a discussion of Wallace's strategy, see Stephan Lesher, *George Wallace: American Populist* (Reading, Mass.: Addison-Wesley, 1994), 194-5.

20. For an extended discussion of how national nominating conventions lost their power to pick or block presidential and vice presidential nominees, see Byron E. Shafer, *Bifurcated Politics: Evolution and Reform in the National Party Convention* (Cambridge, Mass.: Harvard University Press, 1988). William G. Carleton anticipated many of these developments in a prescient analysis of how social and political change had reduced the convention's role well before the reforms of 1968; see "The Revolution in the Presidential Nominating Convention," *Political Science Quarterly* 72 (1957): 224-40.

21. Mayer, "The New Hampshire Primary," 23. Germond and Witcover made a similar argument in *Whose Broad Stripes and Bright Stars*, 133. By 1988, they argued, Iowa had usurped New Hampshire's function of establishing the candidate pecking order, and New Hampshire had become "something more like the semifinals." Since 1976, they concluded, any candidate who did not finish in the Iowa top tier could not hope to compete effectively in New Hampshire.

22. See Sabato, *Toward the Millennium*, 42; also Winebrenner, *The Iowa Precinct Caucuses*. Favorite son Tom Harkin easily won the caucuses in 1992, effectively making them a nonevent.

23. For a discussion of the 1988 events, see Rhodes Cook, *Race for the Presidency: Winning the 1988 Nomination* (Washington, D.C.: Congressional Quarterly Press, 1987). For later developments, see B. Drummond Ayers, Jr., "Political Briefing: Louisiana Tinkers with Calendar Again," *New York Times*, 1 August 1998, A9. In 1996, Louisiana Republicans upstaged the Iowa GOP by scheduling their caucuses for 6 February, six days before Iowa. The Iowa party fought back by pressuring Republican candidates not to campaign in Louisiana, but Pat Buchanan, Phil Gramm, and Alan Keyes refused to comply. Louisiana took on the dimensions of a zero-sum encounter for Buchanan and Gramm. Gramm suffered a devastating defeat that effectively ended his candidacy, while the impact of Buchanan's triumph was felt even in Iowa, where Dole narrowly prevailed. Thus, though assiduously avoided by most candidates, Louisiana's rogue caucuses altered the dynamics of the Republican race before a single vote had been cast in Iowa or New Hampshire. On 30 January 1999, the Republican State Central Committee in Louisiana voted overwhelmingly to preempt Iowa again in 2000.

24. The invisible primary begins when the national press starts speculating about likely candidates. The *New York Times* began naming 1996 Republican possibilities on 11 February 1991. By December 1991, the list of 1996 Republican aspirants included Phil Gramm, Colin Powell, Dick Cheney, James Baker, Dan Quayle, Pat Buchanan (then only days into his bid for the 1992 GOP nomination), Pete Wilson, and Lamar

Alexander. Ostensibly convened to renominate Bush in 1992, the Republican convention in Houston showcased Quayle, Buchanan, Cheney, Baker, Gramm, Wilson, and other 1996 possibilities. See Maureen Dowd, "Stars of War Room Are Auditioning for the Battle to Come," *New York Times,* 11 February 1991, A7; "Washington Wire: Gramm in '96?" *Wall Street Journal,* 20 September 1991, A1; Andrew Rosenthal, "Weary of '92 Campaign? Now Try Pondering '96," *New York Times,* 22 December 1991, A10; Jack Anderson and Michael Binstein, "Buchanan Aims Right toward 1996," *Washington Post,* 3 August 1992; and Andrew Rosenthal, "While in Houston to Help Bush, Many Have Eyes on 1996," *New York Times,* 12 August 1992, A10.

25. See Emmett H. Buell, Jr., "The Invisible Primary," in *In Pursuit of the White House: How We Choose Our Presidential Nominees,* ed. William G. Mayer (Chatham, N.J.: Chatham House, 1996), 1–43. Governor Pete Wilson and Senator Arlen Specter formally declared but withdrew before the selection of a single delegate. Others who seriously considered running and decided not to take the plunge included General Colin Powell, former Defense secretary Dick Cheney, former vice president Dan Quayle, former Housing secretary Jack Kemp, former Labor secretary Lynn Martin, former Education secretary and drug czar William Bennett, and Governor Carroll Campbell.

26. Federal Election Commission data, kindly provided by Robert Biersack, revealed that by 1 January 1996, Dole had already spent $21.6 million of the overall $37.1 million cap on candidates who accepted matching funds. Expensive straw polls and an advertising war with Steve Forbes helped drive up his costs during the 1996 invisible primary.

27. See *Presidential Elections 1789-1996;* also William G. Mayer, "The Presidential Nominations," in *The Election of 1996,* ed. Gerald M. Pomper (Chatham, N.J.: Chatham House, 1997), 58. Lyndon Johnson handily won the two primaries he entered in 1964 and was nominated by acclamation at the Democratic convention in Atlantic City. However, the huge vote cast for uncommitted delegates, favorite sons standing in for Johnson, and others reduced LBJ's share of the total primary vote to only 17.7 percent. New Hampshire gave Nixon his smallest primary vote in 1972, 67.8 percent to 19.8 percent for Paul McCloskey and 9.7 percent for John Ashbrook. Nixon won more than 80 percent in every other primary where his name appeared on the ballot.

28. Adlai Stevenson wisely chose not to contest the New Hampshire primary in 1956, figuring that Kefauver had sewed it up with a campaign that had not ended since 1952. Indeed, Kefauver spent so much time in the state and so often promised to stand up for it in Congress that he became known as New Hampshire's third senator. Kefauver won all the delegates and the beauty contest, but Stevenson garnered enough write-in votes to finish second. See Brereton, *First in the Nation,* 42–4. See also John Bartlow Martin, *Adlai Stevenson and the World* (Garden City, N.Y.: Anchor Books, 1978).

29. Andrew E. Busch, *Outsiders and Openness in the Presidential Nominating System* (Pittsburgh: University of Pittsburgh Press, 1997), 2. Busch defines an "outsider" candidate as "one who (1) is outside the corridors of power, in the sense either of holding no office or of residing outside the 'mainstream' or majority of his party, explicitly rejecting the party's leadership and dominant element; (2) serves as the spokesman or representative of a broader group (political movement) outside the corridors of power; and/or (3) serves as the spokesman or representative of ideas, ideologies, or themes that challenge the dominant element in the party."

Many "outsiders" lack credibility on one or more of these dimensions. Among the 1996 Republicans, for example, career politician Lamar Alexander never convinced many voters either of his radicalism or of his break with the party establishment. Buchanan's passionate assault on moderate Republicanism and its free-trade orthodoxy gave him enough ideological credibility to offset a long history of roaming the corridors of Republican power. Though heir to an enormous fortune and well connected to GOP elites, Forbes enjoyed some credibility as a radical for his flat-tax pitch and associated assault on "Washington insiders."

30. Reagan is a good example of how events can overtake or confound such labels. In 1976, he headed the conservative movement in a battle for control of the GOP. Arguably, by 1980 (if not before), Reagan conservatism dominated the Republican agenda and Reagan himself had evolved into a party insider. Busch notes that many outsiders, like Kefauver, Carter, Hart, Tsongas, Buchanan in 1992, and Forbes, were not movement leaders. Busch and his coauthor, James W. Ceaser, classified Clinton in 1992 as an "insider-outsider," or one who positioned himself precisely at midpoint along this continuum. Clinton also put himself in the middle of the liberal-conservative continuum. See Busch and Ceaser, *Upside Down and Inside Out: The 1992 Election and American Politics* (Lanham, Md.: Rowan & Littlefield, 1993), 1–10.

31. For a good account of 1988 Super Tuesday primary voting, see Barbara Norrander, "The Best Laid Plans," in *Nominating the President*, ed. Emmett H. Buell and Lee Sigelman (Knoxville: University of Tennessee Press, 1991), 72–90.

32. See Lori Sharn, "Buchanan Fails to Win Christians' Faith," *USA Today*, 5 March 1996, A8. Religious right identifiers voting in the Georgia Republican primary supported Buchanan over Dole, 47 to 31 percent. In Texas and Florida, however, Dole led Buchanan in the religious right vote by 10 and 24 percentage points, respectively. See "At the Polls: A Political Profile of GOP Voters in Four States," *New York Times*, 6 March 1996, A13; and "At the Polls: Republican Voters in Florida and Texas," *New York Times*, 14 March 1996, A12.

33. Donald R. Matthews, "'Winnowing': The News Media and the 1976 Presidential Nominations," in *Race for the Presidency: The Media and the Nominating Process*, ed. James David Barber (Englewood Cliffs, N.J.: Prentice-Hall, 1978), 65.

34. David Paletz and Robert Entman, *Media Power Politics* (New York: Free Press, 1981), 36.

35. Elizabeth Drew, *Campaign Journal: The Events of 1983–1984* (New York: Macmillan, 1985), 310.

36. Witcover, *Marathon*, 223.

37. James Perry, *Us and Them: How the Press Covered the 1972 Election* (New York: Clarkson N. Potter, 1973), 83.

38. Jack W. Germond and Jules Witcover, *Blue Smoke & Mirrors: How Reagan Won & Why Carter Lost the Election of 1980* (New York: Viking Press, 1981), 122. Daffodils later went out of business, other hotels now compete with the Wayfarer, and the road to Portsmouth has been improved.

39. On this point, see Michael J. Robinson, "Where's the Beef? Media and Media Elites in 1984," in *The American Elections of 1984,* ed. Austin Ranney (Durham, N.C.: Duke University Press, 1985), 191.

40. Doris R. Graber, *Mass Media and American Politics,* 2nd ed. (Washington, D.C.: Congressional Quarterly Press, 1984), 199.

41. See table 2 in Matthews, "'Winnowing,'" 65.

42. William C. Adams, "As New Hampshire Goes . . . ," in *Media and Momentum: The New Hampshire Primary and Nomination Politics*, ed. Gary R. Orren and Nelson W. Polsby (Chatham, N.J.: Chatham House, 1987), 42–60.

43. Emmett H. Buell, Jr., "'Locals and Cosmopolitans': National, Regional, and State Newspaper Coverage of the New Hampshire Primary," in *Media and Momentum: The New Hampshire Primary and Nomination Politics*, ed. Gary R. Orren and Nelson W. Polsby (Chatham, N.J.: Chatham House, 1987), 61–5.

44. Owing to the Republicans' exceptionally long invisible primary for 1996, I dated early network coverage from 1 January 1995.

45. Michael J. Robinson and Margaret A. Sheehan, *Over the Wire and on TV: CBS and UPI in Campaign '80* (New York: Russell Sage Foundation, 1983), 176-7.

46. Robinson, "Where's the Beef?" 191.

47. New Hampshire's effect also showed up in Alabama and Florida. On 27 February, one day before the New Hampshire primary, a *Birmingham Post-Herald* poll estimated Hart's support at 2 percent and Mondale's at 48 percent. Three days later, Hart stood at 22 percent and Mondale at 36 percent. Likewise, the *Miami Herald* reported that Hart shot up from 1 to 15 percent, while Mondale's rating increased from 37 to 38 percent.

48. Maurice Carroll, "Hart Plans Strong Effort in New York State," *New York Times*, 2 March 1984, A14.

49. Curtis Wilkie, "Candidates Finding a Newly Centrist South," *Boston Globe*, 4 March 1984, A1.

50. Chris Black, "It's Hart Again; Vermont Gives Colo. Senator 3d Straight Win," *Boston Globe*, 7 March 1984, A1.

51. "Democratic Gladiators Enter Hardball Political Arena," *Washington Post*, 17 March 1984, A7; Bill Peterson, "Symbols Clashing in Mondale's State," *Washington Post*, 20 March 1984, A7; "Political Notes," *Washington Post*, 17 March 1984, A8; Sandra Sugawara, "Hart's Surge Portends Spirited Va. Caucuses," *Washington Post*, 21 March 1984, C3; and Wallace Turner, "Hart's Results in New England Turn Out Workers in Seattle," *New York Times*, 9 March 1984, A14.

52. In Gallup's last nationwide poll before the 1988 New Hampshire primary, Bush led the Republican field with 45 percent. The next Gallup poll, taken 10–12 March, gave him 69 percent, but it included the effects of Bush's wins on Super Tuesday. Gallup did take a poll before and just after the New Hampshire primary in Super Tuesday states. In both samplings, Bush led all others with 54 percent. Gallup's polls of likely Democratic primary voters in these states showed Dukakis moving from 8 percent before New Hampshire to 35 percent immediately afterward. See *The Gallup Poll 1988* (Wilmington, Del.: Scholarly Resources, 1989), 27, 45.

53. Peirce, *New England States*, 285–361.

54. See Palmer, *New Hampshire Primary*, 37-43, for a good summary of the census data. William Gardner, New Hampshire's secretary of state, estimates that French-Canadians of one description or another presently make up at least one-third of the population. Data on religious affiliations at the county level come from Martin B. Bradley, Norman M. Green, Jr., Dale E. Jones, Mac Lynn, and Lou McNeil, *Churches and Church Membership in the United States 1990* (Atlanta: Glenmary Research Center, 1992). According to this source, Catholic majorities ranged from 53 percent in Merrimack County to 78 percent in Strafford County.

55. Ralph Jimenez, "N.H. Governor Backs School Aid Amendment," *Boston Globe*, 5 September 1998, B5.

56. Palmer, *New Hampshire Primary*, 37-39. Jules Witcover and Jack Germond in

four coauthored books about the presidential elections of 1980–1992 have also characterized New Hampshire as much more representative of the mainstream than critics allow. See, for example, *Whose Broad Stripes and Bright Stars*, 132–3. See also Witcover's brief commentary about New Hampshire's industrialization in *Marathon*, 222.

57. "2000: Gore, Quayle In; Gephardt Out," cnn.com/allpolitics, 4 February 1999.
58. Drew, *Campaign Journal*, 311.
59. See *Presidential Elections 1789–1996*, 91–127.
60. The data for 1855–1975 come from *Guide to U.S. Elections* (Washington, D.C.: Congressional Quarterly, 1976), 470–1. More recent data are from *Congressional Elections 1946–1996* (Washington, D.C.: Congressional Quarterly Press, 1998), 75. Data for the 1998 Senate election are from www.usatoday.com. New Hampshire senators belong to classes two and three.
61. The data for 1857–1944 come from *Guide to U.S. Elections*, 603–805. The returns for 1946–1996 are found in *Congressional Elections 1946–1996*, 192–322; 1998 House data are from www.usatoday.com.
62. See *Gubernatorial Elections 1787–1997* (Washington, D.C.: Congressional Quarterly Press, 1998), 66–8. This source disagrees with official New Hampshire documents as to when biennial elections for governor began. *Gubernatorial Elections* gives the date as 1880. The state constitution, however, cites 1878 as the date of the first such election, which followed 1877 amendments that changed election day from Town Meeting Day in March to November, replaced annual elections for governor with biennial ones, and abolished adherence to the Protestant faith as a requirement for election as governor. See *Manual for the General Court* 55: 75. For a contemporary overview of state politics in New Hampshire, see Michelle Anne Fistek and Bob Egbert, "New Hampshire," in *State Party Profiles*, ed. Andrew M. Appleton and Daniel S. Ward (Washington, D.C.: Congressional Quarterly Press, 1997), 204–10.
63. Little correspondence shows up between those who register as undeclared and those who identify themselves as independents in the Republican primaries. For instance, only 36 percent of the independents polled after voting in the 1992 Republican primary had registered as undeclared. Fifty-three percent of independents voting in the 1992 Democratic primary reported having registered as undeclared. Recent exit polls provide only slight evidence of a connection between vote choice and undeclared registration.
64. Perry, *Us and Them*.
65. Aides to Mondale quoted in Dennis Roddy, "So Who Will Survive Tuesday Vote?" *Greensburg (Pa.) Tribune-Review*, 17 February 1984. See also Walter Mondale, *The Accountability of Power* (New York: David McKay, 1975); and Jack W. Germond and Jules Witcover, *Wake Us When It's Over: Presidential Politics of 1984* (New York: Macmillan, 1985), 165. Secondary analysis of the 1984 CBS/*New York Times* exit poll of New Hampshire Democratic primary voters upheld Mondale's claim that Hart got a big boost from independents. Among independents, Hart led Mondale 41 to 17 percent. The problem for Mondale was that liberals also favored Hart over him, 42 to 23 percent, as did Democratic identifiers, albeit by a smaller margin of 38 to 33 percent. Mondale ran relatively well among conservatives, winning 24 percent to Hart's 29 percent. Clearly, his problems in New Hampshire carried over to party regulars, liberals, and most other groups.
66. "By the Numbers: Voters in the Republican Primaries," *New York Times*, 31 March 1996, A24.

67. "Recap of the Primaries: How Democrats in 29 States Voted," *New York Times*, 12 July 1992, A18. Eight percent of the New Hampshire turnout consisted of miscellaneous others.

68. The standard question asks respondents to locate themselves on a three- or five-point liberal-moderate-conservative scale. Such a question ignores important differences between free-market and social conservatives, conservatives and libertarians, new and old politics liberals, and so on. For an early discussion of these problems, see William Maddox and Stuart Lilie, *Beyond Liberal and Conservative* (Washington, D.C.: Cato Institute, 1984).

69. Voter News Service (VNS) polled 4,374 voters on Yankee Tuesday (5 March) in Maine, Massachusetts, Rhode Island, and Vermont; 9,911 were polled one week later in Florida, Louisiana, Mississippi, Oklahoma, Tennessee, and Texas on Southern Super Tuesday; and 6,477 were interviewed the following week in Illinois, Michigan, Ohio, and Wisconsin.

70. Emmett H. Buell, Jr., and John P. Resch, "A New Look at the New Hampshire Primary," *Election Politics*, 4 (spring 1987): 2–7. Exit poll comparisons of New Hampshire and other 1980 Democratic primary electorates in this article make the same point. New Hampshire Democrats and independents were more likely to endorse the Equal Rights Amendment and identify themselves as liberals than were their counterparts in Massachusetts, Florida, Illinois, New York, Pennsylvania, New Jersey, and Ohio.

71. "Recap of the Primaries"; and 1992 Voter Research and Surveys (VRS) exit poll of New Hampshire Democratic primary voters.

72. VRS exit polls obtained from the Inter-University Consortium for Political and Social Research (ICPSR).

73. David W. Moore, "The *Manchester Union Leader* in the New Hampshire Primary," in *Media and Momentum: The New Hampshire Primary and Nomination Politics*, ed. Gary R. Orren and Nelson W. Polsby (Chatham, N.J.: Chatham House, 1987), 108.

74. Theodore H. White, *The Making of the President 1964* (New York: Atheneum, 1965), 103; idem, *The Making of the President 1968* (New York: Atheneum, 1969), 129; and idem, *The Making of the President 1972* (New York: Atheneum, 1973), 81.

75. These and other Loeb epithets have been widely quoted over the years. See Witcover and Germond, *Whose Broad Stripes and Bright Stars*, 70; and Eric P. Veblen, *The Manchester Union Leader in New Hampshire Elections* (Hanover, N.H.: University Press of New England, 1975), 160–61.

76. White, *Making of the President 1972*, 82. For more on Loeb's attacks on Muskie, see Jules Witcover, "William Loeb and the New Hampshire Primary: A Question of Ethics," *Columbia Journalism Review* 11 (May/June 1972): 14–25. One reason this incident amplified doubts about Muskie's fitness is that it fit a pattern of temper tantrums observed by the reporters who followed his campaign; see Timothy Crouse, *The Boys on the Bus* (New York: Ballantine Books, 1973).

77. Veblen, *Manchester Union Leader*, 53, 67, 178. For more about the rage Loeb aroused in New Hampshire, see Kevin Cash, *Who the Hell Is William Loeb?* (Manchester, N.H.: Amoskeag Press, 1975).

78. Veblen, *Manchester Union Leader*, 171–4.

79. Christopher H. Achen, *Interpreting and Using Regression* (Beverly Hills, Calif.: Sage Publications, 1982), 17–30.

80. I am indebted to Michael York of the New Hampshire State Library and the Library

and Archives of New Hampshire's Political Tradition for information on *Union Leader* endorsements.

81. *Presidential Elections 1789-1996*, 182–90.
82. Veblen, *Manchester Union Leader*, 174. In one sense, as already noted, Loeb goaded Muskie into a show of emotion that reflected badly on his candidacy and probably hurt him in subsequent primaries. Even so, Muskie won the New Hampshire primary with 46.4 percent of the vote. This compares quite favorably with the votes of both Democratic and Republican winners in other New Hampshire primaries contested by three or more serious candidates, none of whom was an incumbent president. Eisenhower in 1952 was the only candidate in ten such races to win 50 percent of the vote. Reagan came close with 49.6 percent in the 1980 primary. The average for these select primaries is 38.1 percent.
83. Moore, *"Manchester Union Leader,"* 104.
84. Ibid., 112–5. Moore also notes that the paper had begun to promote Reagan well before Bush emerged as his main rival. It launched personal attacks on Phil Crane, called Howard Baker a "political chameleon," and lambasted "Oily John" Connally as "the Arab candidate." Bush got lumped with Baker as "clean fingernail Republicans," wealthy elites who favored tax increases.
85. Ibid., 121.
86. Based on 1992 New Hampshire exit polls conducted by VRS.
87. Owing to the limited number of variables in the exit poll and the nominal level of most available measures, an attempt to replicate Moore's eighteen-variable regression model seemed pointless. Unfortunately, VNS did not ask 1996 primary voters if they read the *Union Leader*.
88. Total registration as a percentage base for standardized subscription rates included Democrats, Republicans, and undeclared. Omitting registered Democrats from the base changed the results only slightly: .394 for Buchanan in 1992, .492 for Buchanan in 1996, -.397 for Bush, -.484 for Dole, and -.058 for Alexander, with all coefficients significant at .001 except in the case of Alexander (p = .449).
89. Jill Zuckman, "The Torch Is Passed," *Boston Globe*, 23 May 1999, B1.
90. See Palmer, *New Hampshire Primary*, for more on the changing media markets of New Hampshire.
91. David W. Moore, "The Death of Politics in New Hampshire," in *The Mass Media in Campaign '84*, ed. Michael J. Robinson and Austin Ranney (Washington, D.C.: American Enterprise Institute for Public Policy Research, 1985), 5–6.
92. Gary C. Jacobson, *The Politics of Congressional Elections*, 4th ed. (New York: Longman, 1997), 69.
93. See Richard F. Fenno, "U.S. House Members in Their Constituencies: An Exploration," *American Political Science Review* 71 (1977): 883–917.
94. For a detailed account of how the 1988 campaigns recruited New Hampshire activists, see Dayton Duncan, *Grass Roots: One Year in the Life of the New Hampshire Presidential Primary* (New York: Viking, 1991).
95. Dana Milbank, "Political Machine: The Gore Campaign Gears Up for 2000," *New Republic*, 25 January 1999, 18.
96. Sabato, *Toward the Millennium*, 79–81.
97. Buell, "First-in-the-Nation."
98. See B. Drummond Ayers, Jr., "Political Briefing: Presidency in 2000: $2,893 an Hour," *New York Times*, 12 January 1999, A17; and Buell, "Invisible Primary."
99. State law authorizes the secretary of state to choose an earlier date if any other state schedules its primary to occur earlier than New Hampshire's or during the

same week as New Hampshire's. Secretary Gardner may schedule an earlier date if Delaware or some other state challenges New Hampshire's insistence not only on voting first, but also on having an entire week to itself. A New Hampshire–Iowa Presidential Election Commission, consisting of former and current officeholders and party officials in both states, has proposed that potential presidential candidates for 2000 commit to signing the following pledge: "I am not currently a candidate for President of the United States. If I should decide to be a candidate, I _____ pledge I will support the first-in-the-nation status of the New Hampshire Primary, and that I will not campaign in or allow declarations of candidacy to be filed in any state or territory that holds its presidential primary earlier than 7 days following the New Hampshire primary." Governor Shaheen endorsed the idea in a press conference held on 8 December 1998. See "Saga of the New Hampshire Presidential Pledge," *2000 Update* (a newsletter circulated by the Library and Archives of New Hampshire's Political Tradition), December 1998, 13. New Hampshire officials exacted a similar pledge from the 1996 Republican candidates, and, in 1984, Democratic Party leaders in New Hampshire and Iowa pressured the Democratic presidential candidates to back their efforts at keeping Iowa and New Hampshire first.

100. For 1996 delegate totals by state, see *National Party Conventions 1831–1996* (Washington, D.C.: Congressional Quarterly Press, 1997), 259–60. See also Jon Matthews, "Head Start for State in Presidential Race," *Sacramento Bee*, 29 September 1998, A1.

101. Dave Lesher, "Governor OK's Early Primary for 2000," *Los Angeles Times*, 29 September 1998, A1.

102. Matthews, "Head Start for State," A10.

103. In March 1996, Californians approved Proposition 198, a blanket primary initiative allowing voters to cast ballots for any candidate regardless of party registration. Both parties opposed the measure. On 20 February 1998, California state senator Jim Costa introduced SB 1999 for the purpose of changing the date of the California presidential primary from June to the first Tuesday in March. Governor Pete Wilson signed an amended version of the Costa bill into law on 28 September 1998. Responding to national party threats not to seat any delegates selected in a blanket presidential primary, state senator John Lewis moved to put a proposition on the November 1998 ballot that would restrict voting in the Democratic primary to registered Democrats and voting in the Republican primary to registered Republicans. Proposition 3 was defeated, 46 to 54 percent. According to New Hampshire's secretary of state, William Gardner, California's ballot coding procedure will be acceptable to the national parties. See "Presidential Primary Schedule Worries Secretaries of State," *Seiler Report*, 5 August 1998, 1; "Governor Approves Early Primary Elections Legislation," *Seiler Report*, 5 October 1998, 1; Mark Babarak, "Prop. 3 Loss May Leave State with No Presidential Nominating Role," *Los Angeles Times*, 5 November 1998, A11; and B. Drummond Ayers, Jr., "Political Briefing: Front-Loading 2000, a Headlong Rush," *New York Times*, 23 November 1998, A12.

104. Richard L. Berke, "Native Son Says He's Running, and Few Are Happy about It," *New York Times*, 19 February 1999, A13.

105. For a discussion of the proposals for a system of regional or cluster primaries put forth by Congressman Albert Quie, Senator Robert Packwood, and others during the 1970s, see Austin Ranney, *The Federalization of Presidential Primaries* (Washington, D.C.: American Enterprise Institute for Public Policy Research, 1978).

106. Lesher, "Governor OKs Early Primary"; and Bill Jones, California secretary of state, "Jones Urges National Reform of Presidential Primary System," news release BJ98: 125, 17 November 1998.

CHAPTER FOUR

The *New* New Presidential Elite

by Jonathan Bernstein

IN 1976, Jeane Kirkpatrick undertook a study of what she called *The New Presidential Elite*. To find important players in presidential politics, she naturally turned to the place where they had always been found: the national nominating conventions. Like others who studied convention delegates, Kirkpatrick was concerned with the effects of reform on delegates. The key question was the extent to which the people chosen to represent their parties at the national conventions would be typical of the party rank and file.

What was less clear at the time than it is now is that party reform had removed the nominating process from the control of conventions. Presidential nominations are now contested by candidate campaign organizations and decided by the votes of large electorates. Those candidate campaign organizations are the "new" presidential elite. In this chapter, I look at the career paths of some of those who make up the pool of activists and professionals from which candidates recruit staff and supporters, asking whether elite political activists and campaign professionals are party loyalists or candidate loyalists.

Candidate-Centered Politics?

The major concern Kirkpatrick addressed was the possibility that the reformed parties would be too ideological.[1] Since that time, however, a different concern has dominated the literature: the possibility that the parties are no longer important actors in a political system dominated by the candidates. It is by now well documented that although formal party organizations are actively involved in general election campaigns, the bulk of the work is organized and carried out within the candidates' campaign organizations. As Leon Epstein has noted, "Candidate-centered organizations . . . [are] dominant in presidential campaigns."[2] What is not documented, but is nevertheless assumed in most discussions of campaigns, is that these organizations are a sign of candidate strength and independence from the parties.

Paul Herrnson summarizes the conventional wisdom (here, in the context of congressional elections):

> Candidates, not political parties, are the major focus of congressional campaigns, and candidates, not parties, bear the ultimate responsibility for election outcomes. . . . In the United States, parties do not actually run congressional campaigns nor do they become the major focus of elections. Instead, candidates run their own campaigns.
>
> Candidates are the most important actors in American congressional elections.[3]

The assumption that elite campaign professionals are not partisans is probably strongest for consultants. For Sandy Maisel, this took the form of surprise that the Republican National Committee (RNC) would turn for its new chair in 1989 to Lee Atwater, "a political consultant—the very essence of an institutional rival to party organization as an influence in the electoral process."[4]

More specifically, the untested assumption concerns the nature of candidate campaign organizations and those involved in them. Most writing on this topic pictures these organizations as basically extensions of the candidate—extra hands, feet, talent, and dollars, as loyal to the candidate as his or her own hands, feet, talent, and dollars. Those associated with candidate campaign organizations are assumed to be either personally loyal or hired guns who are willing to act as if they were personally loyal because they have no other political attachments. Such campaign organizations can therefore comfortably be referred to as "candidates" (as Herrnson does), since they are thought to be (in Epstein's words) "strongly personal campaigns conducted mainly by themselves and their closest associates."[5]

This, then, is one model of candidate campaign organizations: the candidate-loyalty model.[6] A quick glance at any presidential campaign, however, raises questions about the accuracy of this model. After all, even a presumably candidate-centered campaign such as George McGovern's in 1972 included many veterans of other candidates' campaigns, as well as a campaign manager (Gary Hart) with no previous ties to the candidate. And Jimmy Carter's candidate-centered campaign featured a pollster, Pat Caddell, who had worked for McGovern's campaign. Clearly, there is more to candidate campaign organizations than "closest associates."

An alternative to the candidate-loyalty model is that candidate campaign organizations are actually a species of party organization and are therefore likely to be composed of partisan activists and professionals. Such partisans might move between affiliations with formal party organizations and various candidates who share the party label, and they might also be found between campaign seasons on the staffs of elected officials from their party. This model jettisons the assumption that candidate campaign organizations are best thought of as extensions of the candidate; instead, it contends that candidates form complex organizations with a potential for multiple loyalties and motivations. I investigate here the possibility that candidate campaign organizations contain strong partisan elements.

Research Design and Methods

In this study, I examine the career paths of a group of elite activists and professionals: the forty-eight Democrats and forty-two Republicans chosen as *Campaigns & Elections* magazine's "Rising Stars" of 1988.[7] That is, I look at the question of partisanship from the perspective of individuals within campaigns rather than from the perspective of entire campaign organizations.[8]

Career paths furnish information about the behavior patterns of elite political activists and campaign professionals difficult to obtain from a snapshot of current officials. A sizable number of studies have focused on the attitudes of "party elites." In those cases, however, *party* was defined as formal party organizations, and people were surveyed if they held such positions as county party chair or convention delegate. For example, the Southern Grassroots Party Activists Project surveyed southern county party committee members and chairs, asking about both attitudes and behavior. While that project is certainly an important contribution, its conclusions may not hold for those within candidate campaign organizations—the very people most observers believe are crucial to campaigns.[9]

What kind of career paths would be generated by the two models of candidate campaign organizations? If the candidate-loyalist model is correct, it would be reasonable to expect loyalty to individual office-holders over multiple campaign cycles. Some might, of course, eventually move on to a second candidate, but at least there would be what might be called "sequential" candidate loyalty. Support over one election cycle would, for a successful candidate, continue as support while that person is in office and then resume as electoral support in a campaign for reelection or higher office. On the other hand, there would be no reason to expect an activist or professional who is a candidate loyalist to work for a party, hold a party position, or donate funds to parties, or to contribute to large numbers of other candidates.

What would career paths look like for activists and professionals if candidate campaign organizations are really subsets, along with formal party organizations, of a more broadly conceived party? Certainly, it would be reasonable to expect party activists and campaign professionals to move back and forth between positions with candidates and formal party organizations. Partisan violations would be extremely rare; those involved would choose candidates primarily on the basis of party label. Thus, GOP financial supporters would not be expected to support conservative Democrats but would embrace those same politicians if they switched parties. Essentially, the expectation is for broad party support. A Democratic press secretary might work directly for a Democratic presidential candidate in one election cycle, for the Democratic National Committee (DNC) in the next, then serve as communications director for a Democratic governor or spokesman for a government agency in a Democratic administration, and then set up his or her own shop as a consultant to Democratic candidates.

Of course, a further possibility exists that multiple models are true. It would hardly be surprising to come across partisan activists with a particularly strong attachment to a particular politician or professionals primarily committed to one politician but who are also, on occasion, willing to work for other politicians, but only for those of the same party.[10] Still, the analysis should be able to determine whether one or the other pattern is more common.

Candidate loyalists, then, are those who remain supporters of an individual candidate over an extended period of time. Evidence against the proposition that a Rising Star is a candidate loyalist would be multiple simultaneous loyalties, or a position in a formal party organization, or support for a formal party organization. Partisan loyalists are those who directly support formal party organizations *or* those who support many candidates within the same party. Partisan violations are strong evidence against party loyalty.

The people chosen as Rising Stars by *Campaigns & Elections* come from the worlds of electioneering and governing. They include lobbyists and policymakers, pollsters and campaign managers, party staff and party fund raisers. They are treated here as a sample of all campaign elites, with two reservations. As Rising Stars they are obviously atypical, in the sense that most people involved in campaigns do not call enough attention to themselves to be noticed by a national magazine. Nevertheless, they are still a group that can fairly be called representative of a larger population of campaign elites. For example, if Nikki Heidepriem of the political consulting firm of Foreman and Heidepriem is among the group examined, it is fairly likely that Carol Tucker Foreman of the same firm (not a Rising Star) might have had similar experiences. The magazine itself supports the view that this group is in some ways typical. When introducing the first list of Rising Stars in 1988, the editors observed, "*Campaigns & Elections*' list is somewhat subjective. More important, it is invariably limited by space constraints. Consequently, there may be other rising stars that we missed."[11] Moreover, it is reasonable to assume that in many ways, the Stars who rose in 1988 were basically similar to those who were ineligible because they had "risen" in 1984 or 1986, or to those who soared in 1990 or 1992.

Even if these ninety Rising Stars are representative of all elite activists and campaign professionals, *Campaigns & Elections* introduced a second constraint. The magazine deliberately chose partisans, entitling the twin articles "The Democratic Party's Rising Stars" and "The Republican Party's Rising Stars." There is certainly a bias in favor of partisanship. Is that a problem? Only to a limited extent. To begin with, the very fact that all these Rising Stars are explicitly identified as Republicans or Democrats is at least mild support for the proposition that candidate campaign organizations and formal party organizations are often best conceptualized as subsets of a more broadly defined party. Beyond that, however, the partisan nature of the lists does impose a limit to interpretation. Even if the data show that many of those who work in candidate campaign organizations have followed partisan career paths, we could conclude, at most, that some of those in candidate campaign organizations are party loyalists; there may be a second population of staff or supporters who are more candidate-loyal than partisan.

The question, then, is how large that "second population" might be. Even without a systematic study, it is fairly evident that its size is limited. At the highest level, the president's chief of staff appears no more likely to be a personal loyalist (such as Mack McLarty for Clinton, Hamilton Jordan for Carter, or H.R. Haldeman for Nixon) than a partisan (such as

Leon Panetta for Clinton, James Baker and Howard Baker for Reagan, or John Sununu for Bush).[12] A somewhat more systematic test of the proposition can be obtained by looking at those who attended a series of meetings of Bill Clinton's reelection team, as profiled by Richard Berke in the *New York Times*.[13] Of the eighteen Clinton insiders who were mentioned, only consultant Dick Morris had been involved in any of Clinton's campaigns in Arkansas. Three of the eighteen were Rising Stars (Mike McCurry from the 1988 group, and George Stephanopoulos and Bill Knapp from the 1991 list). Of the other fifteen, three were politicians themselves (Al Gore, Henry Cisneros, and Leon Panetta). Some of the rest were too old to have been Rising Stars, but it is easy to imagine their having qualified had such lists been compiled earlier than 1988; among these were media expert Bob Squier and Democratic strategist Ann Lewis, both of whom were veterans of numerous presidential and other campaigns. The rest have profiles similar to those of the Rising Stars—support for a variety of candidates (in this case, Democratic ones), either in campaigns or in office. The question, again, is whether the group selected for study here is essentially typical of all those involved at the high levels of presidential campaigns or whether the editors of *Campaigns & Elections* ignored a second, less partisan group. The evidence from the Clinton reelection campaign suggests that if such a group exists, it is not very large.[14]

The career paths of the Rising Stars have been reconstructed from public records, including the Lexis/Nexis database, Federal Election Commission (FEC) records, editions of the *Congressional Staff Directory* and *Federal Staff Directory*, and other sources, including the original articles themselves (see the appendix to this chapter). For most of the ninety members of the *C&E* class of 1988, this was sufficient to fill in the outlines of their careers, which are mapped through the 1996 campaign cycle. For a few, such as 1992 Clinton campaign manager James Carville and 1996 Dole campaign manager Scott Reed, much more detail was available. It is possible that for a small group, the public search may have omitted significant roles the Rising Stars have played. For example, few are reported as having served on campaign committees for individual candidates; it is possible that the search missed such items, since they are rarely reported in the press. Such omissions are unlikely to affect the results of the study, however, because it seems likely that the positions that are reported— either by the Rising Stars themselves in their entries in the directories or by the press in profile pieces—are central to their careers.[15]

The ninety Rising Stars were coded with respect to several positions; in each case, a positive coding indicates that the Star had held that position at some point in his or her career:

- position in a formal party organization: party chair, member of party committee, delegate to party convention
- staff of a formal party organization: staff for national, state, or local parties, including party legislative committees
- position in a candidate campaign organization: campaign chair or member of campaign committee
- staff of a candidate campaign organization
- consultant to a candidate campaign organization
- candidate or elected official
- governing role: staff of elected officials or political appointees
- member of a party-associated or allied organization; for example, chair of Emily's List or member of executive board of American Conservative Union
- staff of a party-associated or allied organization

The Rising Stars were also coded according to their campaign contributions to formal party organizations, political action committees, and candidates. Those who financially supported candidates directly were coded as donating to a single candidate, two to five candidates, or more than five candidates.

Campaigns & Elections' Rising Stars of 1988

Table 4.1 reports the various roles played by the "Rising Stars." They are most likely to have served as campaign staff (79 percent), followed by consultants (69 percent), governing staff (60 percent), and formal party organization staff (54 percent). Few have held formal party positions, such as delegate or state chair (12 percent) or analogous positions in candidate campaign organizations (3 percent).[16] Obviously, there is overlap; over the course of their careers, Rising Stars are serving in multiple roles.

It should be noted that *Campaigns & Elections* did an excellent job of selecting their rising stars. In 1988, none of the group had any significant ties to Bill Clinton, then governor of Arkansas, and few had ties to Bob Dole. By the 1996 campaign, this was no longer true. Several were involved in Dole's presidential campaign, including Scott Reed, the campaign manager, as well as Deborah Steelman, Linda DiVall, John Buckley, and Jill Hanson. When Dole fired his pollster in February 1996, both the fired pollster (Bill McInturff) and the replacement (Tony Fabrizio) were Rising Stars from 1988. On the Democratic side, Joan Baggett was White House political director from 1993 to 1995; she replaced Rising Star Rahm

TABLE 4.1   BACKGROUNDS OF THE RISING STARS

Position/Contribution	All Rising Stars (%)	Democrats (%)	Republicans (%)
Formal party position	12	15	10
Formal party staff	54	48	62
Candidate organization position	3	4	2
Candidate organization staff	79	81	76
Consultant	69	63	76
Candidate or elected official	4	4	5
Governing staff	60	58	61
Member, party-allied organization	12	19	5
Staff, party-allied organization	36	42	29
Donor to one candidate	13	17	10
Donor to two to five candidates	22	23	21
Donor to over five candidates	22	17	29
Donor to formal party organization	12	12	12
Donor to party-allied organization	17	20	12
Any FEC contribution	63	67	60

Emanuel, who remained at the White House in various positions. Baggett's deputy was also a Rising Star, Joe Velasquez. When Baggett left in 1995, among the rumored replacements was Wendy Sherman, who had worked in the Clinton State Department. Mike McCurry was White House spokesman, and David Strauss is on the vice president's staff. The Clinton campaign in 1992 featured Rising Stars James Carville, Stan Greenberg, Paige Gardner, Emanuel, Frank Greer, and Stephanie Solien. Don Foley was the manager of the 1996 Democratic National Convention.

The Rising Stars also made their mark in Congress. In 1988, none of them were associated with Newt Gingrich. By the time Gingrich ended his first term as Speaker, several, including Deborah Steelman, Linda DiVall, Ed Goeas, Nick Calio, and Wayne Berman, had been described in the press as Gingrich insiders. On the Democratic side, Rising Star Rosa DeLauro, a political consultant in 1988, is now a member of Congress from Connecticut.

Few Rising Stars have dropped entirely out of partisan politics. Of the eighty-nine still living (Otto Bos died in 1991), Katie Boyle has probably traveled the farthest from partisanship and politics. In 1988, she was a writer/producer with the media-consulting firm of Sipple: Strategic Communications, after previously serving in the press offices of the 1988 Dole campaign, Kit Bond (both Senate and campaign staffs), and U.S. Assistant Attorney General Lois Harrington. Later in 1988, she became a producer for CBS News, where she has worked on such programs as *48 Hours* and *Nightwatch*. For other Rising Stars, however, it is harder to say what constitutes a full break with partisan politics. For example, John Buckley (another press secretary), after leaving the National Republican Congressional Committee (NRCC) in 1989, had apparently avoided partisan politics except for occasional campaign contributions, working for several years as senior vice president for communications at Fannie Mae, the home-mortgage services company. When the Dole campaign faltered in the summer of 1996, however, Buckley took a leave from Fannie Mae to serve as Dole's communications director for the fall campaign.

At least on the surface, then, there is no question that the Rising Stars of 1988 fulfilled *Campaigns & Elections'* promise: their stars have risen. Ambition is not the focus here. The magazine also did not hesitate to call their Rising Stars Democrats and Republicans. Does further examination show their behavior to have been primarily partisan?

Candidate Loyalists

What would it mean for a political activist or campaign professional to be a candidate loyalist? Three measures of candidate loyalty are available. A strict test for long-term loyalty requires an attachment of ten years or longer to the same candidate or elected official. This test should capture those who have dedicated large portions of their careers to supporting a single politician. To qualify as a candidate loyalist under a looser conception, five years of continuous association with a single politician is the test. This measure would require, for example, that someone remain with a member of Congress for more than two full election cycles or with a governor for more than one full term. The loosest definition would require an activist or professional to have had a position or served on the staff of a candidate campaign organization or to have made campaign contributions to a single candidate. Only by this very loose measure do many of the Rising Stars qualify as candidate loyalists; indeed, nine out of ten have been attached to a single candidate at some point in their careers (see table 4.2). This indicates, as expected, that candidate campaign organizations are key actors in campaigns; whether partisan or not, most of the Rising Stars have had the experience of being part of such an organization. The two stricter tests yield very different results. Only 17 percent of the Rising Stars have spent at least five years attached to a single politician; when the ten-year test is applied, the number of Rising Stars displaying candidate loyalty shrinks to just four of the ninety. In other words, only four of the ninety have displayed long-term loyalty to a single candidate, but eighty have at times been associated with candidate campaign organizations.

TABLE 4.2   ARE RISING STARS CANDIDATE LOYALISTS?

	Percentage of Rising Stars Who Are Candidate Loyalists
Loosest definition: one-time association with a candidate campaign organization[a]	89
Loose definition: five-year minimum with a single politician[b]	17
Strict definition: ten-year minimum with a single politician[b]	4

[a] Association with a candidate campaign organization includes formal position or staff position and donation to exactly one candidate.
[b] Association with a politician includes formal position or staff position with a candidate campaign committee, staff position with an elected official, or donation to the candidate.

The measure of candidate loyalty that is appropriate depends on the question under consideration. Using the loosest measure, the data can support the proposition that campaigns are conducted by candidate campaign organizations—a proposition no one doubts. The five- and ten-year tests, however, help answer the question of whether those involved in such organizations are primarily loyal to a single boss. Again, only a small number of these Rising Stars seem to display such behavior.

Closer examination of the long-term candidate loyalists is revealing. Only one Rising Star has worked for a single candidate or elected official for at least five years but has not worked or contributed to a formal party organization or held an official party position. This was Otto Bos, who was a reporter in San Diego before going to work for then-mayor Pete Wilson; he remained with Wilson until just before his death in 1991, serving Mayor, Senator, and Governor Wilson and in each Wilson campaign. At the time of his death, Bos was planning to open a consulting firm with two other Wilson staffers. It is easy to imagine that he would have been heavily involved in Wilson's 1994 reelection campaign, as well as his short-lived presidential campaign in 1995. Bos was a member of the Republican Business and Professional Club, but otherwise he has no record of specifically party-oriented behavior. Bos, then, was exactly what is implied by the image of "candidate-centered" politics: his career was dedicated to a politician, not a party.

Of the other Rising Stars who showed long-term candidate loyalty, however, most seem to have been making (relatively) long-term stops in a career that was unfettered by such loyalty. For example, Rosa DeLauro began working for Christopher Dodd in 1979. She managed his campaign for the Senate, served as his chief of staff during his first term in the Senate, and then managed his reelection campaign. Before that, she had held a series of political and government jobs in New Haven; after her work for Dodd, she served as executive director of Emily's List for a year and then was elected to the U.S. House from Connecticut. Was DeLauro a Dodd loyalist, a party loyalist working temporarily for a particular Democrat, or just personally ambitious? All may be true, but it is unlikely that her primary motivation for political involvement has been supporting Christopher Dodd.

Only Don Foley (for Dick Gephardt), Tom Mason and Jann Olsten (for Rudy Boschwitz), and David Strauss (for North Dakota senator Quentin Burdick) approach the candidate loyalty demonstrated by Otto Bos, and even in these cases, each moved on after some time. Only Bos maintained exclusive loyalty.[17] That candidate connections extend beyond a particular job is likely. For example, Terry Michael, Paul Simon's press secretary from 1975 to 1979 and again during Simon's presidential campaign in 1987 and 1988, was widely reported to have attempted to spark a "Simon for Vice President" boomlet prior to the 1992 convention. But describing any Rising Star except Bos as exclusively or even primarily loyal to a single candidate or elected official does not seem justified by the evidence of their careers.

Party Loyalists

There are two ways of judging party loyalty. The first is by identifying those who have a positive affiliation with formal party organizations. Party loyalty can be indicated by formal party position, staff role for a formal party organization, or financial contribution to such an organization. By this measure, two-thirds (68 percent) of the Rising Stars qualify as party loyalists. If donations to five or more (same-party) candidates are also taken as evidence of party loyalty, then sixty-four of the ninety Rising Stars (71 percent) count as party loyalists.

While affiliation with a formal party organization is a strong sign of partisanship, perhaps even better evidence of party loyalty is the absence of partisan violation. Partisan violations are cases of Democratic Rising Stars working for or supporting Republicans, or GOP Rising Stars working for or supporting Democrats. Of the ninety, six have a record of at least one partisan violation. Three of these—all Republicans—involve campaign contributions to candidates of the other party (in these cases, Democrats). Of these, two are lawyer-lobbyists who contribute primarily to Republicans but who have occasionally given to Democrats. Wayne Berman, who has been described as a top GOP money raiser, has contributed to three Democrats—Senator Charles

Robb, Senator Lloyd Bentsen, and Richard Moore, a House candidate from North Carolina.[18] Nick Calio, a Gingrich insider, has contributed to over thirty Republican candidates, to the NRCC, and to the "New Republican Majority Fund"; he has also contributed to Democratic Senator Joseph Lieberman and members of the House Bill Richardson, Robert Matsui, and Daniel Rostenkowski. *Roll Call* has described Calio as follows:

> Nick Calio, President Bush's liaison to the House and a Gingrich insider, can play both sides of the aisle and is considered the paragon of the tax committee, which virtually all lobbyists must learn to navigate. He knew former Chairman Dan Rostenkowski (D-Ill.) well, say colleagues, and because of his ideological bent can work even more easily with the new chairman, Rep. Bill Archer (R-Texas).[19]

Certainly, the cases of Calio and Berman are difficult to interpret. Are they lobbyists primarily interested in being able to work with both Democrats and Republicans? Or are they partisan Republicans who occasionally stray?[20]

The third violation involving campaign contributions raises a different issue. Scott Mackenzie, a Republican political-financial consultant, has been treasurer or deputy treasurer for five different Republican national campaigns (Reagan in 1980 and 1984, Kemp in 1988, and Buchanan in 1992 and 1996). He has given occasional contributions to Republican candidates—but also has repeatedly donated money to a Democratic member of Congress, Frank Pallone of New Jersey.

Rising Star Paul Maslin has a single violation. A Democratic pollster for more than fifteen years, Maslin also polled for Ross Perot's presidential campaign in 1992. While this might not be quite as "traitorous" as working for a Republican, it is still clearly a partisan violation. Like the others, Maslin has not been punished in any visible way for his transgression. (It is certainly possible that he has received fewer references and less consulting work from Democratic formal party organizations, but if so, it has not been reported in the press.)

Geoff Garin presents a different case. Since 1978, Garin has been one of the most visible Democratic pollsters; he is currently president of Garin-Hart Strategic Research, the political arm of Hart Research. Between graduating from Harvard in 1975 and joining Peter Hart in 1978, however, Garin took a job as chief legislative assistant to Republican Senator John Heinz of Pennsylvania. Without further information, it is impossible to conclude much about this case, other than that Garin's career as a Democratic pollster certainly does not seem to have been harmed by his stint with Heinz. Whether or not Garin began as a partisan, he certainly appears to have become one. Heinz was a moderate Republican, but judging from his client list, Garin now applies a partisan, not an ideological, screen for clients.

Thad Garrett presents a very different case from any of the other five. The only African-American among the forty-two Republican Rising Stars, Garrett has worked for a number of Republicans, beginning with a college internship for a member of Congress from Ohio. He served on the staffs of former vice presidents Rockefeller and Bush and was a senior adviser to the Bush campaign in 1988 and the Republican National Committee in 1992. He was twice a delegate to the Republican National Convention and once ran (as a Republican) for the Ohio state legislature.

However, Garrett also served on the staff of Democratic Congresswoman Shirley Chisholm of New York and has made campaign contributions to a number of members of the Congressional Black Caucus, all of them Democrats. Explaining his service on Chisholm's staff, Garrett has said that he called and received approval from Ohio Republican leaders before taking the job.[21] Certainly, these partisan violations did not prevent him from succeeding within the Republican Party, or at least within the formal party organizations, as he demonstrated by winning delegate slots to national conventions, as well as positions in Republican administrations.

Not included in this record of partisan violations are ventures with members of the other party outside the realm of electoral politics. For example, several of the Stars have joined nonpartisan or bipartisan lobbying or public relations firms, and some of the consultants have worked together across party lines—but only when elections were not involved. Two Rising Star pollsters, Democrat Celinda Lake and Republican Ed Goeas, have teamed up for the past five years to produce a series of polls for use by the media, but they do not work together on behalf of candidates.[22] Such relationships are peripheral to the crucial issue of partisan violations. On those, the record is clear. The six cases detailed here suggest, on the whole, that party affiliation may occasionally be one of a complex variety of political and personal attachments. But complexities that strain the boundaries of party are the exceptions, not the rule. Eighty-four of the ninety Rising Stars have been completely loyal to their political parties.

Do those whom I have earlier classified as candidate loyalists violate the norms of party loyalty? Table 4.3 gives the answers for the five-year

TABLE 4.3   RELATIONSHIP BETWEEN CANDIDATE LOYALTY AND PARTY LOYALTY
AMONG RISING STARS

	Formal Party Connection[a]	
	Yes	No
Candidate loyalty (five-year minimum)	14	1
No candidate loyalty	50	25

[a] Formal party connection is formal party position, formal party staff, or donation.
Entries are number of Rising Stars in each group.

test of candidate loyalty. Of those Rising Stars who have supported a candidate or elected official for at least five years, more appear to be party-oriented than those who have not displayed long-term loyalty to a candidate—by a large margin. Two-thirds of those without long-term candidate affiliation have held a party position, worked as party staff, or donated money to a formal party organization. But of those who have been affiliated with a single politician for five years or longer, all but one (i.e., fourteen of fifteen) also have a formal party background. So it would be a mistake to assume that candidate loyalty is incompatible with party support; on the contrary, there is some evidence here that the same people support candidates and parties.[23]

Interparty Differences

Few major differences appear to exist in the career paths of Democratic and Republican Rising Stars (see table 4.1). Republicans in the *Campaigns & Elections* group have been somewhat more likely to be on the staffs of formal party organizations and to have been independent consultants. However, given that the "Rising Stars" are not an independent sample of all activists and campaign professionals, it is probably unwise to conclude anything about Republicans and Democrats in general from such limited data.[24] Although caution is necessary, a case can be made for the Democrats' stronger association with party-allied organizations and interest groups. In three separate measures—membership,[25] staff positions, and financial contributions—Democrats score higher than Republicans by fairly high margins. While it is certainly possible that this is a result of chance in the magazine's selection process, it may suggest that Democrats are more likely to utilize such organizations as Emily's List and the Rainbow Coalition than the Republicans are to be associated with such organizations as the American Conservative Union or the National Conservative Political Action Committee (NCPAC).

It is difficult to make any stronger claims regarding differences (or similarities) between the parties. In general, the evidence suggests the parties are roughly similar; no startling differences emerge from the data. For example, if Republicans primarily held official party positions, while Democrats were all staffers in Democratic candidate campaign committees, it would raise the possibility that formal party organizations were much more central to the Republican Party than to the Democrats. The data cannot rule out such possibilities, but neither do they suggest any such division.

Six Careers

While descriptive statistics paint a general picture of the Rising Stars of 1988 and lead to some important conclusions, it is hard to capture the flavor of the lives of campaign elites in such broad strokes. For a more vivid portrait of the new presidential elite, I turn to detailed profiles of six Rising Stars, three Democrats and three Republicans. I have selected these six for two reasons: (1) they have been sufficiently prominent that fairly detailed biographies are available, and (2) they illustrate the complexities of the categories under discussion. They also cover much of the range of electioneering specialties. Deborah Steelman is a policy expert. Linda DiVall is a pollster. Jann Olsten has been a generalist. Mike McCurry is a press secretary or spokesman. David Axelrod is a media consultant. Susan Estrich has been both a generalist and a policy expert. While it would be too strong to say that all are representative of their specialties, certainly their careers have been influenced by the norms of their specialties. Media experts and pollsters, for example, are likely to become independent consultants because they are able to serve multiple candidates (or organizations) at the same time, while a press secretary is generally limited to one boss at a time.[26]

Deborah Steelman

Deborah Steelman was born in February 1955 in the small town of Salem, Missouri.[27] She inherited her partisan orientation; her father, Dorman Steelman, was a GOP state chair in Missouri, as well as a Republican leader in the Missouri state house and a judge. Deborah Steelman did her undergraduate work at the University of Missouri and earned her J.D. there in 1978.

After a stint as a public defender in Kansas City, Steelman moved permanently into politics in the 1980 reelection effort of John Ashcroft, who was then attorney general of Missouri. Starting as a volunteer, she eventually became campaign manager for the future governor and senator, which earned her a job with the state government. Following a brief role as deputy director of the state's department of natural resources, Steelman embarked on her second major position: lobbyist with Missouri's office in Washington, which marked her transition from Missouri to national politics.

Lobbying for the state of Missouri didn't last long. In late 1981, Steelman began a brief career on Capitol Hill, serving as legislative director for moderate Republican Senator John Heinz of Pennsylvania. From there, it was on to a series of jobs in the Reagan administration: director of intergovernmental affairs at the Environmental Protection Agency under William Ruckelshaus (1982-83); White House office of intergovernmental affairs, first under Mitchell Daniels and then replacing him (1984-85); and associate director of human resources at the Office of Management and Budget under James Miller (1986-87).

Steelman left government in the summer of 1987, taking a lobbying position with a Washington law firm, Epstein Becker & Green. However, she soon returned to campaigning, first volunteering as chair of George Bush's advisory group on health policy in September 1987 and then as director of domestic policy for the Bush campaign (at which point she was noticed by *Campaigns & Elections*). Resuming her lobbying career after the election, she opened her own firm (The Law Offices of Deborah Steelman), which lobbies on a wide range of issues. President Bush recruited her to chair (from 1989 to 1991) the independent Quadrennial Advisory Council on Social Security and Medicare, which issued recommendations for reforming Social Security and health care financing. A Bush insider even though she never joined the administration, she was among those present at Camp David in August 1991 when Bush informed his staff and advisers that he would run for a second term. She then reprised her role as domestic issues adviser to Bush-Quayle '92.

Republican lobbyists no longer had a friend in the White House after 1992, and Steelman shifted her focus to Capitol Hill. Of course, as a lobbyist, Steelman already had a Hill presence. For example, in 1992 she attended a press conference for the Republican Majority Coalition, a moderate group of congressional Republicans. In 1993 and 1994, Steelman's efforts focused on defeating the Clinton health plan; her long list of industry clients included Aetna, Cigna, and Prudential. She worked closely with GOP House members Nancy L. Johnson and Christopher Shays, both of

Connecticut. After the Republican triumph in the 1994 elections, she became one of a group of GOP lobbyists who met regularly with Speaker Newt Gingrich.

Steelman has been a major donor to Republican campaigns, giving to more than thirty Republican presidential, Senate, and House candidates during the 1993–94 and 1995–96 cycles. She gave to incumbents and challengers, moderates (such as Massachusetts governor William Weld) and conservatives (such as Georgia senator Paul Coverdell). She also gave directly to party organizations; she is listed as donating to the RNC and both Republican Hill committees. And she contributed to GOP-aligned committees, including the Republican Network to Elect Women and Bob Dole's leadership PAC. She was one of eleven lobbyists to give more than $10,000 to congressional candidates in 1995, as well as one of five lobbyists who were among the cochairs of the Republicans' $8.5 million House-Senate dinner in June 1996.

In 1996, Steelman once again became involved in presidential politics, this time on behalf of the Dole campaign. First, she was named to Dole's eleven-member "Clinton Accountability Team," designed to attract media attention to the Republican view of the Clinton record, and then she was named RNC senior adviser for policy for the duration of the campaign.

If Deborah Steelman has ever held a formal position within the Republican Party, it has not been widely reported.[28] Her only direct staff position for the party was her 1996 role as an RNC policy expert, but even that was merely the result of the Dole campaign's cash drought between the primaries and the convention; she was working for the Dole campaign in all but name. However, it is clear that Steelman fits the model of party loyalist well. Throughout her career, she has worked for and supported only Republican candidates and elected officials, and though she certainly has forged close working relationships with many of them, she has not displayed long-term loyalty to any. She moved on from Ashcroft to Heinz to Reagan to Bush to Dole (with many stops along the way), apparently remaining on good terms with all but identified particularly with none. She has associated with moderates such as John Heinz and Nancy Johnson, mainstream Republicans such as Dole and Bush, and conservatives such as Reagan and Gingrich. And although she is not a member of the Republican National Committee, she has become a major GOP fund raiser. She appears regularly on television shows as an advocate of Republican policies, particularly on the issues of health care and entitlements.

Linda DiVall

Linda DiVall was born in August 1952 in Mt. Prospect, Illinois, a Chicago suburb.[29] After graduating from Arizona State University in 1974, she headed for Washington, D.C., where she began work doing survey research for the Republican National Committee. After five years, she moved over to the National Republican Congressional Committee as director of survey research and reapportionment; she remained at the NRCC, eventually as director of coalition development, until 1984. In 1984, she left the formal party structure and became president of American Viewpoint, a national polling firm in Alexandria, Virginia, where she has remained ever since.

Her firm has been extremely successful and is considered one of the leading Republican firms. DiVall does not work for Democratic candidates or party organizations. In 1994, she polled for five Republican gubernatorial candidates, six Senate candidates, and twenty-six House candidates; the numbers for 1996 were similar. She has also done plenty of work for Republican Party organizations and GOP-aligned groups. Among her clients in 1987 were the RNC, the NRCC, the National Republican Senatorial Committee (NRSC), the Republican Party of Virginia, and the Republican Governors Association. She polled for the NRCC after the Supreme Court's *Webster* decision on abortion and was part of a volunteer group assembled by RNC chair Lee Atwater to advise the Republican Party on redistricting in 1989. More recently, she was cited as polling for the Florida Republican Party in 1994. She was Speaker Newt Gingrich's pollster for his own House reelection campaigns and has been the pollster for two presidential campaigns: Bob Dole's in 1988 and Phil Gramm's in 1996. Later in 1996, she was among those giving advice to the Dole campaign.

While she is primarily a pollster, DiVall also boasts a prominent speaking career. She is among the Republicans most likely to be seen making the case for the party on television, where she is generally identified as a "Republican pollster." She has been a CBS election-night analyst and appears regularly on such shows as PBS's *Newshour* and CNN's *Crossfire*. Like Deborah Steelman, she was a member of Dole's "Clinton Accountability Team." DiVall has occasionally contributed financially to GOP campaigns, generally supporting one or two candidates in each election cycle; since 1988, she has contributed to six candidates for federal office. In the 1996 election cycle, she contributed to a GOP-aligned committee, "Wish List," which supports women who are Republican candidates.

Although she does not work for Democratic candidates, she has worked with Democratic pollsters. In 1993, she and Mark Mellman (another Rising Star) worked together, polling on behalf of insurance companies. And, in 1996, she and Rising Star Celinda Lake polled together for the League of Women Voters (a nonpartisan organization).

DiVall's career path is similar to those of the other Rising Star pollsters. Although not all of them started out working for a formal party organization, all of them did eventually set up shop for themselves or with partners. Obviously, she is not a candidate loyalist. Her behavior seems exactly what one would expect of a party loyalist. She worked directly for formal Republican Party organizations for ten years; in electoral politics, she works only for Republicans; she appears on television on behalf of Republicans; and she contributes financially to Republican candidates and organizations.

Jann Olsten

Jann Olsten was born in Long Lake, Minnesota, in May 1948. He graduated from Gustavus Adolphus College in 1970 and attended law school at William Mitchell in St. Paul. He practiced law in two Minnesota firms from 1974 to 1978.

While there is no record of Olsten's having had any political involvement before 1978, it is likely that he had been involved in politics in some way, because in that year he emerged as campaign manager of Rudy Boschwitz's improbable run for the U.S. Senate. When Boschwitz won, Olsten followed him to Washington, serving as chief of staff for the new senator from 1979 to 1982. Olsten then left Capitol Hill for a job in the Reagan administration as special assistant for the International Trade Administration, an agency within the Department of Commerce.

After only a few weeks at the ITA, Olsten returned to Minnesota to run Wheelock Whitney's unsuccessful campaign for governor. Following the campaign, he joined a law firm with offices in Minnesota and Washington. In 1984, instead of running Senator Boschwitz's reelection effort as campaign manager, he served as campaign chairman. In 1987, however, with Boschwitz at the helm of the National Republican Senate Committee, Olsten returned to electoral politics as that committee's executive director.

Since then, Olsten has returned to Minnesota, where he has had an active business career. In 1990, he again served as chairman of Boschwitz's reelection campaign. When David Durenberger retired from the Senate in 1994, the press in Minnesota speculated that Olsten might run for the seat himself, but he did not. While Olsten was considering that possibility, Boschwitz (who was also considered a possible candidate) publicly expressed support for an Olsten run.[30]

While his political activities have been fairly quiet since early in the 1994 election cycle, Olsten continues to make campaign contributions. As one might expect, he contributed to Rudy Boschwitz's comeback campaign for the Senate in 1996. He has also contributed to five different House candidates from Minnesota since the 1990 cycle and to three different Senate candidates: Bob Kasten of Wisconsin in 1992 and Slade Gorton of Washington and Spencer Abraham of Michigan in 1994.[31]

Olsten's career illustrates the complexity of sorting out partisan from candidate loyalty. On the one hand, at the national level, Olsten is a good example of candidate loyalty; he has been a campaign manager, campaign chair, chief of staff, and executive director for the same U.S. senator. On the other hand, his loyalty to Boschwitz led him to a party job, as executive director of the NRSC, and in that role, loyalty to Boschwitz meant advancing the goals of the Republican Party. At the same time, Olsten's role in Minnesota is more difficult to explain, at least on the basis of the information presented here. Is he best seen as a candidate loyalist, sticking with his sponsor, Boschwitz, over several election cycles? Would that explain his campaign contributions? Or would it be better to consider him part of a (moderate) faction within the Minnesota GOP? That might be consistent with his contribution patterns, as well as his reported personal electoral ambitions. If the latter, what separates a member of a party faction from a party loyalist? Is the former a subset of the latter, or are they different concepts?

Once we consider opening up the concept of party membership and loyalty beyond formal party organizations—an idea that certainly seems warranted from the cases of Steelman and DiVall—all of these questions become very relevant. At present, unfortunately, party theory is not sufficiently developed to answer such questions.

Mike McCurry

Mike McCurry was born in Charleston, South Carolina, in October 1954.[32] His family moved several times—to Pittsburgh, Lansing, and Chicago—before settling down in the San Francisco suburb of Redwood City in 1964. In 1968, he worked for Robert Kennedy's presidential campaign; he also walked precincts for his social studies teacher's city council campaign. He then attended Princeton University, graduating in 1976.

After writing press releases for Jerry Brown's presidential campaign during his senior year at Princeton, McCurry went to Washington, where he worked as press secretary for Senator Harrison Williams (from 1976 to 1981) and Senator Pat Moynihan (from 1981 through 1983). He moved on to John Glenn's presidential campaign in 1984.

In 1985, McCurry took a brief job as director of public affairs for a business association but returned to politics the next year as press secretary for Bruce Babbitt's presidential campaign. After that campaign folded, he served as press secretary for vice presidential candidate Lloyd Bentsen during the fall campaign. After the 1988 election, McCurry became press secretary for the Democratic National Committee, remaining there until 1990, when he went to work for a public relations firm. Once again, he did not stay away from electoral politics for long; in the 1992 presidential campaign, he served as press secretary for Bob Kerrey. Although as Kerrey's spokesman McCurry had been sharply critical of the Clinton campaign, he nevertheless joined the new administration as State Department spokesman. After two years there, he moved on to become White House press secretary.

McCurry has made two campaign contributions to federal candidates since 1988. He contributed to Bruce Babbitt's presidential campaign in 1988 and to the campaign of Kevin Sweeney, a House candidate in California, in 1992.

Mike McCurry's career is straightforward. Since graduating from college, he has served as spokesman for a series of Democratic candidates, elected officials, and formal party organizations, with only a few short interruptions in the private sector. Like DiVall's, his role seems to be providing a service to the party; while both DiVall and McCurry are presumably well-paid for their services, neither appears likely to become, for example, the chair of a state party—although both have worked on the staffs of formal party organizations. And in both cases, the support service is apparently being provided by someone who is clearly devoting a career to the party. The largest difference between them is probably that DiVall has financially exploited her partisan career as an entrepreneur, while McCurry has earned the more modest income of a high-level government employee.

David Axelrod

David Axelrod was born in New York in February 1955.[33] He worked for Robert Kennedy's Senate campaign in 1964 and John Lindsay's mayoral campaign the next year. Although Lindsay was a Republican, New York's party structure allowed Axelrod to avoid any GOP support. As he put it, "I worked out of Liberal Party headquarters, I didn't want to work for a Republican."[34]

Attending the University of Chicago, Axelrod became a journalist, eventually working for the *Chicago Tribune* for almost a decade after he graduated in 1976, and spending most of that time covering politics. The political beat ultimately led him out of journalism and into a political career. He left the *Tribune* when Paul Simon asked him to serve as press secretary for his 1984 campaign for the U.S. Senate. Axelrod eventually became the campaign manager.

Although Simon offered him a job in Washington, Axelrod stayed in Chicago, where he opened his own media-consulting firm. He soon became highly successful; in 1992, the *Tribune* called him "the premier political media consultant in the Midwest."[35] He has worked for almost every recently successful Illinois Democrat, from Mayors Harold Washington and Richard M. Daley to Senators Carol Moseley-Braun and Paul Simon, as well as for unsuccessful gubernatorial candidate Adlai Stevenson. He has been retained as an adviser to Mayors Washington and Daley between campaigns as well and has even listed Washington and Daley as his "Political Heroes."[36] Although Axelrod specializes in Midwestern races, he has worked for candidates in other parts of the nation, including Mario Cuomo in New York and Gray Davis in California. In presidential politics, he worked for Joe Biden and Paul Simon in 1988, Bill Clinton in the 1992 primaries, and the Clinton-Gore ticket in the 1992 general election. He has also created ads for the Democratic National Committee.

Axelrod occasionally contributes financially to Democratic candidates; in the four election cycles through 1996, he contributed to fifteen federal candidates and the Clinton-Gore 1996 presidential campaign. Despite the Midwestern focus of his business, his contributions have gone to campaigns all over the country, including Patrick Kennedy's race for a Rhode Island House seat in 1994, Josie Heath's race for a Colorado Senate seat in 1990, and Senator Bill Bradley's reelection campaign in New Jersey in 1990. In 1995, he also contributed to the "DNC Services Corporation," an arm of the Democratic National Committee.

Like Mike McCurry, David Axelrod was interested in both journalism and active participation in politics, and through the 1984 campaign, his career path looked similar to McCurry's. However, rather than choosing a Washington career and staff positions, Axelrod became an electioneering businessman. McCurry has worked for a relatively small number of Democrats; Axelrod has worked for dozens. In one sense, it is Axelrod who seems the more partisan of the two: McCurry's career is marked more by serial loyalty to individual candidates or elected officials (all of whom are Democrats), while Axelrod tries to win elections for entire slates of candidates. On the other hand, McCurry's serial loyalty brought him to work directly for the Democratic National Committee; Axelrod has never been directly employed by a formal party organization, although he has contracted with such organizations and contributed to them. Cheryl Lavin's profile in the *Chicago Tribune* raised the issue of party loyalty. Axelrod's response is revealing: "In a primary, you fight to define your party. But I'm a partisan; in a general election I support the Democratic candidate. And just because I work for a candidate doesn't mean I belong to them for life. If someone disappoints me, I move on."

While Axelrod and DiVall are typical consultants in that each has worked with many different candidates, they are atypical in another way: both have stayed put within their own firms. Their experiences tend to understate the degree to which consultants have close ties with each other over time. For example, Rising Star Celinda Lake worked for Peter Hart Research in the mid-1980s (along with Geoff Garin); in 1988, she formed a partnership with Rising Star Stan Greenberg; in 1992, she left Greenberg's Analysis Group and went to work with Rising Stars Mark Mellman and Ed Lazarus at Mellman-Lazarus-Lake; and finally, in 1994, she set up her own firm.[37] Of course, consultants work with each other all the time even without forming businesses together. Major pollsters and media specialists, working for a variety of different candidates, probably know each other better than they do the people in any specific candidate campaign organization.

Susan Estrich

Susan Estrich was born in December 1952 in Lynn, Massachusetts, and grew up in Swampscott, another suburb of Boston.[38] During high school, she worked her neighborhood for the reelection campaign of a local member of the House, Michael Harrington. She received a B.A. from Wellesley College in 1974 and a J.D. from Harvard in 1977, and then clerked at the U.S. Court of Appeals and the Supreme Court.

Following her clerkships, she became involved in Edward Kennedy's 1980 presidential campaign, serving as that campaign's deputy national issues director; she drafted amendments to the Democratic platform designed to woo Carter delegates to the more liberal Kennedy. She spent some time after the campaign on Senator Kennedy's Washington staff but left Washington for a faculty position at Harvard Law School. She remained fully immersed in Democratic Party politics, however. She was an unpaid adviser to Michael Dukakis's comeback campaign for governor from 1981 to 1982, and before the 1984 presidential campaign, she served on the Technical Advisory Committee to the DNC's Commission on Presidential Nominations. Chosen by Geraldine Ferraro as the executive director of the Democrats' platform committee for the 1984 convention, she then served as a senior policy adviser to the Mondale-Ferraro campaign.

Meanwhile, in June of 1984, Estrich was elected to a vacancy on the Democratic National Committee. She remained a DNC member through 1988 and was selected as a delegate to both the 1984 and 1988 Democratic National Conventions. She was the chair of the drafting committee for the Democrats' "Fairness Commission" in 1985–86 and was a member of the compliance review commission charged with enforcing the new nominating rules in 1986. Estrich also served a term as president of the Boston chapter of the ACLU in 1985–86; she has served on the national boards of both the ACLU and Common Cause (the latter from 1983 to 1989). After a brief period of practicing law with a Los Angeles firm, she joined the Dukakis presidential campaign in 1987, eventually becoming campaign manager.

Since the Dukakis campaign, Estrich's role has completely changed. Her active involvement in both formal party organizations and campaigns has been minimal, and while there was speculation that she would have a job in the Clinton administration, nothing developed. She has remained politically active as an attorney, filing briefs in various cases of interest (e.g., abortion cases). In 1994, she joined a public committee dedicated to defending President Clinton against Whitewater charges. But for the most part, her role has been completely different from her pre-Dukakis career: Estrich has become a pundit. At various times, she has been an analyst for the KTLA morning news in Los Angeles, a radio talk show host in Los Angeles, a contributing editor to the *Los Angeles Times* "Opinion" section, and a once-a-week columnist for *USA Today*. Her visibility is high enough that she was selected as one of *Newsweek*'s "Overclass 100" in 1995. A search of Federal Election Commission records revealed only one Estrich campaign contribution since 1988: a contribution in support of her former boss, Senator Edward Kennedy, for his closely contested 1994 race.

What is immediately striking about Estrich, compared with the other five Stars discussed here, is her experience as a member of formal party organizations; she served as a member of the Democratic National Committee for four years and as a delegate to two Democratic National Conventions. She is, in short, the type of person on whom traditional party studies have focused when they examine party activists. That aside, however, her career looks much like the careers of many other Rising

Stars. While she has never been a campaign consultant, she has served on the staffs of candidates and elected officials; indeed, she has displayed more loyalty to a particular elected official (Kennedy) than someone such as DiVall has shown.

Discussion: Rethinking Party

In describing the behavior of the *Campaigns & Elections* Rising Stars, two categories were used: candidate loyalists and party loyalists. I have shown that while temporary employment by or support for a particular candidate or elected official is quite common, long-term loyalty is rare for this group of activists and campaign professionals. And, at least at the national level, such behavior appears to be the norm, as can be seen from the career paths of the many Rising Stars who worked for the Clinton and Dole campaigns and the Clinton administrations and who made up the ranks of Gingrich insiders. While it is likely that many activists and campaign professionals may be originally inspired to enter politics by a single politician, and while it is certainly possible that they may be extremely loyal to a candidate campaign committee during their association with it, long-term loyalty to single politicians does not appear to be an important factor in the behavior of campaign elites. Instead, the Rising Stars followed career paths best described as loyal to their parties. Many worked for or otherwise supported formal party organizations. Most worked for or otherwise supported multiple candidates from their party. And few have committed partisan violations.

Before considering some of the theoretical implications of the party-loyalty model, brief consideration should be given to a third model of campaign professionals, which holds that they are best thought of as mercenaries, willing to work for whoever or whatever will pay them. As Larry Sabato put it in his book on consultants, "They are even less concerned with issues, the parties, and the substance of politics than their clients. They are businessmen, not ideologues."[39]

The problem with this third model, from the perspective of this analysis, is its failure to spell out any clear, testable propositions about how such motivations would affect the behavior of campaign professionals. The problem is that for mercenaries, career trajectories will be determined by the market, and the market will be shaped by the political culture. For example, a nonpartisan pollster might choose to work only for Democrats if both Democratic and Republican candidates only employed pollsters who displayed partisan loyalty. It is even possible to excuse campaign contributions, which would seem a clear sign of a lack of entrepreneurial greed, by supposing that those who financially support candidates (or even parties) reap rewards larger than the cost of the contributions.

Therefore, the evidence here cannot determine whether the Rising Stars are sincere party (or candidate) loyalists or are really in it only for the money and are merely acting as if they were loyal to their parties. What is significant is the possibility that in order to have influence in campaigns, it apparently helps to be a party loyalist; and, in order to help their party, people must become campaign professionals or serve on the staff of governing politicians. A *requirement* that party activists become party professionals places rather severe constraints on the permeability of parties; those without a professional service to offer, or without the intense interest demanded of careers in politics, may find it difficult to participate meaningfully.

Behavior and Attitudes

The method of analysis pursued in this chapter may be vulnerable to the charge that short-term behavior within each campaign is more important than long-term partisan loyalties. In other words, an activist or campaign professional may have an extremely partisan orientation, and therefore work only for formal party organizations or candidate campaign organizations of party candidates, but still act as a candidate loyalist during the time he or she is associated with a campaign.

In a decentralized, nonhierarchical party, it is sometimes difficult to tell when the interests of the party as a whole diverge from the interests of one of the party's candidates. It is easy to imagine that in the heat of a campaign, members of a candidate campaign organization—no matter how loyal they may be to party in the abstract—tend to equate success in that particular campaign with party success, even in a primary; it is easy to imagine even the most jaded ignoring for the time any doubts that this particular candidate is the best hope for the party in that particular district. And, given the nature of American parties, no one exists who can authoritatively argue otherwise. That is, there are no party hierarchies to dictate what the "good of the party" might be.

What remains unclear is whether either the short-term nature of elite "loyalty" to candidates or the long-term nature of loyalty to parties is relevant to the day-to-day functioning of campaigns. It seems unlikely that anyone faced with a task such as writing a polling questionnaire or a piece of direct mail would mull over whether to do it as a Republican or as a partisan of Jones for Congress. Indeed, it is far from certain that there is a Democratic or Republican way to write a poll question or a speech. On the other hand, it is quite possible that if Democrats and Republicans constitute separate networks—separate webs of connected activists and professionals—then each network may develop separate norms and behavior patterns. For example, it seems likely that a pollster who has previously worked for the DNC will have a tendency to poll for cleavages that "work for Democrats," which in turn could influence Democratic candidates to take similar stands on policy issues. It also seems likely that networked parties open up other possibilities for cooperation. When staff members of a presidential campaign need to recommend positions on public policy, they may follow their personal contacts from previous campaigns in deciding which elected officials or think tanks will be helpful. If those contacts are partisan and have had partisan careers, then campaigns will enlist primarily partisan resources in choosing issue positions. The present study cannot reach conclusions about how these contacts operate, but it does strongly suggest that such a web of interrelationships exists within each party.[40]

National Parties

Forty years ago, V.O. Key explained the concept of national parties by quoting President Eisenhower: "Now, let's remember, there are no national parties in the United States. There are forty-eight state parties, then they are the ones that determine the people that belong to those parties. . . . We have got to remember that these are state organizations." Or, as Key summarized, "More than a tinge of truth colors the observation that there are no national parties, only state and local parties."[41] The basic organizational structure of the national parties was already in place at the time, but its components—a national committee and its chair, the quadrennial national conventions, and the separate legislative elections committees—were basically empty shells, temporarily active during elections seasons but inconsequential even then. The most meaningful action of the parties as national bodies, of course, was the nomination of the presidential candidates, but this was done in a national gathering of state and local parties that shared the same label, rather than as a meeting of a national organization.

Key's "tinge of truth" is gone, of course; the national party institutions are no longer empty shells, as Herrnson and others have demonstrated.[42] The present study of the Rising Stars shows that the new national parties have also developed outside of the formal party organizations. The Stars are not only party elites; they are *national* party elites, part of a network of governing and electioneering Democrats or Republicans who concern themselves with national matters—gaining partisan control of Congress and the White House, and then governing or influencing national policymakers. Indeed, unlike the state and local party notables who gathered to bargain over nominations at the pre-reform national conventions, people like James Carville and Frank Greer, Scott Reed and Linda DiVall are truly a *presidential* elite. It is impossible to imagine a serious presidential candidate running, winning, and then governing without the help of these Rising Stars or others like them.

The present study only hints at whether the description of these national Rising Stars is generalizable to state or local parties. There is some evidence of an intersection between the two, since many of the national Stars have strong state or local ties. David Axelrod, for example, specializes in Chicago politics and more generally in Midwestern politics. While he is certainly not a creature of the Chicago Democratic machine, he has worked for both Mayor Washington and the current Mayor Daley, as well as with President Clinton; he clearly has ties to both the Chicago organization and the national Democratic network. Ed Brookover, David Strauss, and Jill Hanson have all been executive directors of state party organizations, and although they have become Washingtonians, all of them presumably still have ties to those states. Moreover, to the extent that local and state party networks feature the same type of circulation of campaigners seen here, anyone who has worked on congressional campaigns is likely to have had at least minimal exposure to local and state activists.

Party Loyalists

This study has advanced loose and strict criteria for defining candidate loyalists, but it has presented only one standard—affiliation with a formal party organization—for defining a party loyalist. About two-thirds of the Rising Stars qualified as party loyalists under that criterion. A strong argument can be made, however, that this is the wrong way of determining party-oriented behavior. If parties are *not* equivalent to formal party organizations, then affiliation with such institutions cannot be the threshold for party affiliation. Instead, any party affiliation, through formal party organization *or* through same-party campaigns, could be considered an indicator of party-oriented behavior.

What would need to be true to make such a broad description accurate? Primarily, it would be necessary to show that candidate campaign organizations are party-oriented. The data presented here begin the job of making that case. They have demonstrated two important factors, or rather one factor seen from two perspectives. From the perspective of the campaign, it is evident that in many candidate campaign organizations, at least some staff and officials (and virtually all consultants) are temporary loyalists drawn from a network of long-term party activists and campaign professionals. And from the perspective of this party elite, any particular campaign is a step along a partisan road.

At the very least, this shows that party ties exist beyond the type of party-performed services generally discussed in studies of parties that are limited to the formal organizations.[43] It points in the direction of a broader idea of party, one that encompasses both formal organizations and partisan networks that extend into candidate campaign organizations and into Congress and the White House. For this sort of party, answers about party activity are as likely to be found in the interactions between activists and campaign professionals over time as they are within the organizational charts of formal party organizations. Questions about whether presidential candidates have been nominated with party support would be answered by examining the partisan ties of their supporters, including paid staff and consultants, volunteers, and fund-raising networks. Candidate loyalties may be rivals to these parties, but the simple fact of organized campaigns directed by the candidates is no sign of party weakness. Parties of this type are as strong as the links that integrate candidates and elected officials along partisan lines, and by that measure American parties are in good health.

Appendix: Sources of Biographical Data

Electronic Sources

The basic sources of biographical information for the ninety Rising Stars were Lexis-Nexis searches of the "News" library. While there is some bias to such searches in that not all newspapers are available through Lexis-Nexis, most major national papers and magazines are available. Particularly helpful for tracing careers in Washington were *Roll Call*, the *National Journal*, and *Campaigns & Elections* (supplemented by a search through printed versions of *Campaigns & Elections* from its first edition in 1980 until its inclusion in Lexis-Nexis in October 1989).

Information on campaign contributions is available in Lexis-Nexis through the campaign finance file in the campaign library. Lexis-Nexis records include contributions to candidates beginning in the 1988 campaign cycle. For the 1995–96 cycle, those records are supplemented by

FECINFO (www.tray.com/fecinfo), which has Federal Election Commission records of individual donations to candidates, parties, and political action committees.

Printed Sources

Printed sources include the following:

- *Congressional Staff Directory*, various editions 1975 through 1996 (Mount Vernon, Va.: Staff Directories, Ltd.);
- *Federal Staff Directory*, various editions 1982 through 1996 (Mount Vernon, Va.: Staff Directories, Ltd.);
- Jeffrey B. Trammell and Steve Piacente, eds., *The Almanac of the Unelected: Staff of the U.S. Congress 1994* (Washington, D.C.: Almanac Publishing, Inc., 1994); and
- *Who's Who in America*, 47th ed. (New Providence, N.J.: Marquis Who's Who, 1992).

Acknowledgments

An earlier version of this chapter was presented at the annual meeting of the American Political Science Association, San Francisco, 29 August–1 September 1996. I am grateful for the comments of Nelson W. Polsby, Bruce Cain, Laura Stoker, and Ben Highton.

Notes

1. Jeane Kirkpatrick, *The New Presidential Elite: Men and Women in National Politics* (New York: Russell Sage Foundation, 1976). Similar concerns about "amateurs" and "purists" have been expressed by James Q. Wilson, *The Amateur Democrat* (Chicago: University of Chicago Press, 1962); and Aaron Wildavsky, "The Goldwater Phenomenon: Purists, Politicians, and the Two Party System." *Review of Politics* 17 (1965): 386–413.
2. Leon Epstein, *Political Parties in the American Mold* (Madison: University of Wisconsin Press, 1986), 110.
3. Paul S. Herrnson, *Congressional Elections: Campaigning at Home and in Washington* (Washington, D.C.: CQ Press, 1998), 6–7.
4. L. Sandy Maisel, "The Evolution of Political Parties: Toward the 21st Century," in *The Parties Respond*, ed. L. Sandy Maisel (Boulder, Colo.: Westview Press, 1990), 310. For more characterizations of "candidate-centered" campaigns that assume a rivalry between candidate campaign organizations and parties, see Epstein, *Political Parties*, especially 109–13; Larry J. Sabato, *The Rise of Political Consultants* (New York: Basic Books, 1981); John H. Aldrich, *Why Parties?* (Chicago: University of Chicago Press, 1995), 159–274; Barbara G. Salmore and Stephen A. Salmore,

Candidates, Parties, and Campaigns (Washington, D.C.: CQ Press, 1989), especially 39–62, 215–75; and Alan Ware, *Breakdown of Democratic Party Organization 1940–1980* (Oxford: Clarendon Press, 1985).

5. Epstein, *Political Parties*, 112.

6. A careful reading of the literature reveals that there are, in fact, two very different notions of "candidate-centered" campaigns. I deal here with the implicit assumption that candidate campaign organizations are composed primarily of candidate, not party, loyalists. A second meaning of candidate-centered campaigns focuses on the content of campaign messages, as opposed to the identity of the messengers, claiming that candidates advertise themselves without reference to party labels. For this meaning, see Martin P. Wattenberg, *The Rise of Candidate-Centered Politics* (Cambridge, Mass.: Harvard University Press, 1991).

7. *Campaigns & Elections*, the professional magazine of the electioneering industry, occasionally recognizes about a hundred young activists and campaign professionals as "Rising Stars." The first such lists appeared in 1988 and were subtitled "the forty-eight [forty-two] people who over the past four years have entered the party's inner sanctums." See "The Democratic Party's Rising Stars," *Campaigns & Elections*, July 1988, 22–6; and "The Republican Party's Rising Stars," *Campaigns & Elections*, August/September 1988, 34–7.

8. Elsewhere, I use the other perspective, examining the backgrounds of those in congressional campaigns; see Jonathan Bernstein, "Partisanship and Candidate Loyalism in Candidate Campaign Organizations" (paper presented at the annual meeting of the Western Political Science Association, Los Angeles, March 1998). I find there that candidate campaign organizations in House races are highly partisan, especially in the most competitive races.

9. Charles D. Hadley and Lewis Bowman, eds., *Southern State Party Organizations and Activists* (Westport, Conn.: Praeger, 1995). See also Warren E. Miller and M. Kent Jennings, *Parties in Transition: A Longitudinal Study of Party Elites and Party Supporters* (New York: Russell Sage Foundation, 1986); and Alan I. Abramowitz and Walter J. Stone, *Nomination Politics: Party Activists and Presidential Choice* (New York: Praeger, 1984).

10. In decentralized, nonhierarchical parties, it may be extremely difficult to distinguish between candidate loyalty, on the one hand, and loyalty that is primarily focused on the party but secondarily focused on a faction within the party. For example, in Virginia, the leading GOP moderate candidates in recent elections have been Marshall Coleman and John Warner, and Warner has actively supported Coleman's campaigns. An activist who worked for Coleman and Warner in successive election campaigns may have done so as an avid moderate Republican or as a Warner loyalist.

11. "Democratic Party's Rising Stars," 22.

12. Just as Clinton included the apartisan consultant Dick Morris in his 1996 reelection team, presidents have been known to reach across the aisle to staff their administrations. These exceptions are exceedingly rare. Under Bill Clinton, they consisted of one experienced presidential adviser (David Gergen, briefly a White House aide during Clinton's first term) and one Republican senator (William Cohen, secretary of defense during Clinton's second term). The most prominent Democrat in the Reagan administration, Jeane Kirkpatrick, became a Republican.

13. Richard L. Berke, "After Hours at the White House, Brain Trust Turns to Politics," *New York Times*, 21 July 1996, A1.

14. A similar result is found in an early profile of the Clinton administration; see Owen Ullmann, "Who Has Clinton's Ear Now?" *Washingtonian*, January 1994, 403–11.

Ullmann, a journalist, describes the president's associates using the metaphor of a series of larger and larger circles. Of those in the innermost circle, three were probably best described as personal loyalists (Hillary Clinton, Bruce Lindsey, and Mack McLarty); one, David Gergen, was a Republican, and two were partisan Democrats with careers separate from Clinton's before the 1992 campaign (Al Gore and George Stephanopoulos). The next circle is entirely composed of partisans: Robert Rubin, Lloyd Bentsen, Robert Reich, Roger Altman, Anthony Lake, Ira Magaziner, Warren Christopher, and Strobe Talbott. While some of these partisans (Reich and Talbott, for example) had long personal ties to the president and one (Lake) had worked in a previous Republican administration, none was introduced to Democratic politics by Bill Clinton. Only three Rising Stars were among the forty advisers mentioned in Ullmann's article (Rahm Emanuel from 1988, George Stephanopoulos from 1991, and Alexis Herman from 1994). That so few were mentioned can be attributed mainly to two factors: most of the forty Clinton advisers were older than the Rising Stars, and many (nine of the forty) were politicians who had previously been elected to office, rather than campaign professionals. As with the reelection team in 1996, the Clinton advisers in 1994 were primarily drawn from traditional Democratic sources, not from Clinton's previous campaigns and gubernatorial administrations. Only five Arkansans—McLarty, Lindsey, Hillary Clinton, Carol Rasco, and Webster Hubbell—were among the forty advisers discussed in that article.

15. Several other omissions are possible. Rising Stars' FEC contributions were compiled, but not donations to state or local candidates and organizations. For those Rising Stars for whom information is comparatively scarce, it is possible that some brief jobs went unreported, although in no case are there obvious gaps in any of the careers studied here. For example, a Rising Star may have temporarily left a job to volunteer or consult with a campaign, without any press notice of the departure or return to the permanent job. In general, such omissions would not affect this study's findings. The tests for long-term candidate loyalty would not be affected. The most likely effect of missing information would be to bias the study against party, as opposed to candidate, loyalty; here, candidate loyalty is essentially the null hypothesis, and therefore missing information would tend to support the null hypothesis against the tested hypothesis of party loyalty.

16. As described more fully in the chapter appendix, information on Rising Star career paths was collected from two kinds of sources: self-reported descriptions, such as those in the *Congressional Staff Directory*, and news reports. It is possible that some Rising Stars have served in other roles, such as party precinct committee chairs or on candidate campaign committees, but that reporters did not find these positions newsworthy nor did the Stars consider these roles worthy of inclusion in their self-descriptions. If this is the case, however, it seems reasonable to assume that those roles had only limited importance.

17. Of these, only Mason did not meet the strict test of candidate loyalty. He did have a long association with Boschwitz, but it was not continuous.

18. Michael Duffy, "Campaign '96 Briefing: The Money Chase; The Secret Primary of 1995 Is a Mad Dash to Raise at Least $100,000 Every Day for the Rest of the Year," *Time*, 13 March 1995, 93; and Kim Masters and Roxanne Roberts, "Vested Interests: GOP's Fete Cats; The Rewards of Mixing Business with Politics," *Washington Post*, 10 February 1995, B1.

19. Alice A. Love, "A Rolodex of GOP's Most Influential Lobbyists, Committee by Committee," *Roll Call*, 23 January 1995, B6.

20. See also Alice A. Love, "Big-Giving Lobbyists Ante Up Campaign Cash for Members," *Roll Call*, 22 January 1996, Special Welcome Back Congress Section.

21. Jacqueline Trescott, "The Power and the Pulpit: The Well-Planned Ascent of Thaddeus Garrett Jr.," *Washington Post*, 22 March 1981, G1.

22. J. Jennings Moss, "Pollsters See from Both Sides Now: Bipartisan Team Touts Honesty," *Washington Times*, 27 December 1993, A4. Partisan "violations" dating back to college years or earlier are also ignored; at least two of the ninety switched parties as young people, after already having volunteered in campaigns for their original party.

23. Three of the four ten-year candidate loyalists are also party loyalists. For the loosest definition of candidate loyalty (those who have had any affiliation with a candidate campaign organization), 68 percent have also worked as party staff, held a position with a formal party organization, or donated to parties, compared with 70 percent of those who have not had an affiliation with a candidate campaign organization.

24. Possible sources of bias include the status of the Republicans as the "in party" with respect to the White House before the Rising Stars were selected; the Republicans' status at the time as the "out party" in Congress, especially in the House; and the results of the 1988 campaign, which presumably boosted the careers of the many Bush supporters selected but may have harmed the careers of many Dukakis supporters.

25. Sources of biographical information almost certainly underreport these memberships. Several sources depend on self-reporting (for example, biographical sketches in the *Federal Staff Directory*), and visual inspection of these sources suggests that some people spend more time filling out spaces for "Memberships" than others; that is, it is not unusual to find no memberships reported in such sources, even though other sources indicate such memberships exist. Furthermore, while elite job changes tend to be reported in specialized press sources, such as *Campaigns & Elections* or *Roll Call*, memberships are not reported, even such high-level positions as chair of a political action committee. On the other hand, it may be reasonable to assume some correlation between the rate at which these positions or memberships are self-reported or mentioned in news articles and the importance placed on them.

26. For more on the various specialties of electioneering, see Sabato, *Rise of Political Consultants*.

27. Sources of special help in this profile include Paul Blustein, "Deborah Steelman on the Women's Appeal: The Domestic Advisor to the Bush Campaign, Stalking the Female Vote," *Washington Post*, 8 August 1988, C1; and Dick Kirschten, "West Wing Player Takes a Swing at OMB Job," *National Journal*, 15 February 1986, 400. In addition, this and the other five extended Rising Star profiles rely on the general sources detailed in the chapter appendix.

28. This includes Steelman's self-description in the *Federal Staff Directory*; if she held any formal party position, she did not consider it important enough to mention.

29. Specific sources for DiVall include Howard Kurtz and Alexandra Siegel, "Capitol Gains: Women in Politics," *Working Woman*, February 1992, 66.

30. Tim Curran and Glenn R. Simpson, "It's D-Day for Senate Retirements in Arizona, Minnesota: Candidates Swarming," *Roll Call*, 20 September 1993, 1.

31. Spencer Abraham of Michigan was a member of the Rising Stars group of 1991; see Bill Whalen, "Rising Stars 1991," *Campaigns & Elections*, March 1991, 22–31.

32. Specific sources for McCurry include David Ellis and Garry Clifford, "Michael McCurry, Sharp Wit and Tongue: The White House Press Spokesman Talks the Talk,"

Time, 23 October 1995, 57; Todd S. Purdum, "Michael Demaree McCurry: Articulate Defender," *New York Times*, 6 January 1995, A19; and Geraldine Baum, "The Smooth Operative: Mike McCurry May Have Just What the President Needs in Press Secretary—a Way with Words," *Los Angeles Times*, 22 December 1994, E1.

33. Specific sources for Axelrod include "Movers and Shakers: David Axelrod," *Campaigns & Elections*, July 1994, 57; and Cheryl Lavin, "Hooked on Politics: Media Consultant David Axelrod Now Shapes the News instead of Reporting It," *Chicago Tribune*, 25 March 1992, C1.

34. Lavin, "Hooked on Politics."

35. Ibid.

36. "Movers and Shakers: David Axelrod."

37. Stuart Rothenberg, "Change Is Good: The Consultant Soap Opera," *Roll Call*, 13 March 1995, 15.

38. Specific sources for Estrich include Robin Toner, "Susan Estrich Brings Assurance and Toughness to Dukakis Drive," *New York Times*, 6 May 1988, A18; Mary Battiata, "Susan Estrich and the Marathon Call: A Seasoned Player, Stepping in to Manage Dukakis' Campaign," *Washington Post*, 16 October 1987, D1; and Bella Stumbo, "Dukakis Aide Estrich: She's More than Most Can Manage," *Los Angeles Times*, 4 June 1988, A1.

39. Sabato, *Rise of Political Consultants*, 6.

40. Jo Freeman's work indicates that the parties have different internal cultures. This tends to confirm the idea that they are separate sets of close networks and may even suggest consequences stemming from their differences. See Jo Freeman, "The Political Culture of the Democratic and Republican Parties," *Political Science Quarterly* 101 (fall 1986): 327–56.

41. V.O. Key, *Politics, Parties, and Pressure Groups*, 4th ed. (New York: Thomas Y. Crowell, 1958), 361n, 362.

42. Paul Herrnson, *Party Campaigning in the 1980s* (Cambridge, Mass.: Harvard University Press, 1988); and idem, "Party Strategy and Campaign Activities in the 1992 Congressional Elections," in *The State of the Parties: The Changing Role of Contemporary American Parties*, ed. Daniel M. Shea and John C. Green (Lanham, Md.: Rowman & Littlefield, 1994), 83–106.

43. See, for example, Herrnson, *Party Campaigning*; and Cornelius P. Cotter, James L. Gibson, John F. Bibby, and Robert J. Huckshorn, *Party Organizations in American Politics* (New York: Praeger, 1984).

CHAPTER FIVE

The Gender Gap in Presidential Nominations

by Jody McMullen and Barbara Norrander

SINCE THE EARLY 1980s, journalists and social scientists have frequently noted differences between men and women in their voting behavior and political attitudes. Men are described as more conservative and as favoring Republican candidates. Women show more liberal tendencies and support Democratic candidates. Women outpace men in voting in elections, but men express a higher interest in politics than women do. Men continue to outnumber women in holding elective offices. In 1998, women held 22 percent of the state legislative seats, 12 percent of the seats in the House of Representatives, and 9 percent of the Senate seats. Women occupied 26 percent of the statewide offices, but only three served as governors. Women more frequently are elected as lieutenant governors, secretaries of state, or heads of a state's education department.[1] No woman has been nominated for president by one of the two major parties, and the only woman ever nominated to be vice president was Geraldine Ferraro in 1984.

Should we expect men and women citizens to behave differently when it comes to presidential nomination politics? Previous studies of the gender gap in elections have focused on differences between men and women across the two parties. Yet the American political parties are not so ideologically cohesive as to preclude differences within each party.[2] Some of these intraparty differences may very well follow gender lines. We may find that men and women prefer different candidates within as well as across the parties. They may also have different reasons for choosing among candidates within the same party. On the other hand, since we are examining preferences within each party, the differences between men and women Democrats or women and men Republicans may be small and infrequent.

A second avenue for citizens to participate in presidential nominations is by becoming a delegate to either the Democratic or Republican National Convention. By 1992, both parties were using their conventions to showcase women candidates for federal and state offices.[3] This same showcasing strategy was carried out again at the 1996 Republican and Democratic National Conventions with speeches by both presidential candidates' wives, as well as by women holding public office.[4] Women speakers at the Democratic convention included Senators Barbara Boxer, Dianne Feinstein, Barbara Mikulski, Patty Murray, and Carol Moseley-Braun. In total, approximately sixty women addressed the 1996 Democratic convention. The Republican convention featured New Jersey Governor Christine Todd Whitman and New York Representative Susan Molinari. With this new emphasis on the inclusion of women at the conventions, do men and women delegates to these conventions differ in their preferences?

The Growth of Gender Differences in Politics

While scholarly and press attention began to focus on gender patterns in the 1980s, the trends responsible for these differences between the sexes emerged earlier. The first gender gap arose on issues concerning the use of force; differences between men's and women's positions on these issues are found in surveys dating back to the 1940s. Women are less supportive of military intervention abroad. At home, men are more favorable toward the death penalty and less supportive of gun control. In the 1970s, a second area of gender differences arose as women began to show more liberal tendencies on compassion issues. Women are more supportive than men of social welfare programs to aid the poor and elderly. On use-of-force and compassion issues the gender gap averages between 3 and 8 percentage points.[5] On women's issues, such as abortion and the role of women in society, men's and women's positions are actually the same.[6] Men and women are equally divided over the abortion issue, and both overwhelmingly favor an active role for women in society. By the 1990s, earlier divisions on issue positions had culminated in differences in ideological self-identifications as well. In the 1996 American National Election Study (ANES), half of the men identified themselves as conservatives, in contrast to only one-third of the women.

In the 1950s, the partisan gender gap actually was the opposite of today's.[7] Men were more likely than women to be Democrats. This occurred primarily because southern white males identified heavily with the Democratic Party, with over two-thirds holding this preference (including independents leaning toward the Democratic Party). Southern women also preferred the Democratic Party, but by 9 percentage points less than men.[8] The Democratic Party of the South in the 1950s was a conservative party rooted in preferences for limited government and a traditionalistic society. Outside the South in the 1950s, men's and women's partisan preferences were the same.

Partisanship began to change slowly in the 1960s as the national Democratic Party adopted a more aggressive stance on civil rights and supported an expansion of social welfare programs. This was clearest after Lyndon Johnson's landslide victory in the 1964 presidential election, which led Congress to pass the Voting Rights Act and the Medicare program. The conservative white base of the southern Democratic Party began to break away and move slowly into the Republican Party. The exodus of southern men from the Democratic Party was much stronger than that of southern women. Thus, by the early 1970s, a gender gap was apparent in southern partisan preferences. Outside the South, northern men also began to change their partisanship preferences and to move away from the Democratic Party. The partisan preferences of women outside the South exhibit no such trend. By the 1980s, the gender gap nationwide stood at 5 percentage points. This partisan gender gap grew to 10 percentage points in 1992 and to 14 percentage points in 1996.[9]

Gender Gap in Primary Voting

In looking for a gender gap in presidential primary voting, two aspects need to be studied. First, do men and women support different candidates? Some candidates may stress issues or personal qualities that resonate more fully with one or the other sex. As a result, the two sexes may develop different preferences. Alternatively, even when both men and women prefer the same candidate, they may do so for different reasons. Candidates adopt a number of issues and themes in their campaigns, and men and women may focus on different aspects. Thus, the second task will be to look for gender differences in the importance of various issues and candidate qualities in explaining primary voters' selection of candidates.

To search for a gender gap in presidential primary voting, we use the exit polls developed for the national media. The national television networks pool their resources with the Voter News Service (VNS) exit polls.

(In 1992, the name "Voter Research and Surveys" was used.) The VNS exit polls are quite short, as compared with the more lengthy major academic polls.[10] The number of candidates listed on each primary exit poll varies. Early presidential primaries attract a large number of candidates, but some candidates receive little support and quickly drop out of the contest. Other candidates remain contestants throughout most of the primary season, and of course, one candidate ultimately wins the nomination. To maintain consistency in the measurement of a gender gap in candidate support, only those candidates receiving the support of 5 percent of survey respondents are included in the figures. Votes for "other" and "uncommitted" also are eliminated from the analysis. The size of the gender gap is measured by subtracting the percentage of men from the percentage of women voting for a candidate. The statistical significance of this gap is measured by a difference in proportions test.

The extent of a gender gap in candidate preferences in the 1992 and 1996 presidential primaries is demonstrated in table 5.1. The most obvious point is that a gender gap was much more prevalent on the Republican side, especially in 1992. In that race, the Republican Party showed a consistent gender gap, as men were 10 percentage points more likely than women to support Buchanan. In an essentially two-candidate race, this meant that women were more likely to support the other candidate, George Bush. David Duke received few votes from either men or women and quickly dropped out of the 1992 Republican contest. However, in two of the three primaries where Duke received five percent or more of the vote, men were more likely than women to support him. In 1996, a statistically significant gender gap in voting preferences occurred in about one-third of the Republican primaries. Once again, men were more favorable than women toward Buchanan. Women were more likely to support Dole and, to a lesser extent, Alexander. The size of the gender gap for these three candidates averaged from 2 to 4 percentage points.

The 1992 Democratic nomination contest evoked even fewer gender differences in candidate preferences. In about one in five primaries, a gender gap appeared in support for Jerry Brown, but on average only 2 percentage points more men than women were attracted to his candidacy. Bill Clinton's support was divided unequally between the two sexes only 14 percent of the time, and on average there was less than 1 percentage point difference between men's and women's support for Clinton. Paul Tsongas's pattern matches that of Clinton, a gender gap only 12 percent of the time and a gap averaging less than 1 percentage point. The short candidacies of Bob Kerrey and Tom Harkin did not produce statistically significant gender gaps in any of the primaries covered

TABLE 5.1   GENDER GAP IN PRESIDENTIAL PRIMARY VOTING

	No. of Primaries in Which Candidate Received 5% of Vote	% of Primaries with Significant Gender Gap[a]	Mean Gender Gap[b]
1992 Democrat			
Brown	28	21	-1.7
Clinton	28	14	0.8
Tsongas	25	12	0.9
Kerrey	4	0	1.8
Harkin	3	0	-1.1
1992 Republican			
Bush	27	93	10.7
Buchanan	27	89	-10.4
Duke	3	67	-3.1
1996 Republican			
Alexander	9	33	1.6
Buchanan	20	35	-3.9
Dole	19	42	4.2
Forbes	18	11	-1.0
Keyes	1	0	1.1

[a] Percentage of primaries in which a statistical significance test for differences in proportions of men and women supporting candidate meets the .05 cutoff level.
[b] Positive mean values indicate more support from women; negative values indicate more support from men.

by the VRS exit polls. Except for the 1992 Republican contest, presidential primary voting is not overly characterized by gender voting patterns. A gender gap appears in approximately one-quarter to one-third of the primary contests. The combination of the Bush and Buchanan candidacies may have been unique in bringing about such a large and consistent gender gap in the 1992 Republican nomination battle. It also is possible that gender gaps emerge more clearly in two-candidate contests.

Gender Differences in Reasons for Candidate Support

The greater prevalence of a gender gap in candidate preferences among Republicans than among Democrats could occur for several reasons. One possibility is that male and female Republicans disagree more on what constitutes important issues and candidate traits, and thus they select different candidates. A second possibility is that relatively equal differences between the sexes on issues and candidate qualities exist within both parties, but that a particular candidate field in one party brings more of these differences to bear on voters' choices. Finally, gender differences on issues and candidate qualities may result not in the two sexes' choosing different candidates, but in their having different reasons for supporting the same candidate.

To investigate gender differences in reasons for supporting candidates, the VNS surveys are again employed. Instead of asking a series of questions on issue positions, these exit polls ask respondents, "Which 1 or 2 Issue(s) Mattered Most in Deciding How You Voted?" In the 1992 surveys, respondents could check off two items from a list of nine. In 1996, respondents were instructed to select only one item from the list. This question format means that voters' issue priorities rather than issue positions are being measured. However, issue priorities may be the more important factor in intraparty contests.[11] Respondents' use of candidate qualities to choose between competitors also was measured by selections from a list of quality priorities. Thus, respondents were asked, "Which 1 or 2 Qualities Mattered Most in Deciding How You Voted?"[12] While some issue and quality options are repeated in every survey, others are asked in some polls but not others. To be included in this analysis, an issue or quality option must have been included in five exit polls.

In looking at an issue or candidate quality, three factors determine how important it is in demonstrating differences between men and women voters. The first factor is how many voters used this issue or quality as a criterion for making their vote choice. If only a few voters select an issue, the issue's overall impact on the election outcome is small even if there is a gender gap in selecting the issue. The second criterion is the presence of a gender gap in selecting an issue or candidate quality as an important decision factor. If 90 percent of men and 90 percent of women select a specific issue as important in their decision making, this issue is important in the overall outcome of an election, but it is not a reason for differences between men and women. The third criterion is that an issue on which there is a gender difference also is connected to support for a specific candidate. Men and women might differ on the importance they attach to an issue, but if this issue does not lead voters to support one candidate over the others, the gender differences do not affect the outcome of the election. Thus, for an issue or candidate quality to produce a significant gender difference in voting, it must be an issue or quality that many voters care about, that men and women select at different rates, and that leads voters to support a specific candidate.

Table 5.2 investigates which issues were selected at different rates by the two sexes and which of these issues also affected candidate support in the 1992 and 1996 primaries. The first column of numbers indi-

TABLE 5.2   PERCENTAGE OF TIMES A GENDER GAP ON ISSUE PRIORITIES
INFLUENCED PRESIDENTIAL PRIMARY VOTES

Part A: 1992 Democratic Candidates

	How Often Issue Was Chosen	How Often Gender Gap Occurred in Picking Issue	Sex That Picked Issue More Often	How Often Gender Gap and Issue Affected Vote	Candidates Selected for This Issue
Economy	51	25	men	11	Tsongas
Deficit	19	56	men	33	Tsongas
Taxes	14	33	men	15	Clinton
Business com- petitiveness	10	69	men	63	Tsongas
Foreign imports	3	64	men	14	Brown & Clinton
Health insurance	30	56	women	26	Clinton
Education	20	56	women	26	Clinton
Poverty	12	71	women	43	Clinton
Welfare	6	27	women	9	Clinton
Government corruption	22	21	men	21	Brown
Crime	19	0	—	0	—
Environment	14	19	men	19	Brown
Race	8	0	—	0	—

Part B: 1992 Republican Candidates

	How Often Issue Was Chosen	How Often Gender Gap Occurred in Picking Issue	Sex That Picked Issue More Often	How Often Gender Gap and Issue Affected Vote	Candidates Selected for This Issue
Economy	38	15	men	8	Buchanan
Deficit	33	100	men	33	Buchanan
Taxes	31	30	men	19	Buchanan
Business com- petitiveness	24	48	men	23	Bush
Foreign imports	6	71	men	23	Buchanan
Health insurance	19	85	women	23	Bush
Education	24	85	women	59	Bush
Welfare	8	5	men	5	Buchanan
Quotas	5	43	men	29	Buchanan
Gulf War	11	26	women	26	Bush

(continued)

TABLE 5.2   *(continued)*

Part C: 1996 Republican Candidates

	How Often Issue Was Chosen	*How Often Gender Gap Occurred in Picking Issue*	*Sex That Picked Issue More Often*	*How Often Gender Gap and Issue Affected Vote*	*Candidates Selected for This Issue*
Economy	23	5	women	5	Dole
Deficit	25	80	men	80	Dole
Taxes	23	35	men	30	Forbes
Foreign trade	5	35	men	35	Buchanan
Education	7	80	women	45	Alexander & Dole
Environment	3	0	—	0	—
Abortion	12	90	women	90	Buchanan
Immigration	6	31	men	31	Buchanan

cates the average percentage of respondents in the primary exit polls who selected an issue as an important reason for supporting a candidate. The second column of numbers lists the percentage of primaries in which a statistically significant gender gap occurred in selecting each issue as a priority. These gender gaps are not necessarily large. A difference of five percentage points between men's and women's selection rates can be statistically significant. So even if an issue shows a gender gap in most of the presidential primaries, it does not mean that men and women are voting on entirely different factors. Rather, it is a case of nuances—men are slightly more likely to pick one factor and women are slightly more likely to select another. The third set of numbers in table 5.2 indicates the percentage of primaries in which an issue showed a significant gender gap and led to a preference for one of the candidates. Again, the distinctiveness of an issue in relation to candidate choice does not have to be large to show a statistically significant pattern. Those concerned about each of the issues always will split their votes among the candidates. The count in this column simply signifies a tendency for more of these voters to support one candidate over the others.

In the 1992 Democratic campaign (table 5.2, part A), men were more likely than women to say they based their votes on some aspect of the economy (overall economy, federal deficit, taxes, business competitiveness, and foreign imports). Usually, these sentiments led more men to support Tsongas, though those concerned about taxes tended to vote for Clinton. Women were more likely to base their votes on some aspect of social welfare policy (health insurance, education, poverty, or welfare).

These types of concerns led to greater support for Clinton. Finally, Brown found a constituency among men who were concerned about government corruption or the environment. These issues reflect themes stressed by the candidates. Tsongas, for example, emphasized a need to make difficult economic choices to balance the federal deficit, and Brown railed against government corruption, especially in campaign contributions. The support for Brown also demonstrates that men, as well as women, can be "green," or environmental, voters.[13] Not to be forgotten, however, is that in only one-quarter of the 1992 Democratic presidential primaries did men and women voters select candidates at different rates. Thus, the results of table 5.2 indicate that men and women voters sometimes have different reasons for supporting the same candidate.

In the 1992 Republican race (table 5.2, part B), men once again showed a greater concern for the economy. In every primary surveyed, men were more likely than women to say they based their votes on concerns over the federal deficit. This does not mean that Republican women were not concerned with the deficit, but only that men were more likely to use it as a reason for their votes while women used it less often. Still, the deficit showed an unusually large gender gap. In general, Buchanan benefited at a greater rate than Bush from this concern about the economy. Women showed more concern over health insurance and education, and this tended to produce more support for Bush. The gender gap on the education issue was the strongest for the 1992 Republicans when considering both the frequency with which voters relied on this issue and the frequency with which it produced a gender gap in support for Bush. A few Republicans based their votes on an opposition to welfare, and these voters tended to be men supporting Buchanan. Quotas and foreign trade also were infrequently cited as reasons for choosing a particular candidate, though once again more often by men who supported Buchanan. George Bush's widely acclaimed leadership in the Gulf War was fading from the public's mind by the time of the Republican primaries, and only one out of ten voters selected this as a reason for their choice. Somewhat unexpectedly, in about one-fourth of the primaries, women were slightly more likely than men to list the Gulf War as a reason for their vote choice. In 1992, the gender gaps in issues affected the Republican contest by producing a gender gap in candidate choice, as was demonstrated in table 5.1. In over two-thirds of the primaries, men and women chose candidates at different rates, and apparently this was due to different issue priorities between male and female Republican primary voters.

In the 1996 Republican contests (table 5.2, part C), men were more likely than women to select three of the four economic issues (federal deficit, taxes, foreign trade). However, in 1996, each of these economic issues was linked to a different candidate. Some men were drawn to support Dole because of concern about the federal deficit, some supported Forbes because of his call for a flat tax, and some supported Buchanan out of concern that foreign trade was costing Americans jobs. The gender gap on the federal deficit was the strongest of all the issues for all three elections covered. Once again, women voters were more likely to pick education as an important issue, but overall this was not a very salient issue in the 1996 campaign. Buchanan's pro-life stance, however, was a salient issue for one in ten Republican voters and particularly women voters. Thus, Buchanan drew support from men because of his economic stance, while more women were attracted to him because of his position on abortion. Although the 1996 Republican race showed some of the strongest gender differences in issue priorities, a gender gap was revealed in vote choice only about one-third of the time. Thus, in this race, a gender gap in issue priorities sometimes led to a gender gap in voting, and sometimes it did not. In the cases in which it did not, men and women voters had slightly different reasons for supporting the same candidate.

Table 5.3 conducts the same type of analysis as table 5.2, but this time for candidate qualities rather than issue priorities. For the 1992 Democratic contest (table 5.3, part A), three candidate qualities produced significant gender patterns. The strongest pattern (considering both the frequency with which a characteristic was selected and the frequency with which a gender gap was associated with support for a particular candidate) was for the trait of courage. Women were more likely than men to say they supported Tsongas because of his personal courage. Tsongas had previously fought a bout with cancer. Men, in contrast, showed a strong pattern in supporting Tsongas because they liked his ideas. Finally, men rather than women expressed a concern with supporting a winning candidate, and these men tended to vote for Clinton. The "horse race," which receives the bulk of the media's attention, apparently is more interesting to men than it is to women.

Four candidate traits stand out as producing significant differences between the two sexes in reasons for supporting individuals in the 1992 Republican nomination contest. Women supported Bush because of his political experience, while men were more likely to support Bush because of his leadership ability and his front-runner status. Men were attracted to Buchanan because he could shake up the political world. In the 1996 Republican contest, men and women used two candidate

TABLE 5.3   PERCENTAGE OF TIMES A GENDER GAP ON CANDIDATE QUALITIES
INFLUENCED PRESIDENTIAL PRIMARY VOTES

Part A: 1992 Democratic Candidates

	How Often Quality Was Chosen	*How Often Gender Gap Occurred in Picking Quality*	*Sex That Picked Quality More Often*	*How Often Gender Gap and Quality Affected Vote*	*Candidates Selected for This Quality*
Cares	27	54	women	43	Clinton
Courageous	24	56	women	50	Tsongas
Truthful	21	13	women	13	Tsongas
Leadership	18	8	women	0	—
Experience	13	14	both	7	Clinton
Handle crisis	9	50	women	25	Clinton
Likes candidate's ideas	34	36	men	29	Tsongas
Represents party	16	25	women	18	Clinton
Family values	10	12	women	6	Tsongas
From my region	10	15	both	15	Clinton
Shake up politics	20	40	men	27	Brown
Win election	11	79	men	71	Clinton
Debate performance	7	20	women	13	Clinton

Part B: 1992 Republican Candidates

	How Often Quality Was Chosen	*How Often Gender Gap Occurred in Picking Quality*	*Sex That Picked Quality More Often*	*How Often Gender Gap and Quality Affected Vote*	*Candidates Selected for This Quality*
Cares	8	19	women	15	Buchanan
Courageous	20	30	women	26	Bush
Leadership	31	33	men	33	Bush
Experience	44	37	women	37	Bush
Likes candidate's ideas	15	19	men	15	Buchanan
Represents party	17	22	men	15	Buchanan
Family values	23	48	women	19	Buchanan
From my region	4	8	women	8	Duke
Shake up politics	12	73	men	73	Buchanan
Win election	13	48	men	48	Bush

(continued)

TABLE 5.3   *(continued)*

Part C: 1996 Republican Candidates

	How Often Quality Was Chosen	How Often Gender Gap Occurred in Picking Quality	Sex That Picked Quality More Often	How Often Gender Gap and Quality Affected Vote	Candidates Selected for This Quality
Experience	16	45	women	45	Dole
Political vision	11	15	men	15	Forbes
Firm beliefs	23	10	both	10	Buchanan
Real conservative	21	15	women	15	Buchanan
Not extreme	8	15	women	15	Dole & Alexander
Win election	16	80	men	75	Dole
Not a politician	5	5	men	5	Forbes

qualities differently. Once again, men were attracted to a winning candidate, this time Dole, while women supported Dole, as they had Bush, because of his experience in government.

A final factor to be considered in primary voters' choices is the role of ideology. In an intraparty contest, party labels cannot be used to select candidates. Perhaps ideology can substitute for party labels as a shortcut for primary voting decisions. However, about one-fifth of Americans are reluctant to select an ideological label for themselves, while almost everyone chooses between the Democratic, Republican, and independent labels. Primary voters also are typical of other party supporters, being no more likely to hold extreme positions or to be ideological than those who do not vote in the presidential primaries.[14] The ideology question in the VNS is a fairly standard self-placement format of five categories from very conservative to very liberal. Fifty-seven percent of the time in the 1992 Democratic primaries, 67 percent of the time in the 1992 Republican primaries, and 80 percent of the time in the 1996 Republican primaries, women voters were less conservative than the men voters in their party. Ideology also significantly influenced voters' choices. In the 1992 Democratic primaries, ideology influenced voters' choices 57 percent of the time. On the Republican side in 1992, the ideological gap influenced the vote in 56 percent of the primaries, and in 1996, the ideology gap influenced voting 80 percent of the time. This ideological gap within the two parties may prove to be the primary-election equivalent of the partisan gender gap in the general election.

In summary, we have seen that the three nomination contests differ in the extent to which a gender gap occurred in voters' choices. The 1992

Republican battle between Bush and Buchanan produced a frequent gender gap in candidate support, while the 1992 Democratic and the 1996 Republican contests usually did not produce a gender gap in candidate support. On the role of issues in shaping voters' selections, however, the three contests are fairly similar. Ideology frequently comes into play, with women holding less conservative positions than men and with ideology often influencing voters' choices. In broad terms, men tend to look to the economic issues of the federal deficit, taxes, and business competitiveness, while women are more likely to focus on social welfare issues in deciding which candidate to support. In terms of candidate qualities, men look for winners, while women support candidates with political experience. Gender differences in the use of issue and candidate qualities sometimes led women and men to support different candidates, and sometimes they provided men and women with different reasons for supporting the same candidate. In the latter case, women and men would hold different expectations for a winning presidential candidate.

A Gender Gap at the National Conventions?

Women have participated in Democratic and Republican nominating conventions since the turn of the twentieth century, even though women could not vote in presidential elections until 1920. In 1900, one woman delegate was present at each party's convention. In 1916, the Democratic Party established a Women's Division, which advocated the right of women to vote in state-level, but not federal, elections.[15] With the passage of the Nineteenth Amendment, a significant number of women started participating in the political conventions.[16]

By the 1950s, women had begun to play a more visible role in the national conventions by giving important speeches, holding top administrative posts in the party, and receiving votes for the presidency or vice presidency. In 1952, six women gave speeches at the Democratic National Convention. In 1972, Republican Anne Armstrong became the first woman to give a national convention's keynote speech. A number of women have taken on leading roles for the parties at their conventions. Josephine Good served as the executive director of the Republican National Convention in 1960. Mary Louise Smith, the first woman chair of the Republican National Committee (1974–77), was a frequent convention delegate and served on committees dealing with the party's platform and rules reform.

Women also have received votes as presidential and vice presidential candidates. Although a few women candidates had received scattered votes for the presidential nomination as early as 1920, Senator Margaret Chase Smith became the first woman to be formally nominated for president at the Republican convention in 1964. At the 1972 Democratic convention, Congresswoman Shirley Chisholm received 152 votes for president on the first ballot. At the same convention, Frances T. Farenthold was nominated for vice president and received 404 votes, coming in second to the eventual nominee, Thomas Eagleton.[17] In 1984, New York Congresswoman Geraldine Ferraro received the Democratic nomination for vice president. The lack of women candidates for president and vice president reflects the fact that few women have held the posts from which presidential candidates are generally recruited. In recent decades, the most successful presidential contenders have been current or former senators or governors. As noted in the opening paragraph of this chapter, though women hold a variety of elective offices, the number of women senators and governors is still quite small. As more women are elected to these offices, we should expect more women candidates for the presidency as well.

Gender and Reform of the Delegate Selection Process

Changes in party rules in the 1970s increased the level of participation by women at the national nominating conventions. The Democratic Party in 1968 began the process of reforming rules for participation in its conventions by appointing the McGovern-Fraser Commission (see chapter 1). This commission found that women and racial minority groups were underrepresented in the delegations sent to the conventions by the various states. In its 1970 report, the commission proposed a system of quotas to remedy this situation. State party organizations were directed to increase the number of women, racial minorities, and people under age thirty in their delegations until they reflected their proportions in the state population. The commission's suggestions were first instituted at the 1972 Democratic National Convention.

At about the same time, the Republican Party also began to discuss reforms to increase the representativeness of its convention delegates. At their 1968 convention, Republicans voted for a rule against discrimination in the selection of delegates. From 1968 to 1972, the Delegates and Organization (DO) Committee was the Republican counterpart to the McGovern-Fraser Commission. Rosemary Ginn of Missouri headed the DO Committee. Although the Republican Party also saw a need to increase the number of women and racial minorities present at its conventions, ideological beliefs dictated that the situation be handled differently than it was in the Democratic Party. Because Republicans are philosophically opposed to quotas, the party instead decided to advocate a system in which women and minorities were encouraged to become convention delegates.

Following their 1972 conventions, both parties evaluated how successful their reform policies had been. By 1976, the Democratic Party had abandoned its quota system for racial minorities and younger delegates, but in 1980 it reintroduced a mandate that one-half of each state's delegation be composed of women. To achieve this goal, "state delegate selection plans [were required to] include numerical goals, timetables, and specific 'outreach' activities."[18] The Republican Party continued its policy of encouraging women to act as delegates without instituting a system of regulations to ensure that there would be a specific number of women delegates.

Figure 5.1 depicts the trend in women's participation in national nominating conventions from 1944 to 1996. In the 1940s and 1950s, women made up approximately 10 percent of the delegates at both the Republican and Democratic conventions. In the 1960s, women's participation grew slightly, and the Republican Party had a greater number of women delegates than did the Democratic Party.[19] With the onset of party reforms in the early 1970s, the number of women participating in the conventions of both parties grew dramatically. Since the Democratic Party mandates equal representation of women, half of the delegates to all of its conventions since 1980 have been women. Women's participation at Republican conventions, in contrast, reached its highest level in 1984 with 44 percent and dropped to 36 percent in 1996.

In many respects, the women who attended these conventions were much like their male counterparts. In general, both men and women convention delegates tend to be more educated and affluent and to hold higher-status jobs than the average voter. However, women delegates may be slightly less affluent than male delegates.[20] In terms of political behavior, "delegates over the years have been more emotionally devoted to candidates, much more active in campaigns, and substantially more ideological than typical Democrats and Republicans."[21]

The 1992 Convention Delegates Poll

The last academic survey of delegates to the Republican and Democratic National Conventions comes from 1992.[22] A mail questionnaire was sent to convention delegates in the summer of 1993. The survey had a 45 percent response rate for a total of 2,853 cases. In contrast to the exit

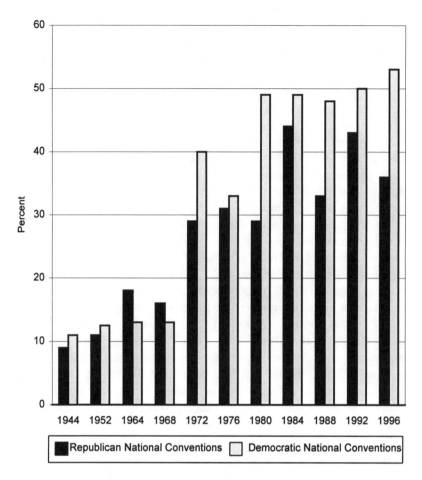

FIGURE 5.1   PERCENTAGE OF WOMEN DELEGATES IN NATIONAL CONVENTIONS,
1944–96

Sources: James W. Ceaser, *Reforming the Reforms: A Critical Analysis of the
Presidential Selection Process* (Cambridge, Mass.: Ballinger, 1982); and Harold W. Stanley
and Richard G. Niemi, *Vital Statistics on American Politics: 1997–1998* (Washington,
D.C.: Congressional Quarterly, 1998).

polls of primary voters, this survey contained numerous questions about
candidate and issue preferences, as well as about the delegates' political
participation.

In the past, women were less politically ambitious than men, though
this seems to be changing.[23] The 1992 Convention Delegate Study
explored the issue of political ambition by soliciting information about
party and elective offices the delegates had held in the past and their

TABLE 5.4   PERCENTAGE OF CONVENTION DELEGATES HOLDING AND ASPIRING
TO HOLD ELECTIVE AND PARTY POSITIONS

	Democratic Delegates			Republican Delegates		
	Male	Female	Significance	Male	Female	Significance
Offices Held in the Past						
Federal elective office	35	24	.00	45	26	.00
Party office	51	52	.59	58	63	.11
Aspirations for Future Public Office						
National public office	20	10		16	8	
State public office	22	20		21	16	
Local public office	13	14	.00	7	6	.00
Aspirations for Future Party Office						
National party office	14	15		9	11	
State party office	20	19		21	20	
Local party office	10	12	.70	10	9	.57

plans for seeking office in the future. One question asked them whether they aspired to hold a national, state, or local elective office or had no future plans for elective office. Another question asked them to choose among the same options for their aspirations for future party office. As can be seen in table 5.4, women delegates in both parties were much less likely than men to have held an elective office. Women delegates also were generally less likely than their male counterparts to aspire to hold a public office in the future, particularly at the national level. Yet, the picture is quite different for party positions. No significant differences exist between men and women delegates in holding past party positions or aspiring to hold future party posts. Women and men delegates to the 1992 convention also had similar histories in regard to participation in past conventions. Two-thirds of the men and women delegates to the Democratic convention were attending a convention for the first time, while half the men and women Republican delegates were at their first convention. These data support a theory proposed by Denise Baer that women have been able to make great strides in the political parties despite the lack of women in elective offices at the national level.[24] Baer argues that to develop a more accurate picture of the political participation and ambition of women, women's involvement in political parties needs to be taken into account.

The Democratic Party's requirement for equal numbers of women and men delegates and the Republican Party's encouragement of greater numbers of women delegates have had a significant impact on how delegates view the process by which they were chosen. Women delegates in 1992 were far more likely than men delegates to believe that their sex, age, or race played a role in their selection as convention delegates. This gap was highly significant in both parties. Sixty-one percent of Democratic women delegates and 29 percent of Democratic male delegates believed that sex, age, or race contributed to their selection. On the Republican side, the numbers were 52 percent for women and 25 percent for men.

Candidate and Issue Differences among Delegates

As is evident in table 5.1, a significant gender gap existed in candidate preferences among Republican primary voters in 1992. Yet only rarely did the two sexes disagree on support for the Democratic candidates. Among the 1992 convention delegates, a different pattern is evident. As table 5.5 shows, a statistically significant gender gap existed among Democratic delegates, but not among the Republican delegates. Sixty-three percent of women Democratic delegates, compared with 56 percent of men, supported Clinton. Male delegates to the convention were slightly more supportive of Harkin, Tsongas, and Kerrey than were their female counterparts. How can the pattern for convention delegates be so different from that for primary voters? One answer is that nearly 90 percent of the Republican delegates supported the renomination of President Bush. Republican delegate distribution rules work to increase the delegate totals of the leading candidate. Thus, Bush won the bulk of convention delegates. With almost all the delegates supporting the same candidate, there is less chance for a gender difference to emerge.

TABLE 5.5   CANDIDATE SUPPORT AMONG MALE AND FEMALE 1992 CONVENTION
             DELEGATES

Democratic Delegates			*Republican Delegates*		
Candidate	*Male*	*Female*	*Candidate*	*Male*	*Female*
Clinton	56%	63%	Bush	86%	87%
Tsongas	14	12	Buchanan	8	6
Brown	13	13	Other	4	5
Harkin	11	8	None	1	2
Kerrey	4	3			
Other	1	2			

Significance: .05   Significance: .49

On ideological positions, however, primary voters and convention delegates present identical patterns, with women being less conservative than men in the same party. The 1992 Convention Delegate Study asked respondents to place themselves on a seven-point ideological scale, in which a value of 1 represented the most liberal ideological position and a value of 7 the most conservative. Among Democratic delegates, the mean ideological position for men was 3.1 and for women a more liberal 2.8. For Republican delegates, men scored an average 5.5, while women averaged a less conservative 5.4. In both parties, these differences met a .01 statistical significance test.

The men and women delegates to the 1992 conventions differed significantly on several political issues, just as men and women voters did in the 1992 primaries. In contrast to the exit polls for the primaries, the 1992 Convention Delegate Study measured delegates' issue positions rather than their issue priorities. Delegates were asked whether they wanted federal spending to be increased, kept the same, reduced, or cut out completely for several programs. Table 5.6 presents the percentages of men and women in both parties who favored increased spending for each of fourteen federal programs. A statistically significant gender gap existed in both parties for the following programs: aid to public schools, Social Security, aid to countries of the former Soviet Union, aid to the homeless, and protecting the environment. For all of these issues, with the exception of aid to countries of the former Soviet Union, a higher

TABLE 5.6   PERCENTAGE OF DELEGATES FAVORING INCREASED FEDERAL
SPENDING ON SELECTED GOVERNMENT PROGRAMS

	Democratic Delegates			Republican Delegates		
	Male	Female	Significance	Male	Female	Significance
Dealing with crime	57	62	.16	56	54	.24
Aid to public schools	69	75	.00	11	15	.03
Social Security	15	19	.00	3	7	.00
AIDS research	56	67	.00	14	12	.07
Aid to former USSR	28	17	.00	16	8	.00
Programs to assist blacks	23	31	.01	2	2	.21
Aid to college students	53	61	.00	7	7	.99
Aid to homeless	51	65	.00	4	8	.01
Child care	59	71	.00	11	12	.31
Welfare programs	15	20	.07	1	1	.65
Protecting environment	45	55	.00	6	7	.00
Aid to big cities	43	41	.88	3	4	.92
Aid to unemployed	47	54	.04	6	6	.96
Aid to poor	42	49	.01	4	4	.06

percentage of women than men in both parties favored increasing federal spending. In addition to these issues in which there was a gender gap for both parties, Democratic women gave significantly greater support than Democratic men to increased spending on AIDS research, programs that assist blacks, aid to college students, child care, programs to assist the unemployed, and aid to the poor. Of the fourteen programs, a gender gap is found among Democratic delegates on eleven of the issues; among Republican delegates, a gender gap is found on five.

This finding of numerous issue differences between men and women delegates differs from Jeane Kirkpatrick's description of the 1972 convention. She found that the views of women delegates were similar to those of men on public policies, including women's issues and social welfare questions. The only difference she found was on military policy, where women were less likely to support the use of force. Kirkpatrick concluded that there were no "consistent differences in the views of women and men delegates concerning which public or private problems were the most important, nor was there a 'women's' position on any of the salient issues of 1972."[25] The growth of gender differences among the public for compassion issues since the early 1970s apparently has increased the distinctiveness of men and women convention delegates as well. Women delegates at both the Republican and Democratic National Conventions show greater support than male delegates for maintaining social welfare programs. Women primary voters also use social welfare issues more often than men in making their voting decisions.

Conclusion

A gender gap does exist within each party. The evidence from two of the three presidential nomination races examined in this chapter suggests, however, that this gender gap is smaller than the one found between the two parties. Somewhat surprising was the finding that among both primary voters and convention delegates, women partisans are less conservative than their male colleagues. If a consistent gender gap does emerge in nomination contests, this gap in ideology may lie at its core. The gender gap also may vary over the course of a single campaign. The 1992 Republican primary contest showed the strongest gender gap in candidate preference, but by the time the Republican convention was convened, a consensus had developed in support of Bush's renomination. Thus, no gender gap was found in the preferences of 1992 convention delegates. In contrast, the less distinctive gender gap found in the 1992 Democratic primaries is replicated among convention delegates, as more male delegates continued to support Clinton's opponents. The size of the gender gap also may vary by the type of nomination contest. The gender gap was much larger in the essentially two-candidate race pitting Buchanan versus Bush. This contest may have been characterized by more protest voting, as Bush's renomination quickly became assured by early primary results. Men may practice this type of protest voting more often than women do.

Even though a gender gap may not be consistently prevalent in the choices of presidential nominees, a number of candidate qualities and issues gave the two sexes different reasons for choosing between the candidates. Women based their voting decisions more often than men on social welfare issues. Men more often than women cited the federal deficit or international trade as reasons for their votes. As for candidate qualities, women looked toward a candidate's political experience and other leadership traits. Men concentrated more on aspects of the political contest, such as a candidate's ability to shake things up or to win.

Women delegates now play a vital role in the national conventions of both parties. Not to be overlooked is that these women delegates are drawn from the ranks of the state and local political parties, where they are as active as men. Only in holding or aspiring to elective governmental office at the national level do women delegates still differ from their male counterparts. Women and men convention delegates do bring with them slightly different issue preferences. Mirroring the divisions in the general public, women delegates in both parties are more supportive than men of a broader governmental role in social welfare policies.

Notes

1. All figures are from Center for the American Woman and Politics (CAWP), "Women in Elective Office 1998," National Information Bank on Women in Public Office, Eagleton Institute of Politics, Rutgers University, 1998, www.rci.rutgers.edu/~cawp/electv98.html.
2. William G. Mayer, *The Divided Democrats: Ideological Unity, Party Reform, and Presidential Elections* (New York: Westview, 1996).
3. Jo Freeman, "Feminism v. Family Values: Women at the 1992 Democratic and Republican National Conventions," *PS: Political Science & Politics* (March 1993): 21-8.
4. Jane Blankenship, Deborah C. Robson, and Maureen S. Williams, "Conventionalizing Gender: Talk by and about Women at the 1996 National Political Conventions," *American Behavioral Scientist* 40 (1997): 1020-48.
5. Robert Y. Shapiro and Harpreet Mahajan, "Gender Differences in Policy Preferences: A Summary of Trends from the 1960s to the 1980s," *Public Opinion Quarterly* 50 (1986): 42-61.

6. Elizabeth Adell Cook, Ted G. Jelen, and Clyde Wilcox, *Between Two Absolutes: Public Opinion and the Politics of Abortion* (Boulder, Colo.: Westview, 1992); Hazel Erskine, "The Polls: Women's Role," *Public Opinion Quarterly* 35 (1971): 275-90; and Rita J. Simon and Jean M. Landis, "The Polls—a Report: Women's and Men's Attitudes about a Woman's Place and Role," *Public Opinion Quarterly* 53 (1989): 265-76.

7. Angus Campbell, Philip E. Converse, Warren E. Miller, and Donald E. Stokes, *The American Voter* (New York: John Wiley, 1960).

8. Barbara Norrander, "Is the Gender Gap Growing?" in *Reelection 1996: How Americans Voted*, ed. Herbert F. Weisberg and Janet M. Box-Steffensmeier (Chatham, N.J.: Chatham House, 1999): 145-61.

9. Karen M. Kaufmann and John R. Petrocik, "The Revenge of the Soccer Moms? Gender as a Party Cleavage in American Politics" (paper presented at the annual meeting of the American Political Science Association, Washington, D.C., 28-31 August 1997); and Norrander, "Is the Gender Gap Growing?"

10. "Voter News Service Presidential Primary Exit Polls, 1996" [computer file], ICPSR version (New York: Voter News Service, 1996), and "Voter Research and Surveys Presidential Primary Exit Polls, 1992" [computer file], ICPSR version (New York: Voter Research and Surveys, 1992); both available from Inter-University Consortium for Political and Social Research, Ann Arbor, Mich. Twenty-eight primaries were analyzed for the 1992 Democratic race and twenty-seven for the 1992 Republican contest. At the time of the analysis, complete codebook information was available for only twenty of the 1996 Republican primaries.

11. John H. Aldrich and R. Michael Alvarez, "Issues and the Presidential Primary Voter," *Political Behavior* 16 (1994): 289-317.

12. The issue and candidate quality questions were turned into a series of dummy variables, with "1" indicating an item was selected and "0" that it was not. These dummy variables were cross-tabulated with sex so that a test of statistical significance could be applied. The frequency with which these bivariate relationships met a standard test of statistical significance was used to measure the existence of gender differences on reasons for supporting candidates in presidential primaries. Pearson's chi square statistic and a cutoff level of .05 were used to judge statistical significance.

13. Sue Tolleson-Rinehart and Mark Somma, "Tracking the Elusive Green Women: Sex, Environmentalism, and Feminism in the United States and Europe," *Political Research Quarterly* 50 (March 1997): 153-71.

14. John G. Geer, "Assessing the Representativeness of Electorates in Presidential Primaries," *American Journal of Political Science* 32 (1988): 929-45; and Barbara Norrander, "Ideological Representativeness of Presidential Primary Voters," *American Journal of Political Science* 33 (1989): 570-87.

15. Barbara Findlen, "Great Moments: We Were There, Even before Women Could Vote," *Ms.*, August 1988, 48-9.

16. Evamarie Socha, ed., *National Party Conventions, 1931-1984* (Washington, D.C.: Congressional Quarterly, 1987).

17. Richard C. Bain and Judith H. Parris, *Convention Decisions and Voting Records*, 2nd ed. (Washington, D.C.: Brookings, 1973).

18. James W. Ceaser, *Reforming the Reforms: A Critical Analysis of the Presidential Selection Process* (Cambridge, Mass.: Ballinger, 1982), 38.

19. Howard Reiter, *Selecting the President: The Nominating Process in Transition* (Philadelphia: University of Pennsylvania Press, 1985).

20. Jeane Kirkpatrick, *The New Presidential Elite: Men and Women in National Politics* (New York: Russell Sage Foundation, 1976).

21. Emmett H. Buell, Jr., and John S. Jackson III, "The National Conventions: Diminished but Still Important in a Primary-Dominated Process," in *Nominating the President,* ed. Emmett H. Buell, Jr., and Lee Sigelman (Knoxville: University of Tennessee Press, 1991), 214.

22. Richard Herrera and Warren E. Miller, "Convention Delegate Study, 1992" [computer file], ICPSR ed. (Ann Arbor, Mich.: Inter-University Consortium for Political and Social Research, 1995).

23. Edmond Costantini, "Political Women and Political Ambition: Closing the Gender Gap," *American Journal of Political Science* 34 (August 1990): 741–70.

24. Denise L. Baer, "Political Parties: The Missing Variable in Women and Politics Research," *Political Research Quarterly* 45 (1993): 547–76.

25. Kirkpatrick, *New Presidential Elite,* 440.

CHAPTER SIX

What Voters Know about the Candidates and How They Learn It: The 1996 New Hampshire Republican Primary as a Case Study

by Tami Buhr

FROM THE EARLY days of the American republic, political theorists have worried about the fate of a democracy whose citizens were ill informed and open to influence from the passions of the day.[1] Despite the Founding Fathers' attempts to insulate political affairs from the vagaries of public opinion, visitors to this experiment in democracy concluded that public opinion had a powerful and generally detrimental effect on government.[2] Early survey-based studies in political science did little to disconfirm the notion of a fickle and ignorant public. Numerous studies documented the American public's lack of knowledge about politics and public affairs.[3] In response, another group of studies attempted to show the rationality of the American public's lack of attention to politics, the meaningful movements of aggregate opinion, and the tendency of citizens to rely on cues and heuristic devices to make political judgments.[4] Still, the consequences of inadequate information and voter shortcuts are just becoming clear.

Why Study Voter Knowledge of Primary Candidates?

Given citizens' lack of attention to politics and resulting low levels of knowledge, are people able to navigate their journeys through the political world when required? Several recent studies have shown that despite citizens' best attempts at low-information rational decision making, lack of political knowledge does matter. In the most comprehensive study of the determinants and consequences of political knowledge to date, Delli Carpini and Keeter show that people with less information about the political world are disadvantaged in the exercise of political power.[5] Poorly informed citizens are more influenced by propaganda, are less able to link their views to evaluations of elected officials, and have difficulty translating their concerns into political action. Based on a spatial model of voting, Alvarez finds that voters who are more uncertain about the candidates' issue positions are less able to base their voting decisions on their own issue preferences.[6] Zaller shows that political knowledge alters the process by which voters form opinions across a variety of issues.[7] In a study of primary elections, Bartels finds that as voters become more informed, they increasingly base their decisions on more substantive criteria, allowing them to make more sophisticated judgments. Better-informed primary voters are better able to judge the candidates on the basis of their own political predispositions and the candidates' issue positions, and they are less likely to project their own issue positions onto the candidates.[8] Bartels extended his examination to the November presidential election and found that information affects more than the decision-making process; less-informed voters cast ballots for different candidates than their better-informed counterparts.[9]

Collectively, these studies show that the amount of information voters have about the candidates influences their decision making. The combined empirical evidence suggests that democratic theorists who worried about the ability of an uninformed citizenry to make quality decisions had cause for concern. Better-informed voters make different and more sophisticated decisions. If much of the public has little interest in politics and remains uninformed, American democracy is weaker as a result. Still, it is important to consider the information environment of modern elections before we blame voters for their ignorance and lack of attention. Writing in response to the first wave of studies that raised serious questions about the ability of voters to cast responsible ballots, V.O. Key noted perceptively that "voters are not fools. . . . [T]he electorate behaves about as rationally and responsibly as we should expect, given the clarity of the alternatives presented to it and the character of the information available to it."[10] Key argued that voters were simply echoing back what the candidates presented, which often is not much. Critics of modern elections often lament the quality of campaign discourse, blaming both candidates and the news media. Candidates run negative and superficial campaigns, while the media focus on the horse race. Those hoping to improve this situation thus focus on the information environment.[11]

A study of the New Hampshire primary presents a unique opportunity to learn about information and voter decision making, as well as to make a significant contribution to ongoing discussions about reform of the nominating process. With the possible exception of Iowans, residents of no other state receive as much information from such varied sources as do the citizens of New Hampshire. The New Hampshire primary combines traditional grass-roots campaigning with more modern media methods. Much of what is prized about contests like Iowa and New Hampshire is the numerous opportunities they allegedly offer ordinary voters to meet the candidates in person and to have direct contact with the campaigns through phone calls and mailings. Advocates of the New Hampshire primary claim that the candidates' retail politicking allows voters to make superior decisions. New Hampshire, they argue, is the gold standard of campaign information. Critics of this primary, on the other hand, call it unrepresentative of the nation as a whole and complain that such a small state has such a large influence. Observers also note that despite its reputation for retail politics, the New Hampshire primary has increasingly been taken over by wholesale campaign techniques.[12]

We know from past work that the New Hampshire primary receives a disproportionate share of the media coverage of the nomination campaign, but quantity does not necessarily mean quality. What are New Hampshire voters learning about the candidates? Are voters learning mainly about the candidates' backgrounds and issue positions or their standings in the polls? Election reformers want to provide voters with enough substantive information to enable them to make high-quality decisions. While it is neither possible nor necessarily desirable to replicate the New Hampshire primary in every state in the nation, reformers should know if the purported gold standard of campaign information is actually that.

If New Hampshire residents are provided with the information necessary to make an informed choice, do they make use of it? Is it possible for them to receive too much of a good thing? Given the large number of candidates running in the primary and the wealth of information reportedly available, the task may be too cognitively complex for all but the most politically sophisticated voters.[13] Given the opportunity, are residents of information-rich New Hampshire able to echo back a responsible vote? Advocates of the New Hampshire primary assert that voters there are more interested and knowledgeable about politics in general than are voters elsewhere. In particular, they are more experienced voters both because of their rich history in presidential politics and because more state and local elections take place in New Hampshire than in any other state.[14] How capable are Granite State voters of making a decision that will affect the rest of the nation? Are they the sophisticated voters their proponents maintain? Most of the debates about the prominence of the New Hampshire primary come down to the quality of the decisions that New Hampshire voters make. Because the results of the New Hampshire primary winnow the field of candidates, the judgments of New Hampshire voters restrict those of voters who come later in the process. If this small group of voters is making poor decisions, the rest of the country has to suffer the consequences. Bartels's finding that informed primary voters cast more sophisticated votes suggests that in order to evaluate the role of the New Hampshire primary, we need to examine the voters' knowledge of the candidates.

This chapter investigates voter knowledge and learning in the 1996 New Hampshire Republican primary. It begins with a brief discussion of past work on political information and learning. According to this work, a combination of contextual and individual factors explains differences in political knowledge—specifically, opportunity, motivation, and ability. The next section asks whether New Hampshire voters had the *opportunity* to learn about the candidates seeking the Republican presidential nomination in 1996. I examine the campaign information environment to determine how much and what type of information about the candidates was presented in the media, the candidates' televised advertisements and interviews, and stump speeches. How active were the candidates' campaigns in phoning and mailing information to voters? I follow this presentation by asking the degree to which New Hampshire residents were *motivated* to learn about the candidates. How much attention did they pay to the campaign, and how frequently did they watch television news or read a newspaper? Next, I examine the *ability* of New Hampshire residents to learn about the candidates. Compared with voters elsewhere, how well educated are New Hampshire voters, and how much existing political information do they bring to the campaign? With this as background, I investigate how much voters knew about the candidates, what they knew, and when and how they learned it.

What We Know about Political Knowledge

According to previous research, the requirements for political learning are similar to those for learning about other subjects. Simply put, people learn when they have the opportunity, the motivation, and the ability to do so.[15] Researchers examining differences in levels of political knowledge have used a number of terms to refer to this concept, including *political sophistication* and *information*. Knowledge of candidates during election campaigns has been characterized as *awareness, familiarity*, or *uncertainty*.[16] The measurement of political knowledge also varies, usually employing one or more of the following: knowledge of political facts, such as the identity of the chief justice of the Supreme Court; interviewer ratings of the respondents; the ability of respondents to answer open-ended questions about the parties and candidates; or the ability to identify candidates' issue positions. Despite differences in terminology and measurement, the theory underlying knowledge acquisition remains the same. People cannot learn about politics if they are not exposed to political information, they will not learn if the subject fails to interest them, and they will be unable to learn if the task is too cognitively demanding.

In reality, of course, these three factors—opportunity, motivation, and ability—overlap to a great extent. The distinction is more conceptual than actual. For example, formal education increases people's ability to learn about politics by sharpening their cognitive abilities. Students are taught political facts that provide context for political information encountered in the real world, thus making it easier to understand. But education also impacts people's motivation to learn about politics by teaching social norms and what it means to be a responsible citizen. In addition, education fosters a feeling of political empowerment or efficacy that motivates people to pay attention to politics.

In New Hampshire, meeting a candidate requires opportunity, but motivation can be important, too, depending on the circumstance. The candidates spend a lot of time in New Hampshire, thus giving residents more opportunity than residents of other states to meet them. It is possible for a voter to happen upon a candidate by chance as she goes about her daily activities, but more motivated voters seek out candidates by attending rallies and speeches or even entertaining candidates in their homes. Such meetings are more likely because of numerous opportunities, but they also require a higher level of motivation than encountering a candidate by chance outside one's place of employment. So, more politically motivated voters will likely learn more from person-to-person contact with a candidate, both because the meeting is likely to be longer and because the candidate will make a more lasting impression, given the voters' preexisting interest in politics.

The idea that the information rich get richer while the information poor get poorer is not new. Communication researchers have long been concerned about a knowledge gap between these two groups.[17] Schema theory from political psychology reaches a similar conclusion.[18] In essence, schema theory argues that people who have prior knowledge of a subject can more easily process new information. Learning is dependent on preexisting knowledge to provide context. This finding is troubling for a representative democracy, because it suggests that traditionally disadvantaged groups will have difficulty achieving political equality. Delli Carpini and Keeter's finding that racial minorities, the poor, and women are consistently less informed is indicative of this concern. But Delli Carpini and Keeter also show that political knowledge is complex. The ability to learn is important, but as discussed above, motivation and opportunity also matter, making it possible, though difficult, for some otherwise disadvantaged groups and individuals to clear society's hurdles. For example, while people tend to be political generalists—that is, their knowledge levels tend to be equivalent across a number of areas—some knowledge is domain-specific. Minorities know more about racial politics, and women know more about school politics. So, sufficient motivation can, to some extent, override deficiencies in opportunity and ability. In addition, Delli Carpini and Keeter demonstrate the importance of opportunity by comparing knowledge levels in different information environments; they find some large differences, even after controlling for individual characteristics. In an experimental setting, Neuman, Just, and Crigler also demonstrate the importance of motivation. People with low cognitive ability but high attention levels learn as much from the news media as those with high cognitive ability but low attention.[19] Hence, all three factors deserve separate and extended examination.

Did New Hampshire Voters Have the Opportunity to Learn about the Candidates?

In a primary election, partisanship—the most common voting cue—is the same for all candidates. Voters thus have the difficult task of distinguishing between a number of candidates who hold roughly similar beliefs. New Hampshire voters have an even tougher assignment because of the large number of candidates on the ballot. Anyone who is willing to pay a filing fee of $1,000 can be on the ballot. As a result, numerous fringe candidates inevitably run; the 1996 New Hampshire Republican primary ballot listed twenty-two names. Of course, the major candidates—the ones who have some semblance of an organization, air advertisements on television, and receive the bulk of media attention—are fewer in number, but the field is still large. In October 1995, ten

Republican candidates were considered serious enough to be invited to debate on WMUR-TV, New Hampshire's only network affiliate. With so many candidates to consider, voters need a lot of quality information to make sense of their choices. What does the information environment of the New Hampshire primary look like? How do direct candidate communications compare with mediated communications? Do these communications provide the necessary amount of quality information for voters to learn who the candidates are and what they would do if elected? In short, are New Hampshire voters given the opportunity to make an informed choice? This section attempts to answer these questions on the basis of content-analysis data collected during the 1996 presidential campaign (see appendix A, pp. 245–7, for details).

Quantity of Information

New Hampshire voters receive information from a combination of media and candidate sources. Despite New Hampshire's retail-politics image, one of the most noted features of its primary is the disproportionate amount of national media attention it receives compared with coverage of nomination contests in other states. Based on a content analysis of CBS and UPI coverage during the 1980 campaign, Robinson and Sheehan found that the New Hampshire primary was the focus of 15 percent of all coverage devoted to state primaries and caucuses.[20] The emphasis on New Hampshire grew in 1984, with 19 percent of nomination stories on ABC, CBS, NBC, and the *New York Times* covering the first primary.[21] Coverage of the 1996 Republican primary emphasized New Hampshire to an even greater extent. Of the 1,115 campaign stories aired on ABC, CBS, and NBC between 1 January 1995 and 26 March 1996, the day Dole clinched the Republican nomination, 25 percent dealt with the New Hampshire primary. If we limit the analysis to the 586 campaign stories specifically mentioning a state primary or caucus, New Hampshire was mentioned in 48 percent.[22]

Though the 1996 New Hampshire primary received more than its share of network news coverage of the presidential campaign, campaign coverage need not focus on New Hampshire for it to be useful to New Hampshire voters. Table 6.1 presents the amount of wholesale campaign information from 20 January through 19 February 1996. If New Hampshire voters had been exposed to nothing but wholesale campaign communications, they would still have received a lot of information. The three networks differed somewhat in the amount of coverage they provided on their evening news programs. ABC aired the most stories

TABLE 6.1   AMOUNT OF WHOLESALE CAMPAIGN INFORMATION,
20 JANUARY–19 FEBRUARY 1996

	Number of Units[a]	Average Length of Units	Total Length of Units
National Media			
ABC evening news	95	1 min. 47 sec.	2 hrs. 49 min.
CBS evening news	88	2 min. 13 sec.	3 hrs. 14 min.
NBC evening news	78	1 min. 51 sec.	2 hrs. 25 min.
Televised candidate interviews	75	8 min. 58 sec.	11 hrs. 13 min.
Local Media			
WMUR news	152	1 min. 19 sec.	3 hrs. 19 min.
Manchester Union Leader	474	9.1 col. inches	4,305 col. inches
Concord Monitor	377	15.0 col. inches	5,637 col. inches
Paid political advertisements	2,432	30 sec.	20 hrs. 16 min.

[a] A unit is defined as an individual television news story, newspaper article, interview, or advertisement.

(ninety-five), but the eighty-eight stories shown on CBS were longer on average, giving CBS the most coverage overall, with a total of 3.25 hours. NBC's stories were somewhat longer than those of ABC, but NBC aired fewer stories than either ABC or CBS, giving NBC the least coverage of the three networks. To help put these numbers in perspective, it is useful to consider what proportion of all network news coverage was devoted to the presidential campaign. Over the course of thirty-one broadcasts from 20 January to 19 February, ABC aired an average of 5.6 minutes of campaign coverage a day, accounting for 25 percent of all news coverage. On an average day, ABC ran three campaign stories, with no stories on only four days and a high of nine stories on 12 February.

For many viewers, local news is their main source of information about politics.[23] Past research comparing network and local news suggests that local news viewers might be at a disadvantage due to the less frequent and more superficial coverage that local outlets provide about government and politics. A study of media coverage of the 1992 presidential election, for example, found that local news focused more on the horse race and less on the issues than did network news.[24] But some recent work indicates that viewers of local news might be on a more level playing field with network viewers. This is not, however, because the quality of local news is improving; rather, with its emphasis on sensational and human interest stories, network news has increasingly come to resemble local news.[25] Advocates of the New Hampshire primary also believe that politics receives special attention from their local news organizations. New Hampshire has only one statewide television channel,

WMUR, an ABC affiliate based in Manchester. Like the state of New Hampshire in general, WMUR is proud of the primary—and of its own coverage of the primary. As WMUR's political reporter Carl Cameron explains,

> New Hampshire reporters have a special expertise. You go to Raleigh-Durham, reporters there can tell you everything there is to know about the Blue Devils. You come here, reporters can tell you everything about politics. It's our local sport. . . . With all due respect, it is almost impossible to scoop us on this. We've covered Lugar every time he's come up here, and he's been coming up here since '92. If national reporters come up here and all of a sudden discover that Lugar isn't getting a response from voters, that's their big story. Well, excuse me, we had that story 18 months ago.[26]

Does WMUR really provide more and better coverage? Table 6.1 provides the answer to the first part of the question. Over the last month of the campaign, WMUR did provide more coverage than any of the networks, but not that much more. Though WMUR aired many more stories than any of the national network news programs, its stories were shorter by an average of half a minute. As a result, WMUR aired only five more minutes of campaign coverage than did CBS, the network with the most coverage. Since these data span only the last month of the campaign, they cannot address Cameron's contention about the plentiful early coverage. No doubt, WMUR was covering the primary when the networks were not. But just because WMUR was covering the campaign months in advance of election day does not mean voters were paying attention then. During the critical last month of the campaign, the networks provided nearly as much coverage as WMUR.

Not surprisingly, the two local newspapers examined in this study ran many more stories on the campaign than were aired by any one television news program. From 20 January through 19 February, the *Manchester Union Leader* ran an astonishing 474 stories on the campaign, including a special election pullout section on 9 February. The *Concord Monitor* ran approximately 100 fewer stories, but they were much longer on average, giving the *Monitor* more coverage overall. Although it is difficult to compare the length of a television story with the length of a newspaper story, a standard conversion formula, based on how long it takes to read the front page of the *New York Times*, equates one inch of newsprint with 18 seconds of television air time.[27] Based on this standard, the average length of the *Union Leader*'s stories was 2.7 minutes, whereas the *Monitor*'s was 4.5 minutes. Both papers' stories were longer than the stories aired on television news, but the *Union Leader*'s shorter stories were not much longer than those aired on CBS. The *Monitor* published the longer stories that we associate with newspapers. Despite the brevity of its stories, the *Union Leader* still conveyed much more information overall than television news because it printed so many stories. Television news programs face a 22-minute limit (30 minutes minus commercials) that newspapers do not. After converting inches to hours, the total amount of campaign coverage during the last month of the campaign was 21.5 hours for the *Union Leader* and 28 hours for the *Monitor*.

A growing source of political information is televised interviews with the candidates. The 1992 campaign popularized such programs due in large part to Bill Clinton's and Ross Perot's successful use of the format.[28] Overwhelmed by scandal, negative press coverage, and attacks from other candidates, Clinton appeared on numerous talk shows to make his case. Similarly, Larry King of CNN is often credited with giving Perot the necessary exposure to launch a full-scale campaign. Other candidates followed suit, taking advantage of the free opportunity to speak more directly to voters. Though an interviewer can ask tough questions and bring up subjects a candidate would rather avoid, a skilled candidate can deflect them. Candidates running for the Republican nomination in 1996 picked up where the 1992 candidates left off. Between 20 January and 19 February, the candidates seeking the Republican nomination appeared on seventy-five interview programs. The candidates made short appearances on early morning talk shows like NBC's *Today* and gave longer interviews on such Sunday morning programs as *Meet the Press*. As in 1992, Larry King conducted a number of interviews. In general, interview programs are the longest format examined here; the average candidate appearance lasts nearly nine minutes. Few voters would likely find the time to tune in to all of these interviews, but with over eleven hours of total television time, there was still plenty of opportunity to catch some of them.

The final wholesale information source is candidates' paid television advertisements. New Hampshire voters were bombarded with ads in 1996. During the last month of the campaign, they were subjected to over twenty hours of ads on WMUR alone.[29] This last month was a frenzied finish to an ad campaign that began in October of 1995. WMUR's figures on the candidates' entire advertisement buys from October 1995 until the primary on 20 February indicate that candidates aired nearly forty-five hours of ads in their efforts to win the primary. Candidates also aired ads on the Boston television stations, which reach voters in southern New Hampshire.

This examination of just one month of the New Hampshire primary campaign from a wholesale perspective shows that voters would have probably been unable to avoid the campaign even if they had tried. But, of course, this is only half the story. New Hampshire is also famous for its retail campaign in which voters come in close contact with the candidates and their organizations. Advocates of the primary argue that there is no substitute for sizing up a candidate in the flesh. As noted earlier, New Hampshire voters have many opportunities to meet the candidates. During the final five weeks of the campaign, Buchanan, Dole, Alexander, and Forbes, the top four finishers in the Republican primary, made a combined fifty-six visits to New Hampshire.[30]

Although the candidates are clearly present in New Hampshire, what proportion of residents actually meet the men who would be president? Figure 6.1 provides an answer to this question. The figure is based on results from five WMUR-Dartmouth College polls of likely New Hampshire Republican primary voters, conducted between 4 October 1995 and 15 February 1996 (see appendix B, pp. 247–50, for survey details). Across all five surveys, around 20 percent of respondents said they had met a candidate running for president or seen one in person. This consistency suggests that the same people were meeting more candidates,

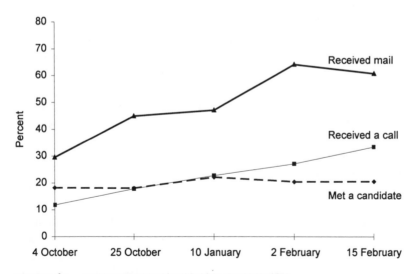

FIGURE 6.1   VOTER CONTACT WITH THE CANDIDATES

Source: WMUR-Dartmouth College poll.

rather than that more people were meeting a candidate for the first time. An examination of the panel component of the surveys gives further support to this idea. The fourth survey, which was conducted at the end of January, was the second wave of a panel that reinterviewed respondents from the two October surveys. Only 9 percent of the respondents who had not met a candidate in October reported having done so by the end of January.

New Hampshire is also unusual in the amount of information voters receive directly from the candidates' organizations. Campaign workers go door to door or stand on street corners and hand out fliers. Candidates also send appeals through the mail. Though much of the printed material voters receive consists of mass mailings, I still consider this form of communication to be retail campaigning. Since these mailings arrive in an individual's mailbox, addressed to an actual person rather than "resident," they take on a more personalized nature than a television ad beamed out to whoever happens to be watching a particular channel at a particular moment. Some of the mailings used in the 1996 campaign might have been especially memorable. Richard Lugar mailed videotapes to voters, and Phil Gramm sent out Christmas cards.[31] Figure 6.1 shows that candidates' local and national organizations were increasingly active in contacting voters as the primary neared. Respondents to the WMUR-Dartmouth College polls were asked if they had received mail from a candidate and if they had received a visit or call from a candidate's campaign organization. The percentage of respondents reporting the receipt of mail was about 30 percent in early October and showed dramatic growth during the campaign. By the end of January, approximately two-thirds of respondents had received mail from a candidate. At the beginning of October, few potential voters—about ten percent—had received calls from the campaigns. By the time of the primary, this number had tripled, with nearly one-third of potential Republican primary voters having received a phone call on behalf of a candidate.

At the presidential level, only the residents of Iowa experience a similar amount of direct attention from the candidates. Iowa differs from New Hampshire, however, in that it holds caucuses instead of a primary, and the campaigns focus their attention on the party activists who are more likely to attend these low-turnout meetings. The retail appeals made in New Hampshire are to a much larger group of voters. New Hampshire residents were very likely to have contact with a presidential candidate or his organization. By the time of the 1996 New Hampshire primary, nearly 70 percent of likely Republican voters had experienced at least one of the three forms of candidate contact shown in figure 6.1. Despite the unusually high levels of candidate contact that New Hampshire voters experience, the constant media campaign that confronts Granite State residents might still overshadow the retail campaign. On the other hand, because the retail campaign is personal and unique, its impact on voters could still be greater.

Quality of Information

As we have just seen, the overall flow of campaign communications to New Hampshire residents during the 1996 primary was constant and abundant. But, again, quantity does not guarantee quality. If voters are provided primarily with poor-quality information, such as where the candidates stand in the horse race rather than where they stand on the issues, voters will have difficulty making a decision that accords with their interests. A small amount of quality information may be superior to a large amount of bad information.[32] Accordingly, this section examines the quality of the information that New Hampshire voters used to make their decisions. The analysis includes all of the wholesale sources listed in table 6.1: network evening news programs, WMUR's local news, the *Manchester Union Leader*, the *Concord Monitor*, televised candidate interviews, and televised advertisements. In addition, one retail source was coded: candidates' campaign stump speeches.

A common criticism of media coverage of campaigns is that it focuses on the horse race and candidates' campaign strategies to the exclusion of more useful topics, such as the candidates' issue positions and backgrounds.[33] Figure 6.2 shows a clear difference in content between the sources of information that were controlled by the media and those controlled by the candidates.[34] The most common topic of news stories in both electronic and print media was the horse race and the candidates' campaign strategies. This focus on "the game" was most pronounced on television. Approximately three-quarters of all news stories aired from 20 January to 19 February on both network and local news mentioned the horse race or strategy. In a primary election with a large number of candidates, some horse-race information is useful for voters who do not want to "waste" their votes. A reasonable decision-making strategy might be to narrow the field to two or three candidates and then cast a ballot for the candidate who is most likely to win.[35] But in order to shrink the field of candidates, a voter would want to compare his own views on the issues with the candidates' positions. In addition to policy information, voters might want information about a candidate's experience and qual-

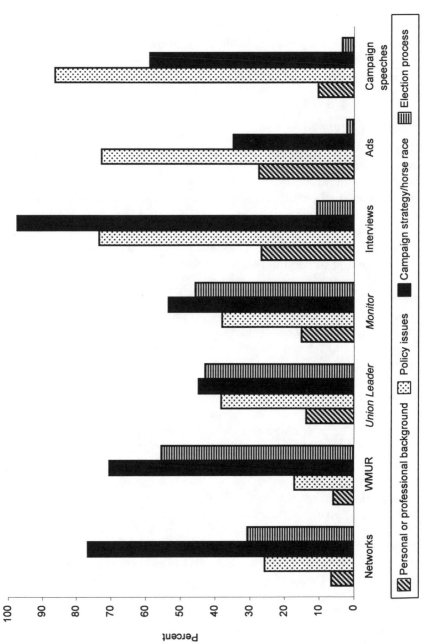

FIGURE 6.2   TOPICS MENTIONED IN CAMPAIGN COMMUNICATIONS

ifications. This type of information is especially crucial for distinguishing among candidates in a primary election, in which candidates often have similar policy positions. Television news did a poor job in conveying more substantive information. Very few television news stories, less than 10 percent, mentioned the candidates' backgrounds; about twice as many stories mentioned a policy issue. The next most frequently mentioned topic on television news was the process of the election. Some election-process stories can help voters understand how the system works and their role in it, but these stories seem to be crowding out stories that could provide information about the candidates. This was particularly true on WMUR, where the process was mentioned in over half of all stories.

Although the *Union Leader* and the *Monitor* also provided a considerable amount of horse-race coverage, their campaign coverage was more balanced across topics. The two newspapers mentioned the horse race less frequently and printed more stories mentioning policy issues than did television news, but they, too, provided little information about the candidates' backgrounds. Like television news, newspaper stories often focused on the election process.

When candidates provided the information, the subjects were quite different. In both ads and speeches, the most common topic was policy issues. The horse race did come up in about two-thirds of the speeches, however. Such references are usually attempts to motivate the audience to support the candidate when he is lagging behind in the polls or appeals for continued support so he can fight through to a victory. While the candidates made reference to the horse race in nearly one-third of all ads, ads provided proportionally more information about the candidates' backgrounds and qualifications than any other source. Candidates did not discuss the election process in either their ads or their speeches.

In terms of format, televised candidate interviews combine features of media and of candidate-controlled communications, so we might also expect them to combine television's fascination with the horse race and strategy with the greater issue content of ads and speeches. Figure 6.2 shows this to be the case. Like television news, interviews apparently cannot avoid talking about the horse race and strategy; the topic came up in nearly all interviews. Given the longer length of interviews, perhaps it is inevitable that the interviewer will eventually mention the candidate's position in the polls. But the longer format also allows discussion of other topics, as evidenced by the more frequent mention of both policy issues and the candidates' backgrounds. As in candidate-controlled communications, the election process was not a common topic of conversation during interviews.

The data in table 6.1 and figure 6.2 suggest that if voters wanted to learn about the candidates' backgrounds and issue positions, they would have been well advised to read newspapers, watch televised candidate interviews, pay attention to political ads, and try to attend some candidate speeches. But a mere mention of an issue does not tell us how richly detailed the communication was. The sources just mentioned have very different formats, and some may therefore not provide the kind of contextual information thought to be useful for learning.[36] One obvious difference between the formats is length. As can be seen in table 6.1, ads are much shorter than the other sources, thus giving candidates less opportunity to provide detailed discussions of their issue positions. Television news stories are shorter than newspaper stories, and interviews and speeches are longer. Did these differences affect the depth of the information provided?

The content analysis of campaign information allows me to examine the degree of detail provided when a candidate's issue positions, policy proposals, or past record on an issue was mentioned. For every such mention, a number of quality measures were coded: whether the topic was given extensive discussion, whether details were provided, whether the issue was placed in a larger context, if societal implications were raised, and if political implications were raised. The first four measures are surely positive attributes of issue information. Their presence in a news story, interview, ad, or speech is likely to be correlated. For instance, a news story that gives an extensive discussion of Steve Forbes's flat tax proposal is likely to include the detail that Forbes's plan calls for a tax rate of 15 percent for all taxpayers regardless of income, to place the tax plan in the context of current graduated tax rates, and to discuss the impact the plan would have on the amount of taxes paid by various people. Discussing the political implications of a policy proposal, by contrast, is not clearly positive or negative. If, in addition to providing other detailed information, a reporter talks about how voters are receiving the proposal and the impact it is having on Forbes's chance of winning, there would be little cause for complaint. But it is often assumed that discussion of the political impact of issues takes time away from other, more useful information like details, context, and societal implications.

How frequently do discussions of the candidates' records, policy proposals, and issue stands include each of the various quality measures? Figure 6.3 allows one to compare the frequency of each measure of qual-

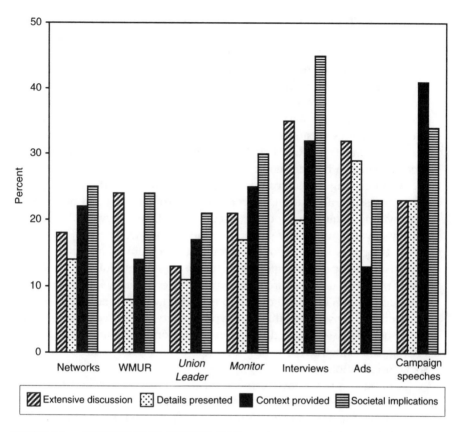

FIGURE 6.3   QUALITY MEASURES IN DISCUSSIONS OF CANDIDATES' RECORDS,
PROPOSALS, AND ISSUE STANDS

ity across information sources, as well as to determine the source with the
highest overall quality.[37] For example, 18 percent of the time when network news mentioned a candidate's records, proposals, and issue stands,
they provided a reasonably extensive discussion of that topic. (An extensive discussion is one in which the issue is allotted more than twenty seconds of a television news story, more than two paragraphs of a newspaper
story, or more than one-third of an interview, ad, or speech.) The depth of
coverage across all sources of information was not very high. Few discussions of candidate issues were extensive, details were generally lacking, little context was provided, and, more often than not, the impact of the issue
on society was ignored. Still, some sources were better than others.
Candidate interviews, one of the longest formats on average, provided the
highest quality of information on candidates' records, proposals, and issue

stands. Such topics received the most extensive coverage, with 35 percent of candidate issue mentions occupying at least one-third of the interview. Since interviews often cover a number of topics, this number could be considered high. In the interviews, nearly half of the discussions involving issues also included talk of the social implications, which is far more than any other information source. Disappointingly, interviewers often let candidates skirt the issues, as evidenced by the lack of detail about candidates' positions and proposals. Interviewers often did not try, and candidates frequently failed, to place issue positions, proposals, and records within a broader context.

Another long format, campaign speeches, provided the next highest quality of issue information. Speeches were strong on context but weaker in providing details and social consequences. Like interviews, speeches usually cover a number of subjects, so few issues were discussed extensively. Length is not the sole determinant of quality, however; political advertisements provided more information about candidate issues than any of the news media sources, all of which were usually longer than ads. Still, only 32 percent of ad discussions of candidates' issue stands qualify as extensive. This means that in a typical thirty-second ad, two-thirds of the issue discussions lasted less than ten seconds. It should not be surprising, then, that ads also provided few details, little context, and few social implications.

Among the news media, the *Concord Monitor* provided the most substantive coverage of the candidates' records, proposals, and issue positions, while the *Manchester Union Leader* provided the worst. The fact that newspapers ranked both best and worst on this dimension, with television sandwiched in between, suggests that editorial policies may have a larger impact on the quality of news coverage than the medium does. Recall that numerous short stories characterized the *Union Leader*'s campaign coverage; this news style appears to have limited the paper's ability to cover the candidates in depth.

Another common criticism of news media coverage of presidential campaigns is that even when issues are mentioned, they are covered in terms of their impact on the horse race and not their impact on the voters.[38] Figure 6.4 shows there is truth to this complaint. In television news coverage of the campaign, the political implications of candidates' records, proposals, and issue stands were much more likely to be mentioned than their social implications. The same is true of newspapers, though to a lesser extent. The political impact of the candidates' policy positions was also discussed frequently during interviews, but the social consequences were a considerably more common topic of conversation

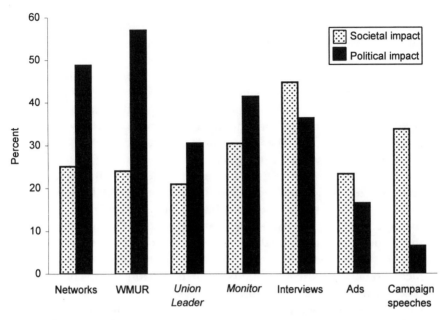

FIGURE 6.4   MENTION OF THE IMPACT OF CANDIDATES' RECORDS, PROPOSALS, AND ISSUE STANDS

on such programs. Candidates infrequently discussed political implications in their ads and speeches. Speeches provided the highest ratio of societal to political talk. For every one mention of the political impact of an issue in a speech, candidates made nearly seven references to its impact on the country.

Does the depth of coverage suffer when journalists and candidates frame an issue in terms of its impact on the campaign? It is often assumed that when reporters talk about the horse race, it comes at the expense of more useful information. By talking and writing about the impact of a candidate's policy proposals on his chances of winning, the argument goes, reporters have less time to cover the impact of the proposals on society or to provide other details regarding the issue. The content-analysis coding allows me to test this assumption by examining the correlation between the mention of political implications and the presence of the positive quality measures. A significant negative correlation between the mention of political implications and the positive quality measures would be confirmation of this assumption. When I calculated this correlation across all of the media and candidate information sources, I found no evidence that discussion of the political implications of a candidate's record, policy proposals, and issue positions reduced the quality of the coverage, but such discussions did not enhance the quality either. All of the positive quality measures are correlated among themselves, meaning that when reporters put an issue in context they are likely to provide details and to discuss the social implications of the issue as well. A discussion of the political implications of an issue position, by contrast, is not associated with a discussion of its social implications or any of the other quality measures. In short, while political discussions do not necessarily hurt campaign communications, they do not help them either.

This analysis so far has focused on the last month of the campaign, but it is possible that information presented early in the campaign is characterized by greater depth and focuses less on the horse race and more on the issues and candidates' backgrounds. Early in the campaign, the outcome is less certain, so news stories might focus on other topics. In addition, because candidates need to spend some time introducing themselves to voters, they may take more time in their early advertisements to detail their backgrounds and issue positions. The content database assembled here, which has information on network news and the candidates' advertisements going back to 1995, can help assess whether early campaign communications are more substantive than later communications. For each network news story and candidate ad, I created a variable to indicate the number of days from when it was aired until the New Hampshire primary on 20 February.[39] I then correlated this date variable with the mention of the four topic categories and the four quality measures shown in figures 6.2 and 6.3.

The analysis finds some slight differences between early and late news coverage and advertisements. Network news stories aired earlier in the campaign were somewhat less likely to mention the horse race and somewhat more likely to mention the election process. Discussion of policy issues and the candidates' backgrounds did not vary across the campaign. In other words, while early network news coverage was a bit less driven by the horse race, the networks substituted process stories rather than stories distinguishing the candidates on substantive grounds. Early candidate ads were somewhat more likely to mention policy issues, while later ads were a bit more likely to mention the candidates' backgrounds. Mentions of the horse race and process did not change over time in candidates' ads. When network news and candidates' ads discussed the candidates' records, proposals, and issue positions, the depth of the discussions differed somewhat over time. Early network stories provided a bit more context and detail than later ones. Ads produced for later in the campaign, on the other hand, were of slightly higher quality than early ads in that they provided somewhat more extensive discussion of the candidates' issue positions. Overall, the networks' early coverage was slightly better than the later coverage. The positive aspects of early ads were canceled out by some negative aspects, making ads approximately consistent in quality over the course of the campaign.

Overall, did New Hampshire voters have the opportunity to learn about the candidates seeking the Republican nomination in 1996? Based on a content analysis of a number of campaign information sources, the answer is mixed. While New Hampshire residents were presented with a constant stream of information coming directly from the candidates and indirectly through the news media, many of these communications focused on the horse race and the candidates' campaign strategies. Information detailing the candidates' issue positions or presidential qualifications was less readily available. When issues were discussed, some sources provided more in-depth information than others did. Candidate interviews and speeches especially stood out. Given the differences in the quantity and quality of information provided by different sources, it is likely that voters' knowledge of the candidates will vary according to their exposure to particular sources.

Were New Hampshire Voters Motivated to Learn about the Candidates?

One of the arguments for maintaining New Hampshire's place at the beginning of the primary calendar is the great interest that New Hampshire residents reportedly have in politics. The claim is that New Hampshire voters are unusually interested in politics and pay close attention to the campaign, with the result that they cast unusually well-informed ballots. As noted above, the literature on political learning indicates that motivation is a key factor in the learning process. In this section, I examine the changing attention levels of New Hampshire voters over the course of the 1996 campaign. Did the primary campaign interest Granite State residents? At what point in the campaign did they start to pay attention? How do the attention levels of New Hampshire residents compare with those of people living elsewhere? Also, what are the media habits of New Hampshire voters? Answers to these questions will help ascertain whether New Hampshire voters paid sufficient attention to learn from the campaign and to make an informed choice.

The WMUR-Dartmouth College poll asked all respondents how much attention they were paying to the 1996 presidential campaign. The survey results show that four and one-half months before the New Hampshire pri-

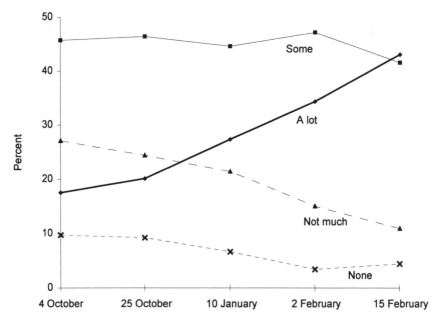

FIGURE 6.5   AMOUNT OF ATTENTION PAID TO PRESIDENTIAL CAMPAIGN:
NEW HAMPSHIRE SAMPLE

Source: WMUR-Dartmouth College poll.

mary, many New Hampshire residents were already paying close attention
to the presidential campaign. At the beginning of October 1995, almost one-
half of the respondents to the poll said they were paying some attention to
the campaign; nearly 20 percent were already paying a lot of attention.
Figure 6.5 shows that as the months passed and the 20 February primary
grew nearer, attention to the campaign increased steadily. In fact, the percentage of people paying a lot of attention continued to increase right up
until the primary, indicating that some people did not start paying a lot of
attention until a decision was imminent. As the previous section noted,
campaign information was plentiful during the last month of the campaign
but somewhat less substantive than earlier campaign information.

Are the attention levels in figure 6.5 high or low? It is difficult to
answer this question without a comparison group. By the end of the primary campaign, 85 percent of the New Hampshire population was paying a lot of or some attention to the campaign. Compared with a national
sample, this level is clearly high. Figure 6.6 shows how respondents
across the nation answered the same attention question in a CBS News/
New York Times poll on two occasions before the New Hampshire pri-

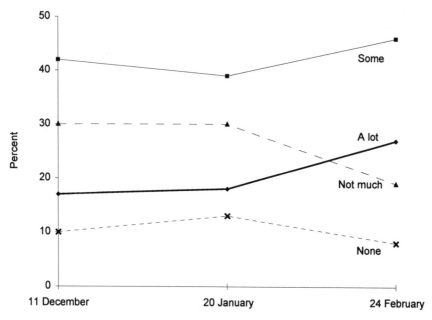

FIGURE 6.6   AMOUNT OF ATTENTION PAID TO PRESIDENTIAL CAMPAIGN:
             NATIONAL SAMPLE

Source: CBS/*New York Times* poll.

mary and again immediately following it. The attention level of the American public in mid-January was similar to that of New Hampshire residents in late October. After the first contests in Iowa and New Hampshire, more people around the country began paying attention, but still not close to the proportion of New Hampshire residents. These differences are not surprising, though, since the amount of campaigning and news coverage of the election is much less in other states. Still, New Hampshire residents are engaged by the campaign and pay attention at the high levels that the primary's supporters maintain.

Motivation has so far been assessed by a self-described attention question that gives an indication of people's changing exposure to campaign information. Another measure of campaign exposure is people's media habits. Where do New Hampshire residents get most of their news? Does their use of the different news media increase as their attention to the campaign increases? Respondents to the WMUR-Dartmouth College poll were asked how often they watched network television news, watched local television news, and read the news pages of a daily newspaper. As can be seen in table 6.2, more New Hampshire residents rely on local

TABLE 6.2   MEDIA USE BY THE NEW HAMPSHIRE REPUBLICAN PRIMARY
ELECTORATE, 1995-96

	4 October	25 October	10 January	2 February	15 February
Network News					
Every day	23.0%	29.8%	24.8%	32.6%	26.0%
Most days	20.1	20.5	22.9	19.8	23.1
Once/twice a week	21.0	21.5	19.3	23.9	20.8
Only occasionally	13.9	14.9	16.6	8.5	15.2
Never	22.0	13.4	16.4	15.1	14.9
Local Television News					
Every day	32.8	39.3	44.0	50.0	42.2
Most days	21.2	20.0	22.7	21.6	22.6
Once/twice a week	17.6	16.9	12.5	12.3	13.8
Only occasionally	11.4	13.5	11.9	8.5	12.0
Never	17.0	10.3	8.8	7.6	9.4
Newspapers					
Every day	45.5	41.8	35.8	44.7	42.8
Most days	14.6	14.3	19.7	15.4	17.0
Once/twice a week	12.1	15.4	13.2	11.3	11.4
Only occasionally	7.5	9.8	11.2	8.5	10.9
Never	20.4	18.8	20.1	20.1	17.9
No. of respondents	(482)	(534)	(512)	(423)	(342)

news sources than on national sources for information. Newspapers and local television news were a much more common source of information than was network television news. Newspapers and local television news also provide the most campaign information. The local news media likely begin covering the primary long before the networks and also provide slightly more coverage in the period just before the primary. The reliance of New Hampshire residents on newspapers bodes well for learning from the campaign, since newspapers provide the most and some of the best coverage among the various news media.

The exposure of New Hampshire residents to the news does not increase steadily during the campaign. Table 6.2 shows that a significant increase in the viewing of both local and network television news took place between the first survey in early October and the second survey in late October, but no significant increases appear in subsequent surveys. There were a few ups and downs in viewing across the later surveys, but none are distinguishable from sampling error. Likewise, newspaper reading remained relatively constant during the campaign, with few changes from survey to survey that are distinguishable from sampling error.

How can we reconcile the increased attention to the campaign shown in figure 6.5 with the steady media habits reported in table 6.2?

One possibility is that the New Hampshire electorate did not increase the frequency with which they used the news media in general, but increased their attention to stories dealing specifically with the campaign. Also, they might have started paying more attention to other sources of information, such as political advertisements or televised interviews with the candidates. Respondents in the last three surveys were asked whether they recalled seeing any political advertisements on television for the Republican presidential candidates. In early January, a large majority of respondents, 82 percent, recalled seeing a political ad on television. A few weeks later, in early February, this number rose to 92 percent, where it remained for the rest of the primary campaign. If this question had been asked in the October surveys, we would likely see even more dramatic changes from the fall to the winter. Finally, recall from figure 6.1 that respondents reported receiving more mail and phone calls from the candidates as the campaign wore on. Heightened attention to the variety of information sources available to voters could explain the increases in attention to the campaign that we see in figure 6.5.

When provided with the opportunity to learn, then, New Hampshire voters pay attention at levels that should facilitate an informed vote. A note of concern is also appropriate, though. While most voters are paying attention by the end of the campaign, the opportunity to learn is not equal across information sources, so what the voters learn might depend on what media they use. Because the quality of late campaign information is somewhat poorer than information provided earlier, New Hampshire voters who pay attention only toward the end of the campaign may be hampered in their ability to make an informed choice.

Did New Hampshire Voters Have the Ability to Learn about the Candidates?

The final requirement for political learning is individual ability. People with more formal education and preexisting knowledge about politics are more likely to learn new political information when they encounter it. New Hampshire residents are better educated than the nation as a whole; in fact, they rank seventh among the fifty states in educational attainment.[40] Based on their formal education alone, the New Hampshire electorate should have the ability to learn from the primary campaign and thus cast an informed ballot.

Advocates of the New Hampshire primary maintain that New Hampshire residents are not only more interested in politics than people elsewhere, but are more knowledgeable as well. Is this claim true, and if so, is it merely a reflection of the state's demographic makeup? That is, are New Hampshire residents more knowledgeable about politics than would be expected on the basis of the state's higher education levels, as well as its wealthier population and lack of large cities? Are Granite State voters the political overachievers their advocates maintain?

My answers to these questions come from a comparison of a 1,002-person national sample of U.S. citizens with a 455-person New Hampshire sample. The New Hampshire respondents were first interviewed in October 1995 and then again in February 1996, just before the primary, as part of the WMUR-Dartmouth College poll. The respondents from the national sample were first interviewed in the summer of 1996, along with the existing New Hampshire panel respondents. A comparison of the political-knowledge levels possessed by New Hampshire and national respondents will shed light on whether New Hampshire residents are more knowledgeable about politics than the rest of the nation.[41]

According to the panel survey, the people of New Hampshire are indeed more politically knowledgeable than the nation as a whole. During the summer telephone survey, respondents were asked five factual political-knowledge questions (see appendix B for the wording of all survey questions). On average, the New Hampshire sample answered 3.9 of these questions correctly, compared with 3.4 correct answers for the national sample.[42] To determine whether the greater political-knowledge levels of the New Hampshire residents were due to population differences or exceptional political intelligence, I regressed political knowledge on age, gender, race, education, income, city size, and whether the respondent was a New Hampshire resident or not. The results are presented in table 6.3. The significant positive coefficient of the New Hampshire dummy variable indicates that New Hampshire residents are

TABLE 6.3   EXPLAINING POLITICAL KNOWLEDGE: IMPACT OF NEW HAMPSHIRE
RESIDENCY

Variable	B	SE B	t
New Hampshire resident	.314	.081	3.86
Age	.014	.002	6.46
Education	.512	.036	14.33
Female	-.669	.070	-9.57
Income	.114	.022	5.19
White	.426	.108	3.94
City size	-.014	.026	-.53
Intercept	.644	.195	3.31
No. of observations	1,317		
R^2	.31		

more knowledgeable about politics than would be expected just on the basis of their demographic characteristics. Controlling for their unique demographic characteristics, New Hampshire respondents still answered more political-knowledge questions correctly than the national sample did.

Voter Learning in the 1996 Republican Primary

The analysis presented in the previous sections indicates that many New Hampshire voters fulfilled the requirements for political learning in the 1996 Republican primary. Attention to the campaign increased steadily as the primary approached. Many voters were motivated to pay attention months in advance, though the majority waited until primary day neared to begin paying a lot of attention. As a group, New Hampshire voters are certainly able to learn about the candidates. The state is populated by people who are well educated and particularly knowledgeable about politics. In terms of opportunity, my findings are more mixed. Both wholesale and retail sources of candidate information provided New Hampshire residents with a large quantity of information, but the quality varied by information source, with candidate communications providing more depth and mentioning more policy issues than media sources. Quality also differed somewhat by date. This section examines survey data to find out how much New Hampshire voters actually learned, what they learned, when they learned it, and what information sources were most effective.

How Much Was Learned?

By 20 February 1996, eight of the ten major candidates invited to WMUR's candidate forum in October 1995 remained in the race. Arlen Specter withdrew on 22 November, and Phil Gramm exited on 14 February after a poor showing in the Iowa caucuses. Eight candidates are still a large field, and it would be a challenge for even the most attentive voter to be knowledgeable about them all. But what exactly qualifies as knowledgeable? At minimum, a person should be able to recognize a candidate's name. The five WMUR-Dartmouth College polls asked likely Republican primary voters whether they had a favorable or unfavorable opinion about each of the eight candidates. Respondents were also given the option of saying they did not know the candidate's name or had not heard enough about him to have an opinion. The last two responses are classified as *not* recognizing a candidate. Respondents who either gave an opinion or said they had enough information but were currently undecided are classified as recognizing a candidate. I then created an overall measure of candidate recognition by counting the number of candidates each respondent recognized. Figure 6.7 is a series of histograms displaying the distribution of this recognition variable for each survey; descriptive statistics appear alongside each figure. The change in the nature of the distributions from slightly skewed to the left in early October to heavily skewed to the right shortly before the February primary shows strong evidence of learning from the campaign. The electorate changed from one in which most voters recognized only a few of the candidates to one in which most voters recognized nearly all eight of them. By the time of the primary, candidate recognition can be thought of as nearly universal.

The means also show the sharp increase in candidate recognition that occurred during the campaign. In early October, likely Republican primary voters recognized an average of 3.87 candidates out of a possible 8. By the time of the primary in February, they recognized an average of 5.67 candidates. Judging from the amount of change in the distributions, the most learning took place during the last six weeks of the campaign. Not only did the average number of candidates recognized increase by nearly one candidate over this period; the standard deviation of the distribution declined slightly as well, meaning that voters were becoming more alike in their knowledge of the candidates. Much of this period was covered by the content analysis presented earlier, and given the large quantity of campaign information presented, it is not surprising that voter recognition of the candidates increased dramatically during this period. But the quality of the information was often poor, and it remains to be seen whether voters learned the type of detailed information about the candidates needed to cast an informed vote.

To vote in such a manner, voters would need to be able to do more than recognize the candidates and offer a general opinion about them; they should have some detailed knowledge of the candidates. Ideally, voters would know something about the candidates' qualifications for office, positions on the major issues, and even where candidates stood in relation to one another in terms of their basic ideological philosophies. Without such knowledge, it would probably be difficult to distinguish one Republican candidate from another. The WMUR-Dartmouth College surveys provide a good measure of voters' detailed knowledge of the candidates. In each survey, respondents who recognized a candidate in response to the favorability question were asked an additional open-ended question about that candidate: "What comes to mind when you

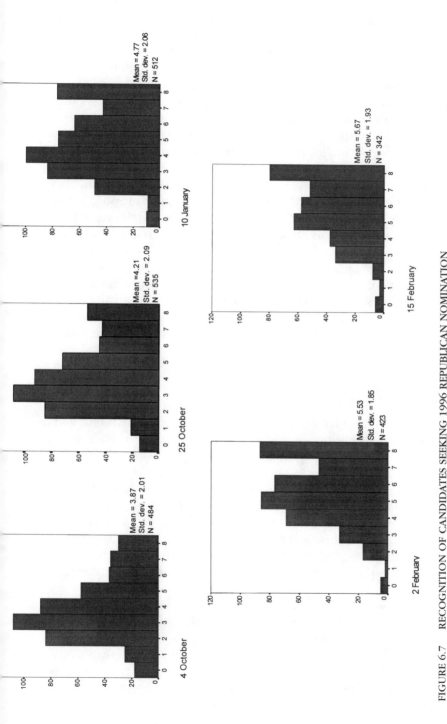

FIGURE 6.7   RECOGNITION OF CANDIDATES SEEKING 1996 REPUBLICAN NOMINATION

Note: Vertical scale shows the number of respondents in each category.

think about [the candidate]?" Interviewers prompted respondents until they had nothing else to say or had given four responses, whichever came first. This question was only asked about the four most recognized candidates—Alexander, Buchanan, Dole, and Forbes—thus allowing for a maximum of sixteen total responses. The total number of responses to these open-ended questions is, then, a measure of the respondents' detailed candidate knowledge. Respondents who were not asked the open-ended question because they did not recognize a candidate were given a score of zero for that candidate, as were respondents who could not provide any response when given the chance.

Figure 6.8 shows that the number of open-ended comments is a much tougher test of knowledge than the recognition measure. The most frequently given number of comments during the first three surveys was zero. Learning did take place, however, and as with candidate recognition, the greatest gains were achieved during the last six weeks of the campaign. But unlike the recognition measures, large gains in detailed knowledge of the candidates were not universal across the electorate. The distribution goes from heavily skewed left in early October to more of a normal distribution in mid-February, shortly before the primary. So, by the end of the campaign, most respondents knew a little about the candidates, but few knew a lot.

What Was Learned?

In a study of the 1976 election conducted in Erie, Pennsylvania, and Los Angeles, Thomas Patterson found that voters' images of the candidates reflected the media's coverage of the campaign.[43] Keeter and Zukin reached a similar conclusion when they examined national voters' knowledge of the 1980 presidential primary candidates. If the New Hampshire primary electorate developed candidate images based mainly on media coverage, they would probably think of the candidates principally in terms of their standings in the polls and campaign strategies. Voters' impressions of the candidates would have little to do with candidates' issue positions and backgrounds. But as we saw in the content analysis, the candidates also presented a lot of information to voters through their ads, interviews, speeches, and mailings. Compared with media coverage of the campaign, candidates' communications focused more on the issues. What types of things did voters learn about the candidates? How well do voters' images of the candidates reflect the information environment? The responses to the open-ended questions about the candidates help answer these questions.

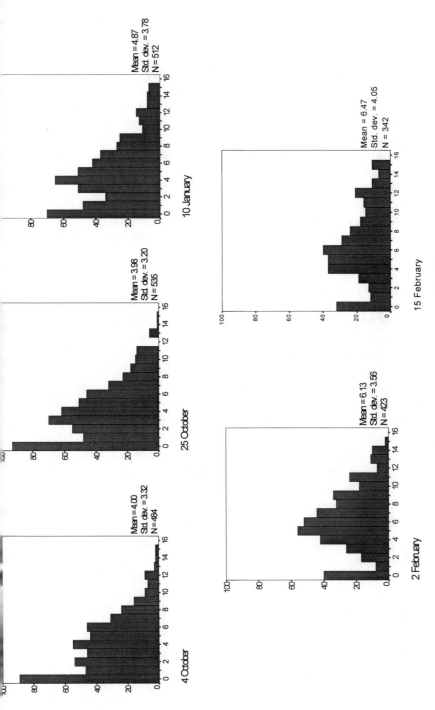

FIGURE 6.8   DETAILED KNOWLEDGE OF CANDIDATES SEEKING 1996 REPUBLICAN NOMINATION: NUMBER OF CANDIDATE COMMENTS

Note: Vertical scale shows the number of respondents in each category.

All responses to the open-ended questions were written down verbatim by the interviewer and later coded as to their subject matter. Starting out with 225 distinct subject codes, responses were ultimately broken down into 9 general areas. Table 6.4 displays the percentage of the responses falling within each of the 9 areas for each survey. In general, voters' images of the candidates were more reflective of the candidates' agenda than of the media coverage. Despite the media's heavy emphasis on the horse race, when voters were asked to talk about candidates, they did so in terms of the candidates' issue positions, the types of people they were, and the candidates' qualifications for the office of president. The focus of voters' comments changed little over the course of the campaign. The campaign itself did come up, but in less than 10 percent of all responses. Recall from figure 6.2 that the horse race was mentioned in over 75 percent of network news stories. Voters, however, are much more preoccupied with the types of subjects they can use to distinguish the candidates and make a voting decision. In short, even in an information environment dominated by the horse race, voters are able to pick up other information about the candidates. This finding is contrary to Patterson's and Keeter and Zukin's, but there are some key differences in the studies. First, we have seen that the New Hampshire electorate is highly motivated and particularly capable of learning. Supporters of the Granite State primary claim that New Hampshire voters are uniquely qualified to begin the winnowing process, and these data suggest that they may be right. Second, with the possible exception of voters in Iowa, New Hampshire voters are exposed to a longer and more intensive campaign than voters anywhere else. They certainly receive more information, and even if the media coverage is sometimes poor, the candidates' lavish attention surely helps compensate.

TABLE 6.4   FOCUS OF VOTERS' THOUGHTS ABOUT THE CANDIDATES

	4 October	25 October	10 January	2 February	15 February
Policy issues	17.9%	17.5%	18.5%	21.9%	19.8%
Character/personality	17.6	16.7	17.0	15.0	13.3
Experience/ability	15.7	16.4	17.2	16.7	21.3
Overall judgment	11.9	11.7	14.0	13.4	9.2
Ideology/party	10.9	10.1	7.9	5.5	7.0
Campaign characteristics	9.0	8.3	9.3	7.9	8.3
Personal background/ characteristics	8.2	9.7	8.2	9.9	11.7
Leadership qualities	4.3	4.8	4.5	5.0	4.6
Group-related perceptions	3.7	3.8	2.5	3.8	3.9
No. of responses	(2,349)	(2,555)	(2,983)	(3,102)	(2,366)

How They Learned It

Though recognition of the candidates was more widespread among the electorate than was detailed knowledge, people learned varying amounts about the candidates on both measures. A few people still did not recognize any of the candidates after months of campaigning. At the other extreme were people who recognized all the candidates in early October and already knew a number of specific things about them. The majority of the electorate, of course, fell somewhere in between and learned more about the candidates as the campaign progressed. Who knew the most, and what factors contributed to voters' knowledge of the candidates? In particular, are some sources of information better than others at educating voters about the candidates? Are some sources more effective at increasing candidate recognition but less effective at providing voters with more detailed candidate information?

To answer these questions, I estimated two models of voter knowledge for each of the five surveys. Specifically, I predicted candidate recognition and detailed candidate knowledge using variables that measure voters' opportunity, motivation, and ability to learn. Unfortunately, as we have already seen, there is a good deal of overlap in the measurement of these three explanations. In the models, I have tried to disentangle the explanations as much as possible by using an array of control variables. For example, exposure to different news media incorporates both opportunity and motivation. On the one hand, by comparing the relative contribution of different media sources to voter knowledge, we get an idea of the learning opportunity each source provided. At the same time, however, people must choose to use the news media. An individual who reads a newspaper will likely have a higher motivation level. So, if newspapers turn out to contribute more to knowledge than network television news does, is it because of the greater quantity and quality of newspaper news, or because the type of people who choose to read a newspaper are more informed from the start? One way to help answer this question is to control for age and education. Older people and people with more education are more likely to read a newspaper and are also more politically knowledgeable. Thus, by controlling for these characteristics, some of the effects of newspaper reading that have to do with individual motivation and ability rather than the content of the paper are removed from the media coefficients.

The models include twelve explanatory variables, seven of which measure exposure to different wholesale and retail information sources. Exposure to the news media is measured by use of network television news, local television news, and newspapers. Exposure to televised interviews is measured by the number of hours of television watched per day. This variable will likely also pick up exposure to political ads. Unfortunately, it is difficult to measure exposure to one information source without picking up exposure to another. Measuring exposure to political ads is particularly tricky. The majority of ads run on WMUR were aired during the local news when the ad buys were more affordable; daytime was the second most often used time period, followed by primetime. So, exposure to local news to some extent captures exposure to political ads, as does hours of television viewed. These variables are also imperfect measures because they do not account for channel flipping during commercials. The ad-recall question reported earlier is a more direct measure, but it was only asked in three surveys, and it lacks variance since nearly everyone recalled seeing at least one ad. This question is unable to measure the number of ads seen or the attention paid to them. Because of these difficulties, a separate variable measuring ad exposure is not included in the models. A cautious interpretation of the results of the media variables is required.

Variables measuring exposure to retail campaign information are also included in the models. Three dummy variables indicate whether the respondent recalled meeting a candidate, receiving mail from a candidate, or receiving a phone call from a candidate's organization. Finally, the models contain a few additional variables that capture motivation and ability. Attention to the campaign is a measure of motivation to learn. Ability is captured by education. Because only one survey asked about preexisting political knowledge, it is not included in the models.[44] The final three variables—gender, age, and ideology—allow a test of some of New Hampshire's interesting features and of primary campaigns in general.

Figures 6.9 through 6.14 display a summary of the models' results.[45] Each graph shows the impact of one set of independent variables on one of the dependent variables over the course of the campaign. The dependent variable for figures 6.9, 6.11, and 6.13 is the number of candidates the respondent recognized. The dependent variable for figures 6.10, 6.12, and 6.14 is the number of candidate comments the respondent expressed. As noted in the figures, each data point is the difference in the number of candidates recognized or number of candidate comments made by two voters who are identical in all respects except for the variable in question. The further the data point is from zero in either a positive or negative direction, the greater the impact of the variable on voters' knowledge of the candidates. For example, the individual-trait fig-

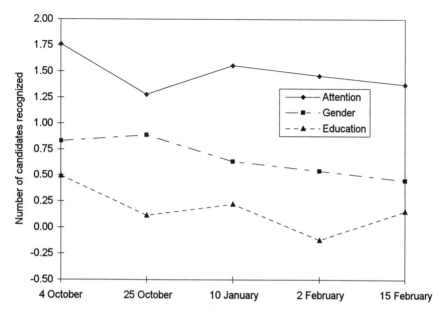

FIGURE 6.9   ESTIMATED EFFECTS OF INDIVIDUAL TRAITS ON NUMBER OF
CANDIDATES RECOGNIZED

Note: Each point is the difference in the number of candidates recognized by two voters
who are identical in all respects except for the trait in question. Attention: a lot versus
not much. Gender: men versus women. Education: college graduate versus high school
graduate.

ures show the estimated effects of three specific characteristics of the
survey respondents. In figure 6.9, the effect of attention can be interpreted as the difference in the number of candidates recognized by two
voters who were identical except that one had paid "a lot" of attention
to the campaign and the other had paid "not much" attention.

Across all five surveys, motivation is the single most important determinant of knowledge of the candidates. Attention to the campaign has
the greatest impact on both candidate recognition and detailed candidate knowledge (see figures 6.9 and 6.10). The impact of attention on
detailed knowledge actually increases over the course of the campaign,
as evidenced by the upward sloping attention line (see figure 6.10). This
is somewhat curious because attention is the only variable that changes
over the campaign. Data presented earlier showed that media use did
not change over the campaign and the demographic characteristics of an

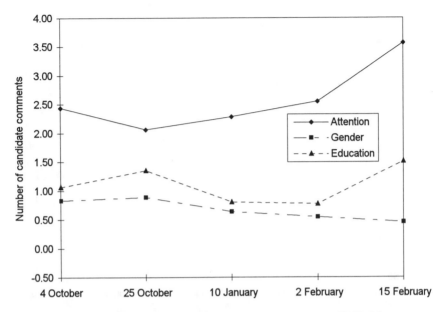

FIGURE 6.10   ESTIMATED EFFECTS OF INDIVIDUAL TRAITS ON NUMBER OF
CANDIDATE COMMENTS

Note: Each point is the difference in the number of candidate comments by two voters
who are identical in all respects except for the trait in question. Attention: a lot versus
not much. Gender: men versus women. Education: college graduate versus high school
graduate.

individual are fixed over such a short period. A person could be in the
low-attention group at the beginning of the campaign but in the high-
attention group at the end, whereas someone is not going to go from
having a high school diploma to a college degree in four months. So, the
types of people making up the high-attention group change during the
campaign, but attention still has the most impact on knowledge. This is
testimony to the importance of motivation and suggests that people who
do not pay a lot of attention until later in the campaign can catch up to
those who have been paying attention for months.

Figures 6.9 and 6.10 also show the impact of education and gender.
Higher education gives an advantage in detailed knowledge of the candidates but not in recognition. Only in the first survey do people with
greater education recognize more candidates. Compared with attention
to the campaign, however, the effect is modest: across the five surveys,
a respondent with a college education is likely to give only about one

more candidate comment than a respondent with a high school education. Consistent with past research, the model results show that gender has a significant, though declining, impact on knowledge over the course of the campaign.[46] Men recognize more candidates than women and have more things to say about the candidates. The work of Verba, Burns, and Scholzman suggests that men may simply have a greater taste for politics. Given the praises sung about New Hampshire's more active retail campaign, one might hope that women are as engaged by it as men, but the results of the knowledge models show this not to be the case.

The impact of age and ideology on knowledge is small and not consistently significant, so the results are not displayed in the figures. An examination of the knowledge levels of different groups of people shows that older people tend to recognize more candidates and possess more detailed knowledge about the candidates than do young people. But the age variable in the models has only a small impact on knowledge and does not

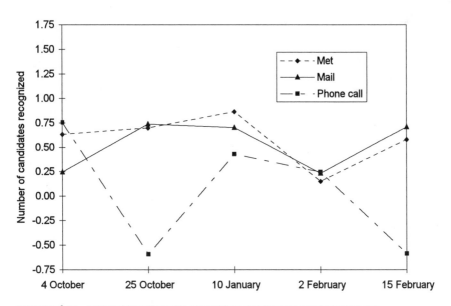

FIGURE 6.11   ESTIMATED EFFECTS OF RETAIL CAMPAIGN ON NUMBER OF
CANDIDATES RECOGNIZED

Note: Each point is the difference in the number of candidates recognized by two voters who are identical in all respects except that one had three contacts of the type in question and the other had none.

consistently achieve statistical significance. It is likely that greater attention and exposure to the campaign accounts for older people's greater knowledge of the candidates. Once these variables are controlled, the impact of age largely disappears. Somewhat surprisingly, ideology has no impact on knowledge of the Republican primary candidates. Conservatives were no more knowledgeable about the candidates than were moderates or liberals.

Figures 6.11 and 6.12 show the impact of contact with the candidates and their organizations on knowledge of the candidates, while figures 6.13 and 6.14 show the impact of exposure to the news media. Overall, respondents learned more from retail communications than from wholesale communications. Candidate mailings, which have an element of wholesale campaigning, were the most effective. A respondent who had received three mailings from a candidate was able to make between one and two additional comments about the candidates, depending on the date of the survey. Meeting three candidates in person

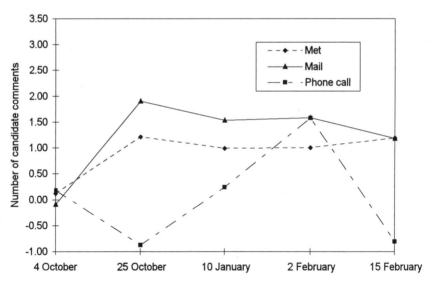

FIGURE 6.12   ESTIMATED EFFECTS OF RETAIL CAMPAIGN ON NUMBER OF
               CANDIDATE COMMENTS

Note: Each point is the difference in the number of candidate comments by two voters who are identical in all respects except that one had three contacts of the type in question and the other had none.

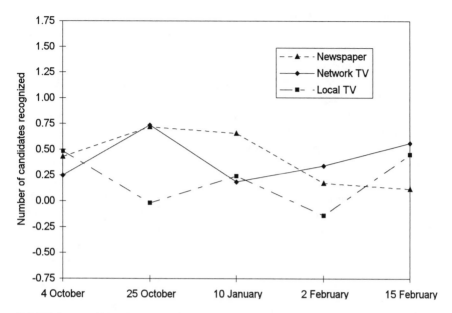

FIGURE 6.13   ESTIMATED EFFECTS OF WHOLESALE CAMPAIGN ON NUMBER OF
CANDIDATES RECOGNIZED

Note: Each point is the difference in the number of candidates recognized by two voters
who are identical in all respects except that one used the media in question every day
and the other never did.

had a smaller effect on detailed knowledge than three pieces of mail, but
as much of an effect on candidate recognition. Receiving phone calls
from the candidates' organizations had an inconsistent and often insignificant impact on knowledge of the candidates.

In general, the impact of exposure to the news media on knowledge
was small and frequently insignificant. Network news had a somewhat
greater effect than the other media on candidate recognition, while
newspaper reading had slightly more influence on detailed candidate
knowledge. In both cases, however, the impact was very small. The figures show the difference between someone who watches the news or
reads a paper every day compared with someone who never does these
activities. At most, watching network news every day allows a voter to
make one additional candidate comment compared with someone who
never watched. Reading a newspaper every day increases one's candidate recognition by three-quarters of a point. Local television news

exposure was rarely significant. Recall that most candidate ads are aired during local news, so this variable was doing double duty, but it still failed to achieve statistical significance. Hours of television watched, another measure of ad exposure and of exposure to televised interviews, was not a significant determinant of knowledge and hence is not displayed in the figures.

The inconsistent and small impact of the media found here is a common theme in research on campaigns and the media. Self-reported measures of media use are known to have significant problems with measurement error, and many scholars disbelieve the null media effects common in the literature.[47] The media variables used in this study, however, were designed to reduce the error associated with the measures that have been traditionally used in the American National Election Studies.[48] The significant coefficients in many of the models presented here suggest that the measures are an improvement, but more work

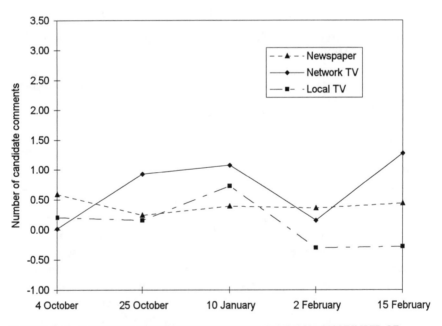

FIGURE 6.14   ESTIMATED EFFECTS OF WHOLESALE CAMPAIGN ON NUMBER OF
CANDIDATE COMMENTS

Note: Each point is the difference in the number of candidate comments by two voters who are identical in all respects except that one used the media in question every day and the other never did.

needs to be done before we can be confident that the news media have such a small influence on voters' knowledge of the candidates.

Conclusion

This chapter has explored the impact of the information environment on New Hampshire voters' knowledge of the candidates seeking the 1996 Republican nomination. I began by asking whether New Hampshire voters were given the opportunity to learn about the candidates by examining the quantity and quality of information available to primary voters. The analysis showed a large amount of information of varying quality. The candidates' agendas, which are communicated through both wholesale and retail channels in New Hampshire, differed significantly from the media's. In their ads, speeches, and appearances on televised interview programs, candidates talked about their policy positions and backgrounds. The candidates also mentioned their prospects of winning and their campaign strategies, but these topics did not dominate all others as they did in television news coverage of the campaign. Newspapers provided coverage of a wider array of topics, but more stories still mentioned the horse race than gave information about what the candidates would do if elected president or their qualifications for the job. Moreover, when the candidates and news media did discuss issues, candidates were more likely than the news media to provide detailed information and to emphasize the impact of their issue positions and record on society. The media, by contrast, stressed the political implications of candidates' issue stances.

Critics of modern election campaigns worry that the media's horse-race–dominated coverage does not give voters enough information on which to base their votes. In a primary, voters have the even more difficult task of choosing among a long list of like-minded candidates. But when I examined voters' images of the candidates, they tended to reflect the candidates' agendas rather than the media's. Those voters who had formed images of the candidates discussed the candidates in terms of their issue positions, character, and qualifications to be president. I found further evidence that candidates may have greater influence than the media in my analysis of the determinants of voters' knowledge of the candidates. The model results revealed that the use of wholesale media has less impact on voter knowledge than does contact with the candidates' retail campaigns. But above all forms of communication, individual motivation matters the most.

This raises the question of whether enough New Hampshire voters paid sufficient attention to the campaign to form the rich candidate images that were possible. In their study of political knowledge, Delli Carpini and Keeter suggested three possible models of how political knowledge is distributed in a democratic society, a typology that can help us evaluate learning in the New Hampshire primary.[49] In the least healthy form, a managerial democracy, most people know a little about politics, but only a few people know a lot. In this case, the few knowledgeable members of society will exercise undue influence over policy. The second model is what they call a pragmatic democracy. Here, the distribution of knowledge is a bell-shaped curve in which a few people are very knowledgeable, a few people are completely uninformed, and most citizens are moderately informed. A pragmatic democracy is the result of a society in which citizens with some cognitive skill can become informed with reasonable effort. This model best describes the American public, according to Delli Carpini and Keeter's examination of national surveys. The final distribution, a strong democracy, is one in which most people are well informed and few are uninformed. "This model conforms most closely with the civic assumptions of democracy in which citizens are able to play an active, even direct role, in governing themselves."[50] According to New Hampshire's supporters, this type of active democracy is what characterizes the state of New Hampshire and its primary.

Does New Hampshire have a stronger democracy than the nation as a whole, thus making it a good place to start the nomination process? Recall figures 6.7 and 6.8, which show the distributions of two measures of voter knowledge. At the beginning of the campaign, the distributions of both candidate recognition and detailed knowledge exhibit the features of a managerial democracy. The masses were uninformed, while a few people were quite knowledgeable about the candidates. But the campaign transformed the electorate. By the time of the primary, the distribution of candidate recognition actually bore a striking resemblance to the strong democracy claimed by New Hampshire's supporters. Yet a voter needs more detailed knowledge of the candidates to play the active role required in a strong democracy, and the final distribution of detailed knowledge fits more with the model of a pragmatic democracy than with that of a strong democracy. While the New Hampshire primary campaign is clearly an educating experience for the electorate, it fails to provide the same level of education for all of its members.

As more and more states hold their primaries at the beginning of the nomination calendar to increase their impact on the outcome, a large-scale change in the nominating process looks more likely. One of the proposed reforms is to hold a small number of regional primaries instead of a large number of individual state contests. Under this reform, Iowa and New Hampshire would no longer start off the nominating process. Some even call for a national primary on one day. The effect of this type of reform would be to turn primary campaigning into a completely wholesale enterprise and eliminate the last remnants of retail campaigning. The media would take on a larger role, and, given the poor quality of campaign coverage detailed here, voters would have an even more difficult time distinguishing among the candidates. While the wholesale campaign in Iowa and New Hampshire becomes more dominant with every election, retail campaigning still exists in these states, and the analysis presented in this chapter indicates that it does have an impact on those it touches. The 1996 New Hampshire primary campaign was generally successful at educating voters about the candidates. But even with a highly motivated and capable electorate who were given unique opportunities to learn, not everyone gained the detailed knowledge necessary for distinguishing among the candidates. Unfortunately, New Hampshire is as good as it gets. Any reform of the nominating process that gives even greater power to the media without a change in how they cover campaigns will hurt the system rather than improve it.

Appendix A: Content Analysis

The content-analysis data of the New Hampshire primary information environment were collected by the Center for Media and Public Affairs for the Consortium for Campaign Media Analysis, with funding from the Pew Charitable Trust. The New Hampshire primary sample runs from 20 January 1996 to 19 February 1996. On each day, the following news media were coded: the evening news on ABC, CBS, and NBC, WMUR's six o'clock evening news, the *Manchester Union Leader*, and the *Concord Monitor*. Every news story that provided twenty seconds or two printed paragraphs of information about the 1996 presidential campaign was coded. In addition, candidate appearances on televised interview programs, such as *Larry King Live*, *Meet the Press*, and *Good Morning America*, were coded. A complete list of interview programs in the New Hampshire primary sample is available from the author upon request. The primary sample contained ninety-three candidate advertisements that were obtained from the Julian P. Kanter Political Commercial Archive at the University of Oklahoma. All ads produced by the Republican primary candidates from 20 January to 19 February were coded. Finally, twenty-eight speeches given in New Hampshire between 20 January and 19 February were coded. The speeches were gathered from Lexis-Nexis, CNN, and C-SPAN. While this is not the entire population of speeches given in New Hampshire during this month, it is a good representation, since candidates tend to give the same speech many times with only slight modifications. In the following description of the variables coded, I often use the term *story* to refer to a single news story, political advertisement, candidate interview, or campaign stump speech.

Topics

All news stories, ads, interviews, and speeches were assigned one or more topic codes. When a story covered more than one topic, as was often the case, multiple codes were assigned. The unit of analysis is the total number of topics mentioned across all stories and not the story itself. For a topic to be coded, it had to have been discussed "extensively"; that is, it must have been the focus of more than twenty seconds of a television news story or interview or more than two paragraphs of a newspaper story or text of a campaign speech. For political advertisements and news stories that were less than sixty seconds or five paragraphs long, an extensive discussion is one that accounts for more than one-third of the item. The twenty-five original topic codes were recoded into the four general categories shown in figure 6.2. The four categories incorporated the following types of stories:

1. *Personal/professional background.* Discussions of the candidates' personal backgrounds, character, temperaments, qualifications for office, professional experience, leadership abilities.
2. *Policy issues.* Candidate issue positions, record in office in dealing with a particular issue, details about a particular issue.
3. *Campaign strategy/horse race.* Candidates' campaign conduct (including negative campaigning), campaign tactics and strategy, discussions of candidates' advertisements, poll results, speculation about election results, speculation about choice of running mates.
4. *Election process.* The workings of the nominating process, commentary on the performance of the process, debates about the role of the media and interest groups, commentary on the campaign finance system, lamentations about voter apathy.

Depth of Discussion of Candidates' Records, Proposals, and Issue Stands

Within a news story, ad, interview, or speech, each separate discussion of a candidate's philosophies, issue positions, specific proposals, and information about his record in public life was coded for the depth of the discussion. A single story could contain multiple issue discussions. Therefore, the unit of analysis is the total number of such discussions across all stories and not the story itself. Each issue discussion was coded for the presence of the following variables:

1. *Extent of discussion.* The issue must have been the focus of more than twenty seconds of a television news story, more than two paragraphs of a newspaper item, or more than one-third of an ad, interview, or speech.
2. *Specificity of discussion.* Specific details such as dollar amounts, implementation mechanisms, time frames, etc., are presented.
3. *Context/background.* The issue is discussed in terms of its broader national context. Some information about the scope of the problem or issue is given.
4. *Societal implications.* The discussion includes assessments or predictions about the national impact of the candidate's past policies or future proposals.
5. *Political context/implications.* The issue is discussed in terms of its impact on the candidate's status in the horse race or in terms of the candidate's strategic motivations for taking the issue position and its impact on various groups' support of the candidate.

Appendix B: Survey Data

Most of the survey data used in this chapter came from five WMUR-Dartmouth College polls conducted by Linda Fowler and myself during the 1996 presidential primary. Table 6.5 displays the interview dates and number of respondents for each survey. The survey population consisted of adult U.S. citizens who were New Hampshire residents. The survey samples were random digit dial samples of New Hampshire phone numbers purchased from Survey Sampling, Inc. To this larger sample of New Hampshire residents, we administered screening questions to identify a smaller sample of likely Republican primary voters. In 1996, the New Hampshire primary allowed same-day voter registration for the first time. Registered independents and Democrats could vote in the Republican primary by switching their party affiliation to Republican before voting.

TABLE 6.5   WMUR-DARTMOUTH COLLEGE POLL INFORMATION

Interview Dates	Total Sample Size	No. of Likely Republican Primary Voters
1–4 October 1995	671	484
22–25 October 1995	700	535
7–10 January 1996	745	512
29 January–2 February 1996	556	420
13–15 February 1996	523	342

Therefore, it would have been unwise to interview only registered Republicans. Self-identified Republicans and independents received a full-length, twenty-minute survey. Most self-identified Democrats received an abbreviated interview. A few Democrats who said they would definitely vote in the Republican primary received the full-length survey. For purposes of preelection prediction, we weighted the smaller sample of likely Republican primary voters based on respondents' answers to a number of questions known to predict voter turnout. The analysis presented in this chapter is based on *unweighted* data.

The WMUR-Dartmouth College polls contained a panel component in which the same respondents were interviewed twice at different times during the campaign. The first wave was made up of a random sample of 100 respondents from the early October survey and all respondents from the late October survey. The fourth survey, conducted from 29 January to 2 February, was the second wave of this panel.

The panel respondents from the WMUR-Dartmouth College poll were included in a separate study of the 1996 general election and reinterviewed up to five more times following the New Hampshire primary. This study, the Project on Campaign Discourse and Civic Engagement, is being conducted by Ann Crigler and Marion Just. In addition to reinterviewing the New Hampshire panel, the study includes a nationally representative sample of U.S. citizens who were also interviewed up to five more times. Four preelection interviews and a postelection survey were conducted. The comparison of the political-knowledge levels of New Hampshire residents with the nation as a whole utilizes the first wave of these panel surveys (see table 6.3).

The questions asked of respondents were worded as follows:

1. *Attention to the campaign.* "How much attention have you been able to pay to the 1996 presidential campaign so far—a lot, some, not much, or no attention so far?"
2. *Candidate recognition.* Candidate recognition ranges from 0 to 8. It is defined as having either a favorable or unfavorable opinion of

a candidate as well as being undecided. Respondents who said they hadn't heard enough yet or volunteered that they did not recognize the name were classified as not recognizing a candidate. The total number of candidates recognized out of a possible 8 is a respondent's overall recognition score. The question was phrased in the following manner: "I'm going to read the names of some presidential candidates and political figures. For each candidate, please tell me whether your opinion of that person is favorable, not favorable, or undecided. If you haven't heard enough about someone, just tell me and we will go on to the next name. How about [candidate's name]? Is your opinion of [candidate] favorable, not favorable, undecided, or haven't you heard enough yet to have an opinion?"

3. *Detailed candidate knowledge.* Respondents who recognized Alexander, Buchanan, Dole, or Forbes were asked an open-ended question about that candidate. Respondents were prompted for up to four responses about each candidate. The total number of responses given about all four candidates is a measure of the respondent's detailed knowledge of the candidates. Thus, the variable ranges from 0 to 16. The responses were also coded for content (see table 6.4). The question was, "Now we'd like to hear your thoughts and ideas about the candidates who are running for president this year. For each candidate that I mention, I'd like you to tell me anything that comes to mind about his abilities, background, issue positions, or anything else. How about [candidate's name]? What comes to mind when you think about [this candidate]? Anything else?"

4. *Exposure to the retail campaign.* "Have you met any of the candidates who are running for president in 1996 or have you seen any of them in person?" "Has anyone called you up or come around and talked to you about supporting a candidate for president?" "Have you received anything in the mail from a candidate who is running for president this year?"

5. *Exposure to the wholesale campaign.* "On a typical weekday, about how many hours of television do you watch during the morning and afternoon?" "How about evening television? About how many hours of television do you watch on a typical weekday evening?" "Do you ever watch national news programs like *World News Tonight* on ABC, *NBC Nightly News*, or *CBS Evening News*?" (If yes) "How often do you watch those types of shows— every day, most days, once or twice a week, or only occasion-

ally?" "Do you ever watch local news programs?" (If yes) "How often do you watch those types of shows—every day, most days, once or twice a week, or only occasionally?" "Do you ever read a daily newspaper?" (If yes) "Many people don't have time to read the entire newspaper. They normally read only certain sections such as the sports pages, the business pages, the entertainment pages, or the news pages. How often do you read the news pages of your daily paper—every day, most days, once or twice a week, or only occasionally?"

6. *Political knowledge.* Political knowledge is a variable that ranges from 0 to 5. The respondent was given 1 point for each correct answer to five knowledge questions. "Here are a few questions about the government in Washington. Many people don't know the answers to these questions, so if there are some you don't know just tell me and we'll go on." The questions were as follows: "Do you happen to know what job or political office is now held by Al Gore?" "Whose responsibility is it to determine if a law if constitutional or not. Is it the president, the Congress, or the Supreme Court?" "How much of a majority is required for the U.S. Senate and House to override a presidential veto?" "Do you happen to know which party currently has the most members in the House of Representatives in Washington?" "Would you say that one of the parties is more conservative than the other at the national level?" (If yes) "Which party is more conservative?"

Notes

1. James Madison, "Federalist Paper No. 10," in Alexander Hamilton, James Madison, and John Jay, *The Federalist Papers,* ed. Clinton Rossiter (New York: New American Library, 1961).
2. Alexis de Tocqueville, *Democracy in America,* 2 vols., ed. Philips Bradley (New York: Vintage Books, 1990).
3. See, for example, Bernard R. Berelson, Paul F. Lazarsfeld, and William N. McPhee, *Voting: A Study of Opinion Formation in a Presidential Campaign* (Chicago: University of Chicago Press, 1954); Angus Campbell, Philip E. Converse, Warren E. Miller, and Donald E. Stokes, *The American Voter* (New York: Wiley, 1960); and Philip E. Converse, "The Nature of Belief Systems in Mass Publics," in *Ideology and Discontent,* ed. David Apter (New York: Free Press, 1964).
4. See Anthony Downs, *An Economic Theory of Democracy* (New York: Harper & Row, 1957); Benjamin I. Page and Robert Y. Shapiro, *The Rational Public: Fifty Years of Trends in Americans' Policy Preferences* (Chicago: University of Chicago Press, 1992); W. Russell Neuman, *The Paradox of Mass Politics* (Cambridge, Mass.: Harvard University Press, 1986); Paul M. Sniderman, Richard A. Brody, and Philip E. Tetlock, *Reasoning and Choice: Explorations in Political Psychology* (Cambridge:

Cambridge University Press, 1991); and James A. Stimson, *Public Opinion in America: Moods, Cycles, and Swings* (Boulder, Colo.: Westview Press, 1991).

5. Michael Delli Carpini and Scott Keeter, *What Americans Know about Politics and Why It Matters* (New Haven, Conn.: Yale University Press, 1996).

6. R. Michael Alvarez, *Information and Elections* (Ann Arbor: University of Michigan Press, 1997).

7. John R. Zaller, *The Nature and Origins of Mass Opinion* (Cambridge: Cambridge University Press, 1992).

8. Larry M. Bartels, *Presidential Primaries and the Dynamics of Public Choice* (Princeton, N.J.: Princeton University Press, 1988), chap. 4.

9. Larry M. Bartels, "Uninformed Votes: Information Effects in Presidential Elections," *American Journal of Political Science* 40 (1996): 194–230.

10. V.O. Key, Jr., *The Responsible Electorate* (Cambridge, Mass.: Harvard University Press, 1966), 7.

11. See Scott Keeter and Cliff Zukin, *Uninformed Choice: The Failure of the Presidential Nominating System* (New York: Praeger, 1983); Thomas E. Patterson, *The Mass Media Election: How Americans Choose Their Presidents* (New York: Praeger, 1980); and Thomas E. Patterson, *Out of Order* (New York: Knopf, 1993).

12. David Moore, "The Death of Politics in New Hampshire," in *The Mass Media in Campaign '84: Articles from Public Opinion Magazine*, ed. Michael J. Robinson and Austin Ranney (Washington, D.C.: American Enterprise Institute, 1985).

13. On this topic, see Doris Graber, *Processing the News: How People Tame the Information Tide* (New York: Longman, 1988).

14. For the virtues of the New Hampshire primary, see Hugh Gregg, "New Hampshire's First-in-the-Nation Presidential Primary," in *State of New Hampshire Manual for the General Court* (Concord, N.H.: Department of State, 1997).

15. For instance, see Stephen Earl Bennet, "Comparing Americans' Political Information in 1988 and 1992," *Journal of Politics* 57 (1995): 521–32; Delli Carpini and Keeter, *What Americans Know about Politics*; Robert C. Luskin, "Explaining Political Sophistication," *Political Behavior* 12 (1990): 331–61; Neuman, *Paradox of Mass Politics*; and Eric R.A.N. Smith, *The Unchanging American Voter* (Berkeley: University of California Press, 1989), chap. 5.

16. Alvarez, *Information and Elections*; Bartels, *Presidential Primaries*; Keeter and Zukin, *Uninformed Choice*; and Patterson, *Mass Media Election*.

17. P.J. Tichenor, G.A. Donahue, and C.N. Olien, "Mass Media Flow and Differential Growth in Knowledge," *Public Opinion Quarterly* 34 (1970): 159–70.

18. For a nice summary of schema theory and its critics, see James H. Kuklinski, Robert C. Luskin, and John Bolland, "Where Is the Schema? Going beyond the 'S' Word in Political Psychology," *American Political Science Review* 85 (1991): 1341–57; and Milton Lodge, Kathleen M. McGraw, Pamela Johnston Conover, Stanley Feldman, and Arthur H. Miller, "Where Is the Schema? Critiques," *American Political Science Review* 85 (1991): 1357–80.

19. W. Russell Neuman, Marion R. Just, and Ann N. Crigler, *Common Knowledge: News and the Construction of Political Meaning* (Chicago: University of Chicago Press, 1992), chap. 6.

20. Michael J. Robinson and Margaret Sheehan, *Over the Wire and on TV: CBS and UPI in Campaign '80* (New York: Russell Sage Foundation, 1983).

21. William C. Adams, "As New Hampshire Goes . . . ," in *Media and Momentum: The New Hampshire Primary and Nomination Politics*, ed. Gary R. Orren and Nelson W. Polsby (Chatham, N.J.: Chatham House, 1987).

22. No other state or regional contest received as much coverage. The Iowa caucuses were discussed in 18 percent of all campaign stories and 34 percent of state stories. The next closest state was California, with 7 percent and 9 percent of all campaign stories and state stories, respectively.

23. A survey conducted by the Pew Research Center in April 1996 found that 65 percent of Americans regularly watch local news while 42 percent regularly watch network news. For statistics on Americans' use of different information sources, see the Pew Research Center's "Biennial News Consumption Survey" at www.people-press.org/med98rpt.htm, which gives the results of both recent and past surveys.

24. Marion R. Just, Ann N. Crigler, Dean E. Alger, Timothy E. Cook, Montague Kern, and Darrell M. West, *Crosstalk: Citizens, Candidates, and the Media in a Presidential Campaign* (Chicago: University of Chicago Press, 1996). On local news, see John McManus, *Market Driven Journalism: Let the Citizen Beware* (Thousand Oaks, Calif.: Sage, 1994).

25. Raymond L. Carroll, "Blurring Distinctions: Network and Local News," in *The Future of News*, ed. Philip S. Cook, Douglas Gomery, and Lawrence W. Lichty (Washington, D.C.: Woodrow Wilson Center Press, 1992).

26. Cameron quoted in Andrew Ferguson, "Live Free or Cry: The Truth about New Hampshire," *Weekly Standard*, 1 and 8 January 1996.

27. For other instances of such a conversion, see Just et al., *Crosstalk*; and S. Robert Lichter and Richard E. Noyes, *Good Intentions Make Bad News* (London: Rowman & Littlefield, 1995).

28. Just et al., *Crosstalk*; and Patterson, *Out of Order*.

29. WMUR ad-buy data were supplied by Samuel Best and Clark Hubbard.

30. Data on candidate visits come from Larry J. Sabato, "Presidential Nominations: The Front-Loaded Frenzy of '96," in *Toward the Millennium: The Elections of 1996*, ed. Larry J. Sabato (Boston: Allyn & Bacon, 1997), 79–81.

31. Both Lugar's videotape and Gramm's card were mentioned by a number of New Hampshire survey respondents.

32. An analogy would be restaurants that provide huge portions of poorly prepared food. Is a bad meal good just because there is more of it? The same applies to candidate information.

33. Patterson, *Out of Order*.

34. Because more than one topic can be mentioned in a news story, ad, interview, or speech, the numbers in figure 6.2 sum to more than 100 percent.

35. A number of studies provide evidence that primary voters base their decisions on a combination of candidate assessments and candidate viability. See, for example, Paul R. Abramson, John H. Aldrich, Phil Paolino, and David W. Rohde, "Sophisticated Voting in the 1988 Presidential Primaries," *American Political Science Review* 86 (1992): 55–69; Bartels, *Presidential Primaries*; Henry E. Brady and Richard Johnston, "What's the Primary Message: Horse Race or Issue Journalism?" in *Media and Momentum: The New Hampshire Primary and Nomination Politics*, ed. Gary R. Orren and Nelson W. Polsby (Chatham, N.J.: Chatham House, 1987); and Patrick J. Kenney and Tom W. Rice, "A Model of Nomination Preferences," *American Politics Quarterly* 20 (1992): 267–86.

36. Neuman, Just, and Crigler, *Common Knowledge*.

37. Some bars in figure 6.3 sum to more than 100 percent because, as noted, an issue mention can contain more than one measure of quality. Alternatively, I could have given each story, ad, or speech 1 point for each measure and computed an average quality score that would have ranged from 0 to 4. The scale on the x-axis turns out

to be equal to such a quality score with 100 representing 1. So, the average quality score for campaign speeches is 1.21 items.

38. Patterson, *Out of Order*, 64.

39. The dates that accompany the political ads are inexact. They indicate the general time frame during which the candidate used the ad in the primary campaign, not the exact dates they were run in New Hampshire.

40. U.S. Department of Commerce, *State and Metropolitan Area Data Book, 1997-98* (Washington, D.C.: Government Printing Office, 1998), table A-14.

41. Because the New Hampshire sample was interviewed two times before the national sample was, it is possible that the New Hampshire sample will show higher knowledge levels simply due to panel attrition. That is, the respondents who were less politically knowledgeable may have already dropped out of the New Hampshire panel. To minimize the unequal effects of panel attrition in the study design, I examine only respondents who completed both the 1996 summer and fall telephone waves, thus similarly dropping national respondents who are less knowledgeable.

42. The difference is statistically significant based on a t-test (t =- 6.62).

43. Patterson, *Mass Media Election*.

44. For this one survey, I ran an additional model that includes political knowledge as an independent variable. The results do not change appreciably, and the conclusions remain the same. Preexisting political knowledge is a significant predictor of candidate knowledge, but it adds to the overall explanatory power of the model and does not reduce the impact of other variables.

45. The dependent variables are counts of the outcome of eight binary variables in the case of candidate recognition and sixteen binary variables for the detailed knowledge variable. This type of variable is often called grouped, or blocked, data. Accordingly, the models were estimated using a procedure that produces maximum likelihood logit estimates for grouped data.

46. Delli Carpini and Keeter, *What Americans Know about Politics*; and Sidney Verba, Nancy Burns, and Kay Lehman Schlozman, "Knowing and Caring about Politics: Gender and Political Engagement," *Journal of Politics* 59 (1997): 1051-72.

47. For example, see Larry Bartels, "Messages Received: The Political Impact of Media Exposure," *American Political Science Review* 87 (1993): 267-85; and Vincent Price and John Zaller, "Who Gets the News? Alternative Measures of News Reception and Their Implications for Research," *Public Opinion Quarterly* 57 (1993): 133-64.

48. See Tami Buhr, Ann Crigler, and Marion Just, "Media Questions on the 1996 Election Study and Related Content Analysis of Media Coverage of the Presidential Campaign," 1995 Pilot Study Reports, www.umich.edu/~nes/resources/psreport/pilotrp.htm#95.

49. Delli Carpini and Keeter, *What Americans Know about Politics*, chap 4.

50. Ibid., 153.

CHAPTER SEVEN

The Role of Televised Debates in the Presidential Nominating Process

by Samuel J. Best and Clark Hubbard

Televised debates have become a cornerstone of American presidential elections. Every presidential campaign since 1976 has featured a series of at least two debates between those candidates who are broadly·construed to be the "major" contenders for the presidency, most frequently the Republican and Democratic nominees.[1] The national prominence afforded these events during the general election season is difficult to overstate. They routinely draw audiences of 60 to 100 million viewers; they feature prominently in water-cooler conversations about the campaign;[2] and they dominate news coverage after their occurrence, to the point that the notion of a "news analysis effect" is commonplace in discussions of debate impact.[3]

In the shadow of the monolithic importance imputed to televised general election debates, however, lies another, quieter American electoral institution: the televised primary debate.[4] These events have a longer televised history than general election debates and are far more frequent in number. Televised debates during the nomination campaign have proliferated since their inception in 1956, and participation in them has become de rigueur for presidential hopefuls, with some would-be nominees participating in as many as a dozen during the months leading up to the national party conventions. As one point of comparison, fourteen presidential candidates have participated in televised general election presidential debates since the 1976 campaign, while at least fifty have participated in televised nomination-season debates during the same period.

While primary debates may not draw the massive audiences or flurry of front-page media coverage associated with general election debates, journalists have begun to regard them as integral to the nomination campaign. Coverage of these events has become a standard part of political reportage during the nomination season, largely because they provide a current-events "hook" that contrasts with the normally humdrum, repetitive nature of nomination campaigns.[5] Political reporters and pundits have attributed to primary debates numerous "turning points" or "defining moments" in nomination campaigns, some of which are discussed below. Given their frequency, high level of candidate participation, and breadth of media coverage, it seems reasonable to conclude that televised debates have become an institutionalized component of the presidential nominating process.

Strangely, however, the vast bulk of the research directed at televised debates has focused specifically on the general election. A review of this material is beyond the scope or focus of this chapter.[6] However, the accumulated scholarly evidence regarding the ability of televised general election debates to affect viewer attitudes is summed up succinctly by Doris Graber, who concludes that "their impact has fluctuated, ranging from inconsequential to decisive."[7] Researchers have had great difficulty establishing that debate viewing alters viewer preferences in any predictable or systematic fashion. Many have concluded that debates serve primarily to reinforce voters' existing preferences, while some dissenters have identified measurable preference changes resulting from debate exposure.[8]

This evidence, however inconclusive, derives entirely from research concerning general election debates. We argue that the contextual differences between general election debates and primary season debates are great enough to discourage drawing conclusions about the effects of the latter from observations about the former. These differences are numerous (more candidates participating, with commensurately less exposure given to each individual candidate; a broader range of issues discussed; a wider variety of formats; a much lower level of public exposure), but they all center on one key difference: the electoral context. Put simply, televised primary debates occur early in the campaign, while general election debates occur late. The temporal precedence of primary debates has profound implications for their effects on the political attitudes of their audiences and therefore for their overall impact on the presidential selection process. We will explore these implications after a brief look at the history of televised primary debates.

A Long-Standing Tradition

Despite the relative lack of scholarly interest in primary-season debates, these events have a long history. In fact, a primary-season debate has the distinction of being the first major televised presidential debate. The American Broadcasting Corporation sponsored and telecast a debate featuring Democratic nomination contenders Adlai Stevenson and Estes Kefauver on 21 May 1956, more than four years before the celebrated Kennedy-Nixon debates. The event garnered a front-page headline in the next day's edition of the *New York Times*—and began a tradition of disenchantment with the utility of televised debates in general:

> Senator Estes Kefauver and Adlai E. Stevenson canvassed their political differences for an hour on television tonight and found very little to disagree about. The nationally televised "debate" found the two chief contenders for the Democratic Presidential nomination taking virtually identical positions on almost every issue discussed.[9]

Since then, televised nomination-season debates have been a feature of every presidential campaign except that of 1964.[10] A historical overview of televised primary debates is presented in table 7.1.

As table 7.1 suggests, televised primary-season debates have become steadily more common over the past ten presidential election cycles. Such events were held sporadically until the 1976 election and then became increasingly common, although considerable year-to-year variation is apparent. The most likely explanation for the increasing number of these events lies in the populist impulses expressed by the McGovern-Fraser Commission reforms of the Democratic Party's nomination system in the early 1970s. That is, as more states hold primaries, debates become relevant for the various state primary electorates, providing an impetus for debate sponsorship that was largely absent when caucuses were the principal mechanism for selecting delegates.

The year-to-year variation in the number of televised debates can be explained by the relative openness of the nomination races in each party. For example, an unusually large number of debates—twenty-one in all— were televised during the 1987–88 nomination season, most likely because the nomination was widely considered to be up for grabs within both parties. On the other hand, 1980, 1984, 1992, and 1996 each saw an incumbent president running for a second term, so debates were held only by the out-party in each of these election cycles. If history is any indication, voters can expect a plethora of televised preconvention debates within both parties leading up to the 2000 election.

TABLE 7.1   TELEVISED PRESIDENTIAL PRIMARY DEBATES

Date	Location	Party	Participating Candidates	Sponsors
5/21/56	Miami	Dem.	Kefauver, Stevenson	ABC
5/4/60	Charleston, W. Va.	Dem.	Humphrey, J. Kennedy	WCHS
7/12/60	Los Angeles	Dem.	Johnson, J. Kennedy	CBS
6/1/68	San Francisco	Dem.	R. Kennedy, McCarthy	ABC
5/28/72	Burbank, Calif.	Dem.	Humphrey, McGovern	CBS
5/30/72	Los Angeles	Dem.	Humphrey, McGovern	NBC
6/4/72	Los Angeles	Dem.	Chisholm, Hardin (for Wallace), Humphrey, McGovern, Yorty	ABC
2/23/76	Boston	Dem.	Bayh, Carter, Harris, H. Jackson, Shapp, Shriver, Udall	League of Women Voters
3/29/76	New York	Dem.	Carter, Church, Harris, H. Jackson, Udall	League of Women Voters
5/3/76	Chicago	Dem.	Church, Udall	League of Women Voters
1/5/80	Des Moines	Rep.	Anderson, Baker, Bush, Connally, Crane, Dole	*Des Moines Register*
2/20/80	Manchester, N.H.	Rep.	Anderson, Baker, Bush, Connally, Crane, Dole, Reagan	League of Women Voters
2/23/80	Nashua, N.H.	Rep.	Bush, Reagan	*Nashua Telegraph*
2/28/80	Columbia, S.C.	Rep.	Baker, Bush, Connally, Reagan	PBS
3/13/80	Chicago	Rep.	Anderson, Bush, Crane, Reagan	League of Women Voters
4/23/80	Grapevine, Tex.	Rep.	Bush, Reagan	League of Women Voters
1/15/84	Hanover, N.H.	Dem.	Askew, Cranston, Glenn, Hart, Hollings, J. Jackson, McGovern, Mondale	Dartmouth College, House Democratic Caucus
1/31/84	Cambridge, Mass.	Dem.	Cranston, Glenn, Hart, Hollings, J. Jackson, McGovern, Mondale	Harvard University, *Boston Globe*
2/3/84	Boston	Dem.	Glenn, Hart, Hollings, J. Jackson, McGovern, Mondale	Emmanuel College, Women in Politics 1984
2/11/84	Des Moines	Dem.	Askew, Cranston, Glenn, Hart, Hollings, J. Jackson, McGovern, Mondale	*Des Moines Register*
2/23/84	Goffstown, N.H.	Dem.	Askew, Cranston, Glenn, Hart, Hollings, J. Jackson, McGovern, Mondale	League of Women Voters
3/11/84	Atlanta	Dem.	Glenn, Hart, J. Jackson, McGovern, Mondale	League of Women Voters
3/18/84	Chicago	Dem.	Hart, J. Jackson, Mondale	Chicago Bar Association
3/28/84	New York	Dem.	Hart, J. Jackson, Mondale	CBS
4/5/84	Pittsburgh	Dem.	Hart, J. Jackson, Mondale	League of Women Voters
5/2/84	Grapevine, Tex.	Dem.	Hart, J. Jackson, Mondale	League of Women Voters
6/3/84	Los Angeles	Dem.	Hart, J. Jackson, Mondale	NBC
7/1/87	Houston	Dem.	Biden, Babbitt, Dukakis, Gephardt, Gore, J. Jackson, Simon	*Firing Line*

TABLE 7.1   *(continued)*

Date	Location	Party	Participating Candidates	Sponsors
8/23/87	Des Moines	Dem.	Biden, Babbitt, Dukakis, Gephardt, Gore, J. Jackson, Simon	n.a.
10/28/87	Houston	Rep.	Bush, Dole, du Pont, Haig, Kemp, Robertson	*Firing Line*
12/1/87	Washington, D.C.	Dem. & Rep.	Babbitt, Dukakis, Gephardt, Gore, J. Jackson, Simon, Bush, Dole, du Pont, Haig, Kemp, Robertson	NBC
1/8/88	Des Moines	Rep.	Bush, Dole, du Pont, Haig, Kemp, Robertson	*Des Moines Register*
1/15/88	Des Moines	Dem.	Babbitt, Dukakis, Gephardt, Gore, Hart, J. Jackson, Simon	*Des Moines Register*
1/16/88	Hanover, N.H.	Rep.	Bush, Dole, du Pont, Haig, Kemp, Robertson	Dartmouth College, Univ. of New Hampshire
1/24/88	Durham, N.H.	Dem.	Babbitt, Dukakis, Gephardt, Gore, Hart, J. Jackson, Simon	Dartmouth College, Univ. of New Hampshire
2/13/88	Goffstown, N.H.	Dem.	Babbitt, Dukakis, Gephardt, Gore, Hart, J. Jackson, Simon	League of Women Voters
2/14/88	Concord, N.H.	Rep.	Bush, Dole, Kemp, Robertson, du Pont	League of Women Voters
2/18/88	Dallas	Dem.	Dukakis, Gephardt, Gore, Hart, J. Jackson	*Dallas Morning News*, KERA-TV
2/19/88	Dallas	Rep.	Bush, Kemp	*Dallas Morning News*, KERA-TV
2/19/88	St. Paul	Dem.	Dukakis, Gephardt, J. Jackson, Simon	*St. Paul Pioneer Press-Dispatch*, WCCO
2/27/88	Atlanta	Dem.	Dukakis, Gephardt, Gore, Hart, J. Jackson, Simon	*Atlanta Constitution*
2/28/88	Atlanta	Rep.	Dole, Robertson, Bush, Kemp	*Atlanta Constitution*
2/29/88	Williamsburg, Va.	Dem.	Dukakis, Gephardt, Gore, Hart, J. Jackson	Democratic Leadership Council
4/12/88	New York	Dem.	Dukakis, Gore, J. Jackson	*N.Y. Daily News*
4/17/88	New York	Dem.	Dukakis, Gore, J. Jackson	WNBC-TV
4/22/88	Philadelphia	Dem.	Dukakis, J. Jackson	Pa. State Democratic Committee
4/23/88	Munhall, Pa.	Dem.	Dukakis, J. Jackson	n.a.
5/25/88	San Francisco	Dem.	Dukakis, J. Jackson	*San Francisco Examinor*, KQED-TV
12/15/91	Washington, D.C.	Dem.	Brown, Clinton, Harkin, Kerrey, Tsongas, Wilder	NBC

(continued)

TABLE 7.1   *(continued)*

Date	Location	Party	Participating Candidates	Sponsors
1/19/92	Manchester, N.H.	Dem.	Brown, Clinton, Harkin, Kerrey, Tsongas	WMUR
1/31/92	Washington, D.C.	Dem.	Brown, Clinton, Harkin, Kerrey, Tsongas	PBS
2/16/92	Goffstown, N.H.	Dem.	Brown, Clinton, Harkin, Kerrey, Tsongas	League of Women Voters, CNN
2/23/92	Sioux Falls, S.D.	Dem.	Agran, Brown, Clinton, Harkin, Kerrey, Tsongas	S.D. Democratic Party
2/29/92	Denver	Dem.	Brown, Clinton, Harkin, Kerrey, Tsongas	n.a.
3/1/92	Atlanta	Dem.	Brown, Clinton, Kerrey, Tsongas	n.a.
3/1/92	College Park, Md.	Dem.	Brown, Clinton, Harkin, Tsongas	n.a.
3/5/92	Dallas	Dem.	Brown, Clinton, Harkin, Tsongas	ABC
3/15/92	Chicago	Dem.	Brown, Clinton, Tsongas	WLS-TV
3/30/92	New York	Dem.	Brown, Clinton	WABC-TV
4/5/92	New York	Dem.	Brown, Clinton	WNBC-TV
4/6/92	New York	Dem.	Brown, Clinton	*Donahue*
10/11/95	Manchester, N.H.	Rep.	Alexander, Buchanan, Dole, Dornan, Forbes, Gramm, Keyes, Lugar, Specter, Taylor	WMUR
1/6/96	Columbia, S.C.	Rep.	Alexander, Buchanan, Gramm, Keyes, Lugar, Taylor	S.C. Republican Party
1/13/96	Johnston, Ia.	Rep.	Alexander, Buchanan, Dole, Dornan, Forbes, Gramm, Keyes,Lugar, Taylor	*Des Moines Register*
2/15/96	Manchester, N.H.	Rep.	Alexander, Buchanan, Dole, Dornan, Forbes, Keyes, Lugar, Taylor	WMUR
2/22/96	Tempe, Ariz.	Rep.	Alexander, Buchanan, Dornan, Forbes	n.a.
2/29/96	Columbia, S.C.	Rep.	Alexander, Buchanan, Dole, Forbes	S.C. Business and Industry Political Education Committee
3/3/96	Atlanta	Rep.	Alexander, Buchanan, Forbes	WSB-TV

Despite increasing reliance on televised debates as a staple of nomination politics, these events are not without their problems, which center largely on formatting issues. Detractors have consistently pointed to one inherent structural feature of preconvention debates as a recurrent difficulty: the large crop of legitimate potential participants. This complaint is summed up nicely by the authors of the Pew Charitable Trust's "Report of the Task Force on Campaign Reform":

> Perhaps the most consequential decision that must be made by any debate sponsor is which candidates should be invited to participate. Here, we see a powerful tension between the competing values of inclusiveness and coherence. On one hand, providing access to minor-party and independent candidates may stimulate interest in the campaign and inject new issues and ideas into the debate. That is all to the good. On the other hand, participation by minor candidates may reduce and fragment the time and attention available to the major candidates, diluting their best opportunity to convey their perspectives and proposals to the electorate. The dangers . . . have been vividly demonstrated in early presidential primary season debates, which sometimes include half-a-dozen or more candidates; the resulting scramble for attention has tended to produce dueling sound bites and mock dramatics better suited to professional wrestling than to political discourse.[11]

Which candidates are legitimate? And should all of them be invited to participate at the expense of coherent, reasonable political discourse? These recurring issues have turned primary debates into something of a laboratory for experimentation with debate formatting. For example, the now-familiar (and widely vilified) "interview format," in which candidates respond to a series of questions from the moderator without direct interaction with each other, was developed in response to the pressures of multiple-candidate primary debates.[12] Far more so than general election debates, in which there have historically been at most three "legitimate" candidates, nomination-season debates face the constant danger of degenerating into "joint press conferences" that emphasize punchy sound bites at the expense of substantive candidate interaction.

On the other hand, table 7.1 reveals that primary debates have traditionally been fairly open to participation by a large number of candidates, although no specific objective or statutory standard has been created to govern entry into these debates.[13] Instead, inclusion and exclusion decisions are made by the debate sponsors on an event-by-event basis. Inconsistency in the inclusiveness criteria results in considerable variation from one primary debate to the next in terms of how many and which candidates are invited. This variation, in turn, has resulted in considerable discontent among excluded candidates.

Despite the inconsistency of eligibility criteria, the fact remains that these events have regularly included as many as a dozen of the party's nomination hopefuls, and, as a result, primary debates have come to be regarded as forums for forging the parties' campaign agendas. Gerald Pomper, for example, says of the 1988 Democratic nomination campaign that "the themes of the candidates had been developed from the first contests and had been honed through a series of debates. . . . The party unity that would be formalized at the party convention was actually forged in the debates and contests held earlier in the year."[14] Hence, there exists a tension between the notion of preconvention debates as tools for "honing" a party's campaign platform (which implies the inclusion of a fairly large number of candidates who wish to affect the issue agenda) and the impulse for coherent, interactive discussion designed to enlighten viewers about prospective nominees (which implies a strict limit on the number of participating candidates). We will bring some empirical evidence to bear on these matters as we explore the effects of primary debates on viewer attitudes later in this chapter.

Primary Debates as Turning Points

Despite the difficulties and complaints surrounding the search for a satisfactory format, primary debates do not lack drama or substance, and they have provided a number of pivotal moments in presidential nomination politics. As far back as 1960, journalists were hailing a televised debate as an important turning point in a primary campaign. In a news analysis of the Democratic primary debate between Senators John F. Kennedy and Hubert H. Humphrey on 4 May 1960, *New York Times* political reporter James Reston wrote that

> the consensus of the reporters covering the Humphrey-Kennedy
> debate here tonight was that Senator Kennedy of Massachusetts
> gained by the encounter. The New Englander went into the
> first television debate of the presidential primary campaign as
> the underdog—and he still is—but the general impression
> here tonight was that he made a more vivid and effective
> presentation of his case than the Senator from Minnesota. . . .
> [W]hile tonight's performance is not likely to relegate the
> Lincoln-Douglas debates into the shadows of history, the general
> impression here was that it was an extremely useful and positive
> encounter.[15]

Primary debates have been the scene of "defining moments" in many contemporary nomination campaigns. In a Republican primary debate held in New Hampshire on 23 February 1980, George Bush arrived at what he thought was a one-on-one confrontation with front-runner Ronald Reagan. The Reagan campaign, however, in what was clearly a public relations stunt, had extended invitations to several of the other candidates as well, without informing the Bush camp. Bush, backed into a corner, refused to allow the others to participate, while Reagan held forth on the populist issue of a broadly inclusive, "fair" debate. Debate moderator Jon Breen instructed the production crew to cut off Reagan's microphone, to which the former California governor (and trained actor) indignantly responded, "I'm *paying* for this microphone, Mr. Green [*sic*]." Bush came across as stiff, self-righteous, and uncomfortable, and at least one author characterizes this as "the event that sealed Bush's fate, and ultimately the outcome of the GOP 1980 race."[16]

In 1984, early Democratic front-runner Walter Mondale unexpectedly lost a string of caucuses and primaries to Gary Hart. During a televised debate in Atlanta, Hart proclaimed his commitment to "new ideas," such as "restoring entrepeneurship" to meet "basic human needs." Borrowing a well-known line from a hamburger chain's ad campaign, Mondale replied, "When I hear your new ideas, I'm reminded of that ad: 'Where's the beef?' " This retort, the most memorable slogan of that year's Democratic primary campaign, is often credited with helping Mondale stop Hart's momentum and win the nomination.

More recent primary debates have also produced some noteworthy political moments. During a televised debate with former California governor Jerry Brown in March 1992, future president Bill Clinton made his famous confession of marijuana experimentation during his college years: "When I was in England I experimented with marijuana a time or two and didn't like it. I didn't inhale and I didn't try it again."[17] Although the admission did little apparent damage to his nomination drive, the ambiguity of Clinton's statement was picked up by his opponents and detractors and has been used ever since as an example of the president's ability (some would say tendency) to equivocate.

In 1996, Republican candidate Alan Keyes engaged in a hunger strike after being excluded from a televised debate in Columbia, South Carolina. A few days later, after being barred entry into another Republican primary debate, a presumably still-hungry Keyes was handcuffed and carted off by the Atlanta police for refusing to leave the premises and repeatedly charging the doors. "Is this America or the Soviet Union? This is a disgrace to

American democracy," the voluble Keyes exclaimed while being led away by police officers, who were called "fascists" by some of his supporters on the scene.[18]

Despite the drama surrounding televised primary debates and the journalistic coverage afforded them, there is little direct empirical evidence as to whether and how these events affect the political attitudes of the viewers.[19] As noted earlier, almost all of the research examining the effects of televised debates has been directed at the late-season general election debates. But primary debates are not general election debates, and the political context in which debates occur has profound implications for their effects. The most notable difference between primary debates and general election debates, of course, is their timing. General election debates occur late in the campaign season, long after most voters have already made a voting decision.[20] Primary debates, on the other hand, occur at a much earlier stage of the campaign, when voters' issue attitudes may not be ossified and voters' candidate preferences may not yet be formed.

The Importance of Being Early

Despite the high level of criticism directed at the recent trend toward "front-loading" the nomination campaign, states have been jockeying for primacy in the nomination calendar since the inception of the McGovern-Fraser reforms.[21] Why governors, legislators, secretaries of state, and other state officials have been trying to move their primaries to the front of the calendar is entirely understandable: state-level politicians have realized that temporal precedence matters in presidential politics.[22] It matters from the perspective of the candidates, who traditionally concentrate their personal appearances in states with early primaries, hoping to catch the elusive wave of momentum. It matters from the perspective of campaign managers, who make spending decisions, formulate methods of media interaction, and construct overall campaign strategies with one eye on the primary calendar.[23] And, most important for our current purpose, being early in the calendar matters from the perspective of voters, who are afforded their first opportunities to judge the qualifications and personalities of the candidates during the early stages of the nominating process. One of the most direct and obvious forums in which voters are afforded these opportunities are the televised primary debates.

Though they may not be aware of it, those who believe that "earlier is better" are also supported by a good deal of scholarly work on public opinion and electoral behavior. Most social-psychological models of attitude formation and change posit a kind of "attitudinal precedence effect," which implies that the longer an attitude has been held by an individual, the more likely that attitude is to be supported by a large amount of evaluative information, and therefore the less likely it is to be changed by new information. Conversely, attitudes that are recently acquired are less well supported and are therefore more susceptible to the persuasive influence of fresh information. This concept is most clearly expressed in the information-integration perspective on attitude change espoused by Norman Anderson.[24] Briefly, the theory holds that attitudes and beliefs are formed and modified as people receive new information and integrate it with their existing attitudes and beliefs. Amount of prior knowledge about a subject serves as a major weighting mechanism that impedes the ability of new information to change existing attitudes; the greater the amount of previous information, the less likely any single piece of new information will cause major changes in the recipient's attitude.[25] This notion has clear and direct implications for the political arena generally, and for the nomination phase of political campaigns specifically.[26]

An appealing metaphor for this social-psychological concept of attitudinal precedence is the physical principle of inertia. Conceptualize an individual's attitudes toward some political object—a presidential nomination seeker, for instance—as a physical mass. A potential voter who has been familiar with the candidate for a reasonable length of time has been exposed to a fairly large amount of information (and concurrently made a fairly large number of judgments) about that candidate, so any new information will have only a marginal impact on moving that large, heavy mass of attitudes. Accumulated attitudes and judgments concerning a relatively unknown candidate, on the other hand, would be small, light, and easily pushed around by new pieces of evaluative information.

The latter situation will be far more prevalent than the former among the mass public during the nomination phase of a campaign, when the candidates are relatively unknown and information about them is scarce.[27] A large amount of empirical research bears out this supposition; during the nomination phase of a presidential campaign, especially in the early stages, large groups of voters are unaware of most candidates and are familiar with others in name only.[28] Hence, voter attitudes toward presidential aspirants during the early stages of the nomination campaign should be weakly held and inchoate, if not nonexistent. Exposure to new information about the candidates during this time frame could lead to dramatic alterations in voters' attitudes toward those candidates. Further, these newly formed attitudes may then serve as "anchors" against which supplementary information encountered throughout the campaign must pull in order to induce additional change in attitude toward the candidates.

The implications of these ideas concerning attitude change are clear in the context of a presidential nomination contest. During the early stages of the campaign, voters are dealing with candidates who are relative unknowns, so voter attitudes are ripe for sizable changes and shifts in preference. A televised primary debate, or a news report concerning it, may be the first time many potential voters are exposed to the candidates and their issue platforms. This is especially true of debates held very early in the season (as was the 1996 Republican debate that we examine in detail in the next section).

We suggest that the types of voter attitudes most open to change from viewing a nomination-season debate can be divided into three main categories. First, exposure to a debate in this context may *stimulate voter interest* in the campaign, which is likely to be quite low during this phase of the election process. Second, nomination-season debates provide the viewing public with the opportunity to *evaluate the candidates* along several different dimensions. Third, these debates can serve as a forum for the candidates to help form and modify the campaign issue agenda, so viewers' *attitudes about policy issues* are likely to be affected.

Debates have long been regarded as a method for stimulating greater public interest in political campaigns. Broadcasting such an event on television can

> create a climate in which even those otherwise disposed to shun political messaging are expected to be able to converse about political data. . . . The social pressure to take a sustained view of both candidates creates a climate more conducive to political learning than any other which the typical voter will seek or chance upon.[29]

Greater public interest in, awareness of, and participation in the nomination campaign has been the general impetus behind the shift from caucuses to primaries, and from closed primaries to open ones.[30] If televising intraparty debates during the primary season can stimulate the kind of increase in campaign interest described above, they may be an important mechanism for further broadening citizen participation in the nominating process.[31]

The second attitudinal function we ascribe to primary debates is that they provide an opportunity for direct exposure to and evaluation of the candidates, an opportunity that becomes ever rarer in the modern age of mediated, sound-bitten, spin-doctored campaigning. This function is mentioned in nearly every discussion of debates as a form of campaign interaction. Its obviousness does not detract from its importance, however. Voters in the era of mass media politicking have few opportunities for direct, unfiltered observation and evaluation of candidates for high office, particularly the presidency. Televised primary debates, occurring as they do when viewer attitudes are still open to change, may thus be a very important source of voter information. These events give many voters their first opportunities to form favorable or unfavorable general impressions of the participants. In addition, debates may allow viewers to form an impression of the candidates' *viability* (what kind of chance they have of winning their party's nomination) because the candidates are seen in an interactive situation, allowing for convenient, comparative evaluations of the party's entire slate of candidates. Numerous scholarly studies of voting behavior in presidential primaries have identified a voter's impression of the candidates' viability as a principal determinant of an individual's vote choice.[32] Debates may also provide viewers with information that helps them evaluate the candidates' *electability* (how well they would run against the other party's nominee in the general election), especially if the other party's nomination is considered to be "locked up." That is, viewers may use a candidate's appearance in a televised intraparty debate to compare that candidate's performance with the campaign skills of the other party's likely nominee, using such a comparison to evaluate how well the debater might perform against an opponent in the general election.

In addition to their potential to stimulate interest in the campaign and the opportunity they afford for candidate evaluation, televised primary debates may also have marked effects on viewers' policy attitudes. In particular, debates may affect what political scientists call the "salience" of an issue: how important the voters believe the issue is and, especially, whether it is something they are likely to take into account when deciding how to vote. This potential to affect issue salience establishes the primary debates as a battleground for the parties' issue agendas during the presidential campaign. Issues that are added to the agenda during the early stages of the nomination campaign may remain important throughout the remainder of the primary season, and perhaps throughout the general election campaign as well. For example, George Bush managed to make crime a major issue of the 1988 election during the nomination campaign, well before the Dukakis campaign was prepared to face the issue.[33] In fact, the nominating process itself can be viewed as a kind of preliminary struggle for control of the campaign agenda.[34] Like their attitudes toward the candidates, voters' attitudes concerning the importance of various policy issues may be more malleable at this early stage of the campaign than during the general election. Hence, we would expect the viewers' policy agendas—the salience of various issues—to be flexible and open to what the candidates say during primary debates.

The combination of these last two areas of potential debate-induced attitude change (candidate evaluations and issue attitudes) speaks to the formatting issue raised earlier. Understanding whether and how certain types of candidates are evaluated in nomination-season debates, and whether they are able to contribute to the issue agenda, can give debate sponsors some leverage in deciding which candidates should be asked to participate. Minor candidates, who have little or no chance of procuring the nomination or even attracting many votes because voters evaluate them and their electoral chances unfavorably, are traditional targets for exclusion from overcrowded primary debates (witness Alan Keyes's predicament). These same "dark-horse" candidates, however, may have the capacity to alter viewers' perceptions of the importance of various issues, thereby making a meaningful contribution to the campaign's issue agenda, and would therefore warrant invitations to participate in the debates. This is an empirical question and is addressed as such below, as we turn to an examination of the effects of viewing a televised primary debate.

Assessing the Impact of Primary Debates

On 11 October 1995, WMUR-TV, the ABC affiliate in Manchester, New Hampshire, invited ten candidates for the Republican presidential nomination to participate in a televised "forum," which most observers—including the *New York Times*—characterized as a debate.[35] A simulcast by the C-SPAN cable network gave the event national exposure. The participants were former Tennessee governor Lamar Alexander, political commentator Pat Buchanan, Senate majority leader Bob Dole, California representative Robert Dornan, businessman Steve Forbes, Texas senator Phil Gramm, radio host Alan Keyes, Indiana senator Richard Lugar, Pennsylvania senator Arlen Specter, and businessman Morry Taylor.

The event was structured in a straightforward "interview" format. Each participant was given two minutes for an opening statement. The moderator, WMUR reporter Carl Cameron, then questioned each candidate for approximately three minutes. The questions were different for each candidate, generally tailored toward specific issue positions adopted by or concerns raised about the candidate. While there was some overlap in topics, each candidate received a unique set of questions. Finally, each participant was given one minute for a closing statement. This type of format—which allows only a minimal amount of direct candidate interaction—is necessary (if unappealing) during a primary-season debate because of the potential for cacophony mentioned earlier. Within the constraints of the debate's format, each candidate pursued his overall campaign image-making strategy:

> In articulating their messages, candidates try to target a different group of potential supporters. Lamar Alexander tried to ride the anti-Washington, anti-big-government bandwagon; Richard Lugar appealed to Republicans interested in foreign policy; Arlen Specter targeted moderates, so-called Rockefeller Republicans who were unhappy with the influence of the Christian Coalition in their party; Phil Gramm appealed to economic conservatives, Alan Keyes to social conservatives, Robert Dornan to national security conservatives, and Pat Buchanan to all three conservative groups. Bob Dole tried to generate a broader appeal as a unifying figure to all Republicans.[36]

Research Design

To evaluate the effectiveness of the debate in changing viewers' attitudes, we had 227 subjects complete paper-and-pencil surveys one week before the debate. These respondents were then randomly assigned to one of two groups. One group, consisting of 126 subjects, viewed a videotape of the debate in a classroom setting one day after the debate; the remainder of the participants, serving as a control group, did not watch the debate. All participants then completed a second survey, largely identical to the first.[37] The questionnaires for both groups included a variety of items that sought to measure campaign interest, candidate evaluations, and policy issue salience. Surveys included questions concerning the respondent's intention to vote in the primary and general elections, standard 0-to-100 feeling thermometer ratings of the candidates, and ratings of the candidates' viability and electability on seven-point continuous-response scales running from "very poor" to "very good."[38] We measured respondents' policy agendas in two ways. First, the participants rated the importance of a predetermined set of policy issues along closed-ended seven-point scales. Second, we asked the respondents to list the "three most important problems facing the nation."

For the sake of generalizability and space considerations, in most of the analysis that follows we do not present the debate's effects on viewer reactions to all ten of the candidates.[39] Instead, we divide the candidates into three distinct "tiers" based on their relative standing in the first wave of our survey: front-runners, contenders, and long shots.[40] Dole's backing far exceeded that of his competitors, making him a first-tier candidate, or "front-runner." Candidates in the survey receiving between 3 and 8 percent support were labeled second-tier candidates, or "contenders." They were Alexander, Buchanan, Forbes, Gramm, Lugar, and Specter. Candidates in the survey with no more than 1 percent support— Dornan, Keyes, and Taylor—were considered third-tier candidates, or "long shots."[41] To facilitate comparisons of opinion change across candidate preference tiers, responses are aggregated within the three tiers.[42] Thus, viability and electability ratings are averaged for all candidates within a given tier. Since we are interested in the impact of the debate on these variables, we subtract the predebate ratings from the postdebate ratings, creating a mean difference score for each candidate preference tier for each variable.[43] The analyses of candidate evaluations presented below are conducted on these mean difference scores.[44]

While these tier divisions are to some extent arbitrary, we assume that candidates considered front-runners or contenders will typically receive invitations to debate.[45] One question we raise here is whether long-shot candidates are evaluated by viewers in a fashion comparable to their evaluations of the major candidates, and whether the long shots can make measurable contributions to the issue agenda and should therefore be invited to participate in these types of debates as well. We now turn to examining the impact of the debate upon viewers' campaign interest, candidate evaluations, and issue agendas.

Stimulation of Campaign Interest

All participants in this study, both viewers and nonviewers, were asked whether they intended to vote in their state's Republican primary election, as well as in the general election in November. Debate viewership prompted a significant increase in turnout intention for the primary election, but not for the general election. Specifically, debate viewers were about 20 percent more likely than nonviewers to say that they were likely to vote in the primary. This effect persisted when controlling for individual differences in party identification, political sophistication, and general campaign interest.[46] Thus, based on this admittedly limited evidence, it appears that exposure to a televised primary debate can generate a greater degree of engagement with the nomination campaign, to the extent of making voting in the primary election more probable. If greater participation in the nominating process is a goal, then televising primary debates (and inducing people to watch them) could be an effective method of achieving it.

Candidate Evaluation

Viewing the debate had a clear and direct impact on respondents' evaluations of the candidates and on their evaluations of the candidates' political fortunes. Judgments about the appeal of each candidate were differentially influenced by debate viewership. Table 7.2 presents the results of a between-subjects analysis of variance of pretest-posttest changes in candidate thermometer ratings by individual candidate. Debate exposure has statistically significant effects for six out of the ten pretest-posttest differences. The magnitude and direction of these changes vary from candidate to candidate, ranging from 11 points in the positive direction (on the 100-point thermometer scale) for Alexander to 21 points in the negative direction for Taylor. As a point of comparison, prior research into the effects of general election debates on viewers' thermometer ratings of the candidates has revealed changes ranging from 2 to 8 points.[47]

TABLE 7.2   CHANGES IN MEAN THERMOMETER RATINGS

	Debate Nonviewers (N = 101)			Debate Viewers (N = 126)			Analyses of Variance Viewer-Nonviewer Contrast (N = 227)	
	Pre	Post	Change	Pre	Post	Change	F	p
Alexander	50.00	47.95	−2.05	50.11	60.88	+10.77	30.48	.00
Buchanan	37.27	40.14	+2.87	39.48	42.74	+3.26	.02	.88
Dole	57.41	58.42	+1.01	51.71	61.50	+9.79	18.85	.00
Dornan	49.18	48.71	−0.47	48.25	38.90	−9.35	10.72	.00
Forbes	49.78	49.18	−0.60	49.17	47.58	−1.59	.09	.76
Gramm	46.10	47.36	+1.26	44.73	51.46	+6.73	3.81	.05
Keyes	48.85	47.59	−1.26	48.95	38.11	−10.84	10.23	.00
Lugar	51.21	51.22	+0.01	48.94	52.19	+3.25	1.78	.18
Specter	45.95	48.25	+2.30	47.85	47.89	+0.04	.71	.39
Taylor	49.18	48.77	−0.41	48.89	27.45	−21.44	55.45	.00

Note: F and p values derived from analysis of variance, thermometer mean difference scores by experimental condition. Degreees of freedom for F-tests (1, 226).

TABLE 7.3   MEAN CHANGE IN FAVORABILITY RATINGS FROM PRETEST TO
POSTTEST BY CANDIDATE PREFERENCE TIER

Candidate Tier	Viewers	Nonviewers	F	p
Front-runner	9.79	1.01	18.85 (1, 226)	.000
Contenders	3.91	.63	4.23 (1, 226)	.041
Long shots	-13.88	-.70	40.52 (1, 226)	.000

Note: F and p values derived from analysis of variance, favorability mean difference
scores by experimental condition. Degrees of freedom for F-tests in parentheses
(explained, residual).

While seemingly unpredictable when examined on a candidate-by-candidate basis, the favorability differences do exhibit some regularity when the results are aggregated into preference tiers as outlined above (see table 7.3). When examined from the perspective of our candidate tier divisions, average thermometer ratings increase by nearly 10 points for the front-runner, while increasing approximately 4 points on average for the contenders. Support for the long shots, by contrast, decreases nearly 14 points after debate exposure.[48] In other words, front-runners and contenders fare moderately well to very well among debate viewers, while the long shots fare quite poorly.

The results are quite similar for respondents' viability and electability ratings, presented in tables 7.4 and 7.5. After viewing the debate, respondents' beliefs about candidates' chances vary inversely as a function of the candidates' predebate favorability ratings (and, by extension, as a function of their predebate poll standings). Viewers' perceptions of the front-runner's chances of winning the nomination or general election rise by nearly three-quarters of a point on a seven-point scale, whereas perceptions of the contenders' chances improve by roughly one-quarter of a point. However, viewers' viability and electability ratings for long shots drop substantially, falling by a full point.[49]

TABLE 7.4   MEAN CHANGE IN VIABILITY RATINGS FROM PRETEST TO
POSTTEST BY CANDIDATE PREFERENCE TIER

Candidate Tier	Viewers	Nonviewers	F	p
Front-runner	.68	-.08	30.67 (1, 226)	.000
Contenders	.24	.13	.89 (1, 226)	.347
Long shots	-1.11	.01	62.06 (1, 226)	.000

Note: F and p values derived from analysis of variance, viability mean difference scores
by experimental condition. Degrees of freedom for F-tests in parentheses (explained,
residual).

TABLE 7.5   MEAN CHANGE IN ELECTABILITY RATINGS FROM PRETEST TO
POSTTEST BY CANDIDATE PREFERENCE TIER

Candidate Tier	Viewers	Nonviewers	F	p
Front-runner	.75	-.06	36.29 (1, 226)	.000
Contenders	.33	.10	4.12 (1, 226)	.044
Long shots	-.98	-.02	46.25 (1, 226)	.000

Note: F and p values derived from analysis of variance, electability mean difference
scores by experimental condition. Degrees of freedom for F-tests in parentheses
(explained, residual).

In the context of this single primary debate, then, there is considerable evidence that watching the candidates debate can have a profound
influence on viewers' evaluations of the participants. The front-runner
and the contenders fare quite well in terms of audience evaluations of
them. But we find no support for the notion that including long-shot candidates in primary debates will improve their chances of being nominated. Not only are respondents less confident that long shots can win
the nomination or general election; they are also generally less favorably
disposed toward them after debate exposure. Clearly, debate participation must be a carefully considered strategic decision on the part of any
nomination hopeful, because large losses in public favor are just as possible as large gains—although it is certainly true that the long-shot candidates have little or nothing to lose (other than self-esteem) and
perhaps much to gain by participating in televised primary debates.

Contributions to the Issue Agenda

Some participants in the presidential nominating process—and, by extension, in nomination-season debates—throw their hats in the ring with no
real expectation of winning or even of attracting a significant number of
votes. Such candidates typically have some sort of ideological or policy
issue they wish to contribute to the campaign agenda; in other words,
they wish to use their candidacies as a "bully pulpit" to preach to the
electorate:

Republicans Dornan and Keyes fell into the pulpit candidacy category in 1996. Each wished to use the nomination campaign as a
platform for his issue agenda and ideological perspective as well
as a vehicle for extending his name recognition and political
influence. With television being the primary vehicle for conducting a large-scale nomination campaign, and with candidates hav-

ing distinctive perspectives and appeals attracting public attention, it is likely that the preconvention process will continue to
be used for purposes other than winning the nomination.[50]

Did the dark-horse candidates, or any of the candidates for that matter, have any success in using the debate to contribute to the campaign
issue agenda to any measurable extent? To examine how the candidates'
statements during the debate affected viewers' issue agendas, we conducted a content analysis of the videotaped debate, dividing candidate
responses into mutually exclusive topical categories and recording the
number of seconds devoted to each topic by each candidate (see chapter appendix for details).

Tables 7.6 and 7.7 present the relative contributions of the three
tiers of candidates to the issue agendas of debate viewers. The first column of table 7.6 lists the closed-ended policy issues that debate viewers
rated as significantly more important than did the control group (nonviewers) in the postdebate survey, indicating that these issues increased
in salience as a direct result of debate exposure. As shown in the second
column of table 7.6, respondents rated four of these issues (state-level
control of welfare, Bosnia, a balanced budget amendment, and Japanese
trade regulations) at least a quarter of a point more important to the
nation in general on a seven-point scale after watching the debate than
they did before. Columns three to five report the percentage of response
time each candidate preference tier devoted to each of these issues out
of the total time each issue was discussed during the debate. For example, the front-runner generated roughly 42 percent of the discussion
about state-level control of welfare, while the contenders were responsible for the remaining 58 percent of the discussion on this issue. The
long-shot candidates did not speak on this topic at all.

Overall, the debate participants were reasonably effective in altering
viewers' ratings of issue importance, and the long shots made a surpris-

TABLE 7.6   CHANGES IN VIEWER SALIENCE AND DISTRIBUTION OF CANDIDATE
RESPONSE TIME FOR CLOSED-ENDED POLICY ISSUES

| | *Mean Change in Importance among Viewers* | *Total Issue Discussion Time* | | |
Policy Issue		*Front-Runner*	*Contenders*	*Long Shots*
State-level control of welfare	.36	42%	58%	0%
Bosnia	.30	0	35	65
Balanced budget	.28	49	30	21
Japanese trade regulations	.25	0	66	34
Universal health care	.02	0	100	0

TABLE 7.7   CHANGES IN VIEWER SALIENCE AND DISTRIBUTION OF CANDIDATE
RESPONSE TIME FOR OPEN-ENDED POLICY ISSUES

Policy Issue	Increase in % of Viewers Mentioning Issue	Total Issue Discussion Time		
		Front-Runner	Contenders	Long Shots
Foreign trade	9%	0%	66%	34%
Jobs	6	0	68	32
Morality	6	1	0	99
Economy	6	33	50	17
Family values	6	7	37	57
Taxes	4	5	90	5
Education	4	0	83	17
Foreign policy	2	21	57	21
Size of government	2	8	75	17

ingly strong impact. They spoke on three of the five issues that viewers perceived as more important following the debate and particularly dominated the discussion on Bosnia. This represents more change in issue salience than was attributable to the front-runner, who spoke the most on the balanced budget but discussed only two of the five issues that were influenced by the debate. Long shots were at least as effective as the front-runner in increasing the salience of policy issues (thereby placing them on the campaign agenda) when given the chance in a televised debate format.

Although closed-ended questions permit more precise measurements, because the researcher must determine them in advance, they may not necessarily reflect the issues that are really most salient to respondents. Therefore, sole reliance on salience ratings derived from closed-ended issue questions may lead to misleading conclusions about the effectiveness of the candidates in shaping the campaign agenda. With this in mind, we also examined changes in debate viewers' responses to a standard open-ended survey question: "In your opinion, what are the three most important problems facing the nation today?"

The first column in table 7.7 identifies the open-ended issues that moved up in importance among debate viewers as a result of debate exposure.[51] For example, 9 percent more viewers listed foreign trade as an important problem in the posttest than in the pretest, 6 percent more viewers named jobs as an important problem, and so on. Columns three, four, and five show the percentage of response time each candidate tier devoted to each of these target issues out of the total amount of broadcasting time devoted to that issue.

The candidates are effective in changing the debate viewers' issue agendas, and once again, the long shots exert a substantial impact. On two of the nine issues that increase in salience, long shots provide most of the discussion. On four other issues, long shots are responsible for the second most discussion. More change in issue agendas is attributable to the long shots than to the front-runner, who does not provide the most discussion on any of the issues that increase in importance from the pretest to the posttest. In fact, the front-runner is responsible for more than 10 percent of the time spent on a target issue in only two cases. While the sheer amount of issue-discussion time taken up by the three long shots is naturally larger than the amount of discussion by the lone front-runner, the important thing to note is that issues brought to the table by long shots are at least as likely to end up on viewers' issue agendas as are the issues brought by the front-runner or the contenders. In other words, simply appearing in a televised debate and discussing an issue is enough to make viewers consider the issue; a candidate's relative chances of success do not appear to be relevant to his potential to have an impact on the issue agenda.

The long-shot candidates all fare quite poorly in terms of debate viewers' evaluations of them, as can be seen in tables 7.3, 7.4, and 7.5. On the other hand, tables 7.6 and 7.7 suggest that minor candidates do have a positive effect in the policy issue arena. Long shots have a measurable impact on the issue agendas of viewers, at least in the short term. Thus, these results suggest that sponsors of televised primary debates should give very careful consideration to determining which candidates to invite and which to exclude from participation. The exclusion of a long-shot candidate may not have much of an effect on viewers' evaluations of the candidates, but it might prevent a legitimate addition to the policy issue agenda.

Conclusion

The results of our experiment suggest that televised primary debates can exercise considerable influence on voter preferences. Debate viewers show increased engagement with the nomination campaign. People are able and willing to evaluate the candidates (either positively or negatively) after being exposed to them in a debate setting, and their evaluations are quite different from the judgments of people who did not see the debate. Finally, viewing a televised primary debate has a measurable impact on viewers' policy agendas. The notion that individuals' attitudes are open to change from exposure to televised debates during the nomination phase of the campaign appears to be borne out by this experiment.

As a result of potential voters' relative openness to change, televised primary debates are likely to act as a nexus for different forms of strategic considerations by the nomination contenders. The debate itself—that is, the interactions among the candidates—represents a public discussion of the party's policy agenda. The candidates put themselves—their appearances, their talents, their speaking ability—on the line. Potential caucus participants and primary voters are watching and evaluating the candidates. Potential donors are watching the voters watch the candidates and are also evaluating the candidates themselves. Mistakes are costly in such an environment, while strong performances can yield large benefits. The fact that several of the participants in the WMUR debate examined here suffered large negative changes in viewers' judgments, while others were viewed favorably, suggests that televised primary debates can provide a proving ground for winnowing the field of nomination contenders. The recent proliferation of these events in the past several election cycles further supports this assertion.

It is surprising, then, that presidential primary debates garner so little attention. In spite of their problems—especially the formatting difficulties that result from the large number of potential participants—televised debates serve as uniquely straightforward, relatively unfiltered forums in which the public can evaluate the candidates and their issue agendas. As such, they should be given more extensive coverage by the media and more careful attention by academics. In a nation in which 98 percent of all households own at least one television, no other forum can expect to expose such a broad audience to the initial, formative stages of the quadrennial presidential contest. Regular, televised debates broadcast to nationwide audiences during the nomination campaign may create a more interested, involved electorate and could quiet some of the national complaints about being stuck with a choice between the lesser of two evils during the general election.

Appendix: Content-Analysis Details

Two coders viewed a videotape of the WMUR broadcast, coding the statements of each candidate for issue topic and amount of time devoted to each topic. Intercoder reliability was quite high, which is unsurprising considering the mechanical nature of the coding. Holsti's intercoder *composite reliability* score, averaged across all candidates and issue categories, equals .96 in this sample.[52]

Coders categorized candidates' opening statements and responses to the moderator's questions into seventy distinct policy issue categories, ranging from abortion, agricultural studies, and the O.J. Simpson verdict to the role of the New Hampshire primary in the electoral process and "women's issues." Candidates spoke for an average of 372 seconds each, ranging from a low of 298 seconds (Buchanan) to a high of 473 seconds (Dornan).

Taxes were the most heavily discussed issue, mentioned by every candidate except Taylor and taking up a total of 348 seconds of screen time (98 of which were attributed to Forbes). Candidate traits—a topic whose status as a "policy issue" is debatable[53]—came in a close second, at 321 seconds. Poverty, drugs, and United Nations involvement in world affairs were discussed the least, at 3 seconds each. A breakdown of the number of issues discussed by each candidate and the number of unique issues discussed by each candidate (mentioned by no others) is provided in table 7.8.

A complete breakdown of the seventy categories of policy issues, the issues discussed by each candidate, and candidates' specific responses to each of the moderator's questions is available from the authors. As a fairly typical example of candidate behavior, consider Lamar Alexander's response to the following question from the moderator:

We have very low unemployment in New Hampshire and welfare is a very small problem, very limited caseload as well. Still, there is an economic insecurity in the Granite State, as there is in the nation, and a dissatisfaction with the current level of wages. What exactly as president can you do to restore that confidence and increase wages?[54]

Alexander's answer lasted 43 seconds and encompassed references to the following policy issues: jobs (8 seconds), candidate background (10

TABLE 7.8   DEBATE POLICY ISSUE CONTENT

Candidate	Number of Policy Issues	Number of Unique Issues	Mean Time per Issue (in Seconds)
Alexander	12	1	12.75
Buchanan	12	2	14.33
Dole	18	5	11.28
Dornan	12	0	8.67
Forbes	9	1	21.44
Gramm	11	1	23.82
Keyes	14	2	25.29
Lugar	11	3	19.45
Specter	15	5	18.93
Taylor	11	1	14.73

seconds), decreasing the size of government (3 seconds), tax cuts (3 seconds), decreased regulation of business (4 seconds), a flat tax (5 seconds), and education (10 seconds). This response, although broader-ranging than some, can be considered fairly typical of the candidates' strategies. As the debate continued, candidate responses came increasingly to refer to earlier statements by other candidates, giving this "joint press conference"–style debate a more interactive character.

Notes

1. John Anderson in 1980 and Ross Perot in 1992 are the only exceptions.
2. See Judith S. Trent and Robert V. Friedenberg, *Political Campaign Communication: Principles and Practices*, 2nd ed. (New York: Praeger, 1991).
3. Some evidence has accumulated to support the notion that debate viewers may alter their beliefs about which candidate won or lost a debate after they watch subsequent media coverage critiquing the candidates' debate performances. For an early look at this phenomenon, see Kurt Lang and Gladys Engel Lang, *Politics and Television* (Chicago: Quadrangle Books, 1968). See also Frederick T. Steeper, "Public Response to Gerald Ford's Statements on Eastern Europe in the Second Debate," in *The Presidential Debates: Media, Electoral, and Policy Perspectives*, ed. George F. Bishop, Robert G. Meadow, and Marilyn Jackson-Beeck (New York: Praeger, 1978); and Michael J. Robinson, "News Media Myths and Realities: What the Network News Did and Didn't Do in the 1984 General Campaign," in *Elections in America*, ed. Kay Lehman Schlozman (Boston: Allen & Unwin, 1987).
4. We use *nomination-season debates*, *preconvention debates*, *primary-season debates*, and *primary debates* interchangeably throughout this chapter, although the first two terms are perhaps the most semantically accurate.
5. For somewhat dated but still relevant discussions of the difficulties of reporting on presidential primary campaigns, see Timothy Crouse, *The Boys on the Bus* (New York: Ballantine, 1973); and Hunter S. Thompson, *Fear and Loathing on the Campaign Trail '72* (New York: Popular Library, 1973)
6. For an overview of studies of general election debates, see Kathleen Hall Jamieson and David Birdsell, *Presidential Debates: The Challenge of Creating an Informed Electorate* (New York: Oxford University Press, 1988); and David J. Lanoue and Peter R. Schrott, *The Joint Press Conference* (New York: Greenwood Press, 1992).
7. Doris Graber, *Mass Media and American Politics*, 4th ed. (Washington, D.C.: Congressional Quarterly Press, 1993), 254.
8. For a review of numerous empirical studies leading to the conclusion that debates reinforce existing attitudes, see David O. Sears and Steve H. Chaffee, "Uses and Effects of the 1976 Debates: An Overview of Empirical Studies," in *The Great Debates: Carter vs. Ford, 1976*, ed. Sidney Kraus (Bloomington: Indiana University Press, 1979). A few exceptions, proffering evidence for debates as instigators of attitude change, include John G. Geer, "The Effects of Presidential Debates on the Electorate's Preferences for Candidates," *American Politics Quarterly* 16 (1988): 486–501; Thomas M. Holbrook, "The Behavioral Consequences of Vice-Presidential Debates: Does the Undercard Have Any Punch?" *American Politics Quarterly* 22 (1994): 469–82; and David J. Lanoue, "One That Made a Difference: Cognitive

Consistency, Political Knowledge, and the 1980 Presidential Debate," *Public Opinion Quarterly* 56 (1992): 168–84.

9. Russell Baker, "Stevenson, Kefauver Find Agreement in TV Debate," *New York Times*, 22 May 1956, A1.

10. By contrast, after the Kennedy-Nixon debates, sixteen years passed before the nation was exposed to another round of general election debates.

11. *Campaign Reform: Insights and Evidence; Report of the Task Force on Campaign Reform* (Princeton, N.J.: Woodrow Wilson School of Public and International Affairs, Princeton University, 1998), 28.

12. See Jamieson and Birdsell, *Presidential Debates*, chap. 6; and Susan A. Hellweg, Michael Pfau, and Steven R. Brydon, *Televised Presidential Debates: Advocacy in Contemporary America* (New York: Praeger, 1992), chap. 1.

13. Some standards do exist for general election–season debates. The League of Women Voters, for example, has adopted three eligibility criteria for would-be participants in presidential debates: constitutional eligibility, ballot eligibility in enough states to have a mathematical possibility of winning the election, and popular support of at least 15 percent in an array of public opinion polls before the debate's scheduled date. See Joel L. Swerdlow, *Beyond Debate: A Paper on Televised Presidential Debates* (New York: Twentieth Century Fund Press, 1984). Clearly, the second and third criteria are inapplicable during the nomination contest. The Commission on Presidential Debates, which sponsored the general election debates in 1992 and 1996, has established eligibility criteria as well; these include evidence of a national party organization, signs of national newsworthiness and competitiveness, and indicators of national public enthusiasm or support. See *Let America Decide: The Report of the Twentieth Century Fund Task Force on Presidential Debates* (New York: Twentieth Century Fund Press, 1995). These criteria, particularly the latter two, *could* be applied to inclusion decisions for primary-season debates. The problem, of course, is their lack of objectivity—one person's lost cause may be another person's dark horse candidate. "Mushy" inclusiveness criteria are essentially useless in the face of a large, undifferentiated pack of early-season candidates, so the onus of making the decisions continues to fall on the individual debate sponsors.

14. Gerald M. Pomper, "The Presidential Nominations," in *The Election of 1988: Reports and Interpretations*, ed. Gerald M. Pomper (Chatham, N.J.: Chatham House, 1989), 48.

15. James Reston, "West Virginia Debate: Humphrey-Kennedy TV Session Is Seen Aiding New Englander," *New York Times*, 5 May 1960, A28.

16. It is worth noting that Reagan *was*, for all practical purposes, paying for the microphone. Although the *Nashua Telegraph* sponsored the event, the Reagan camp supplied the funding. See Niall A. Palmer, *The New Hampshire Primary and the American Electoral Process* (Westport, Conn.: Praeger, 1997), 19.

17. Wendy Benjaminson, "Clinton 'Pot' Use Causes Little Outcry," *Buffalo News*, 30 March 1992, A1.

18. Kevin Sack, "Atlanta Officials Abashed at Arrest of a Candidate," *New York Times*, 5 March 1996, B8.

19. There are, to our knowledge, two exceptions within the recent political science literature: David J. Lanoue and Peter R. Schrott, "The Effects of Primary Season Debates on Public Opinion," *Political Behavior* 11 (1989): 289–306; and Mike Yawn, Kevin Ellsworth, Bob Beatty, and Kim Fridkin Kahn, "How a Presidential Primary Debate Changed Attitudes of Audience Members," *Political Behavior* 20 (1998): 155–81.

20. The classic reference to this contention, of course, is Paul Lazarsfeld, Bernard Berelson, and Hazel Gaudet, *The People's Choice* (New York: Duell, Sloan and Pierce, 1944). An excellent review of the prodigious amount of electoral research since then, much of which has supported the contention that most voters make up their minds well before the final stages of the campaign, can be found in Warren E. Miller and J. Merrill Shanks, *The New American Voter* (Cambridge, Mass.: Harvard University Press, 1996).

21. See William G. Mayer, "The Presidential Nominations," in *The Election of 1996: Reports and Interpretations*, ed. Gerald M. Pomper (Chatham, N.J.: Chatham House, 1997); and Stephen J. Wayne, *The Road to the White House 1996* (New York: St. Martin's Press, 1997), chap. 1.

22. See Drummond Ayers, Jr., "California Is Trying for Early-Bird Vote," *New York Times*, 30 May 1998, A12.

23. The focus of the other eye is presumably divided between the polls and the bottom line of the candidate's war chest accounts.

24. See Norman Anderson, "Integration Theory and Attitude Change," *Psychological Review* 78 (1971): 171–206. For a more comprehensive treatment, see his *Foundations of Information Integration Theory* (San Diego: Academic Press, 1981); and his three edited volumes, all entitled *Contributions to Information Integration Theory* (Hillsdale, N.J.: Erlbaum, 1991).

25. Other widely used attitude change frameworks include the elaboration likelihood model promulgated by Richard Petty and John Cacioppo in *Communication and Persuasion: Central and Peripheral Routes to Attitude Change* (New York: Springer-Verlag, 1986); the heuristic-systematic model first outlined by Shelly Chaiken in "Heuristic versus Systematic Information Processing and the Use of Source versus Message Cues in Persuasion," *Journal of Personality and Social Psychology* 39 (1980): 752–66; and William McGuire's information-processing approach to persuasion outlined in "Attitudes and Attitude Change," in *Handbook of Social Psychology*, vol. 2, 3rd ed., ed. Gardner Lindzey and Eliot Aronson (New York: Random House, 1985), 233–346. These frameworks all posit a similar mechanism of attitude change, which centers on the notion that both strength of attitude commitment and the amount of evaluative information used to formulate an attitude (which will usually be greater the longer an attitude has existed) will result in resistance to change; the implication is that weakly held and short-lived attitudes are more open to change.

26. The explicitly psychological concepts outlined above are clearly reflected in the political science work of Philip E. Converse, "Information Flow and the Stability of Partisan Attitudes," *Public Opinion Quarterly* 27 (1962): 578–99; and "The Nature of Belief Systems in Mass Publics," in *Ideology and Discontent*, ed. David Apter (New York: Free Press, 1964); see also Angus Campbell, Philip E. Converse, Warren E. Miller, and Donald E. Stokes, *The American Voter* (New York: Wiley, 1960). They are also reflected in the political socialization theories put forth in the 1960s and 1970s by Jack Dennis, David Easton, and Fred Greenstein, and in numerous, more recent studies of public opinion and electoral behavior developed from a social-psychological perspective. The latter include Pamela Johnston Conover and Stanley Feldman, "Candidate Perception in an Ambiguous World: Campaigns, Cues, and Inference Processes," *American Journal of Political Science* 33 (1988): 912–40; Milton Lodge, Kathleen M. McGraw, and Patrick Stroh, "An Impression-Driven Model of Candidate Evaluation," *American Political Science Review* 83 (1989): 399–419; and John Zaller, *The Nature and Origins of Mass Opinion* (Cambridge: Cambridge University Press, 1992).

27. Except, of course, among a relatively small group of political "sophisticates" or experts, such as party leaders and activists. For a comprehensive treatment of the attitudes and behavior of these individuals, see Alan I. Abramowitz and Walter J. Stone, *Nomination Politics: Party Activists and Presidential Choice* (New York: Praeger, 1984); see also James A. McCann, "Presidential Nomination Activists and Political Representation: A View from the Active Minority Studies," in *In Pursuit of the White House: How We Choose Our Presidential Nominees*, ed. William G. Mayer (Chatham, N.J.: Chatham House, 1996).

28. In *Out of Order* (New York: Vintage, 1993), Thomas E. Patterson provides a general critique of the relatively low level of voter information during primary season. See also Larry M. Bartels, *Presidential Primaries and the Dynamics of Public Choice* (Princeton, N.J.: Princeton University Press, 1988); Henry E. Brady and Richard Johnston, "What's the Primary Message: Horse Race or Issue Journalism?" in *Media and Momentum: The New Hampshire Primary and Nomination Politics*, ed. Gary R. Orren and Nelson W. Polsby (Chatham, N.J.: Chatham House, 1987); and Scott Keeter and Cliff Zukin, *Uninformed Choice: The Failure of the New Presidential Nominating System* (New York: Praeger, 1983), chaps. 4 and 5.

29. Jamieson and Birdsell, *Presidential Debates*, 5.

30. This is, at least, the populist perspective on these phenomena; see Martin P. Wattenberg, *The Decline of American Political Parties* (Cambridge, Mass.: Harvard University Press, 1984). See Patterson, *Out of Order*, 30–5, for a dissenting contention, that the shift from caucuses to primaries was essentially an unintended consequence of the McGovern-Fraser reforms—although the impulse behind the reforms themselves was unquestionably populist in the first place.

31. Of course, doing so is by no means an uncontroversial goal; see Wattenberg, *Decline of American Political Parties*.

32. See especially Bartels, *Presidential Primaries*; Alan I. Abramowitz, "Viability, Electability, and Candidate Choice in a Presidential Primary Election: A Test of Competing Models," *Journal of Politics* 51 (1989): 977–92; and Walter J. Stone, Ronald B. Rapoport, and Lonna Rae Atkeson, "A Simulation Model of Presidential Nomination Choice," *American Journal of Political Science* 39 (1995): 135–61.

33. The story of the 1988 campaign agenda is told in Kathleen Hall Jamieson, *Dirty Politics: Deception, Distraction, and Democracy* (New York: Oxford University Press, 1992).

34. For an introduction to this perspective, see Holli A. Semetko, Jay G. Blumler, Michael Gurevitch, and David H. Weaver, *The Formation of Campaign Agendas* (Hillsdale, N.J.: Erlbaum, 1991).

35. Richard L. Berke, "G.O.P. Candidates Try to Raise Voices above Dole's in TV Debate," *New York Times*, 12 October 1995, A16.

36. Wayne, *Road to the White House*, 132. Wayne is describing the candidates' image-making strategies throughout the campaign, but the characterizations apply perfectly to the candidates' behaviors in the debate. Morry Taylor, the only participant not mentioned, appeared to be following what is perhaps best described as an "offbeat" version of Alexander's "Washington outsider" strategy. If this was his intent, the strategy certainly worked; Taylor came across as hailing from far, far outside the Beltway.

37. The 227 subjects were recruited from the undergraduate populations of two different universities and were given extra course credit for participating. Before the screening and the postdebate survey, all subjects were asked if they had viewed the debate the night before; none indicated that they had done so. The debate screenings were held in classrooms on both campuses.

38. For a more detailed account of the basic research design, as well as several other analyses not reported here, see Samuel J. Best and Clark Hubbard, "Maximizing 'Minimal Effects: The Impact of Early Primary Season Debates on Voter Preferences," *American Politics Quarterly* (in press).

39. Best and Hubbard, "Maximizing 'Minimal Effects,'" contains a breakdown of all the attitudinal responses to all ten candidates.

40. The most widely recognized method of distinguishing between candidates for presidential debate inclusion is to rely on trial-heat survey results; see Swerdlow, *Beyond Debate*; or the written testimony of Diana Carlin in hearings before the Subcommittee on Elections of the Committee on House Administration, House of Representatives, 103rd Congress, available as a document entitled *Presidential Debates* (Washington, D.C.: Government Printing Office, 1993). This criterion is paramount among considerations of the Presidential Debate Commission when deciding which candidates to invite to the general election debates and has been the primary justification for excluding numerous presidential candidates, including Ross Perot in 1996, from presidential debates.

41. This preference-based division rather nicely reflects the majority opinion of political journalists and pundits concerning the 1996 crop of Republican hopefuls, although the placement of Lugar and Specter is debatable. The preference ordering in this survey is nearly identical to a survey conducted by WMUR-TV during the same week.

42. Examining the candidates individually leads to the same conclusions discussed in the text, with considerably less efficiency or brevity.

43. The mean scores used in the viability and electability analyses do not represent a "canceling out" of one candidate's positive changes with another candidate's negative changes. When these results are disaggregated, all long shots reveal change in a negative direction; all contenders exhibit small positive changes.

44. The use of difference scores as dependent variables for analysis is quite controversial in the social sciences. The basic objection to their use is that spurious independent-dependent variable relationships may appear when change scores serve as dependent variables, because of regression to the mean during the interval between pretest and posttest. Such an effect would cause an independent variable to show a spurious correlation to a difference-score dependent variable if the independent variable were correlated with the dependent variable in the pretest but not in the posttest; see Gregory Markus, *Analyzing Panel Data* (Beverly Hills, Calif.: Sage Publications, 1979). Paul D. Allison, however, in an article entitled "Change Scores as Dependent Variables in Regression Analysis," in *Sociological Methodology 1990*, ed. Clifford C. Clogg (Oxford: Basil Blackwell Press, 1990), demonstrates that regression to the mean, while present within groups, is unlikely to occur between groups. Hence, in certain situations—for example, when dealing with change in attitudinal variables—a difference-score approach is valid and, arguably, superior to the conventional lagged-dependent-variable-as-regressor approach to panel data analysis.

45. There is some evidence that debate organizers classified these candidates in a similar manner. On 3 March, an Atlanta television station invited the leading contenders for the Republican nomination to debate. Of the eight candidates remaining in the race, Lamar Alexander, Pat Buchanan, Bob Dole, and Steve Forbes were invited, while Robert Dornan, Alan Keyes, Richard Lugar, and Morry Taylor were not.

46. A dummy variable for debate viewership yielded a coefficient of .19 (standard error .07, p < .05) when entered into an equation regressing turnout intention, measured

along a three-point scale, upon the variables noted in the text: campaign engagement $_{posttest}$ = a + b_1 campaign engagement $_{pretest}$ + b_2 debate viewership + b_3 party identification + b_4 political sophistication + b_5 campaign interest + e. The debate viewership coefficient (b_2) achieves statistical significance and has a similar magnitude in both ordinary least squares estimation and a more technically correct multinomial logit specification.

47. David J. Lanoue and Peter R. Schrott, "Voters' Reactions to Televised Presidential Debates: Measurement of the Source and Magnitude of Opinion Change," *Political Psychology* 10 (1989): 275–85. The authors conducted an experimental study—similar in design to the one reported here—on the 7 October 1984 debate between Walter Mondale and Ronald Reagan. Viewers increased their ratings of Mondale by an average of 8.24 points on the 100-point thermometer scale, while Reagan's score increased by 1.78 points.

48. Some long-shot candidates fare more poorly than others. Dornan's thermometer rating drops 9.36 points among debate viewers, Keyes's rating goes down 10.84 points, and Taylor's rating plummets a whopping 21.44 points. A sample of Taylor's acumen: "As a businessman who started at the bottom, worked hisself up, you'll have to excuse me if I don't speak, if I ain't as smooth as all of them" (reported by columnist Andrew Merton, "The GOP's Gong Show at WMUR," *Boston Globe*, 15 October 1995).

49. Favorability, viability, and electability ratings for each individual member of the long-shot tier drop among viewers from pretest to posttest. In other words, aggregating the candidates into tiers does not mask any positive change by individual long-shot candidates.

50. Wayne, *Road to the White House*, 149.

51. Pretest-posttest changes in open-ended responses for the control and treatment groups demonstrated no relationship, showing a Pearson product-moment correlation of –.12.

52. For details, see Ole R. Holsti, *Content Analysis for the Social Sciences and Humanities* (Reading, Mass.: Addison-Wesley, 1969).

53. For a discussion of this point, see Patterson, *Out of Order*.

54. Syntax courtesy of moderator Carl Cameron, WMUR-TV.

CHAPTER EIGHT

From the Primaries to the General Election: Does a Divisive Nomination Race Affect a Candidate's Fortunes in the Fall?

by Lonna Rae Atkeson

THE PRESIDENTIAL SELECTION process is a uniquely American institution consisting of two formal stages. The nomination campaign, a highly prolonged event lasting from early February to late June, is the first formal stage. Its purpose is to select a party nominee through a series of intraparty and usually competitive state contests.[1] Most of these contests are presidential preference primaries, in which participation is open to the party rank and file and often to independents as well. Others are caucus contests; of these, Iowa's caucuses are clearly the most famous because of their special status as first in the nation. After a short summer recess and the largely ceremonial media events of the national conventions, the second stage of the presidential selection process—the general election campaign—begins. Although this general two-stage format has been in place for over a hundred years, the rules currently governing the presidential selection process have been in effect only since 1972.

In the years before 1972, a period often called the pre-reform era, state and national party elites controlled the delegate selection process during the nomination campaign; they thus controlled who would be selected as the party's nominee. In this elite-driven process, most delegates aligned themselves not with individual candidates seeking the nomination but with state leaders, often the governor, who had given them delegate status because of their past party work and personal loyalty. Because of this arrangement, state party leaders were the important players at the national conventions. They were free to bargain among themselves to determine who would be the best presidential candidate. With this kind of delegate selection process, potential presidential candidates could pursue an "inside" strategy in their quest for their party's nomination. An inside strategy required candidates to work only with and through party leaders; they had no need to participate actively in primary contests or to take their candidacy to the people.

During this period, the nominating process was by no means as open to participation by the party rank and file as it is today. Caucuses, not primaries, dominated the nominating process, making it easier for state party elites to maintain control. Although in some cases new blood entered the party, as in the case of Barry Goldwater in 1964, the rules, especially in caucus states, were biased in favor of party regulars. Through a number of democratically unfair devices, state elites maintained control and often prevented interested persons from participating in the selection process.

Along with the war in Vietnam and other difficult public issues facing the nation in the 1960s, these procedural irregularities led to a demand for a more open and democratic nominating system. Reformers believed that too much power rested in the hands of the party elites and too little power in the hands of the rank-and-file members of the party. Reformers' demands were recognized at the 1968 Democratic National Convention in Chicago when delegates explicitly called upon the state and national parties to give "all Democratic voters . . . a full, meaningful, and timely opportunity to participate" in the selection of the party's presidential nominee. Protesters outside the convention and many delegates inside it were angered by their perception that Hubert Humphrey was an illegitimate nominee, since he received the party's nomination without having entered a single primary. The reformers' goals were to "weaken the power of traditional party leaders, to reduce the influence of interest groups, and to increase the amount of rank-and-file participation in the nominating process."[2]

Because the clamor and hostility generated by Humphrey's nomination frightened many party leaders, the 1968 Democratic National Convention resolved to appoint a commission to review the presidential nominating system and to make appropriate recommendations. The rules changes recommended by the McGovern-Fraser Commission,[3] as this body became known, were adopted by the Democratic National Committee in 1971 and applied for the first time in the 1972 presidential nominating campaign. The rules changes transferred the responsibility of selecting a nominee from the party professionals to the party rank and file. The underlying purpose of these reforms was to legitimize the party's selection of the presidential nominee by increasing participation and opening the party to underrepresented constituencies.

The result is that today we have a very open and democratic nominating process that emphasizes the preferences of the party rank and file, as established through primaries and caucuses held across the country. This is sometimes referred to as the "candidate-supremacy" or "plebiscitary" model of presidential party nomination.[4] Potential nominees must compete against one another over the course of the nomination season and attract rank-and-file support to win enough delegates to gain the party's nomination. At present, most delegates are elected to the national convention because of their support for a specific candidate. Although delegates are not required to vote for that candidate at the convention, most do. Because of this and because few delegates are selected on an uncommitted basis, the convention outcome is generally known long before the convention begins.

The Divisive Primary Hypothesis

Part of the concern among political scientists who are critical of the reformed nominating process is that changing the rules has changed the game.[5] The shift in emphasis from party leadership to broad party membership has created a candidate-centered nomination contest in which candidates appeal directly to voters and seek support on grounds other than party identification. This, in turn, has led to factionalism within the parties. Because candidates compete directly against one another for rank-and-file support, primary and caucus participants, as well as convention delegates, are often candidate enthusiasts, psychologically committed to supporting a particular candidate and not necessarily committed to a particular party. In this arena, the immediate goal for each would-be nominee is to win the nomination by any means possible, regardless of any future effects on the party or on the eventual nominee's chances in the general election.

In pursuit of this goal, a candidate must create a separate grass-roots organization in every state, both those that hold primaries and those that hold caucuses. The purpose of having these candidate campaign organizations is to identify each candidate's particular constituencies and to help mobilize them to the polls. Such efforts, however, reinforce the division of party members around individual candidates and their ideologies and issue agendas.

Furthermore, the highly competitive nature of the nominating process encourages candidates within the same party to attack one another on both personal and policy grounds. Examples of such attacks are numerous. In 1996, Lamar Alexander attacked Bob Dole as being a weak opponent, one unable to beat an incumbent president. In 1980, George Bush attacked Ronald Reagan's economic policies as "voodoo economics," and in 1984, Gary Hart accused Walter Mondale of being the candidate of special interests. President Jimmy Carter argued that his protracted and hostile nomination battle with Ted Kennedy in 1980 was an important factor in his defeat in the general election. In his memoirs, Carter wrote, "There was no logical reason for [Kennedy] to persist in the debilitating campaign which so weakened his party's chances for success in November. The result of his protracted effort was that Fritz and I were required to spend an enormous amount of time and resources after the convention in winning Democratic voters back to our side. Many of them were alienated permanently."[6]

During the nomination contest, the public infighting and candidate-centered nature of the process create candidate factions. Nomination activists are attracted to specific candidates over the course of the campaign based on their knowledge of the candidate, the candidate's own character and personal qualities, the candidate's performance in previous primaries and caucuses, and his ideology and issue stands.[7] As candidates attract different party factions (e.g., members of labor unions, conservative Christians, or New Democrats), the party naturally divides, but at what cost to the party's eventual nominee? Events that occur during the nomination campaign may affect individual attitudes and behavior during the second stage of the presidential selection process; that is, a divisive nomination campaign may influence citizens' support of the party nominee during the general election. Supporters of losing candidates who witness a hostile nomination campaign may feel less inclined to support their party's nominee in the fall.[8] Nonparticipating observers may also find such divisiveness distasteful and decide that a party candidate who is so controversial may not be someone they want to support. At the very least, enthusiastic supporters of a losing candidate will have to be wooed back into the party fold.

Andrew Hacker, the first scholar to examine the effects of divisive primaries on the outcomes of general elections in a systematic way, stated this argument rather well:

[T]he party whose candidate is obliged to fight a hard primary campaign has an important strike against it upon entering the general election. Common sense, if nothing else, suggests that the very existence of such a primary produces or symbolizes fissures among a party's supporters. The supposition also arises that those who backed the primary loser in the Spring may be less than enthusiastic about aiding his vanquisher in the Fall. And there is reason to believe that voters who are committed to neither party may wonder whether the party that needed to go to the polls to resolve its own leadership problems is fit to hold public office.[9]

The result of drawn-out and competitive nomination contests is that at the end of the nomination season, the party is divided rather than united. Unfortunately, individual candidate factions cannot win a general election. To win in November, the party's nominee must put together a coalition.[10] If the nominating process prevents or hinders the building of a coalition, the nominee may pay the ultimate price and lose the general election. Over the last several decades, this argument has provided the basis for a major body of academic research, generally called the divisive primary hypothesis, which holds that the party with the more divisive nomination contest will find itself significantly handicapped in the general election.

The framework underlying the divisive nomination hypothesis rests on theories and psychological studies relating to group conflict.[11] Social psychologists have found that groups in conflict over scarce resources become loyal to their own group and hostile toward competing groups.[12] Because the party nomination is a scarce resource that can be won by only one group, the nomination campaign stimulates factional loyalties around candidates and creates "in" and "out" groups within the party. Critics of the nominating process and proponents of the divisive nomination hypothesis worry that once the party's nominee has been named, the ingroup-outgroup relationship may persist. Those who backed losing candidates may find it difficult to back their party's nominee; perceptions and attitudes about the nominee formed during the nomination campaign may linger. As Denis Sullivan has noted, "The long pre-convention campaign can only serve to increase the psychological investment each delegate has in his/her candidate. These facts, we think, make it even more difficult for losers to accept the convention outcome and recommit their energies to the winner."[13]

A number of studies have found evidence to support the divisive nomination hypothesis. Because primaries are the standard selection mechanism for many offices besides the presidency, nonpresidential races, including Senate and House elections and gubernatorial races, have been the focus of many of these studies. Such studies have used both aggregate data on election outcomes and survey data on the behavior of individual voters and campaign activists. Both types of studies have attempted to link what happens in the nomination campaign to what happens in the general election.

Robert Bernstein conducted one of the first studies to find an effect of divisive primaries on general election outcomes.[14] Published in 1977, his analysis used data from Senate primaries to explain general election outcomes and included controls for candidate incumbency and partisan orientation of the state. Bernstein defined a divisive primary as any primary in which the winner's margin of victory over the runner-up was less than 20 percentage points. After examining nearly six hundred Senate contests over nine election cycles, he concluded that Senate candidates who faced a heated and divisive nomination contest were less likely to win than those who had minor or no nomination opposition. Nearly a decade later, using regression analysis and a different definition of divisiveness to examine Senate and gubernatorial elections, Patrick Kenney and Tom Rice came to a similar conclusion: the party with the most divisive primary has a more difficult general election fight.[15]

Several scholars have examined the divisive primary hypothesis at the presidential level. James Lengle, Diana Owen, and Molly Sonner used a simple win-lose dichotomy as their dependent variable and a simple divisive primary–nondivisive primary dichotomy as their independent variable.[16] Their definition of a divisive primary was the same as Robert Bernstein's: any primary in which the margin of victory between the winner and the runner-up was less than 20 percentage points. Focusing their analysis on the Democratic nominee, they found that divisive primaries significantly reduced the chances of Democratic success in the fall campaign. Patrick Kenney and Tom Rice also found evidence to support the divisive primary hypothesis in presidential elections.[17] Their study examined states that held presidential primaries between 1912 and 1984. Using multiple regression techniques and a more refined definition of divisiveness that took into account the amount of divisiveness in both parties, they were better able to determine the effect of divisive primaries on general election outcomes. They found that the party with the more divisive nomination battle lost general election votes.

Also supporting the divisive nomination hypothesis are a number of studies that have focused on the behavior of individual party activists (caucus goers and party chairpersons) and primary voters during the nomination and general election stages of the campaign. This research shows that supporters of losing candidates are less active on behalf of the party's nominee than are supporters of the winning candidate.[18] This is often called a "negative carryover effect" and appears to be consistent with the divisive primary hypothesis.

The Revisionist Argument

More recently, however, there has emerged a revisionist view of these matters, which argues that the negative effects of a divisive primary have been substantially overstated.[19] Scholars have made several major arguments challenging the divisive primary literature. The first argument focuses on the need to include measures of candidate quality in models and theories of divisive primaries and their effects on the general election. Candidate quality is particularly important when considering incumbent candidates because not all incumbents are equal.[20] Some are weak; others are strong. Weak incumbents invite nomination challenges and have difficult general election campaigns. By this reasoning, it was not Pat Buchanan's bid for the GOP nomination in 1992 that hurt President Bush, but Bush's political vulnerability that both invited the Buchanan challenge and produced Clinton's victory.

Adding measures of candidate quality to divisive primary models led to conclusions that were quite different from those reached by Bernstein and Lengle. Richard Born's analysis of House elections was the first study to include such measures. With a more fully specified model, Born found that divisive primaries had only a very small effect on general election outcomes and that the effect was "not sufficiently acute in itself to cause defeat."[21] Similarly, after controlling for candidate quality, Patrick Kenney found no independent effect of divisive nomination campaigns on Senate and House races. In a more recent study of Senate races, Mark Westlye found a modest effect of primary divisiveness on general election outcomes, but he also concluded that incumbent vulnerability had a greater impact than incumbent primary divisiveness on general election outcomes. Studies at the presidential level by William Mayer and myself also suggest that prior incumbent vulnerability probably is more important than the modest effects of divisive primaries in explaining general election outcomes.[22]

A second argument made by the revisionists is that proponents of the divisive primary hypothesis have ignored the important role of the general election in bringing voters back to the party fold. During a nomination campaign, division occurs within the party because party members are attracted to different candidates articulating different agendas. The general election campaign, however, is not about internal party decisions, but about which party will win the White House. Thus, while a nomination campaign encourages intraparty factionalism, a general election campaign provides incentives for party members to unite in support of their party's nominee. It entices individuals back to the party fold by focusing attention on the two major candidates and the differences between them. These comparisons allow the members of losing factions to examine the nominee in light of his new opponent—the other party's candidate.

Political pundits also recognize the importance of the general election in refocusing voter attention on the issues at hand and in diminishing the importance of the earlier intraparty fighting. Referring to Bob Dole's race for the presidency in 1996, former Massachusetts governor William F. Weld said, "Primaries always humble candidates, whether they're the incumbent or the front-runner. But when it's over, the winner is seen by the world in a new light. The winner starts to get compared to the nominee of the other party. . . . I don't think [Dole's] been diminished by his having to slog his way through this."[23] I have also found some support for this view.[24] My research shows that while there is clear division in the parties during the nomination campaign, supporters of losing candidates increase their evaluations of the party's nominee during the general election.

Research on small groups also suggests that amelioration of nomination divisiveness is possible. This research shows that when a superordinate goal is introduced, previously competing groups may unite.[25] A superordinate goal is a compelling objective for two or more previously competing groups that can be attained only by their working together. Winning the general election represents such a goal. It requires the creation of a coalition that includes supporters of losing candidates. To pursue their common and superordinate goal of defeating the other party's nominee and winning the election, previously competing factions must put their differences behind them.

Finally, some scholars have suggested that the dominance of the divisive nomination hypothesis and negative carryover effect in research studies has clouded some potentially positive effects of an open and competitive nomination.[26] This line of research suggests that presidential nomination campaigns have the potential to bring new participants into the parties. In this context, the contemporary nominating process facilitates mobilization of new constituencies precisely because the competitive nature of the process forces candidates to build their own personal followings. Jesse Jackson's nomination races in 1984 and 1988 brought many first-time participants into the Democratic Party; Pat Robertson followed a similar strategy in 1988 in his appeals to the religious right. Once these new participants have been mobilized, they may be available to the party and the party's candidate during the fall general election campaign. Thus, there is the potential for a "positive carryover effect"; that is, a contested nomination race may actually *help* a party by mobilizing a sizable number of new participants who then remain active during the general election campaign, even though the candidate they initially supported did not win the party's nomination. For example, Peter Galderisi found that primary voters who supported losing candidates were more apt to vote for the party's nominee than were those who did not participate in the process at all, suggesting that participation in the process may help bind voters to support its outcome.[27] Similarly, Walter Stone, Ronald Rapoport, and I found that political activity in support of losing candidates during a presidential nomination campaign actually stimulated support for the party's nominee in the general election.[28]

These findings indicate another problem with those studies that showed that supporters of losing candidates were less active for the party's nominee during the general election. As the positive carryover research points out, to evaluate the level of participation in the general election, an appropriate baseline or point of comparison is needed. The first wave of studies dealing with the divisive primary hypothesis compared the supporters of losing candidates with supporters of the eventual nominee. Not surprisingly, such a comparison showed that those who had backed one of the defeated candidates were less active during the general election campaign. Stone, Atkeson, and Rapoport chose a different baseline. Our model, in effect, compared the supporters of both losing and winning candidates with party activists who did not work for any candidate during the nomination campaign. Viewed from this perspective, contested nomination races appeared to be a net plus for the parties. The more that activists participated in the nomination campaign, even for a losing candidate, the more they participated in the general election.

In the following sections, I reexamine the divisive primary hypothesis from a variety of angles. First, I consider the role of factionalism in nomination politics and whether attitudes toward the party's nominee created during the nomination campaign are sustained in the general election. Second, I consider whether primaries and caucuses have motivated different types of voting behavior in the pre-reform and post-reform periods. Third, I examine whether primary participants and nonparticipants vote differently in the general election. Finally, while taking into account the context of the election, in particular candidate quality, I consider more closely the role of divisive primaries and their effects on general election outcomes.

Nomination Factionalism

The argument in favor of the divisive nomination hypothesis rests on the notion that primaries divide rank-and-file party members around various candidates and that this causes those who have supported losing candidates to become embittered toward the party's nominee. Martin Wattenberg, a critic of the reforms, stated the problem this way: "One of the key features of the candidate-centered age is the increasingly difficult task of unifying a political party in November when the various factions within it have been competing for so long. Internal animosities stirred up by the reformed nomination process are more likely to continue to haunt the nominee in November."[29] This view suggests that once created, animosities are difficult to mend and leave a nominee who has waged a divisive nomination contest wounded as he enters the general election fray.

Hostilities, however, may not be sustained. The move to a general election campaign, which focuses voters' attention on the two parties' candidates and the differences between them, may cause voters who preferred a losing candidate in the nomination campaign to reevaluate the party's nominee in light of his new opponent. Once voters make this comparison, many of them may realize that their interests are best served by supporting their own party's nominee, regardless of any hostilities created during the nomination campaign. Thus, the party should be able to reunite and rally around its nominee.

One way to address the question of whether factionalism created during the nomination phase endures into the fall campaign is to examine the attitudes toward the nominee held by those who supported this candidate and those who supported the losers. The advantage of examining attitudes is that they gauge how voters are affected by each stage of the presidential selection process. If nominations divide the party, as we would expect, then evaluations of the eventual nominee during the nomination campaign should be higher among his supporters than among those who supported another candidate. If factionalism still exists during the general election campaign, then the attitudes that supporters of losing candidates developed during the nomination campaign should show little change. If, on the other hand, the general election campaign creates a new environment in which to examine the nominee, then attitudes toward him should change and make him a more attractive candidate.

To address this question directly, we need to examine voters' evaluations of the eventual nominee during the nomination campaign and general election stages of the campaign. We also need to identify which candidate voters supported in the nomination campaign so that the voters can be placed in an appropriate comparison group, winner backers or loser backers. Winner backers are those who supported the eventual party nominee during the nomination race; loser backers are those who preferred some other nomination contender. The type of data needed to address this question, then, is a panel study of voters' nomination preferences and attitudes toward the party nominee in the nomination and general election stages of the presidential campaign. Unfortunately, there are very few studies that have such long-term panels. One such study, however, covers the 1976 presidential race.[30] Fortunately, this race is a good contest in which to study intraparty factionalism, because in 1976 both parties had heated nomination contests. On the Republican side, former California governor Ronald Reagan challenged President Gerald Ford for the nomination. The race was highly contested throughout the primary season, which ended with no clear winner. Ford secured the GOP nomination only because of his success in wooing uncommitted delegates during the weeks immediately before the opening of the Republican convention. On the Democratic side, numerous candidates entered the nomination contest, dividing the party rank and file among them. Ultimately, Jimmy Carter came out on top and received the Democratic nomination.

In the 1976 panel, respondents were asked about various attitudes toward the candidates, including an overall evaluation measure that we can use to gauge party factionalism. By comparing the difference in evaluation of the nominee by those who backed the winner and those who backed the loser, we can determine whether factionalism was present during the nomination season and how it responded to the general election campaign. The overall evaluation question was worded as follows:

Now I'd like to get your feeling on those candidates who you
know something about. Please look at Card 2. You can use this

scale to give us an indication of your feelings toward the candidates. If you feel extremely favorable toward a candidate, you would give him the number 1. If you feel fairly favorable, you would give him the number 2. If you feel only slightly favorable, you would give him a 3. If your feelings are mixed between favorable and unfavorable, you would give him a 4. Suppose, however, that you feel unfavorable toward a candidate. You would give him a 7 if you feel extremely unfavorable, a 6 if fairly unfavorable, and a 5 if only slightly unfavorable. First the Democratic candidates. Which number on the scale best describes your feeling about Jimmy Carter? [A similar question was asked about Gerald Ford.]

Figures 8.1 and 8.2 present the evaluations of the nominees by partisan factions—winner and loser backers—for the nomination and general election periods; the scale is reversed so that a higher score represents a more favorable evaluation. Data on nomination attitudes are from April 1976; general election attitudes were obtained in October in the midst of the general election campaign. As is evident from the figures, nomination campaigns do divide the parties. Overall evaluations of the nominee by

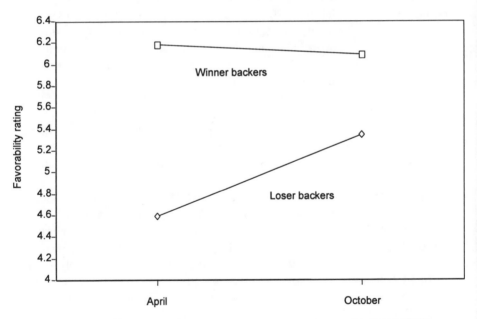

FIGURE 8.1   OVERALL EVALUATIONS OF GERALD FORD IN 1976 NOMINATION AND GENERAL ELECTION CAMPAIGNS, BY THOSE WHO DID AND DID NOT SUPPORT HIM DURING NOMINATION RACE

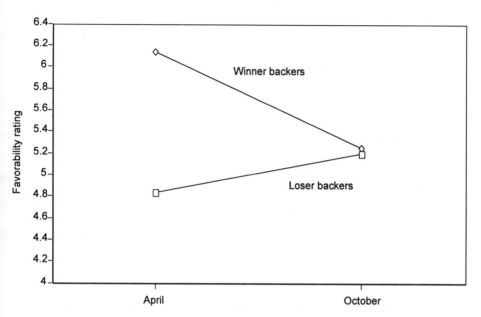

FIGURE 8.2   OVERALL EVALUATIONS OF JIMMY CARTER IN 1976 NOMINATION
AND GENERAL ELECTIONS CAMPAIGNS, BY THOSE WHO DID AND
DID NOT SUPPORT HIM DURING NOMINATION RACE

those who supported the eventual winner and those who did not are
quite different. Winner backers' evaluations of the nominee are much
higher than those of loser backers during the nomination season. For
Democrats, the difference between the two groups was 1.28 (p < .001);
for Republicans it was 1.59 (p < .001). This rather large difference indicates a high level of factionalism within each party.

The level of difference between winner backers and loser backers is
not sustained in the general election, however. On the Democratic side,
loser backers reevaluated Jimmy Carter during the general election and
became significantly more favorable toward him than they had been during the nomination campaign. At the same time, Carter supporters actually decreased their evaluations of the former Georgia governor. The
increase in evaluations of Carter by loser backers and the decrease by
winner backers made the difference in evaluations of Carter between
nomination groups insignificant, meaning that both winner and loser
backers held the same evaluation of Jimmy Carter during the general
election. Thus, for Democrats, the factionalism fostered during the nomination season was not sustained. On the Republican side, the level of
factionalism evident in the nomination period decreased substantially.

The loser backers showed a positive and significant increase of .76 (p < .01) in their overall evaluation of Ford between April and October. The difference between winner and loser backers was thus cut in half, with only a .74 (p < .01) difference between the groups in October.

Overall, the data for both Republicans and Democrats show that attitudes created during a divisive nomination contest are not the final influence on attitudes toward the party's nominee. The change in context from an intraparty nomination campaign to an interparty general election campaign provides voters with the opportunity and perhaps the incentive to reevaluate their own party's nominee in light of his new opponent. The intense interparty battle thus helps alleviate factional differences, bringing winner and loser backers closer together in their evaluation of their party's nominee. These data suggest that amelioration of nomination divisiveness is possible and likely.[31]

Comparing Caucuses and Primaries

As discussed previously, critics of the current nominating process have argued that one unfortunate change in the post-reform period has been an increase in the number of primaries. Critics argue that because of their open and competitive nature, primaries create candidate factions that undermine the political parties. This is because primaries are very public events that attract more candidate spending, media coverage, and voter interest than caucuses.[32] The underlying premise is that caucuses are by nature low-key affairs that produce fewer public fissures and therefore less internal party fighting than primaries. For this reason, general election voters in caucus states are less likely to observe and be embroiled in the party infighting that characterizes a heated primary race and can put the divisive events of a nomination campaign more easily behind them. This suggests that general election voters in caucus states, where the nomination battles are less intense, may vote differently than primary-state voters who have been exposed to a more heated election environment.

In the next few pages, then, I will be examining how the type of nominating mechanism affects voting behavior during the general election. There are three major possibilities. If primaries are more divisive than caucuses and more apt to have lasting effects on voters, then in both the pre-reform and post-reform eras, we should find a significant difference in general election outcomes and voter behavior in primary states and caucus states. By contrast, if the change to a plebiscitary system was the key to primary divisiveness, then we should see that primary states have significantly different voting behavior from caucus states only in the post-reform era. Finally, if we see no difference in general election outcomes and voting behavior in either the pre-reform or post-reform era, then either what happens in primaries is largely irrelevant to what happens in general elections or what happens during the nomination season affects individuals equally in caucus and primary states.

To test whether voters in primary states and caucus states behave differently, I examined data from the American National Election Studies (ANES), a series of major academic polls that have been conducted in every presidential election since 1952. By dividing voters by their party identification and by whether they lived in caucus or primary states,[33] we can compare Democratic voting behavior in primary states with Democratic voting behavior in caucus states, and Republican voting behavior in primary states with Republican voting behavior in caucus states. If primaries are inherently more divisive than caucuses, then we would expect to see more voter defections by partisans in primary states than in caucus states; that is, we would expect party members in primary states to vote for a candidate of the other party more often than do voters in caucus states.

Table 8.1 shows the results. For Republicans, the type of nominating mechanism made no difference in voting behavior. Republicans in both primary and caucus states voted for their party's nominee about 90 percent of the time. A mere 10 percent of Republican identifiers defected and voted for the other party. For Democrats, a slightly different picture emerges. The data show that Democrats in primary states are significantly more likely to vote *for* their party's nominee than are Democratic voters in caucus states. While 24 percent of Democratic identifiers in caucus states defected and voted for the Republican candidate, only 19 percent of the Democrats in primary states defected. This finding is exactly the opposite of what the divisive primary hypothesis would suggest. Thus, if anything, primaries appear to increase support among Democrats for their party's nominee.

Moreover, there is no difference in voting behavior in either party between the pre- and post-reform periods. On the Republican side, primary- and caucus-state residents voted the same in both eras. On the Democratic side, the Democratic candidate did significantly better in primary states than in caucus states in both the pre- and post-reform years. The consistency across periods suggests that changing the rules did not alter partisan voting behavior in primary or caucus states.

Table 8.1 combines data for strong, weak, and leaning party identifiers. It could be, however, that there are differences within partisan

TABLE 8.1   PRESIDENTIAL VOTE BY TYPE OF NOMINATING MECHANISM,
CONTROLLING FOR PARTY IDENTIFICATION

	Democrats		Republicans	
Vote	Caucus	Primary	Caucus	Primary
	Pre-and Post-Reform Eras, 1952–96			
Democrat	76.0%	81.3%	9.7%	9.8%
	(2,303)	(3,411)	(207)	(346)
Republican	24.0%	18.7%	90.3%	90.2%
	(727)	(783)	(1,934)	(3,201)
	Chi-square: 30.15*		Chi-square: .01	
	Pre-Reform Era, 1952–68			
Democrat	77.1%	81.3%	9.4%	9.2%
	(1,424)	(1,013)	(107)	(103)
Republican	22.9%	18.7%	90.6%	90.8%
	(424)	(233)	(1,030)	(1,014)
	Chi-square: 8.01*		Chi-square: .02	
	Post-Reform Era, 1972–96			
Democrat	74.4%	81.3%	10.0%	10.0%
	(879)	(2,398)	(100)	(243)
Republican	25.6%	18.7%	90.0%	90.0%
	(303)	(550)	(904)	(2,187)
	Chi-square: 58.37*		Chi-square: .00	

Source: ANES cumulative file 1952–92, ANES 1996.
Note: N is in parentheses.
* $p < .01$.

camps. Strong partisans may find the other party's opponent less attractive than do weak partisans and may therefore more easily lend their support to their party's nominee. If this is the case, we may be missing a hidden effect of differences between primary and caucus states because we did not control for strength of party identification. Table 8.2 accordingly shows the percentage of strong, weak, and leaning partisans who voted for their party's nominee, both in all presidential election years from 1952 through 1996 and in the pre- and post-reform periods.

Two conclusions are worth noting. First, it is clear that partisanship matters; in all cases, strong partisans voted for their party's nominee more often than did weak and leaning partisans. The combined data for the pre- and post-reform periods show that about 90 percent of strong Democrats, 69 percent of weak Democrats, 76 percent of leaning Democrats,

TABLE 8.2   PERCENTAGE OF PRESIDENTIAL VOTE FOR PARTY NOMINEE BY TYPE
OF NOMINATING MECHANISM, CONTROLLING FOR STRENGTH OF
PARTY IDENTIFICATION

	Democrats			Republicans		
	Caucus	Primary	Significance[a]	Caucus	Primary	Significance[a]
	Pre- and Post-Reform Eras, 1952-96					
Strong	87.8%	91.2%	p < .05	97.4%	96.8%	n.s.
Weak	66.7	71.3	p < .05	85.2	85.5	n.s.
Leaning	71.3	80.3	p < .05	87.5	87.4	n.s.
	Pre-Reform Era, 1952-68					
Strong	88.0%	91.4%	p < .05	97.8%	96.8%	n.s.
Weak	67.5	73.4	p < .05	84.1	84.5	n.s.
Leaning	72.2	75.5	n.s.	88.8	90.9	n.s.
	Post-Reform Era, 1972-96					
Strong	87.5%	91.0%	p < .05	96.8%	96.8%	n.s.
Weak	65.6	70.3	n.s.	86.7	86.0	n.s.
Leaning	70.4	81.9	p < .05	86.5	86.3	n.s.

Source: ANES cumulative file 1952-92, ANES 1996.
[a] n.s. means not significant at .05 level.

97 percent of strong Republicans, 85 percent of weak Republicans, and 87 percent of leaning Republicans supported their party's candidates. Second, the data show no support for the divisive primary hypothesis. Strong, weak, and leaning Republicans voted at about the same rate in both caucus and primary states. On the Democratic side, primary and caucus states do show some statistical differences, but the findings do not support the divisive primary hypothesis. As in table 8.1, the data show that Democratic voters in primary states consistently voted for their party's nominee at higher rates than did Democratic voters in caucus states. Furthermore, all of these results show up in both the pre- and post-reform eras, indicating that the reforms did nothing to change the pattern.

Overall, the data provide very little evidence to support the notion that nominating mechanisms affect voting behavior during the general election. In general, primaries and caucuses lead to very similar rates of party loyalty and defection. The one exception involved the Democratic Party—but the difference was the opposite of that predicted by the divisive primary hypothesis. Democratic candidates retain more of their partisans in primary states than they do in caucus states.

TABLE 8.3   VOTING BEHAVIOR OF PRIMARY PARTICIPANTS AND
NONPARTICIPANTS IN PRESIDENTIAL ELECTIONS

	Democrats' Support for Their Party Nominee			Republicans' Support for Their Party Nominee		
	Primary Nonvoter	Primary Voter	Significance[a]	Primary Nonvoter	Primary Voter	Significance[a]
1972	62.6%	64.2%	n.s.	90.4%	95.1%	n.s.
1976	80.2	83.4	n.s.	89.0	87.2	n.s.
1980	73.6	79.2	n.s.	92.9	96.7	n.s.
1988	81.4	87.0	n.s.	91.6	90.6	n.s.
1992	90.0	93.7	n.s.	87.2	88.6	n.s.

Source: American National Election Studies.
Note: Analysis is limited to the 1972, 1976, 1980, 1988, and 1992 races because these
are the only years in which NES asked about primary voting behavior.
[a] n.s. means not significant at .10 level.

Voting Behavior of Primary Participants and Nonparticipants

Yet another way of examining the divisive primary hypothesis is to see
if there is any difference in partisan loyalty between those who vote in
both the primary and general elections and those who choose to vote
only in the general election. Perhaps there is something about the act of
voting in a presidential primary that symbolizes or solidifies the attachment between a voter and a candidate, such that a voter for a losing candidate would be less likely to support the party nominee than would a
partisan voter who did not participate in the primary process.[34] Table 8.3
shows the percentage of primary voters and nonvoters supporting each
party's nominee in five general elections between 1972 and 1992. There
is no evidence to support the hypothesis that these two groups behave
differently. In each party, those who voted in the primary and those who
voted only in the general election supported the nominee in equal proportions. Once again, we are left to conclude either that primaries and
the events that occur within them have little effect on what happens in
general elections or that the divisiveness that occurs in nominating campaigns affects all voters equally.

Divisive Primaries and Candidate Quality

Some primaries are more divisive than others. For instance, in states that
have early primaries, intraparty factionalism may be quite pronounced
because the field of candidates in these early contests is likely to be large
and the battle to mobilize constituencies is apt to be heated. Divisiveness

also varies by election year. To put it another way, in searching for the effect of the nomination race on the general election, the crucial difference may not be between primaries and caucuses, but between divisive primaries and nondivisive primaries. To test this hypothesis, I collected data on state primary and general election outcomes from 1936 to 1996.[35]

In comparing divisive and nondivisive primaries, divisiveness needs to be measured in a way that takes into account what happens in the primaries of both parties. This is because it is not the divisiveness of one party that matters, but how divisive one party is in relation to the other.[36] If the Democratic Party in one state has a divisive primary and the Republican Party in that state does not, then the more divided Democratic Party is disadvantaged during the general election. If, however, both parties have equally divisive races, then neither party is advantaged as it enters the general election campaign. Therefore, to calculate divisiveness, I subtracted the eventual Republican nominee's percentage of the state primary vote from the Democratic nominee's primary vote percentage. This gives a divisiveness index that ranges from -100 (when Republicans are completely advantaged) to 100 (when Democrats are completely advantaged).[37] To simplify this measure, I recoded it into three categories: Republicans advantaged, Democrats advantaged, neither party advantaged. The Republicans are advantaged when the divisiveness index has a value between -100 percent and -25.1 percent. The Democrats are advantaged when the divisiveness value is between 25.1 percent and 100 percent. Neither party was considered advantaged if the divisiveness value was between -25 percent and 25 percent.

Table 8.4 shows the relationship between this divisiveness measure and which party's presidential candidate carried the state in the general election. The results clearly *favor* the divisive primary hypothesis. When the Republicans had a less divisive primary than the Democrats in a given state, they won that state 80 percent of the time. Results for the

TABLE 8.4   STATE OUTCOMES IN PRESIDENTIAL GENERAL ELECTIONS BY LEVEL OF PRIMARY DIVISIVENESS, 1936–96

Winner	Republicans Advantaged	Neither Party Advantaged	Democrats Advantaged
Democrat	19.5%	41.7%	74.6%
Republican	80.5%	58.3%	25.4%
	(123)	(139)	(63)
		Chi-square: 53.24*	

Note: N is in parentheses.
* p < .001.

Democrats are similar; nearly 75 percent of primary states supported the Democratic candidate when the Democratic Party had the less divisive primary. But these results do not take into consideration the context of the election and, in particular, the quality of the candidates—something that opponents of the divisive primary argument have deemed important in understanding both divisive primaries and general elections.

The context of the election, including the quality of the candidates and the nature of the times, is important because some years overwhelmingly favor one party over the other. This can be seen in table 8.5, which breaks down the results in table 8.4 by election year and rearranges the data so that instead of looking at relative nomination divisiveness between the two parties, we examine nomination divisiveness between the incumbent party and the challenging party. This is necessary because elections in which an incumbent president is running are different from elections in which there is an open race. An incumbent president brings his record and the power of his position to the election. Notice that when an incumbent president runs for reelection, the challenging party almost always has a more divisive nomination race. Because the out-party has no obvious candidate with a lock on the nomination, more candidates enter the race, creating more divisiveness for the party's eventual nominee. For this reason, in years when an incumbent is running, our measure of divisiveness rarely favors the challenging party (the lone exception is

TABLE 8.5   PERCENTAGE OF PRIMARY STATES FAVORING THE INCUMBENT PARTY, THE CHALLENGING PARTY, AND NEITHER PARTY, 1936-96

	Incumbent Party Advantaged	*Neither Party Advantaged*	*Challenging Party Advantaged*	*N*
1936	75.0%	16.7%	8.3%	12
1940	58.3	41.7	0.0	12
1944	33.3	66.7	0.0	12
1948	66.7	33.3	0.0	12
1952[a]	61.5	30.8	0.0	13
1956	70.6	29.4	0.0	17
1960[a]	50.0	42.9	7.1	14
1964	53.3	26.7	20.0	15
1968[a]	64.3	35.7	0.0	14
1972	90.0	10.0	0.0	20
1976	23.1	65.4	11.5	26
1980	3.3	70.0	26.7	31
1984	100.0	0.0	0.0	23
1988[a]	42.4	57.6	0.0	34
1992	32.4	67.6	0.0	37
1996	62.9	31.4	5.7	35

[a] Indicates open races, in which no incumbent ran.

1980). But table 8.5 still shows substantial relative variation in nomination divisiveness, with some years providing a clear advantage to the incumbent party and other years providing no advantage to either party. What is the reason for this difference?

To answer this question, let us compare the last two presidential elections. In 1996, Bill Clinton, the incumbent president, was basically unchallenged in the nomination campaign. Meanwhile, the Republicans had a highly divisive race, in which a number of candidates competed for the nomination. By the divisiveness measure, 1996 was a bad year for the Republicans; 63 percent of primary states favored Clinton and another 31 percent favored neither party. Now consider the election of 1992, when George Bush, another incumbent president, ran for office. Bush was mildly challenged by a single candidate, Pat Buchanan, who received 23 percent of the primary vote. Bush won the primaries easily, with 72 percent of the total vote. The out-party's contenders in 1992 included Bill Clinton, Jerry Brown, Tom Harkin, Paul Tsongas, and Bob Kerrey. With so many contenders, the slice of the primary pie that each received was often quite small. In the end, Clinton, the eventual Democratic nominee, received 51 percent of the total primary vote, but he lost eight states to other contenders. According to our divisiveness measure, 32 percent of primary states favored Bush, while the remaining 68 percent favored neither party.

In both the 1992 and 1996 races, then, an incumbent president ran for reelection, but the electoral context that these candidates found themselves in was distinctly different. By the relative divisiveness measure, a majority of states were neutral in 1992, while a majority of states favored the incumbent president in 1996. Why was this the case? Obviously, it has to do with the competition Buchanan posed for Bush in 1992 and Clinton's noncompetitive 1996 run. But why the difference? What was the reason President Bush was challenged and President Clinton not challenged?

The differences between the two candidates are due to the specific factors of the election, including the nature of the times and the economy, which affect overall perceptions of candidate quality.[38] One measure of candidate quality is the presidential approval question developed by the Gallup organization. On a regular basis over the past sixty years, Gallup has asked the public, "Do you approve or disapprove of the way [president's name] is handling his job as President?"[39] Table 8.6 shows the percentage of respondents approving of the president just before the nomination campaign began and whether the presidential race was open or whether an incumbent president was seeking another term. The

TABLE 8.6   PRE-NEW HAMPSHIRE PRESIDENTIAL APPROVAL RATINGS AND NUMBER
OF MAJOR CANDIDATES IN PRESIDENTIAL ELECTION YEARS

	Presidential Approval	Type of Race	No. of Incumbent Party Candidates with 15% or More of Primary Vote	No. of Challenging Party Candidates with 15% or More of Primary Vote
1936	55%	Incumbent	1	2[a]
1940	63	Incumbent	1	3[a]
1944	56	Incumbent	1	2[a]
1948	46	Incumbent	1	2[a]
1952	29	Open[b]	1[a]	3
1956	77	Incumbent	1	2
1960	64	Open	1	2
1964	76	Incumbent	1	2
1968	41	Open[b]	2[a]	2
1972	52	Incumbent	1	3
1976	46	Incumbent	2	2
1980	55	Incumbent	2	2
1984	55	Incumbent	1	3
1988	49	Open	2	2
1992	47	Incumbent	2	3
1996	52	Incumbent	1	2

[a] Eventual nominee did not run in the primaries or did not get 15 percent of the primary vote.
[b] Incumbent initially sought nomination but dropped out after New Hampshire primary.

fourth and fifth columns in the table show the number of candidates who received at least 15 percent of the total primary vote. The data show that in years in which presidential approval was above 50 percent, the incumbent president faced little or no challenge in the nomination race. In years in which presidential popularity was below 50 percent, such as 1976 and 1992, the incumbent president's challengers received substantial primary support.[40]

The connection between presidential popularity and a nomination challenge suggests that candidate quality is an important factor in understanding presidential elections and divisive primaries. When presidential popularity was below 50 percent, the average state had a presidential divisiveness measure of 6 percent, but the average was 43 percent when presidential approval was above 50 percent. Thus, popular presidents, like Bill Clinton in 1996, evidently fare well in the nomination campaign, while unpopular presidents, like George Bush in 1992, encourage a nomination fight.

These findings are important because they suggest that the real factor in understanding general election outcomes is not what happens in

TABLE 8.7 PERCENTAGE OF STATES WON BY INCUMBENT PRESIDENT, BY
RELATIVE DIVISIVENESS, CONTROLLING FOR PRESIDENTIAL APPROVAL

	President Advantaged	Neither President nor Challenger Advantaged	Challenger Advantaged	Chi-Square	N
Presidential approval > 50%	89.3%	81.1%	83.3%	1.71[a]	146
Presidential approval < 50%	29.6%	40.3%	8.3%	4.93[a]	106

[a] Not significant at .05 level.

primaries, but how the incumbent president is evaluated in the first place. When a presidential incumbent faces a hard-fought nomination contest, it is an early indication of his weakness and failures in office, which makes him both open to challenge in the nomination campaign and extremely vulnerable in the general election. Carter in 1980 fits this picture, as does Bush in 1992. Table 8.7 shows the percentage of states that were carried by an incumbent president when his party was advantaged, disadvantaged, or neither according to the relative divisiveness measure presented earlier, controlling for the president's popularity (whether his approval rating just before the New Hampshire primary was above or below 50 percent). The results indicate that divisiveness no longer has the strong effect that was so noteworthy in table 8.4. When the president's approval rating is above 50 percent, he wins about as many races in states where he has an advantage according to the relative divisiveness measure (89 percent) as he does in states where the challenger is advantaged (83 percent). When presidential approval is below 50 percent, the president loses a majority of states, regardless of whether he was advantaged or disadvantaged by the nomination campaign. In fact, by controlling for presidential approval, we find no significant effect of relative divisiveness on general election outcomes. This finding suggests that candidate quality is a much stronger predictor in explaining general election outcomes than is the divisiveness of a presidential nomination contest.

Conclusion

Over the past three decades, critics of the post-reform era have made a strong case against the greater intraparty democracy mandated by the reforms. In particular, many critics have come out strongly against presidential preference primaries because of their divisive nature. The results presented here, however, suggest that the critics may be overstating the power of the rules changes. First, those who supported losing candidates during the nomination campaign improve their evaluations of their party's nominee during the general election campaign, indicating that the level of intraparty division produced during the nomination is not sustained in the general election. Second, despite some arguments that caucuses are better coalition builders than primaries, there is no evidence, either before or after the reforms, that primaries and caucuses produce different general election outcomes. Third, there is no difference in the voting behavior of primary participants and nonparticipants, suggesting that any divisiveness that occurs in a primary affects both groups equally. Fourth, candidate quality is the most important feature in understanding both general election outcomes and divisive primaries. When incumbent presidents are weak, they inspire presidential aspirants within their own party to challenge them; conversely, when they are strong they prevent a challenge from within their own party. Furthermore, when an incumbent president is weak, his reelection chances are also weak, regardless of the level of divisiveness of the primary contest.

What about elections in which no incumbent president is running? This is a much harder question to answer because there have been very few open races in the last sixty years and only one such race (1988) since the presidential nominating reforms. This may be the area in which nomination divisiveness does make a difference. If both parties have equally long, drawn-out nomination races with a great deal of intraparty animosity, then neither party may realize an advantage. However, if one party excites less intraparty divison than the other and its front-runner is determined early on, forcing opposition to drop from the field quickly, then that party may have an advantage. In this respect, it is worth noting that the rules governing the nominating process are somewhat different for each party. The Democrats insist on rules that allocate delegates on the basis of proportional representation, while many Republican contests have winner-take-all rules, which may limit factionalism within the party and allow a front-runner to emerge more quickly. In open contests, such rules may help favor the Republicans over the Democrats.[41] Future races, like that in 2000, should help scholars assess what role divisive primaries play in open contests.

Notes

1. In the post-reform era (from 1972 on), the party not in power has always had a competitive nomination contest. *Competitive* is defined here as two or more party hopefuls receiving at least 15 percent of the primary vote. When there has been an

open contest, the party currently holding office also has had a competitive campaign. However, when an incumbent has run for reelection, there has been a competitive in-party nomination contest in only half the elections since 1972 (i.e., 1976, 1980, and 1992).

2. James W. Ceaser, *Reforming the Reforms* (Cambridge, Mass.: Ballinger, 1982), 31.

3. The commission's official title was the "Commission on Party Structure and Delegate Selection," but it is commonly called the McGovern-Fraser commission after its two chairs, Senator George S. McGovern of South Dakota and Representative Donald M. Fraser of Minnesota.

4. James W. Ceaser, *Presidential Selection* (Princeton, N.J.: Princeton University Press, 1979).

5. For a recent overview, see Elaine Ciulla Kamarck and Kenneth M. Goldstein, "The Rules Do Matter: Post-Reform Presidential Nominating Politics," in *The Parties Respond*, 2nd ed., ed. L. Sandy Maisel (Boulder, Colo.: Westview, 1994).

6. Jimmy Carter, *Keeping Faith: Memoirs of a President* (New York: Bantam, 1982), 531-2.

7. Walter J. Stone, Ronald B. Rapoport, and Lonna Rae Atkeson, "A Simulation Model of Presidential Nomination Choice," *American Journal of Political Science* 39 (1995): 135-61; Thomas R. Marshall, "Evaluating Presidential Nominees: Opinion Polls, Issues, and Personalities," *Western Political Quarterly* 36 (1983): 650-9; Patrick J. Kenney and Tom W. Rice, "A Model of Nomination Preferences," *American Politics Quarterly* 20 (1992): 267-86; Barbara Norrander, "Correlates of Vote Choice in the 1980 Presidential Primaries," *Journal of Politics* 48 (1986): 156-67; Daniel Williams et al., "Voter Decisionmaking in a Primary Election: An Evaluation of Three Models of Choice," *American Journal of Political Science* 20 (1976): 37-49; James E. Campbell, "Candidate Image Evaluations: Influence and Rationalization in Presidential Primaries," *American Politics Quarterly* 11 (1983): 293-313; Scott Keeter and Cliff Zukin, *Uninformed Choice: The Failure of the New Presidential Nominating System* (New York: Praeger, 1983); Thomas E. Patterson, *The Mass Media Election: How Americans Choose Their President* (New York: Praeger, 1980); and John G. Geer, *Nominating Presidents* (New York: Greenwood, 1989).

8. See Lonna Rae Atkeson, "Moving toward Unity: Attitudes in the Nomination and General Election Stages of a Presidential Campaign," *American Politics Quarterly* 21 (1993): 272-89.

9. Andrew Hacker, "Does a 'Divisive' Primary Harm a Candidate's Election Chances?" *American Political Science Review* 59 (1965): 105.

10. For a good review, see Martin P. Wattenberg, *The Rise of Candidate-Centered Politics* (Cambridge, Mass.: Harvard University Press, 1991); Nelson W. Polsby, *Consequences of Party Reform* (New York: Oxford University Press, 1983); Austin Ranney, "Changing the Rules of the Presidential Nominating Game," in *Parties and Elections*, ed. Jeff Fishel (Bloomington: Indiana University Press, 1978); and Kamarck and Goldstein, "The Rules Do Matter."

11. This framework was first proposed by Patrick J. Kenney and Tom W. Rice, "The Relationship between Divisive Primaries and General Election Outcomes," *American Journal of Political Science* 31 (1987): 31-44.

12. See Lewis A. Coser, *The Functions of Social Conflict* (New York: Bantam, 1956); Jacob M. Rabbie and Murray Horwitz, "Arousal of Ingroup-Outgroup Bias by a Chance Win or Loss," *Journal of Personality and Social Psychology* 13 (1969): 269-77; Henri Tajfel, "Experiments in Intergroup Discrimination," *Scientific American* 223 (November 1970): 96-102; Bernadette Park and Myron Rothbart,

"Perception of Out-Group Homogeneity and Levels of Social Categorization: Memory for the Subordinate Attributes of In-Group and Out-Group Members," *Journal of Personality and Social Psychology* 42 (1982): 1051-68; Myron Rothbart and Oliver P. John, "Social Categorization and Behavioral Episodes: A Cognitive Analysis of the Effects of Intergroup Contact," *Journal of Social Issues* 41 (fall 1985): 81-104; and Caroline Kelly, "Intergroup Differentiation in a Political Context," *British Journal of Social Psychology* 27 (1988): 319-32.

13. Denis G. Sullivan, "Party Unity: Appearance and Reality," *Political Science Quarterly* 91 (1977-78): 637.

14. Robert A. Bernstein, "Divisive Primaries Do Hurt: U.S. Senate Races, 1956-1972," *American Political Science Review* 71 (1977): 540-5.

15. Patrick J. Kenney and Tom W. Rice, "The Effect of Primary Divisiveness in Gubernatorial and Senatorial Elections," *Journal of Politics* 46 (1984): 904-15.

16. James I. Lengle, Diana Owen, and Molly Sonner, "Divisive Nominating Mechanisms and Democratic Party Electoral Prospects," *Journal of Politics* 57 (1995): 370-83. See also James I. Lengle, "Divisive Presidential Primaries and Party Electoral Prospects, 1932-1976," *American Politics Quarterly* 8 (1980): 261-77.

17. Kenney and Rice, "Relationship between Divisive Primaries and General Election Outcomes."

18. See Donald Bruce Johnson and James R. Gibson, "The Divisive Primary Revisited: Party Activists in Iowa," *American Political Science Review* 68 (1984): 67-77; John Comer, "Another Look at the Effects of the Divisive Primary," *American Politics Quarterly* 4 (1976): 121-8; Walter J. Stone, "Prenomination Candidate Choice and General Election Behavior: Iowa Presidential Activists in 1980," *American Journal of Political Science* 28 (1984): 361-78; Walter J. Stone, "The Carryover Effect in Presidential Elections," *American Political Science Review* 80 (1986): 271-80; Priscilla L. Southwell, "The Politics of Disgruntlement: Nonvoting and Defection among Supporters of Nomination Losers, 1968-1984," *Political Behavior* 8 (1986): 81-95; Emmett H. Buell, Jr., "Divisive Primaries and Participation in Presidential Campaigns: A Study of 1984 New Hampshire Primary Activists," *American Politics Quarterly* 14 (1986): 376-90; and Lengle, "Divisive Presidential Primaries."

19. For a good overview, see Alan Ware, *The Logic of Party Democracy* (New York: St. Martin's Press, 1979).

20. See Lonna Rae Atkeson, "Divisive Primaries and General Election Outcomes: Another Look at Presidential Campaigns," *American Journal of Political Science* 42 (1998): 256-71; Walter J. Stone, Lonna Rae Atkeson, and Ronald B. Rapoport, "Turning On or Turning Off? Mobilization and Demobilization Effects of Presidential Nomination Campaigns," *American Journal of Political Science* 36 (1992): 665-91; and William G. Mayer, *The Divided Democrats: Ideological Unity, Party Reform, and Presidential Elections* (Boulder, Colo.: Westview, 1996).

21. Richard Born, "The Influence of House Primary Election Divisiveness on General Election Margins, 1962-76," *Journal of Politics* 43 (1981): 640-61.

22. Patrick J. Kenney, "Sorting Out the Effects of Primary Divisiveness in Congressional and Senatorial Elections," *Western Political Quarterly* 41 (1988): 756-77; Mark C. Westlye, *Senate Elections and Campaign Intensity* (Baltimore: Johns Hopkins University Press, 1991); Atkeson, "Moving toward Unity"; and Mayer, *Divided Democrats*.

23. Dan Balz, "The Once and Future Front-Runner," *Washington Post National Weekly*, 11-17 March 1996, 12.

24. Atkeson, "Moving toward Unity."

25. Roderick M. Kramer, "Windows of Vulnerability or Cognitive Illusions? Cognitive Processes and the Nuclear Arms Race," *Journal of Experimental Social Psychology* 25 (1989): 78-100; and Muzafer Sherif, O.J. Harvey, B. Jack White, William R. Hood, and Carolyn W. Sherif, *The Robbers Cave Experiment: Intergroup Conflict and Cooperation* (Middletown, Conn.: Wesleyan University Press, 1988).

26. Stone, Atkeson, and Rapoport, "Turning On or Turning Off?"; Atkeson, "Moving toward Unity,"; and James A. McCann, Randall W. Partin, and Walter J. Stone, "Presidential Nomination Campaigns and Party Mobilization: An Assessment of Spillover Effects," *American Journal of Political Science* 40 (1996): 756-67.

27. Peter F. Galderisi, "Is the Direct Primary a Threat to Party Maintenance? The Divisive Primary Revisited, Again" (paper presented at the annual meeting of the Midwest Political Science Association, Milwaukee, Wis., 28 April-1 May 1982).

28. Stone, Atkeson, and Rapoport, "Turning On or Turning Off?"

29. Wattenberg, *Rise of Candidate-Centered Politics*, 46.

30. The study was called the "Presidential Campaign Impact on Voters" and was directed by Thomas E. Patterson. Data were made available by the Inter-University Consortium for Political and Social Research. Respondents were selected from samples of residents in Los Angeles and Erie, Pennsylvania. They were interviewed in February and again in April, June, August, and October. The study also included a sixth wave of telephone interviews after the election, in which respondents were asked about their actual vote choice.

31. See Atkeson, "Moving toward Unity"; and Lonna Rae Atkeson, "Divisiveness or Unity? Reassessing the Divisive Nomination Hypothesis in the Presidential Selection Process" (Ph.D. diss., University of Colorado, 1995).

32. For discussions of candidate spending, see Paul-Henri Gurian, "Primaries versus Caucuses: Strategic Considerations of Presidential Candidates," *Social Science Quarterly* 74 (1993): 310-21; and Rhodes Cook and David Kaplan, "In 1988, Caucuses Have Been the Place for Political Passion," *Congressional Quarterly Weekly Report,* 4 June 1988, 1523-7. On media coverage, see David S. Castle, "Media Coverage of Presidential Primaries," *American Politics Quarterly* 19 (1991): 33-42; Gurian, "Primaries versus Caucuses"; William Crotty and John Jackson III, *Presidential Primaries and Nominations* (Washington, D.C.: Congressional Quarterly Press, 1985); and Audrey A. Haynes, "Antecedents of National and Local News Coverage" (paper presented at the annual meeting of the Southern Political Science Association, Atlanta, November 1996). Caucus participation levels rarely exceed 10 percent of the eligible electorate; normal turnout is less than 5 percent. Primaries have a much higher turnout, often averaging above 20 percent and in competitive contests often reaching 30 percent or more. Turnout in primaries depends on numerous factors, including the number of candidates in the race, the sequence of the primary, and the number of delegates at stake. For an examination of the factors that influence turnout in these contests, see Jack Moran and Mark Fenster, "Voter Turnout in Presidential Primaries: A Diachronic Analysis," *American Politics Quarterly* 10 (1982): 453-76; and Barbara Norrander, "Measuring Primary Turnout in Aggregate Analysis," *Political Behavior* 8 (1986): 356-73.

33. Party identifiers include strong, weak, and leaning identifiers. States are defined as caucus or primary states when *both* parties used that type of delegate selection mechanism. When one party used one type of mechanism and the other party used the second type, the state was deleted from the analysis.

34. A closer look at primary voters who support losing candidates would be useful. However, it has been shown that the ANES data have a large bias toward the party

nominee, suggesting that these data are unreliable; see Lonna Rae Atkeson, "More Errors in Voting Behavior: Overreport of Vote for the Party Nominee in the National Election Studies" (Department of Political Science, University of New Mexico, 1998, typescript). But looking simply at the data for voters and nonvoters should provide us with a clear picture of their support for their party's nominee.

35. I chose 1936 because that is the year the Gallup poll first began measuring presidential approval.

36. This measure was developed by Kenney and Rice, "Relationship between Divisive Primaries and General Election Outcomes."

37. A complete examination of the data using the full divisiveness scale was done by Lonna Rae Atkeson, "Divisive Primaries and General Election Outcomes." The analysis that follows draws heavily on this article.

38. The importance of candidate quality in understanding divisive primaries and general election outcomes is also examined by Mayer, *Divided Democrats*.

39. All presidential approval measures are based on Gallup survey data. For 1936 and 1944, it was necessary to use the presidential trial heat survey data; at that time, Gallup had not made the complete transition to the use of the presidential approval variable.

40. With a presidential approval rating of 55 percent in 1980, Carter looks like an exception to this rule. However, Carter's January rating is artificially high because the Iranian hostage crisis provided a brief surge in public support for the president; see Richard Brody, *Assessing the President* (Stanford, Calif.: Stanford University Press, 1991). With only a 46 percent approval rating in 1948 and no serious nomination challenge, President Truman also looks like an exception. Of course, in Truman's day, the parties controlled conventions and convention delegates, so candidates did not necessarily have to run in the primaries to win their party's nomination.

41. But see Mayer, *Divided Democrats*.

CHAPTER NINE

A Brief History of Vice Presidential Selection

by William G. Mayer

THERE ARE TWO challenges in writing an article about the vice presidency. One is to write the article; the other is to convince anyone else that it is worth reading.

Through most of American history, it has been possible to write a perfectly good textbook about our national government that barely mentions the vice presidency.[1] The pattern was set as early as 1885, when a young political scientist named Woodrow Wilson published a highly acclaimed book called *Congressional Government*. A path-breaking attempt to go beyond the formal laws and rules and examine how American government really functioned, Wilson's treatise devoted all of one paragraph to the vice presidency. Indeed, said Wilson, in concluding his account, "The chief embarrassment in discussing [the vice president's] office is, that in explaining how little there is to be said about it one has evidently said all there is to say."[2] Seventy-one years later, in an important book entitled *The American Presidency*, Clinton Rossiter all but apologized for according the vice presidency a somewhat more extended treatment: "I trust it will be thought proper in a book of 175 pages on the Presidency to devote four or five to the Vice-Presidency, although even this ratio is no measure of the gap between them in power and prestige."[3]

As a general matter, Rossiter probably had the proportions about right. But a stronger case can be made, I believe, for giving some attention to the vice presidency in a book on presidential selection. At the most minimal level, vice presidential candidates clearly are a part of the same system that designates the presidential contenders. At least in recent years, the choice of a running mate has been made by the presidential nominee himself; it must then be ratified by the same delegates, at the same convention, that formally name the presidential standard-bearer. Once selected, moreover, the presidential and vice presidential candidates run as a team. Though there is evidence in recent years that many people might have preferred to vote for a Republican presidential candidate and a Democratic vice president, the operations of the electoral college effectively foreclose such a choice. And this, in turn, raises at least the possibility that a presidential aspirant's choice of a running mate may have some effect on his chances in the general election: that putting a particular individual on the ticket may help or hurt the party by attracting or repelling certain constituencies or by affecting the voters' judgment about the presidential candidate's own competence and abilities.[4]

A second and clearly more substantial reason for studying the vice presidency is that this office has now become perhaps *the* preeminent incubator of presidential nominees: the single best stepping-stone to the White House. As we will see later in this chapter, this has not always been the case. Through most of this country's history, vice presidents ascended to the White House only if the president died in office. If the president stayed healthy, the vice presidency was a dead-end job. Over the last fifty years, however, a quite different pattern has emerged. Today, a sitting vice president almost automatically becomes a prime contender—usually, in fact, the front-runner—in his party's next open presidential nominating contest.

From this perspective, the single most important event in George Bush's successful quest for the 1988 Republican presidential nomination probably took place on 16 July 1980, when Ronald Reagan selected Bush as his vice presidential candidate. To be sure, there was nothing inevitable about what happened over the next eight years; Bush himself clearly worked hard to take advantage of his opportunity. But it is not an exaggeration to say that Reagan's 1980 decision made Bush the early favorite for the 1988 nomination. Similarly, there should be no mystery as to why, as this book goes to press, Al Gore is the clear front-runner for the Democratic nomination in 2000. Gore's own strengths and abilities notwithstanding, he is at the front of the Democratic pack today primarily because of a decision that Bill Clinton made in the summer of 1992.

Historical perspective provides, I believe, a third reason for taking a closer look at how we choose our vice presidential nominees. A little more than twenty-five years ago, the vice presidential selection process suffered two very conspicuous failures. In the summer of 1972, Democratic presidential nominee George McGovern chose Senator Thomas Eagleton as his vice presidential candidate—only to find out within the next several days that Eagleton had been hospitalized three times for what was variously described as depression and nervous exhaustion. After almost three weeks of confusion and unfavorable publicity, McGovern was finally compelled to drop Eagleton from the ticket and find another running mate. Though the Republicans made great sport of McGovern's discomfiture, it turned out that they also had a highly flawed vice presidential nominee that year; fortunately for the GOP, those flaws did not become public until after the election. But in October 1973, Vice President Spiro Agnew pled guilty to income tax evasion and resigned from office.

The upshot of these two incidents was to focus a good deal of needed publicity on the way that the two major parties selected their vice presidential candidates. Whatever its other flaws, the *presidential* selection process at least allowed for some measure of public discussion about the strengths and weaknesses of the rival contenders. The vice presidential candidate, by contrast, was generally chosen through a very secretive process, without any careful or systematic investigation of the alternatives. In the wake of the Eagleton and Agnew revelations, a small flood of articles, reports, and study commissions poured forth, all aimed at figuring out what was wrong with the current system and how it might be fixed.[5]

The final years of the twentieth century thus seem like a good time to take another look at the vice presidential selection process, and whether and how it has changed since its embarrassing performance in 1972. Did the nation and its two major political parties profit from the Eagleton and Agnew experiences—or is the vice presidency still one of the most glaring weaknesses in the American constitutional system, a disaster just waiting to happen again?

Like the presidential nominating process, vice presidential selection procedures can be examined from a variety of perspectives. The approach taken in this chapter is primarily historical. Before undertaking one more round of reforms, I would argue, we should know more about how vice presidents have been chosen at other points in American history and how the process evolved into its current form. To date, this subject has received surprisingly little serious attention. While there are a fair number of biographical studies of the vice presidents and vice presidential candidates,[6] as well as historical accounts of how particular candidates were slated for the position, the mechanics and politics of vice presidential selection have not generated the kind of sustained, analytical examination that has been accorded almost every other American political institution.[7] This chapter attempts to fill that hole.

The Original System and Its Modification

As befits an office whose principal problem has been its failure to be taken seriously, the vice presidency was, from the very beginning, something of an afterthought. When the delegates to the Constitutional Convention gathered in Philadelphia in May 1787, they were overwhelmingly agreed on the need to establish a chief executive; that position, in one form or another, was part of every major plan submitted to the convention. But the need for a *vice* presidency was never mentioned until quite late in the deliberations—and even then, the position seems to have been created less because of its own merits than as a way of helping settle a dispute over the mechanics of *presidential* selection.[8]

As is well known, the central line of cleavage at the Constitutional Convention—the single most divisive set of issues the delegates confronted—was not about what powers to give the new national government or how democratic it should be, but about the relative power and influence that should be given to small states versus large ones. Most famously, this conflict was reflected in the structure of the legislative branch, in which the membership of the House of Representatives was apportioned on the basis of population while the Senate gave an equal vote to all states. But the same tension haunted the convention's discussions of how to elect the president. Here, too, small states wanted a system that gave all states an equal say, while larger states sought a selection process that emphasized population.

The creation of an electoral college was one way of compromising the differences, since the number of electoral votes each state received took account of both statehood and population. But even with this mechanism in place, small states worried that presidential elections would come to be dominated by large states, each of which would simply cast all of its electoral votes for one of its own citizens; hence, the provision in Article II, Section 1 of the Constitution, that each member of the electoral college would vote for "two Persons," at least one of whom "shall not be an Inhabitant of the same State with themselves." Still, someone pointed out, what was to prevent large-state electors from casting one meaningful vote for a candidate from their own state and then deliberately throwing away the other vote on some obscure nonentity?

The only way to remedy this deficiency was to make sure that the second vote also served some meaningful function. Thus, the electoral college was made responsible for choosing *two* distinct officials. The person who received the greatest number of electoral votes—if the number he received was a majority of the total number of electors—would become president. And the person with the second largest number of votes would become vice president.

The vice presidency, to be fair, also solved some other problems: it provided a method of succession in case the president died, resigned, or was impeached; it allowed the Senate to have a presiding officer without compelling any state to forfeit one of its votes.[9] But at least one delegate, Hugh Williamson of North Carolina, who served on the committee that first came up with the idea, insisted that "such an officer as vice-President was not wanted. He was introduced only for the sake of a valuable mode of election which required two to be chosen at the same time."[10]

Under the original provisions of the Constitution, then, there was no distinct process or system for nominating or electing vice presidents. The vice president was simply the runner-up in the presidential voting. And thus, it was assumed, he would also be a person of presidential caliber: ideally, the second most qualified presidential prospect in the country.

This system worked approximately as it was expected to in the first three presidential elections held under the new Constitution. For its first twelve years, the vice presidency was occupied by two remarkable men who were undeniably of presidential stature: John Adams and Thomas Jefferson. More generally, the system the framers devised might have worked tolerably well in a world without political parties, which is what most of the Constitution's architects clearly hoped for and expected.[11] But the new United States was not to be such a place. By the mid-1790s, according to most accounts, partylike organizations had already come into existence. The pivotal figures in this development were both members of George Washington's cabinet: Secretary of the Treasury Alexander Hamilton and Secretary of State Thomas Jefferson. Hamilton's followers came to be known as the Federalists, and Jefferson's adherents as the Republicans or Democratic-Republicans.

Once parties had come to play a significant role in the presidential selection process, the electoral system just described was vulnerable to two forms of dysfunction. On the one hand, the electoral college might elect a president and vice president from different parties, thus creating a situation in which the president's heir apparent was also his chief critic and the leader of the opposition. Were the president to die or resign in such circumstances, moreover, the existence of the vice presidency, far from providing for a smooth and orderly transition, would more likely lead to an abrupt change in policies and personnel. Alternatively, and more seriously, the electors affiliated with one party might cast an equal number of votes for two different candidates, thereby throwing the election into the House of Representatives and possibly allowing the other party to play a major role in breaking the tie.

As it so happened, the first of these undesirable contingencies occurred in the election of 1796, the second in 1800. The latter election, in particular, was a near traumatic experience for the new nation, leading to a prolonged deadlock in the House, the near election as president of a man later indicted for treason, and threats by various state militia to march on Washington if the matter were not resolved properly. To prevent a recurrence of such events, in 1803–04 Congress passed and the requisite number of states ratified the Twelfth Amendment to the Constitution, which rewrote the provisions dealing with presidential selection in a way that had rather minor effects on the nature of the presidency but radically transformed the character of the vice presidency.

The Twelfth Amendment's solution to this "defect in the constitution"[12] was to require the members of the electoral college to cast separate votes for president and vice president. While in one sense an obvious remedy, this provision further complicated the already uneasy status of the vice presidency. If the office had been created "only for the sake of a valuable mode of election," what was its purpose now that this mode of election was about to be terminated? A fair number of those who helped frame the Twelfth Amendment drew what would seem to be another obvious conclusion. As Senator Jonathan Dayton of New Jersey put it, "The reasons of erecting the office are frustrated by the amendment. . . . It will be preferable, therefore, to abolish the office."[13] But this proved to be a minority viewpoint. Both the House and the Senate explicitly rejected such a proposal.

The result, as Arthur Schlesinger has noted, was to send "the Vice Presidency into prompt decline. . . . After the [Twelfth] amendment the Vice Presidency became a resting-place for mediocrities."[14] In fact, such a tendency had already begun to emerge in the election of 1800. Of the two candidates nominated by the Republican Party that year, it was widely understood that only Thomas Jefferson was of presidential caliber.[15] The other candidate, Aaron Burr, was added to the ticket as a way of providing regional balance and rewarding Burr for the vigorous and successful campaign he had just directed to win a Republican majority in the New York state legislature.[16] No one in the Republican leadership seriously wanted him to serve as president. But with the passage of the

Twelfth Amendment, the subordinate, instrumental character of the vice presidency became even more pronounced. Much as one senator had predicted during the debate over the amendment, "Character, talents, virtue, and merit will not be sought after, in the candidate. The question will not be asked, is he capable? is he honest? But can he by his name, by his connexions, by his wealth, by his local situation, by his influence, or his intrigues, best promote the election of a President?"[17]

A good example of this emerging tendency was the man who replaced Burr on the 1804 Republican ticket, George Clinton. A member of the Second Continental Congress, former general, and seven-term governor of New York, Clinton at one time would have been—in fact, was—regarded as a legitimate presidential prospect. By 1804, however, he was sixty-five years old and well past his prime. Indeed, he was widely regarded as senile.[18] But from the perspective of the so-called Virginia dynasty (Jefferson, Madison, and Monroe held the presidency in an unbroken line between 1801 and 1825), Clinton was an almost ideal choice for the second slot. He provided regional balance to the ticket, but without posing any serious competition for the next Virginian who aspired to the White House. And having found a successful formula, the Virginia-led Republicans stuck with it. In 1808, they renominated Clinton—against his wishes—this time as the running mate of James Madison. In 1812, shortly after Clinton died in office, the Republicans nominated a remarkably similar figure for the vice presidency: seventy-one-year-old John Langdon of New Hampshire. When Langdon declined the honor, the party turned to a younger man: sixty-eight-year-old Elbridge Gerry of Massachusetts. Like Clinton, Gerry died in office.

A Transitional Period: 1804–40

Beyond noting the rather unimpressive quality of the nominees, it is difficult to generalize about vice presidential selection in the years immediately after the passage of the Twelfth Amendment. If one "system" had come to an end, it was less clear what was going to replace it. Perhaps the best way to characterize the years between 1804 and 1840 is to say that the country's political leaders were searching for a legitimate and reliable method of nominating candidates for national office and that it took them the better part of forty years to settle upon a single, stable alternative. In the meantime, they experimented with an intriguing variety of arrangements.[19]

For the first half of this period, the best-known method of nominating presidential and vice presidential candidates was the *congressional caucus*, a specially called meeting of all the members of Congress who were affiliated with a particular party. But a closer look at these years suggests that the caucus was never quite as dominant or well established as many present-day writers seem to think.

If the congressional caucus really was *the* crucial screening mechanism facing those who seriously aspired to the presidency during this period, that claim rests largely on its role in the Republican Party. In every election between 1800 and 1816, the two candidates nominated by the Republican congressional caucus went on to be elected president and vice president. In most of these cases, however, it can plausibly be argued, at least with respect to the presidential nominee, that the caucus was merely registering a consensus that already existed among the nation's Republicans.[20] As John W. Taylor, a Republican member of Congress, put it, "Should they [the congressional caucus] ever attempt to *control* the public sentiment instead of *expressing* it, their doings would have little influence in the nation other than to embitter party animosity and to sharpen the edge of political strife." A correspondent of Taylor similarly argued, "Let a caucus once nominate him who is not the favorite of the people, and then it will be seen that a caucus nomination does not make the president of these United States."[21] Nor did a person's failure to win the caucus's endorsement necessarily signal an end to his candidacy. In 1812, for example, just eleven days after the Republican congressional caucus had unanimously endorsed Madison for reelection, ninety out of ninety-five Republicans in the New York state legislature voted to nominate DeWitt Clinton for president.

Questions of authority and influence aside, even during its heyday, the Republican congressional caucus had a remarkably precarious and uncertain existence. From the very beginning, its legitimacy was under constant attack. As one reflection of its problematic status, the congressional caucus never developed a stable set of rules and procedures. Even on such basic matters as who had the authority to organize and convene the caucus, there was surprisingly little continuity from one election to the next. Republican caucuses were also plagued by poor attendance.

As for the Federalists, who held the first congressional nominating caucus in May 1800, they never held another one. In 1804, the Federalists did not formally nominate anyone, though there may have been an informal agreement to support Charles Cotesworth Pinckney and Rufus King. In both 1808 and 1812, the Federalists held a secret conference in New York that brought together representatives from about half the states, in what some historians have called "the first national nominating conventions."[22] In both instances, however, the conference decision was poorly communicated to state and local parties, many of which attempted to pursue a different course.

However vigorous the congressional caucus may once have been, there is no dispute that it came to an end in the early 1820s. In 1820, the Republican caucus was in effect cancelled because of poor attendance. The Federalist Party, as least at the national level, was defunct; the few electors who were chosen under the Federalist label that year voted for the Republican candidates. In 1824, any semblance of an organized process broke down completely. A congressional caucus actually was held that year—the last of the breed—but all indications are that it was seen less as a meeting of the Republican Party than as a gathering of the supporters of one particular candidate. That candidate was William H. Crawford of Georgia; and his caucus nomination notwithstanding, four other major candidates—all claiming to be Republicans—eventually took the field against him: John Quincy Adams, Andrew Jackson, Henry Clay, and John C. Calhoun. (Calhoun eventually withdrew and ran for the vice presidency.) These noncaucus candidates were nominated in an amazing variety of ways: state legislative caucuses, resolutions by the full state legislature, state party conventions, and local mass meetings.[23] Any remaining doubts about the value of a caucus nomination were settled by the final results. In a field of four candidates, Crawford finished last in the popular vote and a weak third in the electoral college.

The diversity in presidential nominating mechanisms continued in 1828. Not until 1832 did the supporters of Andrew Jackson and the supporters of Henry Clay (it is not clear that either yet deserved to be called a "party") hold national conventions to nominate their presidential and vice presidential candidates. The Jacksonians also held a national convention in 1836, but the Clay supporters, now generally known as the Whig Party, decided not to hold one, instead allowing each of the party's state affiliates to back one of a group of regional favorites. In 1840, both parties again held conventions, but this time the Jacksonians, now known as Democrats, chose not to name a vice presidential candidate, again leaving that decision to the state parties.

The Partisan Era: 1844–1916

After an initial period of experimentation, then, by the 1840s American presidential elections had finally developed a reasonably stable set of institutions and practices, most of which had not been spelled out in the Constitution or clearly anticipated by its framers. The two most important pillars of that process were, of course, a two-party system and the use of national delegate conventions to nominate the candidates for both parties' national tickets. And for the next seventy years or so, that system operated in a quite coherent and predictable manner, sufficiently so that one can reasonably refer to the years between about 1844 and 1916 as a distinct and well-defined era in vice presidential selection. For reasons that will soon become clear, I call this period the "partisan era."

From our present-day perspective, the most noteworthy feature of vice presidential nominations during the partisan era is that *presidential candidates rarely, if ever, played any role at all in choosing their running mates*. Indeed, after a close examination of every major-party vice presidential nomination between 1844 and 1916, I have been unable to find a single instance in which a presidential nominee was involved in selecting his party's vice presidential candidate. Instead, there seems to have been a strong expectation—an unwritten rule of conduct for presidential candidates—that they were not to meddle in the convention's choice of vice president.

One possible exception to this characterization is the Republican vice presidential nomination of 1864. At that year's Republican National Convention, the delegates made what turned out to be a fateful decision: they elected not to renominate Hannibal Hamlin of Maine as Abraham Lincoln's running mate, selecting instead Andrew Johnson, then the military governor of Tennessee. Though Lincoln never expressed any public preference between the two men, some historians have claimed that he was actively involved behind the scenes, covertly working through trusted intermediaries to dump Hamlin and add Johnson to the ticket.[24] My own reading of the evidence runs strongly *against* this theory. But even if it is true, it was a quite exceptional decision, made under clearly exceptional circumstances. I can find no other case that is even remotely similar.

These years were, in general, a time of fairly weak presidents and presidential candidates, the period that James Bryce had in mind when he wrote his famous essay "Why Great Men Are Not Chosen Presidents."[25] But even on those occasions when a party selected a strong and activist candidate, one power that nominee did not presume to exercise was to choose his own running mate. Henry Clay, for example, exercised an extraordinary measure of leadership over the early Whig Party, a dominion that has few parallels in American history. Yet, when Clay himself was the Whig presidential candidate in 1844, he made no attempt to intervene in the party's choice of a vice president.[26]

An even more telling demonstration of the point, perhaps, is provided by the Democratic National Convention of 1900.[27] That conclave, as one historian has noted, "belonged to" William Jennings Bryan "from the first item on the agenda to the adjournment."[28] Having won the party's presidential nomination in 1896, the Great Commoner was a prohibitive favorite to do it again four years later. In the end, he received a unanimous vote on the convention's only presidential roll call. No shrinking violet he, Bryan was not shy about using his position to make sure that the convention adopted a platform exactly to his liking. Though he did not actually attend the convention—this, too, was considered inappropriate conduct in a presidential aspirant—Bryan stayed in constant contact with it by telephone and telegraph, carefully going over the wording of each plank and resolution. But when it came to choosing a vice presidential candidate, Bryan declined to express a preference, even though the man ultimately selected, Adlai Stevenson, greatly complicated Bryan's plans for the general election.[29]

If the presidential nominee was not involved in selecting the vice president, who did make this decision? The short answer is that it was made at the national party convention by party leaders and ordinary delegates. What needs to be emphasized, though, is that the vice presidential candidate truly was a *partisan* choice during this period. The decision was made by the party operating as a collective entity; no one individual, no small "inner club" of well-connected insiders, could pronounce a final judgment on the matter.

A particularly good example of how the system worked is provided by the nomination of Theodore Roosevelt at the Republican National Convention of 1900.[30] To provide just a bit of background: In 1896, the Republican Party had reclaimed the White House with a ticket featuring William McKinley of Ohio as the presidential candidate and a little-known businessman and former state legislator from New Jersey named Garret Hobart as the vice presidential nominee. McKinley's first four years in office were, from the party's perspective, an enormous success; Hobart, however, died in 1899. Thus, as the Republicans approached their 1900 convention, McKinley's renomination was taken for granted; the vice presidential contest, by contrast, was wide open.

Popular histories of this era have sometimes claimed that Roosevelt was added to the 1900 Republican ticket so that Thomas Platt, the Republican Party boss in New York, could get him out of the governor's office. And there is a kernel of truth to this story, particularly as it regards Platt's own motivation. In 1898, Platt had pushed the New York Republican Party to nominate Roosevelt for governor—only to find that Roosevelt was considerably more independent and activist than Platt had expected. By early 1900, several major interests connected with the

Platt machine were quite upset about Roosevelt's conduct in office, and Platt was looking for an uncontroversial way to avoid having Roosevelt in the governor's office for another two years. The best way to do this, Platt finally decided, was to "kick Roosevelt upstairs" by having him nominated for the vice presidency.

To end the story here, however, greatly overestimates the ability of Platt—or any other individual—to control the workings of a national party convention. In fact, Roosevelt was an attractive vice presidential prospect on a number of grounds. To begin with, in the closing decades of the nineteenth century, any prominent politician from New York was likely to receive at least some consideration for a spot on his party's national ticket. The Empire State was not only the largest single bloc of electoral votes at that time, but also one of the few states where the parties still competed on fairly even terms. (Between 1876 and 1916, fifteen of twenty-two major-party vice presidential candidates came from just two states: New York and Indiana.) Roosevelt was also a war hero, the leader of the fabled Rough Riders during the recently concluded Spanish-American War. Finally, Roosevelt had a substantial following among western Republicans, who were beginning to chafe over the party's persistent failure to include candidates from the West on its national tickets. Though a resident of New York, Roosevelt had spent a good deal of time in the West and had written several well-received books about the region.

Not everyone in the Grand Old Party was enamored of Roosevelt, however. In particular, he had one quite formidable opponent, who shuddered at the very thought of putting the New York governor on the ticket. That man was Mark Hanna, U.S. senator from Ohio, chairman of the Republican National Committee, and close friend and political advisor to President McKinley. But all of Hanna's advantages notwithstanding, he alone did not have the power to veto Roosevelt's nomination. So he tried to persuade other party leaders that Roosevelt was a risky choice—to no avail. Finally, in desperation, Hanna appealed to President McKinley, urging him to come out against Roosevelt's selection. But McKinley refused to get involved in the decision. Instead, he sent the following message to the convention:

> The President's friends must not undertake to commit the
> Administration to any candidate [for vice president]. It has no
> candidate. The convention must make the nomination; the
> Administration would not if it could. The President's close friends
> should be satisfied with his unanimous renomination and not

interfere with the vice-presidential nomination. The Administration wants the candidate of the convention, and the President's friends must not dictate to the convention.[31]

With great misgivings, Hanna threw in the towel. His final thoughts on the matter are conveyed in a letter he later sent to President McKinley: "Your *duty* to the Country is to *live* for four years from next March."

To say that the vice presidential nomination was a collective partisan decision, however, only raises further questions. If we have learned nothing else from the work of the so-called rational-choice school of political analysis, it is that collective decision-making processes are rarely very simple. How was it, then—in a convention with several hundred or a thousand delegates, facing dozens of vice presidential possibilities—that a majority of the delegates were able to agree on a single individual?[32]

Part of the answer lies in the process. The national conventions allowed the delegates a number of opportunities to assess the level of support enjoyed by the various contenders and then to coordinate their votes informally. Especially if the presidential nomination had been contested, there was usually an adjournment or recess before the vice presidential selection began, during which the delegates could caucus and confer with one another. (On a number of occasions, the convention proceedings indicate that this recess was called for the explicit purpose of permitting, as one party leader put it, "the most mature deliberation possible under the circumstances.")[33]

In addition, in about half of the conventions held during the partisan era, it required more than one ballot to choose a vice presidential candidate. In general, multiballot vice presidential nominations were a process of elimination and consolidation. After the first ballot had shown who the major contenders were and what kind of support they enjoyed, many of the candidates would withdraw, and various state delegations would shift their votes to the front-runners until one candidate finally achieved the requisite majority.[34]

Most of all, agreement on a vice presidential nominee was made easier by what seem to have been a number of widely shared assumptions about what was needed in a vice presidential candidate. One such assumption, as we have seen, was that the vice presidency was overwhelmingly viewed in terms of immediate electoral advantage; that is, the principal criterion for evaluating vice presidential contenders was whether they brought additional votes to the party's presidential ticket. This is not to say that *no* attention was given to a vice presidential candidate's abilities or policy views—the convention proceedings do provide occasional evidence of such concern—but quite clearly these were secondary considerations.

One indication of how thoroughly electoral motives dominated the vice presidential selection is the nature of the nominating speeches that were given at the national conventions. When a New Jersey delegate nominated Garret Hobart for the vice presidency in 1896, for example, his speech to the Republican convention never mentioned Hobart or his qualifications for the position until the very end. Instead, most of the speech is a detailed recounting of the Republican Party's recent electoral successes in New Jersey, designed to emphasize how fragile the party's position in that state currently was and how much it would therefore benefit from having a New Jersey resident on the national ticket. Especially to contemporary ears, the most striking feature of this address is how open and undisguised is the speaker's concern with his party's electoral fortunes. The speech begins, for example, "I rise to present to this Convention the claims of New Jersey to the vice-presidency. We come because we feel that we can for the first time in our history bring to you a promise that our electoral vote will be cast for your nominees. If you comply with our request, this promise will surely be redeemed."[35]

The dominance of electoral considerations, along with the generally partisan nature of American politics during this period, points to another widely held belief: that one important function of the vice presidential nomination was to help promote party unity. More specifically, both parties sought vice presidential candidates who would provide *balance* to their national tickets—people whose selection would offer some support, consolation, or recognition to those interests and factions within the party that had not prevailed in the presidential balloting.

In some cases, presidential ticket balancing was done openly and explicitly. The 1860 Democratic convention, for example, featured a long, knockdown battle between the northern and southern wings of the party.[36] When the northerners finally prevailed in the presidential balloting, the convention invited the remaining southern delegates—most had walked out by this time—to caucus and choose the party's vice presidential candidate. When the southerners announced that they had agreed upon Benjamin Fitzpatrick of Alabama, the convention approved the selection by a vote of 198½ to 1. (Fitzpatrick, however, declined the position.)[37]

But even when the balancing act was not quite so blatant as this, the importance of party unity was clearly reflected in the types of candidates who were nominated. At a time when state and regional affiliations loomed especially large in American politics, the most obvious form of balance observed in the construction of national tickets was *geographic*. Of the thirty-eight major-party tickets nominated between 1844 and 1916, there is exactly one that was clearly unbalanced in regional terms. In 1868, the Republicans chose a presidential candidate from Illinois (Ulysses S. Grant) and a vice presidential candidate from Indiana (Schuyler Colfax). There are also one or two borderline cases.[38] In every other instance, however, the two nominees came from what were clearly regarded as different regions of the country. In the elections between 1840 and 1852, both Whig and Democratic tickets invariably included one person from the Northeast or Midwest and one from the Deep or Border South. After the Civil War and Reconstruction, when the South was no longer a politically competitive region, *every* Republican ticket between 1872 and 1924 and about three-fourths of the Democratic tickets paired one candidate from the Northeast with another from the Midwest.

But the concept of ticket balancing went far beyond an attention to region. In races in which the personal followings of one or more candidates played a major role, the vice presidential nominee was frequently someone closely associated with one of the defeated presidential contenders. At the Democratic National Convention of 1852, for example, two candidates dominated the early presidential balloting: James Buchanan and Lewis Cass. When neither of these men could win the necessary two-thirds vote, the convention, on the forty-ninth ballot, finally turned to a dark horse, Franklin Pierce of New Hampshire. As a sop to the Buchanan supporters, however, the party's vice presidential nomination was conferred upon William R. King of Alabama, Buchanan's close personal friend and long-time roommate. (Indeed, Whig newspapers of the time often intimated that the two men were lovers.)[39] The Democrats did this, it might be noted, even though King was widely known to be quite sick; in fact, he died just a month and a half after Pierce's inauguration.

Great attention was also paid to the need for *ideological balance*. If a party was sharply divided over some major issue, the side that lost the presidential balloting was generally given the vice presidency as a consolation prize. Indeed, vice presidential selections during this period are a good guide to the major cleavages, divisions, and fault lines within the two major parties. When the Republican Party was first established, for example, it sought to bring together former members of the Whig and Democratic parties around a common platform of opposition to the extension of slavery. Not surprisingly, every Republican ticket through the end of the Civil War consisted of one former Whig and one former Democrat.

Of course, as any number of recent major-party tickets demonstrate, vice presidential selection is still used in part as a way of reaching out to those factions and groups within the party that are uncertain about the presidential candidate. But especially over the last forty years, the ideological distance between a party's presidential and vice presidential nominees has tended to be reasonably small. During the partisan era, by contrast, national tickets often tried to bridge gaps that were positively breathtaking.

In 1864, for example, the northern Democratic Party was sharply divided between two factions: War Democrats, who wanted to win the war but felt that Lincoln's attempts to link it with the slavery issue were hurting the North's military effort; and Peace Democrats, who thought the war was a bad idea and favored an immediate cessation of hostilities. How were these two groups to be united behind a single national ticket? The solution the Democrats contrived at their national convention was to nominate a presidential candidate who was a conspicuous War Democrat (former general George McClellan) and a vice presidential candidate who was a prominent Peace Democrat (Ohio congressman George Pendleton).[40]

Similarly, both historians and contemporary observers agree that Martin Van Buren was an all but prohibitive favorite to win the 1844 Democratic presidential nomination—until the party split over the annexation of Texas. Van Buren opposed immediate annexation, while the southern wing of the party insisted on it. Indeed, southern support for annexation was so strong that Van Buren was unable to win the two-thirds majority the Democrats then required for nomination. On the ninth ballot, the convention finally turned to annexation supporter James K. Polk. But no sooner had the party nominated Polk than they unanimously offered the vice presidential slot to Silas Wright, a close friend of Van Buren's who also opposed annexation. (Wright turned the nomination down, however.)[41]

From Partisan to Candidate-Centered Selection: 1920–60

After 1916, the system I have just described began to change in one enormously significant way: presidential candidates became more and more actively involved in selecting their running mates. Though the transition occurred gradually, the total change was quite substantial. By the 1960s, the choice of a vice presidential candidate was widely viewed as the personal prerogative of the presidential nominee. Party leaders were usually *consulted* about the decision, but even this appeared to be an increasingly pro forma process, an opportunity to ratify a choice that had already been made.

What took place during these years was not entirely without precedent. In 1832, with both the party system and the presidential nominating process in disarray, Andrew Jackson had vigorously supported the nomination of Martin Van Buren as his vice presidential candidate.[42] But with that lone exception, the first case I can find in which a presidential candidate was even minimally involved in selecting his running mate occurred at the Democratic National Convention of 1920.[43] At the top of the Democratic ticket that year—it had taken the convention forty-four ballots to put him there—was James M. Cox, newspaper publisher and governor of Ohio. Later on the day of Cox's nomination, after a lengthy recess, the vice presidential nomination was conferred upon thirty-eight-year-old Franklin Delano Roosevelt, then the assistant secretary of the navy.

Such are the bare facts, but there is less agreement on how much of a role Cox played in Roosevelt's selection. In his memoirs, which were published in 1946, Cox claims to have selected a running mate almost entirely on his own initiative. Like almost all presidential aspirants before 1932, Cox himself did not actually attend the 1920 convention, which was held in San Francisco; he did follow the proceedings closely by telegraph, however, from his newspaper offices in Dayton. Shortly after he himself was nominated, Cox says, he received a telephone call from Edmond H. Moore, who had managed the Cox forces at the convention, asking the Ohio governor if he had any "preference for vice-president." As Cox has recorded his reply:

> I told [Moore] that I had given the matter some thought and that my choice would be Franklin D. Roosevelt of New York. Moore inquired, "Do you know him?" I did not. In fact, so far as I knew, I had never seen him; but I explained to Mr. Moore that he met the geographical requirement, that he was recognized as an Independent and that Roosevelt was a well-known name. I knew that his relations with the organization in his state were not friendly. . . . This made it necessary for Mr. Moore to consult Charles F. Murphy, head of New York's organization, explaining to him what had moved me to this selection, but saying that if it were offensive, we would abandon the idea and go to Edward T. Meredith of Iowa.
>
> Mr. Roosevelt knew nothing of all this. The story of his nomination has been so badly bungled by biographers in the last few

years that I think it appropriate to put in the records the exact facts.[44]

Even by his own account, Cox's intervention in the vice presidential selection process was not—at least by today's standards—an act of vigorous self-assertion. Notice in particular the conditional nature of Cox's choice: he wants Roosevelt only if the choice is acceptable to Boss Murphy of Tammany Hall. If Murphy objects, Cox will go with someone else.

But as the final sentence in Cox's account suggests, there is another version of the story. In particular, there is good reason to think that Cox's memoirs—which were published, after all, twenty-six years after the convention and a year after Roosevelt's death—slightly inflate his own role in these events. So far as I can determine, no contemporary account of the 1920 Democratic vice presidential nomination portrayed Cox as a central player in the drama. Instead, the key decision makers seem to have been a group of party leaders and delegates, including both the formal leaders of the Cox convention forces, such as Moore, and a number of state party leaders, such as Murphy of New York and George Brennan of Illinois, who had supported Cox at a crucial point in the presidential balloting. In a series of meetings that were held before and just after the convention was gaveled to order that morning, these leaders had canvassed the various vice presidential prospects and the preferences of their own delegations, and gradually reached a consensus that Roosevelt was the strongest available candidate. As the next day's *New York Times* put it, Governor Cox was "consulted" on the matter, but rather than choosing Roosevelt on his own, his role seems to have been a bit more passive: he simply ratified a choice that already had a great deal of support among the delegates and party leaders. To quote the *Times*, "His [Cox's] advice as to a running mate was asked. He wanted to know who was in the field. When the list was given, he was also informed that Mr. Roosevelt was acceptable to the leaders, and he gave his approval."[45]

To undercut the significance of Cox's actions just a bit further, it is not clear from the historical record how widely Cox's views were made known to the convention delegates. While a small number of party leaders were apparently aware of the nominee's preferences, there appears to have been no attempt to make them generally and publicly known.[46] In particular, *there is not a single reference to Cox's views in the official convention proceedings*. Of the half dozen or so speeches by which Roosevelt's nomination was made and seconded, not one describes him as being Cox's personal preference for the position. Five other candidates were officially nominated for the vice presidency; all eventually withdrew before a roll call vote was taken—but again, none of the withdrawal speeches suggest that that step was being taken in deference to Cox's wishes.[47]

Like most nominations made during the partisan era, then, Roosevelt's selection by the 1920 Democratic convention was probably not the decision of just one individual. Instead, like his uncle Theodore in 1900, Franklin was an attractive vice presidential candidate from a variety of perspectives. He came from the still crucial state of New York; he provided the ticket with both geographic and ideological balance; his last name was perhaps the most magnetic in American politics. As the assistant secretary of the navy, he had played some part in America's successful performance in World War I; he was associated with the Wilson administration—but not too closely associated with it. Roosevelt himself had also conducted a low-key campaign for the position; many close friends and supporters of his were quite active in those early morning meetings. Of course, Roosevelt was not the only plausible vice presidential prospect in the Democratic Party. In this sense, the support he received from the Cox forces may have given him an important final push toward the brass ring. But as one of Roosevelt's friends wrote just one day later, "Franklin's nomination . . . really didn't require much shoving from anyone."[48]

It is a bit of an overstatement, then, to suggest that James Cox *personally selected* Franklin Roosevelt as his running mate. But Cox's actions in 1920 were nevertheless a break with a long-established precedent. Since the institutionalization of national nominating conventions in the early 1840s, this seems to be the first instance in which a presidential candidate made any attempt at all to become involved in the vice presidential selection process.

For all its obvious idiosyncrasies, Franklin Roosevelt's selection as a vice presidential candidate in 1920 is, in a number of respects, quite typical of how such nominations were made for the next twenty years or so. A few presidential nominees, such as Al Smith in 1928, continued to insist that the selection "be made by the convention itself."[49] But of most presidential candidates between 1920 and 1940, it can be said that, like James Cox, they were involved in the vice presidential selection decision—but they weren't that involved.

Both contemporary and historical accounts suggest that the process generally went something like this: After the presidential candidate had been nominated, a meeting (or meetings) would be held to canvass existing opinions about the vice presidential nomination and to evaluate the alternatives. Who took part in this meeting varied from convention to convention; since the meetings were private, it is usually impossible to establish a definitive list of the participants. In general, however, four categories of people appear to have played a major role in these deliberations: (1) the convention managers and other personal representatives of the presidential nominee; (2) the heads of the major state delegations that had supported the nominee; (3) other important party leaders, such as the Speaker of the House or the chairman of the national committee; and (4) anyone else who could worm his way into the proceedings. After taking into account both their own preferences and those of the other delegates, and briefly discussing the strengths and weaknesses of the major contenders, this group would reach a consensus. During or immediately after this meeting, the presidential nominee would be contacted—usually by telephone—and asked for his own preferences or informed of the candidate agreed upon by the party leaders. Assuming the presidential candidate approved of this choice—and there is no evidence that any nominee sought to exercise a right of veto—the matter was effectively settled. Word would then be spread among the rest of the convention delegates. Though a number of other candidates were generally nominated for the second slot, this was usually just a way of honoring previous commitments and grabbing a few precious moments of national radio time. Almost all of these other contenders would withdraw before the roll was called, and the leaders' candidate would then breeze to a lopsided victory on the first ballot.

The notion that presidential nominees could select their own running mates took a giant step forward at the Democratic National Convention of 1940. And in this case, there is not a shade of doubt or ambiguity: Franklin D. Roosevelt personally chose Henry Wallace as the Democratic vice presidential candidate. It was, in fact, a quite naked display of political power.

While Wallace was generally regarded as an effective secretary of agriculture and was popular among a narrow stratum of hard-core liberals and intellectuals, he had remarkably little support among Democratic Party leaders or rank-and-file voters. As one of Roosevelt's biographers has noted, Wallace "was almost, if not quite, the least acceptable [choice] to the delegates that [Roosevelt] could have made."[50] Wallace excited opposition on a variety of counts. Conservative Democrats, especially in the South, thought he was too liberal. The political professionals and big-city bosses were leery of him because he had never run for office before. Many throughout the party felt he was a mystic and a dreamer, who had an inordinate fascination with spiritualism and theosophy. The final blow, to many delegates, was that Wallace had been a Republican for most of his life, not changing his party registration until 1936.[51]

But Roosevelt insisted, and in 1940 he had a lot of leverage to work with. Not only was he the greatest Democratic vote-getter in memory— possibly of all time—but he had also managed, in various ways, to make sure that no other Democrat had emerged as a plausible successor. Having been nominated for an unprecedented third term in the White House, Roosevelt then let the delegates know, through his convention managers, that unless Wallace was also on the ticket, the president would refuse his own nomination. That this message was successfully communicated is clearly indicated in the convention proceedings. For the first time in the history of American national conventions, a candidate for the vice presidency is explicitly identified as being the personal preference of the presidential nominee. Indeed, such claims appear in at least five different speeches. To quote from three of them:

> It seems to me that if the President of the United States desires Henry Wallace as his running mate, that we should respect his request, because, after all, Roosevelt is the individual who is going to carry the load.

> As far as the junior Senator from Michigan is concerned, he feels that the President of the United States desires the nomination of the Honorable Henry A. Wallace and the junior Senator will cast his vote in the Michigan delegation in favor of the Honorable Henry A. Wallace.

> [Roosevelt] is my commander-in-chief. I follow his wishes, and I am here to support his choice for Vice President of the United States.[52]

Even then, it was a near thing. On the vice presidential roll call, Wallace won just 57 percent of the votes. Indeed, so strong was the opposition to him that, at the urging of Roosevelt's convention managers, Wallace decided not to deliver his acceptance speech.

It is probably a mistake, however, to make too much of this one nomination as a precedent that other candidates could readily follow. As the preceding account should indicate, Roosevelt won his point only because of a variety of special circumstances. Indeed, Roosevelt himself was considerably more restrained when selecting a running mate in 1944. How and why that year's Democratic convention decided to drop Wallace from the ticket and replace him with Harry Truman remains a subject of some historical dispute.[53] But one point that does seem clear is that in 1944, Roosevelt did not state a single, unambiguous preference for the vice presidential nomination, much less exert the kind of pressure that would have been necessary to force it upon the convention. Instead, Roosevelt assumed a more passive role, allowing his advisors and other party leaders to argue the merits of the various contenders, apparently content to run with whichever candidate was most widely acceptable to all the elements in the New Deal coalition. In the end, Roosevelt sent (at least) two different messages to the convention, one saying that he "personally would vote" for Wallace, the other saying that he would "be very glad to run" with either Harry Truman or William Douglas.

Whatever the impact of what Roosevelt did in 1940, there is a clear pattern during this period of presidential nominees being more and more actively involved in the selection of their running mates. One reason for this trend is the simple fact that beginning in about 1940, most major presidential contenders were physically present at their party's national convention. As a result, when the major party and delegation leaders got together to discuss the vice presidency, the nominee himself could sit in on the meeting.

Yet, if the right of a presidential nominee to become involved in the vice presidential selection decision was by now reasonably well established, candidates varied in how seriously they took this new responsibility. The 1948 election provides a good example of the diversity. On the Republican side, presidential nominee Thomas E. Dewey was clearly the central player in his party's vice presidential selection process. Not only did Dewey personally choose California governor Earl Warren as his running mate; when Warren showed some reluctance to accept the position, it was Dewey himself who helped apply the pressure that led Warren to change his mind.[54] In the Democratic Party, by contrast, Harry Truman was, to the great consternation of his advisors, not especially concerned about who became his running mate.[55] In an effort to appease the restive liberal wing of his party, Truman had initially attempted to recruit Supreme Court justice William O. Douglas as the vice presidential candidate. When that effort proved unsuccessful, Truman seemed content to run with whomever the convention wanted. As it turned out, a rousing keynote address by Senate minority leader Alben W. Barkley helped set in motion a movement to draft Barkley for the position; Truman, by all accounts, did little more than indicate a willingness to go along with the bandwagon. As one of Truman's aides recorded in his diary, "The president said he never did care much who was nominated to run with him. . . . He indicated he did not feel Barkley was the best candidate but that if the delegates wanted him, let them have him."[56]

If the "candidate-centered" vice presidential selection process emerged rather gradually, the final gasp of the system it replaced can be dated quite precisely. The last occasion when a presidential nominee refused to get involved in selecting his own running mate was the Democratic National Convention of 1956. The Democratic standard-bearer that year was Adlai Stevenson, and shortly after his own nomination, he suddenly appeared on the convention rostrum. What he said, by all accounts, "shocked" and "electrified" the delegates:

> I have concluded to depart from the precedents of the past. I have decided that the selection of the Vice Presidential nominee should be made through the free processes of this Convention so that the Democratic Party's candidate for this office may join me before the Nation not as one man's selection but as one chosen by our Party even as I have been chosen. . . . The choice will be yours.[57]

From some candidates, such words might have been only a smoke screen: an attempt to cover up an extensive, behind-the-scenes effort to secure the nomination of an otherwise controversial running mate. But by all accounts, Stevenson was true to his word; he and his campaign managers made no further effort to intervene in the process.[58]

By 1956, as the first line in Stevenson's speech indicates, it was the candidate who *stayed out* of the vice presidential selection who was bucking tradition. Indeed, many of Stevenson's top advisors and other party leaders had argued strongly against his decision. (One of the sharpest critics was Speaker of the House Sam Rayburn, who called Stevenson's proposed course of action "the damnedest fool idea I ever heard of.")[59] But a number of special circumstances convinced the usually cautious Stevenson that in 1956, the risk was worth taking. As the Democrats looked ahead to the general election, most saw little reason to think that Stevenson could defeat Eisenhower in a one-on-one contest. The same two candidates had squared off four years earlier, after all, and the result had been an easy Republican victory. But the GOP ticket was considerably more vulnerable at the vice presidential level. Large numbers of Americans—including many within his own party—felt that Richard Nixon was not a suitable occupant of the Oval Office. Moreover,

Eisenhower had had two serious and highly publicized health problems during his first term in office: a heart attack in September 1955 and an intestinal inflammation that required emergency surgery in June 1956. Stevenson declined to pick his running mate, in short, not because he thought it was inappropriate or unimportant, but as a deliberate strategic gambit. By turning the decision over to the convention, he hoped to call greater attention to the position and to contrast his own party's "open" selection system with what were generally seen as the more monolithic, "steamroller" procedures employed by the Republicans.

If nothing else, what followed was enormously entertaining. After one night of furious campaigning, seven names were formally presented to the convention. By the end of the first ballot, two candidates had opened up a sizable lead over the rest of the field: Senator Estes Kefauver of Tennessee and Senator John Kennedy of Massachusetts. By the end of the second roll call, Kennedy was narrowly ahead of Kefauver but still short of a majority. Before a third ballot could begin, however, a flurry of states announced that they wished to change their votes; and when the dust had settled, these switches gave the nomination to Kefauver.

In retrospect, Stevenson's experiment seems to have been generally successful; at the very least, there is no compelling reason to think that it hurt either his candidacy or his party. Press reaction also tended to be quite favorable. As Arthur Krock noted four days later in the *New York Times*, "Stevenson scored emphatically against the Republicans with his maneuver"—sufficiently so that the Republicans were now looking for ways to make it appear that they, too, had an "open" convention.[60] There is some evidence that Stevenson had a mild (though unexpressed) preference for Kennedy;[61] but all of the leading convention vote-getters were among the top prospects that Stevenson and his advisors had considered before opting not to make the choice themselves. The Democrats still lost decisively in the general election, of course, but in retrospect, it seems most unlikely that any vice presidential choice would have significantly altered that result.

To future presidential candidates and campaign strategists, however, it is likely that these events carried a somewhat different moral. From their perspective, the bottom line was that (1) Stevenson's decision was the product of quite special circumstances, and (2) even in those circumstances, it had not brought the kind of clear, tangible benefits that might have encouraged emulation. By 1960, in any event, neither presidential nominee sought to maintain even a pretense of noninvolvement. On the Republican side, Richard Nixon convened a late-night meeting of twenty or thirty party leaders shortly after his own nomination. According to Nixon's own account, he had already reached the conclusion that Henry Cabot Lodge, then the U.S. ambassador to the United Nations, "would be the strongest vice presidential nominee we could select," but he "did not make the final decision until meeting with the party leaders."[62] Other participants in that meeting had a different impression. Then-congressman Gerald Ford, one of the Republican leaders in attendance, came away convinced that the meeting was a "sham," that Nixon had already made up his mind and was merely "pretending that his options were still open."[63] Whichever view is correct, there is little doubt about who controlled the process. As Theodore White noted in the first of his *Making of the President* books, "Richard M. Nixon had been chosen as Republican Vice-presidential nominee at just such a meeting in 1952 . . . but Mr. Eisenhower had not participated personally in that meeting and had left the selection to his strategy board. In 1960, Nixon was present himself; he did not propose to leave the choice of Vice-president to the consensus of others."[64]

Similarly with the Democrats: There remains a good deal of controversy as to exactly how and why it was that John Kennedy selected Lyndon Johnson to be his running mate. Particularly problematic is Kennedy's own motivation. By some accounts, he genuinely wanted Johnson as his running mate—or, at least, was talked into it by his father. Another version, however, holds that Kennedy offered the vice presidency to Johnson because he expected him to turn it down—only to find that Johnson actually wanted the job and that, once the offer had been made, it would have been politically disastrous to withdraw it.[65] But all accounts agree on at least one point: the key decisions in the process were made by John Kennedy himself. It was he who decided to meet with Johnson early on the morning after his own nomination, it was he who then broached the possibility of adding the Texas senator to the ticket, and it was Kennedy who issued the press release that finally resolved the matter. While Kennedy did confer with an assortment of party and interest-group leaders, in most cases it appears that these meetings were designed less to seek their advice than to sell them on a decision that had been all but finalized.

And so it has been in *every* presidential election since then. Whatever other controversies exist about the vice presidential selection process, there is no doubt about where the responsibility currently lies. Presidential nominees choose their own running mates—even when there is considerable doubt about the wisdom of their choice.

Changes in Vice Presidential Power and Resources

Up to this point, the analysis in this chapter has focused rather narrowly on changes in the mechanics and politics of vice presidential selection. But significant changes have also occurred in other aspects of the vice presidency—changes that would ultimately have an important effect on how vice presidential candidates were chosen. Two such changes are particularly worth noting: the gradual increase in the power and resources of the vice presidency, and the emergence of the vice presidency as a preeminent stepping-stone to the White House.

Besides the framers' failure to anticipate the rise of political parties, the vice presidential office they created had one other signal deficiency. Having created a position that was supposed to be filled by the second-best presidential prospect in the country, they neglected to give this person anything much to do.[66] The Constitution assigned just two duties to the vice president: he was to "discharge the powers and duties" of the presidency in case of the president's removal, death, resignation, or inability; and he was made the "president" (i.e., presiding officer) of the Senate, though he was granted no speaking privileges there and could vote only in case of a tie. The upshot was quickly apparent. As John Adams, the office's first occupant, lamented, "My country has in its wisdom contrived for me the most insignificant office that ever the invention of man contrived or his imagination conceived."[67]

If the vice presidency was to be anything more than an empty sinecure, then, this would occur only because other constitutional actors found that having an active and influential vice president served *their* interests—that granting the vice president additional resources and responsibilities was useful to *them*.[68] One possibility was to fortify the vice president's role as president of the Senate. Legislatures vary enormously in the powers they invest in their presiding officers. Some presiding officers merely recognize speakers and moderate debates; other play a considerably more active role—formulating the agenda, appointing committees, participating in the discussion. His complaints notwithstanding, John Adams actually exercised most of these latter powers. Had the Constitution's framers merely given the vice president a regular vote, it is conceivable that the office might have evolved into something like the role now played by the Speaker of the House of Representatives. But without a vote—or any other reason to be taken seriously—the vice president gradually, inevitably became a very weak presider. Even when there is a contested point of parliamentary procedure, the vice president is generally expected to follow the recommendation of the Senate parliamentarian.[69] Or, as Senate majority leader Mike Mansfield told Vice

President Ford in 1973, "Here, presiding officers are to be seen and not heard."[70]

For the first hundred years or so after the ratification of the Constitution, there was little reason to think that the president would be any more willing to confer power on the vice president than the Senate was. Whatever advantages a "balanced ticket" provided for a political party, it also generally guaranteed that the president and vice president were not natural allies. Frequently, as we have seen, the two men came from opposite wings of the party or disagreed on the most important issues of the day.

Not until the early twentieth century did vice presidents begin to play a more active role in the workings of the executive branch. Table 9.1 lists some of the major milestones in the growth of vice presidential power and resources. Perhaps the most significant point revealed by this table is how slowly and gradually the change took place. There is no single, sharp turning point in the evolution of the office, no one vice president who can claim that he alone revolutionized the position.

Three factors are principally responsible for the trend shown in table 9.1. To begin with, the president's own powers were growing rapidly throughout this period, and as this occurred, presidents quickly discovered that they needed help. They received that help from a variety of sources, but making greater use of the vice president had, from the president's perspective, a number of important advantages. The situation has been summarized nicely by Joel Goldstein:

> The White House became the active initiator of domestic programs. Groups directed demands there and expected a response. Presidents often expressed their interest by establishing committees within the Executive Office. Frequently they named the Vice President as chairman, at once giving him something to do and adding prestige to the effort. . . . America's increased involvement in world affairs also enhanced the vice presidency. Presidents were expected to travel abroad more, an activity simplified by the development of the airplane. They could not accommodate all invitations they received. The Vice President often served as a surrogate head of state, his high rank making him an appropriate representative. . . .
>
> Close association with the executive branch also made the Vice President a useful administration spokesman. Presidents could not devote much of their time to defending their record or educating the public on certain issues. Nor could they often

TABLE 9.1   MAJOR MILESTONES IN THE GROWTH OF VICE PRESIDENTIAL POWER
AND RESOURCES

Vice President	Term	Additions to Power and Resources
Calvin Coolidge	1921-23	First vice president invited to attend cabinet meetings on a regular basis[a]
John Nance Garner	1933-41	First vice president to travel abroad on president's behalf
Henry Wallace	1941-45	First vice president to be given a major policy assignment by president
		First vice president to serve as a major spokesman for president's program
Alben Barkley	1949-53	Vice president made a statutory member of National Security Council
Richard Nixon	1953-61	Vice president serves as his party's major campaign spokesman during off-year elections
		Significant increase in foreign travel as presidential emissary
Lyndon Johnson	1961-63	Vice president given suite of offices in Executive Office Building[b]
Hubert Humphrey	1965-69	Twenty-Fifth Amendment clarifies vice president's status in case of president's death or disability
Spiro Agnew	1969-73	Vice presidency receives its own line item in the executive budget
Gerald Ford	1973-74	Substantial increase in budget for vice presidential staff
Nelson Rockefeller	1974-77	Vice president given private, weekly meeting with president
		Vice president given an official residence
Walter Mondale	1977-81	First vice president to participate in a nationally televised debate during a presidential campaign
		Vice president given an office in West Wing of White House
		Receives authority to attend all presidential meetings and access to all papers going to and from president
George Bush	1981-89	First vice president to become acting president under the disability provisions of the Twenty-Fifth Amendment

[a] This practice was discontinued during the Coolidge and Hoover administrations, but reinstituted by Franklin Roosevelt and followed by every subsequent president.
[b] Prior to this time, the vice president's only office was in the Capitol Building.

attack their critics without seeming too sensitive and unpresidential. Among the functions of the vice-presidential candidate were echo, defender of the standard-bearer, and attacker of opponents. Once in office, he performed these same roles.[71]

A second factor responsible for the growing influence of the vice presidency was the change in the vice presidential selection process described in the previous section. Allowing a presidential candidate to select his own running mate did not guarantee that the president would trust the vice president or respect his abilities—but it did make that eventuality more likely than a system in which the president had no say in the matter. Equally important, the new selection process greatly increased the vice president's incentive to remain loyal to the president.

Finally, presidents gave more work to their vice presidents because of the sharply increased political costs of having a poorly prepared successor. As the president's governing responsibilities grew, especially in the international arena, so did Americans' concern with ensuring a smooth transfer of power in cases of presidential death or disability. For those who were not yet convinced, the events of early 1945 provided an especially vivid illustration of what was at stake. On 12 April of that year, Franklin Roosevelt died of a cerebral hemorrhage, and Harry Truman, after serving less than three months as vice president, was suddenly elevated to the top job. During the next four months, Truman made some of the most significant foreign policy decisions in American history, including approving the final changes necessary to create the United Nations, negotiating with Stalin and Churchill at Potsdam, and deciding to drop the atomic bomb on Japan.

Presidents, in short, could no longer afford to ignore their vice presidents. If only as a public relations ploy, they had to reassure Americans that the vice president was ready to take over in a crisis: that he was performing important duties, that his voice and counsel were taken seriously within the administration, that he was "in the loop" on all the most pressing issues confronting the president.

From Dead End to Stepping-Stone

A second important change in the vice presidency concerns its status as a "stepping-stone" to the White House. Under the original presidential election system, as we have seen, the vice president was simply the runner-up in the presidential voting. Thus, the vice president was generally a presidential contender in his own right—and hence a logical candidate for the top spot in the next election. Indeed, if we may generalize on the basis of a very small number of cases, the vice presidency quickly emerged as a sort of "natural path" to the presidency. When George Washington retired from public life, he was succeeded by his vice president, John Adams, who in turn was beaten four years later by his vice president, Thomas Jefferson.

With the ratification of the Twelfth Amendment, however, the vice presidential slot took on a very different character, with particularly important implications for the vice president's standing as a presidential contender. Simply put, for the first century and a half after the Twelfth Amendment, vice presidents were generally *not* seen as the "heir apparent" to the presidency. As shown in table 9.2, between 1805 and 1952, thirty-two different men served as vice president; eight later became president. But of these eight, only one—Martin Van Buren in 1836—succeeded to the presidency by getting elected. The other seven advanced to the chief executive's position because the previous incumbent died in office. Indeed, with the exception of Van Buren, no incumbent vice president during this period even received a major-party presidential *nomination*. Put another way, for almost a hundred and fifty years, a vice president could generally look forward to one of two career paths. If the president died in office, the vice president would be elevated to the top spot. But if the president remained healthy and served out the entirety of his term(s), the vice president's future usually consisted of retirement and continued obscurity. There was virtually no chance that a vice president could win a presidential nomination on his own.

TABLE 9.2   VICE PRESIDENCY AS A STEPPING-STONE TO THE PRESIDENCY, 1789–1992

	1789–1804	*1805–1952*	*1953–1992*
Total no. of individuals who served as vice president	3	32	9
No. who eventually became president	2	8	4
No. who succeeded to presidency on death or resignation of the incumbent	0	7	2
No. who first assumed presidency by getting elected in their own right	2	1	2
No. who were nominated for presidency by a major party but lost the general election[a]	0	0	3

[a] Includes only those who had not previously been elected president.

As the data in table 9.2 also indicate, however, a quite different situation has prevailed in the years since 1953. Two vice presidents were elected president on their own (Nixon in 1968 and Bush in 1988); three (Nixon in 1960, Humphrey in 1968, and Mondale in 1984) won their party's nomination but then lost in the general election. If Al Gore appears, at this writing, to be the front-runner for the next Democratic nomination, such would almost certainly not have been the case fifty years ago.

The most striking demonstration of whether the vice presidency can serve as a stepping-stone to the White House occurs when a president reaches the end of his second term and/or announces well before the election that he will not be seeking another term in the Oval Office. This situation occurred four times between 1900 and 1953, and *not once* did the incumbent vice president receive his party's presidential nomination.[72]

For example, shortly after getting elected president in his own right in 1904, Theodore Roosevelt publicly declared that he would *not* be a candidate in the 1908 presidential contest. And though there is some evidence that he later came to regret this pledge, Roosevelt faithfully kept his commitment. But TR had no qualms about becoming very actively involved in the selection of his successor. Roosevelt apparently considered throwing his weight behind a number of potential candidates, including Charles Evans Hughes and Elihu Root, before finally settling on William Howard Taft, his secretary of war and all-purpose troubleshooter. But one name that never entered into Roosevelt's calculations was that of his own vice president, Charles Fairbanks. Perhaps this was not unexpected; the two men had never been close, either personally or politically. Indeed, Fairbanks had been added to the 1904 Republican ticket precisely because his conservatism was thought to balance Roosevelt's progressive views. But there were a large number of Republicans in 1908 who were suspicious of Roosevelt's progressive tendencies, and none of them seem to have regarded Fairbanks as a natural champion, either. In the end, Fairbanks finished fifth on the presidential ballot at the 1908 Republican convention, receiving just 40 of the 979 votes cast.[73]

Similarly in 1928: Charles Gates Dawes, Calvin Coolidge's vice president, is easily one of the most accomplished individuals ever to hold that office. Before being elected vice president in 1924, Dawes had been, at one time or another, a civil engineer, lawyer, businessman, bank president, the author of several well-regarded works on economics, a brigadier general in World War I, holder of several major appointive positions within the federal executive branch (among other things, he was the first director of the Bureau of the Budget), and the chairman of an international commission on war reparations. For the last of these services, he won the Nobel Peace Prize in 1925. Yet, when President Coolidge issued his famous declaration in August 1927 that he did "not choose to run for president in 1928," there are no signs of any great movement within the Republican Party to rally around Dawes as Coolidge's successor. The Republican nomination went instead to a different figure in the administration: Secretary of Commerce Herbert Hoover. In the thirteen Republican presidential preference primaries held that year, Dawes never won more than 2 percent of the vote; on the presidential roll call at the convention, he received just four votes.[74]

By contrast, since 1953 there have been three cases in which an incumbent president decided or was forced not to seek another term in office—and in every single case, his party's presidential nomination was conferred upon his vice president. When Dwight Eisenhower finished his second term, then–vice president Richard Nixon easily won the 1960 Republican presidential nomination. When Lyndon Johnson announced in March 1968 that he would not be a candidate for reelection, the Democratic Party turned to Vice President Hubert Humphrey. And after Reagan had served eight years in the White House, the next Republican nominee was, unsurprisingly, George Bush, who had been Reagan's ticket mate in 1980 and 1984.

A number of factors explain this change in the vice president's status as a presidential possibility. Most obviously, as we have just seen, the vice presidency is a more active and influential position than it once was. As a major administration spokesman, campaign surrogate, foreign envoy, and sometime governing official, the vice president gains a lot more useful experience—and publicity—than he did just by presiding over the Senate. As one reflection of this new role, public opinion data regularly show that the vice president is, after the president, probably the single best-known person in American national politics.[75]

The vice president's ability to project himself as the heir apparent to the president also received a substantial boost from the passage in 1951 of the Twenty-Second Amendment to the Constitution, which prohibited a president from serving more than two terms. Prior to that time, there were distinct limits on what a sitting vice president could do to promote his own presidential ambitions. Except in those comparatively rare instances when the president had made his intentions clear well in advance of the election, any overt attempt by the vice president to organize a presidential campaign was likely to be interpreted as an act of rank disloyalty toward the man currently holding that job. Nor, it appears, did the vice president derive much cover from the so-called two-term tradition. Though only one person actually served more than two terms as president, many others contemplated doing so. (Examples include Ulysses S. Grant, Theodore Roosevelt, Woodrow Wilson, and Harry Truman.) But the Twenty-Second Amendment made at least this aspect of the vice president's job considerably easier; like it or not, two terms was all a president got. This freed Nixon in 1960, Bush in 1988, and Gore in 2000 to make an all-out assault on the White House without any lingering sense that they were stepping on the toes of the most popular and influential person in their own party.

Between about 1920 and 1960, then, the vice presidency changed in three major ways. Presidential nominees became more and more actively involved in choosing their party's vice presidential candidates; there was a significant increase in the powers and resources of the office; and the vice presidency emerged as perhaps the single best vantage point for launching a presidential candidacy. And though we have thus far examined each of these trends independently, quite clearly they were interrelated. As has already been pointed out, changes in the vice presidential selection process were one important factor that helped make the office more powerful. When presidents could select their running mates, they were more likely to accord them significant governing responsibilities. Equally important, as the vice presidency became more influential and a better stepping-stone to the presidency, it became increasingly easy to get talented, high-quality people to run for the position. No longer were parties forced to give the nomination to some obscure, second-rate politico simply because no one else would take it.

A Decision in Search of a Process: 1960–72

To resume the main story, by the 1960s it had become clearly established that the presidential nominee would have the major, often the sole, voice in determining who would become his party's vice presidential candidate. But the decision remained a haphazard and chaotic one, less because of who made it than because of the circumstances in which it was made.

Reading through the historical and journalistic accounts of vice presidential selections up through 1972, one is hard pressed to find anything that could reasonably be described as systematic, advance planning. In a real sense, there was no vice presidential selection *process*. There was simply a decision that had to be made—a decision in which the time allotted for serious thought and deliberation was usually less than twenty-four hours, in which the chief participants were generally sleep-deprived and under enormous pressure, and in which there was very little in the way of careful research or reliable information. If the choices that were finally made were sometimes problematic, the wonder is that this did not happen more often.

That vice presidential selection decisions were made under such unpromising conditions was partly a reflection of the traditional inattention under which that office has always labored. But it also resulted from the confluence of two other characteristics of American presidential politics during this period. In the first place, it was (and probably still is) impossible to begin serious consideration of vice presidential prospects until the presidential nomination had been settled. Until then, the all-too-limited time and energy of the candidate and his top staff were necessarily focused on securing the top spot on the ticket.

There were also a number of strategic reasons to delay the vice presidential decision until the presidential nomination race was resolved. For the presidential aspirant who needed a few final votes to achieve or protect his majority, the vice presidential spot on the ticket was an invaluable piece of bait that could be used to attract last-minute support from favorite sons, second-tier candidates, interest-group representatives, and state party leaders. The catch, of course, was that the vice presidential card lost most of its value once a presidential candidate made a firm, public commitment. Only while the final decision was still in doubt could the candidate make what Theodore White called "half-promises, half-commitments" to a variety of different hopefuls.

The final stages of a nomination race might also communicate important, new information to a presidential contender about his own electoral strengths and weaknesses and which groups in the party needed to be appeased or reassured. In particular, once the presidential race was officially resolved and the passions of battle had cooled a bit, one of the nominee's erstwhile opponents might suddenly appear to be a very strong potential running mate. Choosing a defeated presidential contender as the party's vice presidential candidate has not, in general, been a common practice in American political history—but it did occur reasonably often in the middle decades of the twentieth century. (Examples include the Republican national tickets of 1928, 1936, and 1944, and the Democratic tickets of 1932, 1956, and 1960.)

It is no accident, then, that the only vice presidential selection in this period that seems to have been the product of extensive deliberation and consultation and a systematic attempt to gather the requisite information was Lyndon Johnson's decision to add Hubert Humphrey to the

Democratic ticket in 1964.[76] By all accounts, Johnson behaved quite boorishly toward the Minnesota senator in the six months or so that preceded his nomination. But Johnson also conducted a very thorough and rigorous selection process. He considered a large number of potential running mates, consulted extensively with party leaders, kept the press and public reasonably well informed about the people he was considering, and even had aides conduct extensive checks on Humphrey's personal life. But Johnson was willing and able to initiate such procedures because he was the incumbent president, who faced essentially no opposition to his own nomination. Just four years earlier, when Johnson had sought the presidential nomination under more typical conditions, there is no evidence that he devoted any more attention to thinking about a running mate than had any other candidate of this era.

Unfortunately for both the candidates and the country, races that were uncontested or had been clearly resolved well before the convention were the exception during this period. Through the first seven decades of the twentieth century, only incumbent presidents running for reelection were likely to enjoy an easy, untrammeled ride to the nomination.[77] In all other circumstances, the rule was that presidential nomination races generally remained uncertain and unsettled all the way up to the actual convention voting. Even when a candidate prevailed on the first ballot, the nomination was much less a "sure thing," and the convention much less a symbolic media event, than would be the case in the 1980s and 1990s. Without the current consensus that the most popular candidate in the primaries deserves the nomination, and with most convention delegates not formally pledged to a particular candidate, an atmosphere of drama and uncertainty still hovered over most national conventions. *Usually*, the preconvention front-runner would prevail— but a considerable range of last-minute developments and maneuvers might still intervene to break his hold on the brass ring: credentials challenges, rules changes, platform fights, behind-the-scenes negotiations by would-be kingmakers, bandwagons generated by outside events or well-received convention speeches. All of this only further delayed the point at which a presidential nominee could finally begin to concentrate on selecting a running mate.

The most notorious example of all these shortcomings was the selection of Thomas Eagleton as George McGovern's running mate at the Democratic National Convention of 1972.[78] McGovern's road to the Democratic nomination was a quite lengthy one; he formally announced his candidacy in January 1971. Yet there is little indication that he gave much attention to the vice presidential question until the convention was almost over. And when he did contemplate the matter, most of his thoughts apparently centered on the quixotic belief that he could somehow persuade Edward Kennedy to run for vice president. Even after mid-June, when the long string of Democratic primaries finally came to an end, McGovern and his campaign organization were compelled to devote most of their efforts to fending off a credentials challenge that sought to deprive them of 151 delegates they had won in the California primary. McGovern finally, officially won the 1972 Democratic presidential nomination at 11:58 P.M. on 12 July. Shortly thereafter, the South Dakota senator placed a call to Ted Kennedy, asking him to accept the vice presidential nomination. Not at all surprisingly, Kennedy declined—as he had on several other occasions when McGovern had broached the subject. And only then, on 13 July, did McGovern finally set the real vice presidential selection process in motion.

More specifically, the process began with a meeting of McGovern staffers and supporters at nine o'clock the next morning. The atmosphere of that meeting has been memorably described by Theodore White:

> Some twenty-plus people gathered on Thursday morning, July 13th, between 8:30 and 9:00 in a downstairs conference room at the Doral Hotel—all tired from overwork and celebration, some with only two or three hours' sleep, a good number hung-over, others with only a quick dip in the ocean at dawn to clear their sleep-starved minds.
>
> Frank Mankiewicz was to chair the meeting, and earlier in the week, on Tuesday, Mankiewicz had discussed with McGovern the calling together of a small group—himself, Hart, Stearns, Salinger, Van Dyk, Wexler—to sift the choices. On Wednesday night after the nomination, McGovern had instructed other staff members to round up a full panel. "I showed up," said Mankiewicz, "and, Christ, there were about twenty-four people there. What was I going to do? The door would open and someone would say, 'George told me to show up here.'"[79]

The meeting began with what one participant later described as "an invitation to free association: 'Let's bring up every name we can think of.'"[80] That list of thirty or forty prospects was then pared to seven finalists: Senators Walter Mondale (Minn.), Abraham Ribicoff (Conn.), and Thomas Eagleton (Mo.); Governor Patrick Lucey (Wis.); Mayor Kevin White of Boston; Democratic Party chairman Larry O'Brien; and Sargent

Shriver, who had held a number of top-level positions in the Kennedy and Johnson administrations.[81] Gary Hart, McGovern's campaign manager, would later claim that each name on the original list received "serious, deliberate, often exhaustive scrutiny,"[82] but it is difficult to credit this assertion. In a meeting that lasted less than three hours, there simply would not have been time to do anything more than skim the surface as to each prospect's individual strengths and liabilities. And even if there had been time, it is far from clear that this particular meeting was qualified for the task. The group in the hotel conference room consisted of McGovern campaign staffers, prominent supporters, and sympathetic interest-group leaders, but no senators, governors, or big-city mayors—no one who might reasonably have been described as a party leader.

A better indication of how this meeting functioned is to observe what happened when Eagleton's name was brought up. Rick Stearns of the McGovern campaign said that he had had a recent conversation with a national political reporter—unfortunately, he couldn't remember which one—who said that there were "strong rumors of alcoholism or mental illness—or both—in his [Eagleton's] background." Was there any substance to the allegations? No one in the room knew Eagleton very well, certainly not well enough to answer such a personal question. Eventually (there is some dispute as to whether this occurred before or after Eagleton's name was added to the list of finalists), Gordon Weil, another McGovern staffer, spent ninety minutes on the telephone trying to learn more about Eagleton and one other contender.[83] Whom Weil spoke with has never been reported, but his contacts apparently did not include anyone on Eagleton's staff or the reporter who first brought the issue to Stearns's attention. To further vitiate his efforts, Weil seems to have spent most of his time chasing the wrong scent. His principal concern was to check out the rumor that Eagleton had a drinking problem, which did turn out to be false. As for the mental health issue, Weil had interpreted Stearns's comments—especially the phrase "in his background"—as referring to other members of Eagleton's family, not to the senator himself.

Well researched or not, the list was given to McGovern shortly before noon. McGovern spent the next hour and a half consulting with leaders of the principal interest groups that had supported his nomination campaign. By now, it was half-past one, and according to party rules, the nominee's name and filing papers had to be delivered to the national committee offices by four o'clock. And then things really got chaotic.

McGovern's first call went to Walter Mondale, whose name was on the list even though almost nobody believed he would actually accept the nomination (he was running for reelection to the Senate that year). As expected, Mondale declined.

It now appeared "almost certain," Gary Hart has written, that the vice presidential nomination would go to Kevin White. McGovern called White to ask if he was interested; White's name was even written in on one set of filing petitions. But then opposition to White developed from two sources. First, Ted Kennedy seemed uncomfortable with White, and McGovern felt he needed Kennedy's enthusiastic support in the fall campaign. Then McGovern received a call claiming that the Massachusetts delegation was unanimously opposed to White and might even walk out of the convention to protest his selection. Though there is evidence that the objections within the Massachusetts delegation were greatly overstated, there was no time to make a more systematic inquiry. White was out.

Besides helping put the kibosh on White, Kennedy's conversation with McGovern complicated the selection process in one other way. With White as the apparent choice, Kennedy said he wanted time to "think it over"—a comment that McGovern interpreted to mean that Kennedy was reconsidering his own decision not to run. Thirty precious minutes went by before Kennedy called back, said he was still less than enthusiastic about White—and reaffirmed that he himself had no interest in the vice presidency.

Meanwhile, other names were also being dropped from consideration. Sargent Shriver was eliminated because he was traveling in the Soviet Union on business and could not be reached. Ribicoff had already told McGovern he did not want the job. O'Brien looked too much like a "professional politician." Lucey was apparently ruled out because his wife was too outspoken.

With time running out, McGovern turned to a name that was not on the list: Senator Gaylord Nelson of Wisconsin, one of McGovern's closest friends in the Senate. But Nelson, too, turned him down.

And so, almost by default, McGovern chose Thomas Eagleton. By all accounts, neither McGovern nor anyone else on his staff knew much about Eagleton, but he did have some obvious political assets. He was young, Catholic, with strong ties to organized labor. Senators Kennedy, Nelson, and Ribicoff all spoke highly of him. And in a nationally televised interview just one day earlier, Eagleton had made clear that he *did* want the nomination. So the call went out to Eagleton, who quickly accepted. Before hanging up, McGovern handed the phone to Frank Mankiewicz, one of his senior advisors, who asked Eagleton—the exact wording of the query would later become a subject of some controversy—whether he had any skeletons in his closet. When Eagleton said no, the deal was done.

When Richard Nixon chose Spiro Agnew to be his running mate, it can at least be said that Agnew's history of corrupt dealings was a reasonably well buried secret—that even after he became vice president, it took five years for the truth to come out. In Eagleton's case, by contrast, at least two major news organizations were in hot pursuit of his medical records within days of his selection. On 25 July, with the story about to break, Eagleton and McGovern held a joint press conference at which the Missouri Senator said that he had been hospitalized on three different occasions for "nervous exhaustion and fatigue." On further questioning, he admitted that he had twice undergone electroshock therapy as treatment for "depression."[84] In the fallout of the next few days, it soon become clear that the McGovern campaign had no good options. It could keep Eagleton on the ticket and have his health problems overshadow the rest of the campaign, or it could drop him from the ticket and acquire a reputation for both heartlessness and incompetence. On 31 July, it chose the latter course.

Before pronouncing judgment on the Eagleton affair, it is worth taking a briefer look at a second, and in some respects more typical, vice presidential selection decision from this period: Hubert Humphrey's choice of Senator Edmund Muskie as his running mate in 1968.[85] Like almost all presidential candidates of this era, Humphrey later claimed that he had been thinking about the vice presidential question for months before his own nomination. At the most literal level, this statement is undoubtedly true; what is unclear is how much time Humphrey devoted to the matter and how concrete his thinking was. If contemporary press coverage is any indication, the choice of a running mate was certainly not a front-burner issue for Humphrey. At least in the pages of the *New York Times*, Humphrey made only one public statement on the topic before the opening of the Democratic National Convention—and that was in answer to a question posed by a television interviewer.[86]

Though there is no evidence that Humphrey or his aides did any real research on the running-mate question, their preconvention speculations do seem to have narrowed the choice to a manageable number of alternatives. Four names were apparently at the top of the list: Governor Richard Hughes (N.J.), Senator Fred Harris (Okla.), Senator Edmund Muskie (Me.), and Sargent Shriver, then the U.S. ambassador to France. One notch lower were San Francisco mayor Joseph Alioto and former North Carolina governor Terry Sanford. Shortly after his nomination, in the early morning hours of 29 August, Humphrey met with several delegations of Democratic Party leaders. After three and a half hours of sleep, Humphrey and his top aides held one final meeting on the subject. For both positive and negative reasons, Muskie quickly emerged as Humphrey's preference. On the positive side, Humphrey had worked with Muskie in the Senate for ten years and genuinely liked and respected him. As a Polish Catholic, moreover, Muskie might help shore up Democratic support among both Catholic and white ethnic voters. And all the other top contenders raised opposition on one count or another: the southern wing of the party disliked Hughes; Harris was only thirty-seven years old; and the Kennedys were less than enthusiastic about Shriver.

So Humphrey summoned Muskie to his hotel suite—only to find, in the course of a brief conversation, that Muskie did have one potential question mark in his background: one of Muskie's daughters, though unmarried, was pregnant. After delaying his announcement for several hours and consulting with other party leaders, Humphrey finally convinced himself that this was not a sufficient reason to change his mind. Muskie it was.

On one very important level, Humphrey's choice of Edmund Muskie was quite different from McGovern's selection of Eagleton: adding Muskie to the ticket turned out to be a huge political success. By the end of the campaign, the Democrats were prominently mentioning the vice presidential candidates in their television advertising. Yet in most respects, the differences between these two selections are less striking than the similarities. Humphrey's preconvention ruminations about a running mate were considerably more realistic than McGovern's. With that exception, it is difficult to disagree with McGovern's assertion that "the selection of Tom Eagleton as my running mate was made with as much care and reason as traditionally was applied to the selection of vice-presidential candidates."[87]

The Contemporary System: 1976–present

The Eagleton selection fiasco took place in July 1972; Agnew's resignation came in October 1973. And for the next several years, reforming the vice presidency was a growth industry. A dizzying array of proposals were put forward, concerning every aspect of the office. Just with respect to vice presidential *selection*, the major alternatives included the following:

- Having the presidential nominee submit a list of three or four acceptable vice presidential candidates to the convention, with the delegates then making the final choice.
- Allowing the presidential candidate to defer the vice presidential selection until several weeks after the convention, with the national committee then required to approve his decision.
- Having presidential and vice presidential candidates run for their party's nomination as a team, by requiring all presidential contenders to name their running mates before the start of the primaries.
- Having the runner-up in the convention's presidential balloting automatically become the party's vice presidential candidate. Other variants of the same idea would have required the presidential candidate to select his running mate from among the top three defeated presidential contenders or from among those persons who had entered at least one presidential primary that year.
- Lengthening the national convention or rearranging its schedule to give the presidential nominee more time to select his running mate.
- Requiring candidates for the vice presidency to compete in state primaries and conventions, just as presidential candidates do, and then using these results to advise or bind the national convention delegates. As a further guarantee that the convention's decision would not be dictated by its presidential nominee, some reformers also recommended that the vice presidential roll call vote be held *before* the presidential balloting.
- Creating an advisory committee within each party several months before the convention to compile a list of vice presidential prospects, collect background information on them, and perhaps make recommendations.
- Allowing presidential candidates to authorize FBI investigations of prospective vice presidential candidates.
- Amending the Constitution so that only the president would be elected by the members of the electoral college (or by popular vote). The victorious presidential candidate would choose a vice president after the election, subject to confirmation by both houses of Congress.
- Abolishing the vice presidency altogether, with presidential vacancies to be filled by special election.[88]

Were any of these proposals put into effect? Has the vice presidential selection process improved since the Eagleton and Agnew episodes raised such a firestorm of criticism?

The answer to the first question is no. None of the proposals listed above was ever adopted. In fact, none even came close. Perhaps the furthest along anyone got was when the Democratic National Committee appointed a special commission on vice presidential selection, chaired by Hubert Humphrey, in 1973.[89] In December 1973, after conducting hearings and apparently entertaining some quite radical proposals, the commission issued a set of rather modest recommendations: the creation of an advisory "screening" committee; adding an extra day to the convention calendar; and allowing the presidential candidate to request a delay of up to three weeks before announcing his vice presidential choice. The party's executive committee rejected the first recommendation and took no action on the others. In particular, none of the commission's suggestions was incorporated into the first national charter of the Democratic Party, which was adopted at a midterm convention in December 1974. As Humphrey himself would later say, "We went to the mountain and gave birth to a mouse."[90]

Ironically, however, the answer to the second question is yes. Since 1976, the vice presidential selection process has been, on the whole, considerably more rational and deliberative than the one that existed during the 1950s, 1960s, and early 1970s. Though the formal rules are unchanged, in practice the system works quite differently.

Two factors are principally responsible for recent improvements in vice presidential selection. To begin with, presidential candidates and their advisors simply take the process a lot more seriously than they once did. As the demands on the presidency have increased, and as the need for a smooth transition in case of a president's death or disability has grown, presidential aspirants have apparently concluded that the voters are at least somewhat more concerned than they once were about the quality of the vice president. The Eagleton affair also seems to have sent a message about standards of media behavior. From here on in, the press would give some measure of scrutiny to the vice presidential candidates. If the parties could not find someone of clear and obvious presidential stature to fill the second spot on the ticket, at least they needed a person with no major scandals or embarrassments attached to his name.

The second—and, I believe, more important—source of change in vice presidential selection over the last three decades is the changes that have taken place in the *presidential* selection process. As Michael Hagen and I have shown in chapter 1, between 1969 and 1974, the rules of the presidential nominating process were changed in two highly significant ways. In the wake of its 1968 convention, the Democratic Party completely recast its delegate selection rules. And in 1974, in response to Watergate, Congress rewrote the national campaign finance laws. The result, as we have seen, was a sweeping transformation of the presidential nominating process. And while some of the changes that ensued were purposeful and intended, others—such as the increased length of the nominating race and the rise of front-loading—quite clearly were not. These latter were often described, in what quickly became a mantra of the new presidential politics, as the "unanticipated consequences" of reform.

Though it seems not to be widely appreciated, changes in the vice presidential selection process are yet one more of these unanticipated consequences. Under the new rules, it will be recalled, losing candidates dropped out of the race more quickly and the delegate selection calendar became more front-loaded. Those delegates who were selected, moreover, were more likely to be pledged to one of the major presidential contenders and less likely to attend the convention uncommitted or as supporters of a favorite son candidate.

The upshot of these changes is that contemporary presidential nomination contests are settled much earlier in the election cycle than they generally were under the old rules regime. Table 9.3 shows one indicator of this development: the date on which one candidate had won enough pledged delegates to guarantee a first-ballot victory at the convention. As these data indicate, in only one race during the last six election cycles—the Republican contest in 1976—has the presidential nomination been a live issue all the way up to the beginning of the national convention.[91] In every other case, one candidate had effectively clinched the nomination at least one month before the convention was gaveled to order.

All of this effectively solved what had been, by wide agreement, the worst single aspect of the old vice presidential selection process: the remarkably compressed time period in which the decision was generally made. Now, suddenly, presidential candidates had lots of time available. To be sure, there were other things on their agendas, and many continued to treat the vice presidential choice as a rather low priority. But it was something they had to face eventually; both the press and the voters would pay some attention to their decision; and, in any event, much of the real work could be delegated to campaign aides and consultants (who also had less to do during this period).

TABLE 9.3   DATES ON WHICH PRESIDENTIAL CANDIDATES IN CONTESTED
RACES CLINCHED THEIR PARTY'S NOMINATION, 1976–96

Year	Date Nomination Clinched[a]	Opening Day of National Convention
Republicans		
1976	16 August	16 August
1980	24 May	14 July
1988	26 April	15 August
1992	5 May	17 August
1996	26 March	12 August
Democrats		
1976	8 June[b]	12 July
1980	3 June	11 August
1984	6 June	16 July
1988	7 June	18 July
1992	2 June	13 July

Source: Delegate counts are taken from contemporary reports in the *New York Times* and *Congressional Quarterly Weekly Report*.
[a] Date shown is day on which candidate won enough pledged delegates to guarantee a first-ballot convention victory.
[b] Date given for Carter in 1976 is not precisely analogous to the others shown here. When the 1976 Democratic primaries were concluded on 8 June, Carter had only 1,100 pledged delegates, about 400 shy of a majority. But all his major opponents save Jerry Brown withdrew from the race within the next few days and endorsed Carter, and contemporary press coverage openly declared him the "all but certain" nominee. As one reflection of Carter's position, after 8 June, so far as I can determine, no major media organization maintained an active count of Democratic delegate preferences.

The first presidential candidate to confront this new environment was Jimmy Carter in 1976. Besides clinching the Democratic nomination in early June, at least three other factors made Carter's vice presidential selection a propitious occasion for breaking new ground.[92] First, the costs of making a poor choice were still fresh in everyone's mind. As the *New York Times* noted in mid-June, "'No more Eagletons,' has become a [Carter] staff motto, occasionally augmented by 'no more Agnews.'"[93] If politicians, like generals, are prone to refight the last war, in this case that tendency may have worked to the system's advantage. Second, as someone who was a new entrant on the stage of national politics—was, in fact, almost completely unknown to most Americans just six months earlier—Carter sensed that the press and public would pay unusual attention to his choice, treating it as, in effect, his first major presidential decision. Third, whatever Carter's other weaknesses as a political leader, this was precisely the sort of task at which he excelled: a single, multi-faceted decision, with lots of lead time, that demanded such qualities as patience, thoroughness, and intelligence.

After extended deliberation on the matter, Carter and his advisors devised a vice presidential selection process that consisted of five major components:

1. *Compiling an initial list of prospects.* In early and mid-June, shortly after clinching the nomination, the Carter campaign staff assembled a comprehensive list of potential vice presidential candidates. By all accounts, this list contained the names of three hundred to four hundred persons: Democratic members of the House and Senate, governors, big-city mayors, and so forth. Several days of preliminary discussion pruned the pool to more manageable proportions: about two dozen persons.

2. *The first round of consultation and interviews.* A more systematic effort to collect information and evaluate the prospects began in the last two weeks of June. That effort apparently proceeded along two major fronts. First, Carter himself called a list of forty-five "distinguished Americans" in politics, business, labor, and the media to solicit their opinions and get their assessments of the various contenders. Second, Carter sent Charles Kirbo, a lawyer and trusted confidant, to Washington on an extended fact-finding expedition. Like Carter, Kirbo consulted with a variety of party and governmental leaders. More important, he conducted preliminary interviews with all of the top vice presidential prospects. On the basis of what they learned from these inquiries, Carter and his advisors then narrowed their search to seven final candidates: Senators Edmund Muskie (Maine), Walter Mondale (Minn.), John Glenn (Ohio), Frank Church (Idaho), Henry Jackson (Wash.), and Adlai Stevenson III (Ill.), and Representative Peter Rodino (N.J.)

3. *Background investigations.* Each of the finalists was next asked to fill out a lengthy questionnaire that sought detailed information about such matters as their financial and medical history, marital status, family problems, past campaign contributions, whether they had ever been arrested or undergone psychiatric treatment, and, in general, whether there was "anything in your personal life or that of a near relative which you feel, if known, may be of embarrassment." Prospective running mates were also asked to supply the Carter campaign with copies of their income tax returns for the last five years and the results of a complete physical examination. All such materials were then scrutinized by a team of lawyers and tax accountants working under Kirbo's direction.

4. *Interviewing the finalists.* The most publicized phase of Carter's vice presidential selection process began in early July, when Carter himself held lengthy one-on-one meetings with each of the seven finalists. To some extent, these meetings were made necessary by Carter's lack of experience in national politics; he had little previous acquaintance with most of the men he was considering. But this stage of the process also reflected Carter's belief that one important requisite in a vice presidential candidate was some measure of "personal compatibility" with the presidential nominee. That is, if the vice president was to become an active participant in the work of the executive branch, he needed to be someone whom the president trusted and respected. Beyond their individual abilities, the two men had to be able to work effectively together.

5. *Maintaining adequate publicity.* When vice presidential selection decisions were no longer made by the party as a collective entity, they also became, as we have seen, a very private affair. Deliberation and effective choice were confined to a small number of individuals, working behind closed doors, with little more than rumors available as to who was being seriously considered. If Carter's selection method did not expand the circle of decision makers, it was at least a considerably more public process. The one-on-one meetings, in particular, were all announced in advance and followed by a joint press conference. The meetings thus effectively established a public list of finalists. Besides enhancing Carter's own image as a careful decision maker, such publicity also added a useful element of public deliberation to the selection process. The press had time to discuss each contender's major strengths and weaknesses; late-breaking rumors and allegations could be investigated before a decision was made; and party and interest-group leaders who had not been privately consulted could offer their opinions, either directly to the Carter campaign or indirectly through the media.

By all accounts, it was the one-on-one meetings that played an especially important role in Carter's decision to select Walter Mondale as his running mate. Mondale was not among the front-runners when the process began. Carter knew relatively little about him, and what few impressions he did have seem to have been based primarily on Mondale's own short-lived run for the 1976 Democratic presidential nomination. Where Carter felt that both he and the country were well served by the eighteen months he had spent on the campaign trail, Mondale, after testing the waters in 1974, decided he did not want to spend the rest of his life "living in Holiday Inns" and finally, in November, opted not to make the race at all. As he told the press at the time, he "did not have the overwhelming desire to be President which is essential for the kind of campaign that is required."[94] A year and a half later, many within the Carter camp wondered if Mondale had the "heart" for a long and grueling campaign.

To overcome his initial disadvantages, Mondale prepared for his meeting with Carter with great thoroughness. He carefully studied Carter's record as governor and the positions he had taken during the campaign; he even read Carter's autobiography. Equally important, Mondale came to the meeting with well-developed ideas about how to make the vice presidency a more productive job and the kinds of institutional support he hoped for from Carter. As several commentators have noted, Mondale's painstaking preparation was exactly what Carter himself would have done if he were being considered for the vice presidency. The two men hit it off right away, and Mondale soon became the odds-on favorite to receive the nomination.

By virtually every criterion, Carter's decision was a huge success. In immediate electoral terms, Mondale's selection helped unify the Democratic Party. His presence on the ticket was especially pleasing to the party's liberal constituency groups, many of which were still suspicious of Carter. Carter's own handling of the selection process also drew highly favorable reviews, especially when it was compared with the more traditional method employed later that year by the Republicans.[95] According to the polls, Mondale also was the clear winner in a nationally televised debate with Robert Dole, his Republican counterpart. Once in office, moreover, Mondale proved to be, according to almost every scholar who has studied the office, one of the most effective and influential vice presidents in American history.[96] While Carter and Mondale often took differing positions on policy questions, their personal relationship proved to be a strong and enduring one.

Every subsequent vice presidential selection decision has proceeded along the same general lines. Given the large number of candidates to be considered and the substantial amount of research that is ultimately required, contemporary presidential candidates generally begin their search for a running mate by setting up some kind of formal structure to conduct the search process or by designating one individual to oversee it. Michael Dukakis, for example, specifically entrusted most of the work in his vice presidential selection to Paul Brountas, his campaign chairman and longtime friend. In 1992, Bill Clinton appointed a three-person search committee whose members were drawn from outside the formal campaign organization. The next step is to canvass and then narrow the field: to establish a manageable list of prospects who will receive more serious consideration. Every presidential campaign has also made some attempt to conduct background investigations on each of the major contenders, examining their financial and medical histories and trying to make sure, at a minimum, that they have not been involved in any obvious scandals. And either because of leaks or as a matter of deliberate policy, the names of the finalists have usually been made public.

The most variable and controversial element in recent selection decisions has been the individual meetings between the presidential candidate and each of the major vice presidential contenders. In 1984, when Walter Mondale himself was a presidential candidate, he, like Carter, chose to hold lengthy, well-publicized meetings at his home in Minnesota with a succession of vice presidential hopefuls. Republicans, by contrast, have usually regarded such meetings as "undignified" and "humiliating." Neither Ronald Reagan in 1980 nor George Bush in 1988 made any systematic attempt to meet individually with the people they were considering as running mates. In 1992, Bill Clinton sought a compromise procedure: he met with all of the vice presidential finalists but tried (though not very successfully) to keep the meetings secret.

A well-designed search process can increase the likelihood that a presidential candidate will select a qualified and capable running mate. But no process, no matter how artfully constructed, can save a candidate from his own faults and misjudgments. When one examines the vice presidential choices of the last twenty years, what appears to separate the more successful from the less successful is not the formal structure of the process, but the attitude of the presidential nominee: how much priority he attaches to his decision and, especially, how seriously he weights the governmental dimensions of the vice presidency.

Such, I would argue, is the key to understanding what is, by wide agreement, the least meritorious vice presidential selection decision of the last two and a half decades: George Bush's choice of Dan Quayle in 1988.[97] At one level, one could argue—many within the Bush campaign *did* argue—that the process Bush used to select a running mate was not very different from that employed by every other presidential nominee of this period. Though Bush effectively clinched his party's presidential nomination in March, his search for a running mate did not really begin until mid-July, when Democratic presidential candidate Michael Dukakis announced his vice presidential decision (the Democratic convention took place one month before the Republican convention). Then, working with various aides and advisors, Bush developed a "short list"—about a dozen names, by most accounts—of people who would receive serious consideration. Bush then appointed Robert Kimmitt, a lawyer and former general counsel to the Treasury Department, to interview each of the major contenders and gather financial and other background information about them. Bush reportedly read all of this material and conferred with a variety of advisors and top party officials before finally making his decision: Senator J. Danforth Quayle of Indiana.

When one takes a more detailed look at the way this search actually transpired, however, it soon becomes apparent that it had a number of significant shortcomings. To begin with, it seems clear that the background research on the vice presidential prospects was not very thorough. The most striking demonstration of its inadequacy is that one day after the selection was announced, when a controversy developed about Quayle's service in the National Guard, the campaign had almost no solid information on the matter. Instead, shortly after midnight, on the same day that Bush would deliver his own acceptance speech, the Bush high command had to send two people over to Quayle's hotel room to grill the Indiana senator about what exactly he and his family had done to get him into the National Guard and how it could be squared with his outspoken support for the war in Vietnam.

Why was the Bush campaign so unprepared to deal with such an obviously sensitive issue? According to some observers, the fault lay primarily with Bush's decision to put Robert Kimmitt, a man of relatively limited political experience, in charge of the vetting process.[98] But this was only one symptom of a much larger problem: the extraordinarily secretive nature of the Bush selection process. From the very beginning, Bush repeatedly proclaimed his determination that the process not turn into a media circus—that it not be "demeaning" to the people being considered. But this basically laudable goal was carried to such extremes that it interfered with the proper flow of needed information. Whatever Kimmitt did or did not ask Quayle, the more significant point is that there was very little opportunity to supplement or challenge his judgment; when the background reports were completed, Bush was the only person allowed to see them. Everyone else who was advising Bush on the vice presidential question did so without knowing what Kimmitt had learned.

In a further effort to keep the process out of the headlines, Bush decided not to interview any of the top contenders. Bush justified this decision by saying that he already knew the candidates quite well—a characterization that was probably true with regard to most of the people on his short list, but not with regard to Quayle.[99] Bush's obsession with secrecy also denied him the kind of public deliberation and feedback that might have provided some advance warning about how Quayle's selection would be received. Not only did Bush seek to dampen press coverage of his impending decision; all of his top advisors say that *they* had no idea what Bush was thinking, either. There were many people within the Republican Party who doubted Quayle's suitability as a vice presidential candidate, but little of this sentiment was ever communicated to Bush or his top advisors because few thought that Quayle was seriously being considered for the job. With one notable exception—an article in the *New York Times* that appeared two days before the opening of the Republican convention—contemporary press coverage of the process provides almost no foreshadowing of Bush's final choice.[100]

The greatest problem with Bush's selection process, however, was the attitude that informed it. In reaching a final decision, Bush seems to have had two types of considerations in mind. On the one hand, he felt—not at all unreasonably—that he wanted someone with whom he was personally compatible. Unfortunately for Bush, this ruled out the two most highly regarded people on his list: Robert Dole and Jack Kemp. Both had broad support within the Republican Party; and since both had recently been candidates for the presidency, their records and backgrounds had already received extensive scrutiny from the press. But Bush was not comfortable with either man and so eventually dropped them from consideration.

Beyond personal compatibility, however, Bush seems to have based his decision almost entirely on the most narrow, short-term electoral considerations. When Bush and his aides were asked to explain and defend the Quayle selection in the days immediately after it was announced, their answers dealt overwhelmingly with the image that Quayle would supposedly bring to the ticket and the groups he would appeal to.[101] Quayle would help George Bush look "bold," "exciting," and "future-oriented"; he would attract votes from young people (because he was forty-one) and Midwesterners (because he was from Indiana); he was a good campaigner. Several Bush advisors even appear to have believed that Quayle would help the Republican ticket among women voters because he was good-looking. By contrast, there is no evidence that the Bush campaign spent much time worrying about Quayle's legislative record or the way he was regarded by Senate colleagues. One symptom of these priorities was the composition of the group that Bush relied upon most heavily for advice. Though most of Bush's inner circle have been understandably reluctant to talk about their role in the selection process, according to most reports, the two people pushing Quayle hardest were Roger Ailes, Bush's chief media advisor, and Robert Teeter, his pollster. The problem, of course, is that both men knew Quayle only as a campaigner; neither had any reliable basis for pronouncing judgment on his governing abilities.

Ironically, the Bush campaign's preoccupation with short-term electoral considerations led to a vice presidential choice that was a signal failure in electoral terms. Far from expanding the appeal of the 1988 Republican ticket, the evidence is strong that Quayle cost Bush a significant number of votes. Whatever pride young people or Midwesterners may have felt from seeing one of their own on the Republican ticket was overwhelmed by the perception that this particular young Midwesterner was simply not qualified for the job. While it is difficult to estimate the precise impact of a vice presidential candidate on the outcome of a presidential election, the best single study of this issue, by Martin Wattenberg and Bernard Grofman, has concluded that Quayle's presence on the 1988 ticket reduced the Republican popular vote by more than 2 percentage points—the most costly vice presidential choice in all the elections for which they have data.[102]

Conclusion

At a time when there are widespread lamentations about the declining state of American politics, a good case can be made that the vice presidency functions better today than it has at any previous point in our nation's history. To be sure, the system does not work perfectly. But in at least three significant respects, I find it difficult not to conclude that the contemporary vice presidency, warts and all, is demonstrably superior to that which existed in the 1880s, 1920s, or 1960s.

First, the process through which vice presidential candidates are selected is substantially more rational and deliberative. No longer are presidential candidates or party leaders forced to choose a vice presidential nominee without the benefit of serious research or reliable information, nor is the decision-making process crammed into a period of less than twenty-four hours.

Second, once the vice president has been elected, we actually give him something to do. If the office is still not as powerful as some would have it, it has acquired, through a combination of custom and statute, a considerable range of resources and responsibilities. In particular, the vice president is now kept thoroughly informed about ongoing issues and events, thus greatly increasing the likelihood of a smooth transition if the president should die or be disabled.

Finally, though it is not the sort of point that can be readily quantified, there is reason to believe that the general quality of vice presidents and vice presidential candidates is higher today than it has been at any time since the ratification of the Twelfth Amendment. If Dan Quayle's presence on the 1988 Republican ticket was a source of concern to many voters, they reacted that way precisely because Quayle was an exception to the rule—because the Indiana senator was thought to fall well below the standard that the voters had lately come to expect. People of far less experience and capacity than Quayle were routinely nominated for vice president during the nineteenth century and no one batted an eye.

Since the vice presidency has long been regarded as one of the least well constructed features of American national government, many readers may reasonably feel that it is no great endorsement to say that the office works better now than it has in the past. There is much to be said for the verdict of Joel Goldstein, in what is probably the best single book on the modern vice presidency: "The vice presidency remains a dangerous office. Its recent growth has mitigated but not removed its harmful potential. On balance, the office continues to merit a negative assessment."[103]

Can we do better? Is it time to dust off all those reports and proposals from the early 1970s and reconsider some of the changes they recommended? Whether and how we should change the vice presidency are, as I have already suggested, large and complicated questions. A remarkable diversity of "reforms" have been proposed; a variety of different issues and values must be taken into account. A full treatment of such matters is beyond the scope of this chapter. But the analysis presented here does carry some important lessons for future reformers.

One of the most frequent criticisms of the current selection process is that it vests the choice of a major-party vice presidential candidate almost entirely in the hands of one person. To be sure, that person has just won (or is about to win) his party's presidential nomination. But he is still a quite fallible human being. In general, the American governmental system, with its emphasis on checks and balances, presumes that decision processes are more likely to yield good results when many different persons are involved in them. Accordingly, many of the proposed changes in vice presidential selection procedures attempt, in various ways, to spread out the decision-making responsibility a bit more.

As the history recounted here suggests, however, giving the presidential candidate a dominant role in the vice presidential selection process also has important benefits. Given the peculiar nature of the vice presidency, especially its almost complete lack of formal powers, qualities of initiative and independence that we might value in other elected officials are not necessarily a virtue in the vice president. The less say a presidential candidate has in choosing his running mate, the less likely it is that the president will give the vice president significant governing responsibilities and access to important information or that he will take the vice president's advice and counsel seriously.

And if the presidential candidates have a reduced role in vice presidential selection, who will take up the slack? Far and away the most common answer is political parties. In theory, of course, the parties already make vice presidential nominations, but, in practice, everyone recognizes that parties do little more than rubber stamp the choices of the presidential candidates. According to many critics, the parties need to have a more significant and independent voice in the selection process.

As a general matter, I tend to be favorably disposed toward proposals that seek to increase the role of parties in the American political system. At the very least, presidential nominees would be well advised to consult with a diverse cross-section of their own party's members—and to take these consultations seriously in reaching a final decision.

Before we go too far down this path, however, a note of caution is in order. Many advocates of strong party government have an unfortunate tendency to compare the realities of contemporary American politics with a highly idealized portrait of how political parties might behave. As we have seen, parties were at the center of the vice presidential selection process from about 1840 to at least 1920, and the results they produced were hardly an advertisement for the glories of American government. All of the criticisms now leveled at the vice presidential choices made by presidential candidates—in particular, that they focus too narrowly on short-term electoral considerations and not enough on matters of governance—were even more true of the way parties performed in their heyday. To be sure, American parties are not the same creatures today that they were in the nineteenth century—but neither are they a magic wand that will instantly solve all our problems.

Notes

1. Even today, after what almost all observers agree has been a significant increase in the vice president's power and visibility, most introductory textbooks devote only three or four pages to the topic. See, for example, Morris P. Fiorina and Paul E. Peterson, *The New American Democracy* (Boston: Allyn & Bacon, 1998), 313-5,

439; and Everett Carll Ladd, *The American Polity: The People and Their Government*, 5th ed. (New York: Norton, 1995), 195–8.

2. Woodrow Wilson, *Congressional Government: A Study in American Politics* (1885; Baltimore: Johns Hopkins University Press, 1981), 162.

3. Clinton Rossiter, *The American Presidency* (New York: Harcourt, Brace, 1956), 104.

4. Whether and how much the vice presidential candidates affect voting in presidential elections has not received a great deal of attention from political scientists. Two exceptions are Martin P. Wattenberg, "And Tyler, Too," *Public Opinion* 7 (April/May 1984): 52–4; and Martin P. Wattenberg and Bernard Grofman, "A Rational Choice Model of the President and Vice-President as a Package Deal," in *Information, Participation, and Choice: An Economic Theory of Democracy in Perspective*, ed. Bernard Grofman (Ann Arbor: University of Michigan Press, 1993), 173–7.

5. Major examples include *Report of the Study Group on Vice-Presidential Selection* (Cambridge, Mass.: Institute of Politics, Kennedy School of Government, Harvard University, 1976); American Bar Association Special Committee on Election Reform, "Symposium on the Vice-Presidency," *Fordham Law Review* 45 (1976–77): 703–804; and Allan P. Sindler, *Unchosen Presidents: The Vice-President and Other Frustrations of Presidential Succession* (Berkeley: University of California Press, 1976).

6. Among the best books of this type are Louis Clinton Hatch and Earl L. Shoup, *A History of the Vice-Presidency of the United States* (New York: American Historical Society, 1934); and L. Edward Purcell, ed., *The Vice Presidents: A Biographical Dictionary* (New York: Facts On File, 1998).

7. The major exception is a book by political reporter Jules Witcover; see *Crapshoot: Rolling the Dice on the Vice Presidency* (New York: Crown, 1992).

8. On the origin and evolution of the vice presidency in the Constitutional Convention, see John D. Feerick, *From Failing Hands: The Story of Presidential Succession* (New York: Fordham University Press, 1965), chaps. 2 and 3; Richard P. McCormick, *The Presidential Game: The Origins of American Presidential Politics* (New York: Oxford University Press, 1982), 20–3; and Arthur M. Schlesinger, Jr., "On the Presidential Succession," *Political Science Quarterly* 89 (fall 1974): 475–505.

9. When the vice presidency was discussed during the ratification debates—and it was never a central subject of dispute—it was this last point that seems to have been offered most frequently in its defense. See Feerick, *From Failing Hands*, 51–5.

10. Max Farrand, ed., *The Records of the Federal Convention of 1787*, vol. 2 (New Haven, Conn.: Yale University Press, 1966), 537.

11. On the attitudes of the Constitution's framers toward political parties, see especially Richard Hofstadter, *The Idea of a Party System: The Rise of Legitimate Opposition in the United States, 1780–1840* (Berkeley: University of California Press, 1969), chaps. 1 and 2.

12. The phrase is Alexander Hamilton's and was pronounced as early as 1789. See his letter to James Wilson in *The Papers of Alexander Hamilton*, ed. Harold C. Syrett, vol. 5 (New York: Columbia University Press, 1962), 248.

13. Quoted in Feerick, *From Failing Hands*, 73.

14. Schlesinger, "Presidential Succession," 492.

15. Burr was unquestionably a man of great intelligence and ability; it was his morals that were in doubt.

16. Since the New York legislature selected the state's presidential electors, the Republican triumph in the spring legislative elections effectively guaranteed that the Republican presidential ticket would win the state's electoral votes in the fall.

17. Senator Samuel White of Delaware, as quoted in Schlesinger, "Presidential Succession," 491.

18. As William Plumer described Clinton a few years after the latter was elected, "He is an old man—time has impaired his mental faculties as much as it has the powers of his body. He is too old for the office he now holds; little as are its duties—he is from age rendered incapable of discharging them"; quoted in McCormick, *Presidential Game*, 87.

19. The following discussion draws on a variety of sources, especially McCormick, *Presidential Game*; James S. Chase, *Emergence of the Presidential Nominating Convention 1789-1832* (Urbana: University of Illinois Press, 1973); M. Ostrogorski, "The Rise and Fall of the Nominating Caucus, Legislative and Congressional," *American Historical Review* 5 (January 1900): 253-83; Arthur M. Schlesinger, Jr., Fred L. Israel, and William P. Hansen, eds., *History of American Presidential Elections 1789-1968*, vol. 1 (New York: McGraw-Hill, 1971); David Hackett Fischer, *The Revolution of American Conservatism: The Federalist Party in the Era of Jeffersonian Democracy* (New York: Harper & Row, 1965); Arthur M. Schlesinger, Jr., ed., *History of U.S. Political Parties*, vol. 1 (New York: R.R. Bowker, 1973); and Purcell, *Vice Presidents*.

20. An especially strong defense of this position can be found in Chase, *Emergence of Presidential Nominating Convention*, 18-28, from which much of the following analysis is drawn.

21. Both are quoted in Chase, *Emergence of Presidential Nominating Convention*, 22.

22. John S. Murdock, "The First National Nominating Convention," *American Historical Review* 1 (July 1896): 680-3; and Samuel E. Morison, "The First National Nominating Convention, 1808," *American Historical Review* 17 (July 1912): 744-63.

23. For a good account of this diversity, see James F. Hopkins, "Election of 1824," in *History of American Presidential Elections*, ed. Arthur M. Schlesinger, Jr., Fred L. Israel, and William P. Hansen, vol. 1 (New York: McGraw-Hill, 1971), 349-81.

24. The controversy over how Andrew Johnson became the Republican vice presidential candidate in 1864 stretches back more than a century. For two particularly good summaries of the events surrounding this nomination and the evidence concerning Lincoln's role in it, see James F. Glonek, "Lincoln, Johnson, and the Baltimore Ticket," *Abraham Lincoln Quarterly* 6 (March 1951): 255-71; and Don E. Fehrenbacher, "The Making of a Myth: Lincoln and the Vice-Presidential Nomination in 1864," *Civil War History* 41 (December 1995): 273-90. Both articles conclude that Lincoln was not involved in the decision. For other recent readings of the evidence, see David Herbert Donald, *Lincoln* (New York: Simon & Schuster, 1995), 503-7; John C. Waugh, *Reelecting Lincoln: The Battle for the 1864 Presidency* (New York: Crown, 1997), chap. 15; and Mark Scroggins, *Hannibal: The Life of Abraham Lincoln's First Vice President* (Lanham, Md.: University Press of America, 1994), chap. 8.

25. The essay appears as chap. 8 in James Bryce, *The American Commonwealth*, 3rd ed., vol. 1 (New York: Macmillan, 1900), 78-85.

26. On the Whig vice presidential nomination in 1844 and Clay's role in it, see Robert V. Remini, *Henry Clay: Statesman for the Union* (New York: Norton, 1991), 642-5; William Southworth Hunt, "Theodore Frelinghuysen: A Discussion of His Vice Presidential Candidacy in the Clay-Polk Campaign of 1844, and Its Reasons," *Proceedings of the New Jersey Historical Society* 56 (January 1938): 30-40; and Glyndon G. Van Deusen, *The Life of Henry Clay* (Boston: Little, Brown, 1937), 366.

27. The following account draws on Paolo E. Coletta, *Political Evangelist, 1860-1908*, vol. 1 of *William Jennings Bryan* (Lincoln: University of Nebraska Press, 1964),

255-62; Lewis W. Koenig, *Bryan: A Political Biography of William Jennings Bryan* (New York: Putnam, 1971), 318-24; and William Jennings Bryan and Mary Baird Bryan, *The Memoirs of William Jennings Bryan* (Chicago: John C. Winston, 1925), 119-28.

28. David D. Anderson, *William Jennings Bryan* (Boston: Twayne, 1981), 110.

29. Bryan had hoped to form a fusion ticket with what remained of the Populist and Silver Republican Parties. Both groups were favorably disposed toward Bryan but markedly less enthusiastic about Stevenson.

30. Detailed accounts of the 1900 Republican vice presidential nomination can be found in Edmund Morris, *The Rise of Theodore Roosevelt* (New York: Coward, McCann & Geoghegan, 1979), 711-29; Margaret Leech, *In the Days of McKinley* (New York: Harper & Brothers, 1959), 529-42; and Lewis L. Gould, *The Presidency of William McKinley* (Lawrence: University Press of Kansas, 1980), 207-19.

31. Quoted in H. Wayne Morgan, *William McKinley and His America* (Syracuse, N.Y.: Syracuse University Press, 1963), 496.

32. Democrats faced an even more daunting task. Throughout this period, Democratic party rules required a two-thirds majority to nominate presidential and vice presidential candidates.

33. The quotation is from Governor Stone of Missouri, in *Official Proceedings of the Democratic National Convention Held in Chicago, Ill., July 7th, 8th, 9th, 10th and 11th, 1896* (Logansport, Ind.: Wilson, Humphreys, 1896), 330.

34. For a parallel argument about how the sequencing of primaries helps the parties reach agreement on their presidential candidates, see Larry M. Bartels, *Presidential Primaries and the Dynamics of Public Choice* (Princeton, N.J.: Princeton University Press, 1988), chap. 12.

35. *Official Proceedings of the Eleventh Republican National Convention Held in the City of St. Louis, Mo., June 16, 17, and 18, 1896* (n.p., 1896), 133.

36. Indeed, the intraparty fighting was so bitter that the Democrats actually had to hold two conventions in 1860. The first gathering took place in Charleston, South Carolina; after struggling for ten days to nominate a presidential candidate, the party finally decided to adjourn and to meet again a month and a half later in Baltimore. It was only at this second conclave that Stephen A. Douglas became the presidential candidate of what was now regarded as the Northern Democratic Party.

37. See William B. Hesseltine, ed., *Three Against Lincoln: Murat Halstead Reports the Caucuses of 1860* (Baton Rouge: Louisiana State University Press, 1960), 254-9; and Robert W. Johannsen, *Stephen A. Douglas* (New York: Oxford University Press, 1973), 767-72.

38. The cases I regard as borderline are the 1900 Democratic ticket, in which the presidential candidate was from Nebraska and the vice presidential candidate was from Illinois; the 1904 Democratic ticket, which had a presidential candidate from New York and a vice presidential candidate from West Virginia; and the 1908 Democratic ticket, which had a presidential candidate from Nebraska and a vice presidential candidate from Indiana. Whether these tickets are classified as unbalanced depends on how one divides the United States along regional lines. Today, for example, most observers would probably classify both New York and West Virginia as belonging to the Northeast; but there is some evidence that in 1904, West Virginia was considered a Border state. Similarly, at the 1900 and 1908 Democratic conventions, the comments made about regional balance during the vice presidential nomination speeches suggest that the most important line of division at that time was between

states east of the Mississippi River and states west of it. From that perspective, both of these tickets are regionally balanced.

39. On the 1852 Democratic convention, see Daniel Fate Brooks, "William Rufus de Vane King," in *The Vice Presidents: A Biographical Dictionary*, ed. L. Edward Purcell (New York: Facts On File, 1998), 122-8; Larry Gara, *The Presidency of Franklin Pierce* (Lawrence: University Press of Kansas, 1991), chap. 2; John M. Martin, "William R. King and the Vice Presidency," *Alabama Review* 16 (January 1963): 35-54; and Roy Franklin Nichols, *Franklin Pierce: Young Hickory of the Granite Hills* (Philadelphia: University of Pennsylvania Press, 1931), 202-8.

40. On the predicament of the Democrats in 1864, see Waugh, *Reelecting Lincoln*; and Stephen W. Sears, *George B. McClellan: The Young Napoleon* (New York: Ticknor & Fields, 1988), 367-78.

41. The 1844 Democratic convention is discussed in Charles Sellers, *James K. Polk, Continentalist, 1843-1846* (Princeton, N.J.: Princeton University Press, 1966), chap. 3; and John M. Belohlavek, *George Mifflin Dallas: Jacksonian Patrician* (University Park: Pennsylvania State University Press, 1977).

42. Even in this case, there is some dispute—not about Jackson's preferences, but about how important his support was for getting Van Buren nominated. See, for example, Chase, *Emergence of Presidential Nominating Convention*, 243-50, 253-63; and Robert V. Remini, *Andrew Jackson and the Course of American Freedom, 1822-1832* (New York: Harper & Row, 1981), 355-8.

43. In addition to the other sources listed below, the following account draws on Kenneth S. Davis, *FDR: The Beckoning of Destiny, 1882-1928* (New York: Putnam, 1971), 607-14; Geoffrey C. Ward, *A First-Class Temperament: The Emergence of Franklin Roosevelt* (New York: Harper & Row, 1989), 492-512; James E. Cebula, *James M. Cox: Journalist and Politician* (New York: Garland, 1985), 107-8; and Wesley M. Bagby, *The Road to Normalcy: The Presidential Campaign and Election of 1920* (Baltimore: Johns Hopkins Press, 1962), 120-2.

44. James M. Cox, *Journey through My Years* (New York: Simon & Schuster, 1946), 232.

45. *New York Times*, 7 July 1920, 1. A more detailed description of how Roosevelt came to be nominated appeared five days later; see *New York Times*, 12 July 1920, 1. Based on comments by Timothy Ansberry, a close friend of Cox who gave Roosevelt's principal nominating speech at the convention, this story also suggests that Cox played only a minor role in the affair.

46. The best account of the vice presidential maneuvering at the 1920 convention is Frank Freidel, *Franklin D. Roosevelt: The Ordeal* (Boston: Little, Brown, 1954), chap. 4. Freidel specifically notes, "When the delegates returned to the auditorium at about noon, they knew nothing of Cox's choice" (p. 66).

47. See *Official Report of the Proceedings of the Democratic National Convention Held in San Francisco, California June 28, 29, 30, July 1, 2, 3, 5, and 6, 1920* (Indianapolis: Bookwalter-Ball, 1920), 427-52.

48. Grenville T. Emmet, quoted in Freidel, *Roosevelt: The Ordeal*, 51.

49. The quote is from Smith's memoirs; see Alfred E. Smith, *Up to Now: An Autobiography* (New York: Viking, 1929), 378. For other accounts that also emphasize Smith's lack of involvement, see Donn C. Neal, *The World Beyond the Hudson: Alfred E. Smith and National Politics, 1918-1928* (New York: Garland, 1983), 264-5; and Oscar Handlin, *Al Smith and His America* (Boston: Little, Brown, 1958), 127.

50. Kenneth S. Davis, *FDR: Into the Storm, 1937-1940* (New York: Random House, 1993), 599.

51. On Wallace's political background and his relationship with other elements in the Democratic Party, see Edward L. and Frederick H. Schapsmeier, *Henry A. Wallace of Iowa: The Agrarian Years, 1910-1940* (Ames: Iowa State University Press, 1968), 261-72; and Mark L. Kleinman, "Henry Agard Wallace," in *The Vice Presidents: A Biographical Dictionary*, ed. L. Edward Purcell (New York: Facts On File, 1998), 297-305.

52. The speakers are, respectively, Scott Lucas, Prentiss M. Brown, and Paul V. McNutt. All quotations are from *Official Report of the Proceedings of the Democratic National Convention Held at Chicago, Illinois, July 15th to July 18th, Inclusive, 1940* (n.p., 1940), 224, 235, 237-8.

53. See, among others, David McCullough, *Truman* (New York: Simon & Schuster, 1992), 292-321; Alonzo L. Hamby, *Man of the People: A Life of Harry S. Truman* (New York: Oxford University Press, 1995), 274-84; and Frank Freidel, *Franklin D. Roosevelt: A Rendezvous with Destiny* (Boston: Little, Brown, 1990), 529-38.

54. On Warren's selection, see Richard Norton Smith, *Thomas E. Dewey and His Times* (New York: Simon & Schuster, 1982), 497-501; Ed Cray, *Chief Justice: A Biography of Earl Warren* (New York: Simon & Schuster, 1997), 186-9; and *New York Times*, 26 June 1948, 1, 3.

55. My account draws on Hamby, *Man of the People*, 448-50; McCullough, *Truman*, 632-41; Robert J. Donovan, *Conflict and Crisis: The Presidency of Harry S. Truman, 1945-1948* (New York: Norton, 1977), 405-406; Harry S. Truman, *Years of Trial and Hope*, vol. 2 of *Memoirs* (Garden City, N.Y.: Doubleday, 1956), 189-91; and Alben W. Barkley, *That Reminds Me*—(Garden City, N.Y.: Doubleday, 1954), 198-202.

56. Eben A. Ayers, *Truman in the White House: The Diary of Eben A. Ayers*, ed. Robert H. Ferrell (Columbia: University of Missouri Press, 1991), 265.

57. As reported in *Official Report of the Proceedings of the Democratic National Convention, Chicago, Illinois, August 13 through August 17, 1956* (Richmond, Va.: Beacon, 1956), 420.

58. My analysis of the Democratic vice presidential nomination in 1956 draws primarily on John Bartlow Martin, *Adlai Stevenson and the World* (Garden City, N.Y.: Doubleday, 1977), 349-52; Jeff Broadwater, *Adlai Stevenson and American Politics: The Odyssey of a Cold War Liberal* (New York: Twayne, 1994), 161-3; Joseph Bruce Gorman, *Kefauver: A Political Biography* (New York: Oxford University Press, 1971), 249-65; and contemporary coverage in the *New York Times*.

59. As quoted in *Time*, 27 August 1956, 28.

60. *New York Times*, 21 August 1956, 28.

61. On Stevenson's own preferences, see Martin, *Adlai Stevenson and the World*, 350.

62. Richard M. Nixon, *Six Crises* (Garden City, N.Y.: Doubleday, 1962), 317-8.

63. Gerald R. Ford, *A Time to Heal: The Autobiography of Gerald R. Ford* (New York: Harper & Row, 1979), 72-3.

64. Theodore H. White, *The Making of the President 1960* (New York: Atheneum, 1961), 206.

65. This last view is particularly associated with the work of Arthur M. Schlesinger, Jr.; see *A Thousand Days: John F. Kennedy in the White House* (Boston: Houghton Mifflin, 1965), 39-58; and *Robert Kennedy and His Times* (Boston: Houghton Mifflin, 1978), 206-11. For other reconstructions of the decision, almost all of which concede that it is impossible to be certain just what happened, see White, *Making of the President 1960*, 172-7; Thomas C. Reeves, *A Question of Character: A Life of John F. Kennedy* (New York: Free Press, 1991), 176-81; Theodore C. Sorensen, *Kennedy* (New York: Harper & Row, 1965), 162-6; Robert Dallek, *Lone*

Star Rising: Lyndon Johnson and His Times, 1908-1960 (New York: Oxford University Press, 1991), 574-82; and Witcover, *Crapshoot*, 147-58.

66. The growth of vice presidential power and resources is one of the few aspects of the office that has been studied extensively. See especially Joel K. Goldstein, *The Modern American Vice Presidency: The Transformation of a Political Institution* (Princeton, N.J.: Princeton University Press, 1982), chaps. 6-8; Marie D. Natoli, *American Prince, American Pauper: The Contemporary Vice Presidency in Perspective* (Westport, Conn.: Greenwood, 1985), chaps. 5 and 6; Paul C. Light, *Vice-Presidential Power: Advice and Influence in the White House* (Baltimore: Johns Hopkins University Press, 1984); and *A Heartbeat Away: Report of the Twentieth Century Fund Task Force on the Vice Presidency* (New York: Priority Press, 1988).

67. Letter of 19 December 1793, quoted in *The Works of John Adams, Second President of the United States: With a Life of the Author*, vol. 1, ed. Charles Francis Adams (Boston: Little, Brown, 1856), 460.

68. For a good recent statement of this argument by the dean of modern-day presidential studies, see Richard E. Neustadt, "Vice Presidents as National Leaders: Reflections Past, Present, and Future," in *At the President's Side: The Vice Presidency in the Twentieth Century*, ed. Timothy Walch (Columbia: University of Missouri Press, 1997), 183-96.

69. See Goldstein, *Modern American Vice Presidency*, 142-6.

70. Quoted in Light, *Vice-Presidential Power*, 8.

71. Goldstein, *Modern American Vice Presidency*, 140-1.

72. The cases I am referring to are the Republican nominations of 1908 and 1928, and the Democratic nominations of 1920 and 1952.

73. My account of the 1908 Republican presidential nomination draws primarily on Judith Icke Anderson, *William Howard Taft: An Intimate Biography* (New York: Norton, 1981), 90-104; George E. Mowry, *The Era of Theodore Roosevelt, 1900-1912* (New York: Harper & Brothers, 1958), 226-9; Lewis L. Gould, *The Presidency of Theodore Roosevelt* (Lawrence: University Press of Kansas, 1991), 271-4, 283-5; and Ray E. Boomhower, "Charles Warren Fairbanks," in *The Vice Presidents: A Biographical Dictionary*, ed. L. Edward Purcell (New York: Facts On File, 1998), 237-41.

74. On Dawes's role in the 1928 nomination race, see Robert A. Waller, "Charles Gates Dawes," in *The Vice Presidents: A Biographical Dictionary*, ed. L. Edward Purcell (New York: Facts On File, 1998), 272-82; David Burner, *Herbert Hoover: A Public Life* (New York: Knopf, 1979), 190-200; and Herbert Hoover, *The Memoirs of Herbert Hoover: The Cabinet and the Presidency 1920-1933* (New York: Macmillan, 1952), 190-5.

75. For a good review of public opinion data on the vice presidency, see Goldstein, *Modern American Vice Presidency*, 250-9.

76. For good accounts of how Johnson selected Humphrey, see Gerald Pomper, "The Nomination of Hubert Humphrey for Vice-President," *Journal of Politics* 28 (August 1966): 639-59; Carl Solberg, *Hubert Humphrey: A Biography* (New York: Norton, 1984), chap. 23; Theodore H. White, *The Making of the President 1964* (New York: Atheneum, 1965), chap. 9; and Witcover, *Crapshoot*, chap. 12.

77. It is worth noting the ironic situation that thus confronted the Democratic and Republican Parties during this era. The only type of presidential candidate who usually had the opportunity to conduct a thorough and deliberate search for a running mate was an incumbent president. But that opportunity was generally of little value because most incumbents already had a vice presidential candidate—the person

they had run with four years earlier. Johnson is an exception to this pattern only because he had first ascended to the presidency in 1963 upon the death of John Kennedy.

78. My account of the Eagleton selection process is based on George McGovern, *Grassroots: The Autobiography of George McGovern* (New York: Random House, 1977); 188-216; Gary Warren Hart, *Right from the Start: A Chronicle of the McGovern Campaign* (New York: Quadrangle, 1973), 238-65; Gordon L. Weil, *The Long Shot: George McGovern Runs for President* (New York: Norton, 1973), 156-94; Theodore H. White, *The Making of the President 1972* (New York: Atheneum, 1973), 193-217; and Haynes Johnson, "The Eagleton Case," *Washington Post*, 3-6 December 1972.

79. White, *Making of the President 1972*, 194-5.

80. Hart, *Right from the Start*, 238.

81. The list given here is what might be described as the consensus of the major published accounts. For slightly different lists, see Weil, *Long Shot*, 163; and White, *Making of the President 1972*, 195.

82. Hart, *Right from the Start*, 239.

83. Hart claims that Weil was sent on his investigative mission while the meeting was still in progress; see *Right from the Start*, 239. But both Theodore White and Weil himself indicate that Weil conducted his researches only after the meeting broke up—and on his own initiative. See White, *Making of the President 1972*, 196; and Weil, *Long Shot*, 163-5.

84. For a transcript of this press conference, see *New York Times*, 26 July 1972, 20.

85. My discussion of Muskie's selection draws on Theodore H. White, *The Making of the President 1968* (New York: Atheneum, 1969), 303-5; Hubert H. Humphrey, *The Education of a Public Man: My Life and Politics* (Garden City, N.Y.: Doubleday, 1976), 390-3; and Solberg, *Hubert Humphrey*, 366-7. It also draws on *New York Times*, 12 August 1968, 24; 27 August 1968, 1; 29 August 1968, 1; and 30 August 1968, 1.

86. *New York Times*, 12 August 1968, 24.

87. McGovern, *Grassroots*, 190-1.

88. For various proposals and/or discussions of other people's proposals, see *Congressional Quarterly Weekly Report*, 12 January 1974, 48-50; Natoli, *American Prince, American Pauper*, 52-8; Goldstein, *Modern American Vice Presidency*, chap. 12; Schlesinger, "Presidential Succession"; Robert P. Griffin, "On Choosing Vice-Presidents," *Christian Science Monitor*, 13 November 1973, 16; Endicott Peabody, "For a Grassroots Vice-Presidency," *New York Times*, 25 January 1974, 33; "The Role of the Vice Presidency," *Current*, October 1972, 49-52; *Time*, 7 August 1972, 19; *New York Times*, 7 August 1972, 20; *Report of the Study Group on Vice-Presidential Selection*; and Joseph L. Rauh, Jr., "Choosing Vice Presidents: 'Something Is Amiss,'" *Washington Post*, 3 December 1974, A17.

89. Coverage of this commission and its recommendations was exceptionally spotty, even in the sorts of journalistic outlets that normally pay attention to such matters. See, however, *Congressional Quarterly Weekly Report*, 23 June 1973, 1631, and 15 December 1973, 3290; *Washington Post*, 15 February 1974, A2; and *New York Times*, 8 November 1973, 42, and 15 December 1973, 20.

90. Quoted in *Congressional Quarterly Weekly Report*, 3 July 1976, 1727. Another instance worth mentioning was the attempt by supporters of Ronald Reagan to add a provision to the 1976 Republican rules requiring all presidential candidates to announce their vice presidential choices before the start of the presidential roll call

vote at the convention. But this proposal, which was eventually defeated, was clearly put forward as a strategic gambit to help Reagan win the presidential nomination, not as a serious attempt to reform the vice presidential selection process. Four years later, when Reagan had a lock on the nomination and could easily have gotten such a provision enacted, he made no attempt to do so.

91. One other race that could arguably be classified as remaining contested until the opening of the convention is the Democratic nomination race of 1980. Though Carter had won a clear majority of the delegates by the final day of primaries, Edward Kennedy refused to concede, claiming that many of the Carter delegates actually wanted to vote for him—and would do so if one particular provision in the national party rules were changed. Though many in the media treated Kennedy's challenge seriously, my own opinion is that it was based much more on wishful thinking within the Kennedy campaign organization than on any real sentiment among the convention delegates. When the issue was finally brought to a vote, on the first night of the convention, the Kennedy position was decisively rejected. In any event, in terms of the argument being made here, this "contest" had no effect on the vice presidential selection. As an incumbent president, Jimmy Carter had effectively selected his 1980 running mate, Walter Mondale, four years earlier.

92. My account of Carter's vice presidential selection decision draws primarily on Jules Witcover, *Marathon: The Pursuit of the Presidency 1972-1976* (New York: Viking, 1977), chap. 24; Martin Schram, *Running for President 1976: The Carter Campaign* (New York: Stein & Day, 1977), 200-11; Jimmy Carter, *Keeping Faith: Memoirs of a President* (New York: Bantam, 1982), 35-40; Peter G. Bourne, *Jimmy Carter: A Comprehensive Biography from Plains to Postpresidency* (New York: Scribner, 1997), 329-34; Steven M. Gillon, *The Democrats' Dilemma: Walter F. Mondale and the Liberal Legacy* (New York: Columbia University Press, 1992), chap. 9; and contemporary coverage in the *New York Times*.

93. *New York Times*, 18 June 1976, A13.

94. For an account of Mondale's aborted presidential campaign and its denouement, see Gillon, *Democrats' Dilemma*, 149-53; and *New York Times*, 22 November 1974, 1, and 1 December 1974, sec. 4, 5.

95. Just within the pages of the *New York Times*, the Carter selection process was the subject of three different editorials, all very favorable. See *New York Times*, 9 July 1976, A26; 13 July 1976, 32; and 16 July 1976, A20.

96. See especially Light, *Vice-Presidential Power*; Goldstein, *Modern American Vice Presidency*; and Witcover, *Crapshoot*, chap. 16.

97. My analysis of how and why Bush selected Quayle draws primarily on Jack W. Germond and Jules Witcover, *Whose Broad Stripes and Bright Stars? The Trivial Pursuit of the Presidency 1988* (New York: Warner, 1989), chaps. 24 and 25; Peter Goldman and Tom Mathews, *The Quest for the Presidency 1988* (New York: Simon & Schuster, 1989), 314-30; Herbert S. Parmet, *George Bush: The Life of a Lone Star Yankee* (New York: Scribner, 1997), 343-9; David R. Runkel, ed., *Campaign for President: The Managers Look at '88* (Dover, Mass.: Auburn House, 1989), 205-18; Witcover, *Crapshoot*, chaps. 18 and 19; and contemporary coverage in the *New York Times*.

98. See, for example, Goldman and Mathews, *Quest for the Presidency*, 316-7; and the comments by Edward Rollins in Runkel, *Campaign for President*, 211-2.

99. See, for example, Witcover, *Crapshoot*, 338-9.

100. The article referred to, which was reportedly based on information leaked by Bush's campaign manager, James Baker, is Gerald M. Boyd, "Bush Prunes Running-

Mate List; Dole, Quayle and 3 Others Stay," *New York Times*, 13 August 1988, 1. This article actually did prompt several Republican operatives—most notably, James Lake—to admonish the Bush campaign that Quayle's selection would cause problems. But none of Bush's advisors acted on these warnings—because, so far as they knew, there was little chance that Quayle would be chosen. See Germond and Witcover, *Whose Broad Stripes*, 377-9; and Goldman and Mathews, *Quest for the Presidency*, 320.

101. See, for example, *New York Times*, 17 August 1988, A1; and 18 August 1988, A1 and A24.
102. See Wattenberg and Grofman, "Rational Choice Model," 174-5.
103. Goldstein, *Modern American Vice Presidency*, 311.

Tables and Figures

Index

About the Contributors

LONNA RAE ATKESON is an assistant professor of political science at the University of New Mexico, having received her Ph.D. from the University of Colorado at Boulder. Her research on elections and political behavior has appeared in the *American Journal of Political Science* and the *American Political Science Review*. She has received funding from the National Science Foundation and the Emerging Scholar Award from the Political Organizations and Parties section of the American Political Science Association.

JONATHAN BERNSTEIN received his Ph.D. in political science from the University of California, Berkeley. He is coeditor of *Campaigning for Congress: Politicians at Home and in Washington*.

SAMUEL J. BEST is an assistant professor of government at the University of Notre Dame, where he specializes in public opinion and electoral behavior. His research has appeared in a variety of academic journals, including the *Journal of Politics*, *American Politics Quarterly*, and the *American Political Science Review*. He received his Ph.D. in political science from the State University of New York at Stony Brook.

EMMETT H. BUELL, JR., directs the Richard G. Lugar Program in Politics and Public Service and teaches courses on American politics at Denison University. His list of publications on presidential selection includes a 1991 book, *Nominating the President*, coedited with Lee Sigelman, and a chapter on the "invisible primary" for the 1996 book *In Pursuit of the White House*. He is currently working on several projects, including a massive study of negative campaigning in presidential elections with Sigelman.

TAMI BUHR is a Ph.D. candidate in government at Harvard University. She has published articles and presented papers on political communication, public opinion, and presidential selection. She was the pollster for the WMUR-Dartmouth College Poll during the 1996 New Hampshire Republican primary, which is the subject of her dissertation.

ANDREW E. BUSCH is an associate professor of political science at the University of Denver. He is the author of *Outsiders and Openness in the Presidential Nominating System* and *Horses in Midstream: U.S. Midterm Elections and Their Consequences, 1894–1998*, as well as coauthor with James Ceaser of *Upside Down and Inside Out: The 1992 Elections and American Politics* and *Losing to Win: The 1996 Elections and American Politics*. He received his Ph.D. in government at the University of Virginia in 1992.

MICHAEL G. HAGEN is a teacher and researcher at the Annenberg School for Communication at the University of Pennsylvania. He holds a Ph.D. in political science from the University of California, Berkeley. He is coauthor of *Race and Inequality: A Study in American Values* and *Reasoning and Choice: Explorations in Political Psychology*, as well as a contributor to *The Iowa Caucuses and the Presidential Nominating Process*. His articles have appeared in a variety of academic journals.

CLARK HUBBARD is an assistant professor of political science at the University of New Hampshire, where he specializes in mass media and public opinion in American politics. Most of his recent work has concentrated on the New Hampshire primary. He holds a Ph.D. in political science from the State University of New York at Stony Brook.

WILLIAM G. MAYER is an associate professor of political science at Northeastern University, having received his Ph.D. from Harvard University. He is the author of four books, including *The Changing American Mind* and *The Divided Democrats*. He has also published numerous articles on such topics as public opinion, voting behavior, political parties, and media and politics.

JODY MCMULLEN is a graduate student in political science at the University of Arizona. Her research interests include political participation and judicial politics.

BARBARA NORRANDER is a professor of political science at the University of Arizona. She earned her Ph.D. from the Ohio State University. She is the author of *Super Tuesday* and a variety of articles on presidential nominations published in the *American Journal of Political Science*, *Journal of Politics*, and *Political Research Quarterly*.